ALEXANDER
MOODY STUART

— Alexander Moody Stuart, D.D. —
1809–1898

ALEXANDER MOODY STUART

A MEMOIR,
PARTLY AUTOBIOGRAPHICAL

By His Son
Kenneth Moody Stuart

With an Appendix containing
Selected Sermons and Documents

THE BANNER OF TRUTH TRUST

THE BANNER OF TRUTH TRUST

Head Office
3 Murrayfield Road
Edinburgh, EH12 6EL
UK

North America Office
610 Alexander Spring Rd
Carlisle, PA 17015
USA

banneroftruth.org

First published 1899
This retypeset edition with additional material
first published by The Banner of Truth Trust in 2023

© The Banner of Truth Trust, 2023

ISBN
Print: 978 1 80040 250 8
EPUB: 978 1 80040 251 5
Kindle: 978 1 80040 252 2

*

Typeset in 10.5/13.5 Adobe Garamond Pro
at The Banner of Truth Trust, Edinburgh

Printed in the USA by
Versa Press Inc.,
East Peoria, IL.

Endpapers:

Front: Looking west along Edinburgh's George Street towards
St George's Church, late 19th century. *Credit: Chronicle/Alamy*

Rear: View from Buda across the Danube to Pest,
late 19th century. *Credit: Chronicle/Alamy*

Contents

Contents

Illustrations

Foreword

SOME books belong to the category of 'must have'. *Alexander Moody Stuart: A Memoir* belongs to that category, and perhaps especially for ministers of the gospel it is a 'must read'. It becomes clear soon enough why Robert Murray M'Cheyne on first hearing him preach was immediately anxious for his close friends Andrew and Horatius Bonar to come under the influence of his ministry too. For Alexander Moody Stuart exemplified the famous *bon mot* of E. M. Bounds, the American Civil War chaplain (and prisoner-of-war): 'Men are God's method. The church is looking for better methods; God is looking for better men.' These pages, then, part biographical, part autobiographical, tell the story of such a man whose memorable preaching, pastoral counselling, and consistent lifestyle left an abiding impression on a generation of Christians.

The story of the Christian church is punctuated by the names of great men and women. We know their names. But often the names of those who influenced them are forgotten. Although it may seem that God has worked in the lives of individuals *only*, the truth is that when he works in new and fresh ways he characteristically brings together a 'brotherhood' of men: In the fourth century Augustine was surrounded by his friends; in the sixteenth century John Calvin formed the closest of bonds with other ministers; in the seventeenth century men were very conscious that they belonged to an entire 'Puritan brotherhood'; while in the eighteenth century men like Jonathan Edwards and George Whitefield belonged to an entire network of like-minded men, while John Newton, hymnwriter extraordinaire, regularly gathered with his friends in the Eclectic Society. We know these names, while the names of others in these spiritual brotherhoods have been too easily forgotten. So it is also with the remarkable brotherhood that was raised up in Scotland in the first half of the nineteenth century. Who can forget Robert Murray M'Cheyne? Many know of Andrew Bonar only because of his memoir of his friend; thankfully, we still sing Horatius Bonar's great hymns. But—perhaps partly because the present biography has been too long left to gather dust in the lower shelves of old libraries, the name of Alexander Moody Stuart, whom they all esteemed so much, has been forgotten. Yet it took only one encounter with his preaching for Robert M'Cheyne to say, 'I have found the man.'

The best Christian biographies do three things for us: they instruct us; they challenge us; and they inspire within us a desire, not to clone ourselves in the image of the subject, but to follow him in the ways he followed Christ. *Alexander Moody Stuart* does that for us. It comes from an era when God raised up a wonderful variety of men with diverse personalities and gifts shaped by individualized providences, and gave each of them a spiritual burden to discharge in their lives and ministries, while drawing them together in a fellowship and work they all sensed was larger than themselves. Here is a biography that conveys a sense of what it is like for the hand of God to be on a man's life, calling him, shaping him, and using him to minister to others. And, like Andrew Bonar's memoir of their mutual friend Robert M'Cheyne, there is a touch of heaven about these pages.

There is much in *Alexander Moody Stuart* that helps to recalibrate our Christian lives. There is much in it that ministers of the gospel will find speaks directly to them. And all this is because there is so much in it that breathes love for the Lord Jesus Christ.

Is it any wonder it is a 'must have' and a 'must read'?

SINCLAIR B. FERGUSON

March 2023

Publisher's Introduction

APPROXIMATELY halfway between the Scottish cities of Perth and Dundee, on the southern slope of the Sidlaw Hills above the fertile landscape of the Carse of Gowrie, nestles the small settlement of Kilspindie. Next to its seventeenth-century parish church stands the walled family tomb of the Stuarts of Annat. On the far interior wall of this grey dynastic monument, out of reach behind locked iron gates, is a tablet marking the resting place of Jessie Stuart (1821–91), and her husband—the subject of this *Memoir*—Alexander Moody Stuart (1809–98). That most of the inscription under the latter's name was, at the time of the present publisher's visit, rendered unreadable by the intrusion of self-seeded shrubbery, seemed appropriate on a memorial to a man whose memory has become obscured by the passage of time, and the absence of a literary gardener to cut back the weeds of neglect.

The book now in your hands will hopefully serve as that gardener. It was originally published in 1899, this being the first time it has been re-issued in a new edition in well over a hundred years. Some, especially those not connected to Scotland, may well question the value of reading such a memoir as this, its time and space being perceived as distant and foreign to our own contemporary circumstances. It would be a grave mistake, however, to pass this book by on the basis of such perceptions. Biographies are not just paper and ink, but the preservers and carriers of the ideas and events which shaped the lives of their subjects. Circumstances naturally change, but good ideas, rooted in biblical truth, outlive changing circumstances. The ideas contained in this memoir, about the fundamental character and shape of an enduringly fruitful Christian ministry, have much to say to our contemporary scene. Indeed, the pages that lie before you contain not only an interesting record of a significant yet relatively unknown nineteenth-century ministry, but will serve as a window into the living piety and gospel vision which sustained that ministry through many decades.

This record is 'partly autobiographical' in that the earlier chapters consist mostly of Alexander Moody Stuart's own words, written with the intention of publication, in the hope that 'they may prove profitable.' His eldest son Kenneth, himself a minister, served as editor of these early chapters, and author of the subsequent narrative recounting the middle and later years of his father's life and labours. He does an admirable job—unlike some biographies of a similar vintage which now appear tediously detailed, this one moves at a pace. Indeed, there are places when you will likely wish that the son had lingered a while longer on certain aspects of the father's life. Nevertheless, the opinion of John Macleod, the erudite and profoundly well-read principal of Edinburgh's Free Church College during the first half of the twentieth century, is well worth bearing in mind as you begin to read this volume: 'There are few ministerial biographies that are better worth reading than Moody Stuart's Life by his son.'

When those words of Principal Macleod first appeared in his *Scottish Theology*, a certain proportion of his older readers would have possessed a living memory of Moody Stuart's ministry. That is not the case today. It is likely that those who have come across the name of Alexander Moody Stuart have done so in the form of passing references which appear in the memoirs of his friends Andrew Bonar and Robert Murray M'Cheyne. These relatively few references hide the true extent of the influence of Moody Stuart's own long ministry amongst his contemporaries, both at home and overseas. Indeed, in the estimation of his colleagues in the Free Presbytery of Edinburgh, 'Few were honoured to wield an influence so profound and far-reaching.'

At home his church became, again in the words of John Macleod, 'a rallying centre of the most exercised Christians of his generation in Edinburgh.' Whilst Moody Stuart was an unashamed adherent to the Presbyterianism of his homeland, and a resolute defender of the biblical doctrines expounded in the *Westminster Confession of Faith*, his was no dull or formulaic orthodoxy. The personal testimonies of those who sat under his preaching and who experienced his personal counsels, contained in the following pages, bear witness to his evangelistic zeal and warm-hearted pastoral instincts. His ministry was, in Macleod's estimation, 'an eminently spiritual one.' He possessed a weak voice, yet his preaching, marked by 'earnestness' and 'originality', met a felt need amongst his hearers, and remained fresh over many decades. The secret to this spiritual freshness will be discovered in these pages.

Alexander Moody Stuart's vision extended far beyond his own congregation, and his own country. The 1830s witnessed a renewed interest in missionary endeavour within the Church of Scotland, and Moody Stuart early became associated with the cause of mission to the Jews. As noted above, he was in the same circle as Andrew Bonar and Robert Murray M'Cheyne, who would form part of the party which was sent to Palestine to undertake an enquiry into the possibility of a mission to the Jews—a trip which would lead to the establishment of a mission not in Palestine, but in Hungary. Moody Stuart's subsequent championing of the cause of mission to the Jewish populations of Europe became a marked feature of his life's work. A lecture delivered by him on the 'Obligation under which the Gentile Believer has been Laid to Love and Honour the Jew', delivered in 1839, has been included in the appendix, together with sample addresses from his four decades as convener of the Free Church's committee for mission to Jews. Moody Stuart's long involvement in this work was marked by the conviction that it was at heart a *spiritual* endeavour—it was, in his understanding, part of the divine plan for the conversion of the world to Christ.

The 'eminently spiritual' character of Moody Stuart's ministry goes some way toward explaining his involvement in two church controversies—the debate which took place between 1863 and 1873 surrounding a proposed union between his own Free Church of Scotland and the United Presbyterian Church, and that which surrounded the 'Higher Criticism' movement of the later nineteenth century. In both these debates, and especially in the latter, he perceived that the authority of Scripture was at stake, and so was prepared to take a stand. For Moody Stuart, the Bible and its integrity lay at the heart of the church's purpose and missionary success. It was, therefore, no wonder, with all his pastoral and missionary interests, that he was prepared to enter into the debate and defend what he considered to be an affront to the evangelical heart of the church. These debates were of their time, yet involved principles which remain at the core of what it is to stay faithful in ministry when the tide of opinion is moving in a contrary direction.

These are just a few of the noteworthy aspects of Alexander Moody Stuart's long ministry, in which he variously was a missionary, church planter, pastor, and promoter of world mission. Biographies are not their subjects, and to some extent there will always be aspects of Moody Stuart's life and thought, the warmth of his personal interactions with his family, friends, and congregation, that will remain for us in the shadows of the past. But it is hoped that the republication of this *Memoir* will go some way to lift Alexander Moody Stuart, as a servant of Christ worthy of imitation, out of relative obscurity—a man who, in his allotted time and circumstances, exercised a deep and penetrating ministry of the word. The character and aroma of that influential ministry, often vividly brought to life in the following pages, contain much to stimulate and inspire those engaged in that same spiritual work in the twenty-first century.

An extensive appendix has been included in this edition, containing samples of sermons and addresses, and other documents of interest. Publisher's footnotes (marked —*P.*) have also been included to clarify context and provide other information of interest. Footnotes by the original editor are marked '—*KMS.*' and those few by the subject himself are marked '—*AMS.*'

THE PUBLISHER

Edinburgh,
March 2023

Preface to the First Edition

WHILE the subject of this memoir had not contemplated that any formal biography would be published, he had prepared for the press recollections of his earlier years (from 1809 to 1835), and had also indicated his desire that portions of the devotional diary which he kept during the last few years of his life might along with these early reminiscences be given to the public in the hope of their proving profitable. These are contained in chapters one to four and nineteen of this memoir. As, however, such a memorial volume would have omitted no less than sixty years of Dr Moody Stuart's life, it seemed desirable that this material should be incorporated in a memoir taking more or less the form of a regular biography. The diary, besides what is given in chapter nineteen, has occasionally been made use of by the editor in other portions of the book. Besides these chapters, those describing his visits to Madeira in Brazil, to Ireland during the famine, and to Hungary and Bohemia, that on the Jewish mission, as well as those containing his letters, and the short extracts from his sermons, are given almost entirely in his own words (i.e. chapters 5, 6, 8, 11, 15, 17), so that more than half the volume may be said the be from Dr Moody Stuart's own pen.

The following was written by him as a preface to the reminiscences of his early life to the close of his Holy Island ministry:

'In the leisure of old age and being laid aside from active work the days of youth come back to the memory with the Lord's manifold mercies in them; and to the praise of his grace, which is so far above all praise of ours, I desire to recall a few of these mercies in years so long gone by that they may be reckoned as belonging to an age now past.

'In the retrospect of a long life, not the mercies only recur to the memory, but the sins and the mistakes; the feet sometimes "well-nigh slipping," the offences great and little, the self-pleasing, the inconsiderateness for others, and the grievous neglects both personal and ministerial. These constrain the frequent confession: "Mine iniquities are more than the hairs of my head, therefore my heart faileth me"; yet grace much more abounding inspires the thanksgiving: "How precious are thy thoughts unto me, O God! how great is the sum of them! If I should count *them*, they are more in number than the *sand*."

'In the unknown depths of his love the God of peace "casts all our sins behind his back, whilst his own works he has made to be remembered." At times, indeed, we can see little else but sin; and in rather a new light we have come to understand that all our sins have been directly against God, against Christ, against the Holy Spirit. At the same time, while almost shrinking from saying "I lay my sins on Jesus", my whole heart consents to God laying them all on him; to the great central truths that he has been wounded by them and for them; that he has borne the guilt of each and the shame of each as if they had been his own; that his blood cleanses gloriously from all sin, making both the conscience clean and the heart pure; and that his robe of righteousness, of which he stripped himself on the cross when he was numbered with the transgressors and suffered as if unrighteous, clothes us from head to foot with "fine linen and white." "God manifest in the flesh" has become to me more wondrous and more near; the Creator of heaven and earth, "without whom was not anything made that was made," "bearing our sins in his own body on the tree."

'Through sins and through mercies, through chastenings and rebukes and pardons, it has been my ambition by the conviction, the enlightening and the renewing of the Holy Spirit, "to *follow after* righteousness, godliness, faith, love, patience, meekness," and my consolation to believe that whom the Lord loveth "he loveth unto the end." In that end, as so often before, he washes his disciples' feet from the countless stains of our course from our birth to our death; and when called from this earth I trust that he will say to me, as to the dying penitent on the cross, "Today thou shalt be with me in Paradise."

'Annat, 1888.'

At the end of the section on Holy Island Dr Moody Stuart wrote: 'And now in nearing the end of my pilgrimage I desire to say in childlike simplicity of faith, "Into thy hands I commend my spirit: thou hast redeemed me, O Lord God of truth!"'

To this he appends a Latin extract from Bengal: 'O ample grace, potent faith, which in the midst of the world, in the midst of sin, among so many snares of Satan, in such incredible weakness of the flesh, yet sanctifies, yet supports and preserves!

'Annat, 1890.'

The Editor conveys his warm thanks to all those whose names occur in the course of the narrative as having furnished contributions, and also to the Revs. Dr Milne Rae, secretary of the Jews' Conversion Committee, and James Kennedy, librarian of New College for helpful assistance; also to Rev. J. Storie, late of Hobart, and Mr F. A. Brown Douglas, advocate, and to Miss Buchanan, Mrs Macdonald, Mrs T. Stothert, Miss Alice Whitehead, Miss Cousin, Miss J. M. Gillies, Miss Meister, Miss Elder and others for kindly sending notes of sermons and reminiscences.

He desires also specially to thank the Revs. Robert Cowan, Elgin; J. G. Cunningham, D.D.; J. Hood Wilson, D.D.; Robert Logan,

Moffat, and W. Somerville Reid, as well as members of the family, for valued assistance given in revising portions of the manuscript or in correcting the proof sheets.

In presenting this memoir to the public, I do so with considerable diffidence, conscious of many defects in the work of compiling, yet trusting that through the divine blessing it may help to keep in memory and continue the influence of one who was felt by many to have been during a long life 'a good and faithful servant of Jesus Christ.'

To those who may justly feel that the memoir fails to reproduce the subject of it as they remember him, I must apologise in the words of Southey:

> And what if there be those, who in the cabinet
>   Of memory hold enshrined a livelier portraiture;
> And see in thought as in their dreams
>   His actual image verily produced?
> Yet shall this memorial convey
>   To strangers and preserve for after-time
> Something that else had passed away.

KENNETH MOODY STUART
Moffat,
23 November 1899

xxvi

Parentage and Boyhood

Respect the fountain of whose waters thou
And all of thine have drunk. Today
Is yesterday's apt scholar, and tomorrow
The docile, pensive pupil of today.
Our fathers mould us, and we mould our sons.

—Horatius Bonar

THE busy town of Paisley, some eight miles west of Glasgow, has been best known to the public for its shawl-weaving in a past generation, and for its great thread industries in the present. But this manufacturing centre has produced not a few men by whose genius and energy threads of another sort have been spun and woven into our modern Scottish history, without which the texture of our national life would lose something that has contributed materially to its excellence and beauty. Among those who have strengthened and adorned the life of their native land, there are several who claim Paisley as their birthplace.

It may not be too much to say that a service similar to what his townsmen, Alexander Wilson,[1] did for natural science, Prof. John

---

[1] Alexander Wilson (1766–1813), the son of a Paisley weaver, became a respected ornithologist, and the author of, among other things, *The American Ornithology.*—P.

Wilson[2] for literature, Tannahill[3] and Motherwell[4] for poetry, and David Stow[5] for education, has been rendered by *Alexander Moody*, the subject of this memoir, to the deeper spiritual religious life of Scotland. One so well qualified to express his opinion on this as the late Prof. Blaikie, D.D.,[6] wrote: 'There are still not a few among us who know how much we owed to Dr Moody Stuart, especially in those early days when the possibilities of the spiritual life were but beginning to be appreciated even in Christian circles'; while ministers of a succeeding generation, who did not make his acquaintance until in old age he had wholly retired from public life, have testified to their being impressed by his being one who in a very unusual degree was 'endued with power from on high.'

ALEXANDER MOODY was born in Paisley on 15 June 1809. The day of his birth was memorable from a shower of snow which took place on it. He was the sixth and youngest son of Mr Andrew Moody, a leading citizen of that town. Mr Moody was a thread manufacturer when the spinning mills were driven by horsepower, some of them by oxen. After steam was introduced he devoted himself to banking business, being partner and manager of the Union Bank of Paisley. The fact that when a youth he skated from Paisley down the Cart, and up the Clyde to the Broomielaw, reminds one of how recent origin the great shipping trade of Glasgow is. It was said of him that he was 'the strachtest man you wud see ga'en.' The esteem in which he was held by all classes of his fellow townsmen is proved by the fact that he was chosen Chief Magistrate of the burgh, in which

[2] John Wilson (1785–1854), the son of a Paisley manufacturer of gauze, was an early contributor to the Scottish Tory *Blackwood's Magazine*, and in 1820 was elected to the chair of moral philosophy at Edinburgh University.—*P.*

[3] Robert Tannahill (1774–1810), son of a Paisley silk-weaver and Ayrshire farmer's daughter, became a well-known song-writer and poet.—*P.*

[4] William Motherwell (1797–1835), a poet, born in Glasgow and educated in Paisley. In 1828 he became editor of the *Paisley Advertiser*, before moving to do the same at the *Glasgow Courier*.—*P.*

[5] David Stow (1793–1864), son of a Paisley merchant and magistrate, was an educational writer and founder of the Glasgow Normal School.—*P.*

[6] William Garden Blaikie (1820–99) was Professor of Apologetics and Pastoral Theology at New College, Edinburgh, from 1868 to 1897.—*P.*

capacity he cut the first turf of the Glasgow and Paisley Canal, and was a Justice of the Peace of the County of Renfrew. He was beloved by the poor, as he did much for them, and sold them large quantities of potatoes, which he raised on some moss-land, at low prices during the time of scarcity about 1800. In the Radical Riots of the year 1819, when the mob, making a demonstration against the tax upon corn, was parading the streets of the town and breaking the windows, the rioters paused abruptly in their work of destruction opposite his house, one who was on the street heard the leader shout, 'miss Bailie Moody's house! He's a good sowl, Moody.' These rioters did not content themselves with breaking windows. A maid was washing the doorstep near his house in the morning when a man passing remarked, 'Yes, you may wash the step clean, but there will be blood on it before night.'

Mr James Macdonald, W.S.,[7] who accompanied Dr Moody Stuart to Paisley in 1876, to appear before the Presbytery as a representative of St Luke's congregation in their call to Mr Cunningham of Lochwinnoch, recollects his minister pointing out the spot where he had seen Sir Alexander Boswell, who was in command of the troops that had been sent to keep order, strike with the flat of his sword a great burly miller, who was breaking through the lines. The crowd shouted 'Shame! Shame!' as the miller was unarmed, whereupon Sir Alexander leaped from his horse, threw his helmet and gauntlets on the ground, and squared up to the offender with his fists. This elicited loud cheers from the crowd, and he took the opportunity then of addressing them, and urging them to disperse quietly. This officer was killed in a duel with Stewart of Dunearn, the last death from duelling in Scotland. Dr Moody Stuart pointed out another part of the street where from his father's windows he had seen the soldiers bayoneting some of the mob.

Bailie Moody's pedigree is traced back for 200 years in the county of Renfrew, the founder of the stock having according to family

---

[7] The postnominal initials W.S. denote 'Writer to the Signet', that is, a member of the ancient society of solicitors in Scotland.—P.

tradition come from England in the army of the Commonwealth. In the old churchyard of Killallan there is a tombstone to one of the family, Matthew Moody, Farmer, Fodstone, who died in 1720, with the inscription (composed in a style long characteristic of the family): 'A gravestone is a memorial of the dead, and a memento to the living, putting them in remembrance of that which all should be concerned to remember.'

Bailie Moody was married to Margaret Fulton McBrair, daughter of Mr Archibald McBrair, Glasgow, who had a family of seventeen children by his wife Jean Miller, thirteen of whom grew up and sat together round the family table.

My father said that he and his brothers and sisters were brought up religiously with the daily observance of family and personal prayer, and were under the preaching of Evangelical ministers, and the high moral standard of the elder members of the family had its leavening influence upon them all. When they first went to school they said in their simplicity that 'they did not tell lies,' and the boys laughed at them as worse than themselves, who would not have uttered so great a falsehood. But in boyhood he could not recall any time of more special religious impression, except on one Sabbath, when he was seven or eight years old, and had been detained from church by some slight ailment. During part of the time of service, being alone in the bowling-green at the foot of their garden, he had a vivid sense of sin and of the coming judgment. It took the form of an earnest wish that it were possible to begin life anew, with all the past blotted out, but without the least conception that this is actually the case when we receive the forgiveness of sins in Christ Jesus; for their religious teaching had not been impressively clear and full on the doctrines of grace.

His father owned for a time the estate of Muirshiel, in the uplands of Renfrewshire. This property embraced the upper part of Calder Glen, and a wide expanse of solitary moorland, the heather-clad heights of which command magnificent views on every side. The romantic scenery of these Renfrewshire hills, where they used to spend their holidays, was doubtless a factor in the education of one whose preaching and writing were characterised by an intensely appreciative love of nature.

When he was ten or eleven years old, spending the summer holidays here, he experienced a remarkable deliverance from drowning, which, looking back on his youth from his extreme age, he describes as 'the most memorable of the providential events of a long life,' and the remembrance of which was a continual source of thanksgiving to God. In his own narrative he writes:

'In our holidays we had for years been bathing daily in the Calder, but always in the same pool, which we called the bathing pool, it having been chosen for us by our revered father for its breadth and safety. As we grew bigger, and were set on learning to swim, we found it rather shallow; and being allowed much liberty in such things, one of my older brothers proposed that we should look out for one that was deeper and yet safe. Amongst shallower pools, and others of a hidden depth, into which we delighted afterwards to plunge, we found one, a beautiful basin cut out of the smooth water-worn rock from one side of the stream to the other, while its floor of the finest gravel shone temptingly through the clear moss-coloured water. Its one defect was that its depth sloped gradually from about two feet at one end to six or seven at the other; and this we hoped triumphantly to overcome.

'Taking two of the land steward's boys with us, we set to work with barrows and shovels to fill up the dangerous depth. Filling our barrows with gravel, we emptied them from the rock into the pool with great zeal for a whole day. In the afternoon of a second, or perhaps third day, we began to be impatient to bathe in our new pool. The day was bright, the water attractive, and believing it now to be safe, we felt it to be irresistible. Having stripped on the grassy bank at the shallow end of the pool, my brother ran impetuously into the water, never doubting that he could wade to the rock on the opposite side. I looked up, and was overwhelmed with alarm to see that he had got beyond his depth, and was drowning, preserving his life for a few minutes by leaping incessantly from the ground, so as to get his mouth above the water for a moment's breath, and then sinking out of sight.

'In my alarm, while the two boys looked on in stupid callousness, I rushed at once into the water, blindly hoping to help him without knowing how. When quite near him I was over the head, and with the unreflecting impulse of desperation, he stood on my shoulders, and being an agile leaper, sprang to the rock and was safe.

It was a supremely awful moment as I sank in the pool under his feet, saving him, but utterly helpless to save myself. But the Lord now gave me presence of mind far above what was natural to me, and very different from the impetuous alarm about my brother. Either to stand up or to move forward was certain death; but having been pressed to the bottom on my hands and knees, my hope of safety was by continuing in the same position, but turning round toward the bank we had left. This I did without fear or the least misgiving; and so crept along crab-like, on hands and feet, without raising my head till in very shallow water. So it came to pass in the Lord's signal providence that my dear brother saved my life as well as his own; for if he had not made use of my nearness to him, I must have been drowned by trying to keep my head above the water; but when down on my hands and knees, it seemed quite natural to creep along the bottom instead of trying to rise to the surface as he had done. Many a time since I have inwardly said of this deliverance: "I was brought low, and he helped me"; but although neither of us omitted secret prayer morning and night, I did not then know the Lord as my Saviour.'

When Dr Moody Stuart went in the spring of 1876 to Lochwinnoch (the town nearest to Muirshiel), the Rev. J. G. Cunningham[8] accompanied him in revisiting those scenes of his boyhood, and

---

[8] John George Cunningham (1835–1907) was ordained as a minister at Lochwinnoch Free Church in 1859, and in 1876 became assistant to Alexander Moody Stuart at Free St Luke's in Edinburgh. He was also one of Moody Stuart's successors as convener of the Free Church's Committee for the Conversion of the Jews.—P.

he has told me how they knelt down together on the bank of that pool, and gave God united thanks for his providential care over them during their past lives, extending in my father's case to nearly sixty years from the date of this providential deliverance, and who had often since 'drawn them out of many waters which would have overflowed them.'

On this occasion also Dr Moody Stuart told his companion how, when he was seventeen years old, he and one of his brothers had gone up to visit Muirshiel in the early spring of 1827. Snow began to fall, and calling on their way on their friend Mr Wright at Calder Park, in the hilarity of their spirits they passed many a joke at the possibility of their being detained by the snow at Muirshiel. Little did they imagine in their merriment what the event was to be. That was the beginning of the long-remembered snowstorm of 1827, following the 'dry summer' of 1826, which covered the whole country with its deep wreaths for many a long week, when Muirshiel was entirely cut off from all communication with the outside world, and the two storm-stayed brothers had to subsist entirely on the grain and livestock in the farm town.

In recalling these early days he writes:

'In my father's taste for the improvement of waste land he employed a number of labourers on his moorland property, some of whom were in the habit of returning to their homes in Lochwinnoch on the Saturday nights, taking with them their spades and other implements of field labour. The distance was four miles, and one evening, in passing a wood half-way, they bethought themselves of laying aside their burdens, and concealing them under the trees till the Monday morning. The land steward's collie had followed them, and observing what they had done, he laid himself down of his own accord beside the spades, unnoticed by the workmen. On the Monday morning, to their great surprise, they found the dog keeping faithful watch over their spades which, unbidden and unobserved, he had been guarding for nearly thirty-six hours. The dog was of a rather wayward nature, and his action must have been mainly instinctive, as he owed little to any careful training. Yet notwithstanding this apparent approach to a sense of duty and to conscience, this collie had no more capacity than a sheep for any true fellowship with man, or for the appreciation of his character or thoughts.' Man, as he often said, is nearer to the infinite God in his nature than to any of the lower animals who approach nearest to him, for he can hold communion with his Creator, and can have no true communion with the most intelligent animals.

Another reminiscence of Muirshiel has a special interest, because only a month or two before his death Dr Moody Stuart embodied it in a booklet, and made it the basis of what was to be the last testimony, given when nearly ninety years of age, on behalf of the duty of cultivating Christian union and mutual love.

'In our holiday home in the country, two of us, along with a shepherd boy, took a ramble for miles over the heathery hills till we reached a stretch of the moor extremely remote and desolate. There we saw with surprise a flock of our sheep which had formed themselves into a square, the rams and the old sheep with their horns facing outwards, and the lambs carefully encircled in the living enclosure, as the deer in the Alps form a circle against the wolves. We could not think how to account for it till we saw a fox with a lamb in his mouth, running with all his might, leaping over every obstacle, and already far off with his prey.

'The flock now presented an interesting sight, having without any leader arranged themselves into this form, as in a skilful military evolution, by a singular concord amongst themselves. If one of them had broken the ranks, either a second fox might have got in through the opening to the lambs, or a lamb might have escaped from the protecting walls and have fallen an easy prey to another watching his opportunity.

'The sheep looked first to their fleeing foe, watching the fox for themselves, and directing us to see it; and then they looked to us with a bleating appeal for our sympathy and aid, but we were powerless to help them, as we had no dog with us.

'How good it will be when all the Lord's people shall form one loving flock, with a close union that will serve for a wall of defence against the roaring lion and the evening wolf that prowl around us watching for some dividing discord that will open a break in our wall by which they can enter to devour.'[9]

Bailie Moody's sons received their early education in school at Paisley, and they finished it in the Grammar School of Glasgow, where Alexander joined the rector's class (Dr Chrystal's). He was described to me by one of his school-fellows as 'a remarkably clever boy.' In Glasgow he took the second place in his class, William Wingate, who afterwards was again associated with my father as a devoted and much-esteemed missionary to the Jews in Hungary, under the Free Church, gaining the first prize, but as he said himself, 'I had a hard tussle for it.' Among other branches he took prizes for writing and dancing, which is somewhat remarkable, as he never afterwards excelled in either. Dancing, indeed, he did not countenance on principle, holding that, like card-playing, it formed an easily recognised line by which amusements, which were worldly in their character, and had at least associations and tendencies which were injurious to spiritual life, might be distinguished from those that might be safely indulged in. But while his penmanship, of which during his long life he made such good use, was not careless or irregular, it was very difficult to read. My grandmother told me that when he wrote to her expressing his desire to marry her daughter she could not make out what the note was about, and handed it at the breakfast-table to the governess, who was slowly deciphering it, when they were astonished to find that its contents were of a very confidential nature, and it was hastily closed for more private perusal!

---

[9] The tract founded on this incident is published by the Religious Tract Society (No. 284).—*KMS.*

— 2 —

College Days and Conversion

The Lord's invisible hands have been today
Laid on a young man's head;
And evermore beside him on his way,
The unseen Christ shall tread:
Beside him at the marriage feast shall be,
To make the scene more fair;
Beside him in the dark Gethsemane
Of pain and midnight prayer.

—*Henry Wadsworth Longfellow*

A T what he calls 'the too early age' of twelve, Alexander Moody entered the Glasgow University, where he studied Latin under Prof. Walker, Greek under Sir Dan. K. Sandford, Logic under Prof. Buchanan, and Moral Philosophy under Prof. Mylne, in all of which subjects he carried off prizes. He finished his Arts course in 1826, taking his degree of M.A. a year or two later. In 1829 he attended Prof. Jameson's[1] Lectures on Natural History. His father's death, which took place in Glasgow in 1826, followed soon after by the deaths of his two oldest brothers,

[1] Robert Jameson (1774–1854), mineralogist, in 1804 became Regius Professor of Natural History at Edinburgh University. The *Dictionary of National Biography* notes that 'as a teacher he attracted numerous pupils, excited their enthusiasm, keenly measured their abilities, and retained their friendship in after-life.'—*P.*

Matthew and Archibald, coupled with an adverse change in the circumstances of the family, brought, he says, much serious reflection, and the time had come for his deciding as to his future course in life. His sister Jane, who was now left the eldest of the family, had at this period been going through a deep religious experience.

In a fragmentary diary in 1823 she writes: 'I often felt that I was beginning to see light, as the blind man did who saw men as trees walking. The burden of sin I for long felt to be taken away, but could not be satisfied till I knew him by whom it was taken away.'

She passed through a period of spiritual darkness and temptation, but was brought out into the liberty of God's children by a young lady who said to her: 'Oh, do not look back; it will never do. Come to the cross of Christ as the vilest of the vile!' Her diary closes with the petition: 'And, oh, may I not dishonour his Holy Name!'

Never was petition more fully answered than was this; for she adorned the gospel which she now received in its fullness, and laboured quietly for her Redeemer to the close of a long life. She told me that during the last two years of her life she had derived great comfort from thinking upon the ministry of angels, which dispelled all feeling of loneliness. The last words she said to me were: 'It is sweet to lie in the Lord's arms, and to leave all to him. It is good to have his presence here, and then to go to be in his presence above. There will be many very sweet meetings up there!'

My father's narrative, with which his sister's experience is not unconnected, is now continued in his own words:

'After a good deal of thought I decided for the ministry, but not without a struggle. I took the step with a clear conscience, having a steadfast religious persuasion for myself and a conscientious desire for the salvation of others. After serious self-examination I had become a communicant and firmly believed in the necessity of conversion, which I trusted to have passed through by a gradual transformation. In this state I entered the Divinity Hall, and after giving my name to be enrolled my mind was lifted up with a buoyancy and joy of a kind never known before. The fact of having engaged myself to be "a servant of the God of heaven" I felt to be so high a privilege and honour that I could hardly restrain myself, and took a back lane on my way to college to give free scope to my exultation by running along it; it could not be called 'the joy of the hypocrite'; it lasted for ten days. Yet I was a stranger to the covenant of promise and to the new birth by the Holy Spirit, had never known forgiveness through the blood of the Lamb, and had not the spirit of adoption to be "as a son that serveth" his heavenly Father.

'After two years in the Hall at Glasgow I went to Edinburgh to study under Dr Chalmers.[2] My eldest sister, whom we looked up to as the most religious in the family, had recently come under deep convictions, and warned us faithfully that she had never undergone a saving change; and although we thought it too severe a judgment on herself, we knew that if this were true of her, our case must be still worse. For myself, I was constrained to conclude that any apparent tokens of grace might be accounted for by moral training and religious teaching combined with the dictates of natural conscience without any saving work of the Holy Spirit in the heart. But these doubts were quieted by evading the question.

'One night I had a deeply solemn dream. The dream took the form of thinking that I was dead, but not yet buried; that my life was past and irrevocable, but my eternal state not yet begun; and I sat down on my bed beside my coffin to examine myself and to ask if the soul was lost or saved, and I knelt down to cry for mercy although the time for prayer was for ever past. Surprised at my folly in making the attempt I rose from my knees and sat down to force myself to examine the question: Lost or saved? The effort was in vain, and I knelt again to cry for mercy, only to rise again and renew the hopeless inquest. When I awoke in the morning this frightful dream had gone from my memory; but whilst sitting in my room in the course of the day I dreamed it all over again, with

---

[2] Thomas Chalmers (1780–1847), the highly influential minister and philanthropist, and leader of the Evangelical party in the Church of Scotland. He held at this time the Chair of Theology at Edinburgh University.—*P.*

the waking consciousness that it was a dream, yet only to recall it as a stern reality. Of course there was no thought of any revelation in this vision of the night; yet "in a dream, in a vision of the night, in slumberings upon the bed, he openeth the ears of men and sealeth their instruction." The sealed instruction was to consider the state for eternity and to ask if the soul were lost or saved. Accordingly I made the attempt, but with the very same result as in my dream. The great question I asked but could not answer. My judgment was against myself, but I feared to pronounce it, and still hoped that I was not utterly without "part or lot in this matter."

At this time I sat under an esteemed minister in the New Town,[3] whose preaching I admired and valued, but when awakened to my own want of spiritual life I longed to hear some truth not yet learned, or of some path in the soul's history not yet trodden. At the close of the sermon the familiar words would recur to the memory: "All these things have I kept from my youth; what lack I yet?" And I would have been grateful to be told my lack, but it was not disclosed to me. One day on going over to the Old Town to hear Dr Gordon,[4] he told, to an unwilling ear, of conversion as a process, not of building up, such as I had earnestly desired, but of breaking down, by one stroke after another, till the whole gave way. The preacher's meaning was very clear, and it was equally clear that I had never known what he described, and was most averse to receive it. His words, however, by the grace of God, reached my heart as no words had ever done before; and I resolved not to forget them. Dark as they were, it was a new light in the soul's path for which I have ever thanked the Lord.

---

[3] The centre of Edinburgh has an 'Old Town' consisting of the environs of the castle and 'Royal Mile' running down to Holyrood Palace, and a 'New Town' on the north side of the former Nor Loch (drained in the early nineteenth century to form the present Princes Street Gardens), built between 1767 and 1850.—*P.*

[4] Robert Gordon (1786–1853) was a leading evangelical in the Church of Scotland. He exercised an influential ministry in the High Church of Edinburgh, continuing as minister of the Free High Church after the Disruption in 1843.—*P.*

'About this time I took up *Marshall on Sanctification*,[5] which I had put into my trunk on leaving home, but had never read; and to this book, under the Spirit's teaching, I owed my instruction in the doctrines of grace. The two great lessons I learned from it were,— the entire sinfulness of fallen man, the utter worthlessness of all that he can do; and over against this the infinitely perfect righteousness of Jesus Christ given for all and to all who believe on him "without even a pepper-corn of acknowledgment" from anything of ours. More than all this, this provision of a complete righteousness in the Lord Jesus Christ for us by his work and by his sacrifice convinced me of my own worthlessness and nakedness in the sight of God. I now thoroughly understood and believed these truths, although the conviction of guilt was not in the definite and agonising sense of sin as often since, but in a profound sense of the absolute want of all good and of the guilt of unbelief.

'These discoveries cast me to an infinite and helpless distance from God and from Christ. I was lost and dead, without any power either to pray or to believe; there was free salvation in Jesus Christ for the chief of sinners in believing on him, but in him I never had believed, and could not now believe. Standing stripped and ashamed, with no power to put on the clothing of the Lord Jesus Christ, I could do nothing, and made no attempt. Morning and night the Bible was read, and the knee bowed as before; but only as a duty, and not supposing that I could read or pray to any saving effect, for I was dead. I looked out from my window to the lofty and distant sky; and by such a distance felt myself to be "a great way off" from God, from Christ, from heaven.

'It was the time of the Spring Communion[6] in Edinburgh in 1829, and on the Fast Day,[7] my cousin, along with whom I then lodged,

---

[5] The reference is to *The Gospel Mystery of Sanctification* by the English presbyterian Walter Marshall (1628–80), a classic Puritan work on sanctification and justification.—*P.*

[6] A pattern had developed in Scotland whereby it was the norm for the Lord's Supper to be celebrated in parishes twice per year.—*P.*

[7] A typical communion 'season' consisted of a series of meetings over several

in receiving a token for himself, asked one also for me. It was taken without my knowledge, and vexed me when put in my hand, but I had no thought of using it because I had no part in Christ. Next day found me downcast and sad, but with a fixed resolution to care for nothing till I should find salvation, although it might not be for years. As I sat musing sorrowfully my Bible caught my eye, and I wondered if there could be anything in it for me. Taking it up listlessly, I held it in my hand and it was a dark sight, for I thought I had known it, but now it was a sealed book from beginning to end. It was all one to me where to read, for all was equally dark, and I opened it without looking where; but as I read I came to these words in Ephesians 5:14. "Awake *thou that sleepest*, and arise from the dead, and Christ shall give thee light." They came to me like a flash of lightning in the sudden awakening, but with infinite sweetness of light in Christ; they were spoken to *me*, of whom I supposed no one could be thinking. They were addressed to the *sleeper*, and if any one in the whole world was sleeping it was myself.

'I was lost and dead, yet was not in agony, was not praying, was not even anxious, but was sleeping sadly in death. Can this be the Bible? Can this be the book I have been reading from childhood? Having turned it over to make sure that it was my own very Bible, I rejoiced in the sight of the well-known volume, read again to make sure of the words, then closed the book in wonder and peace and joy. I had been darkness, but now was light in the Lord, the darkness past, and the true light now shining, the saving righteousness of Christ now my own. From that hour I could say, "Thy testimonies have I taken as an heritage for ever, for they are the rejoicing of my heart." His "word had quickened me," and I trust that he has never "taken it utterly out of my mouth."

'By God's own gift the word must have been "mixed with faith" in reading, but it awoke and enlightened me with resistless power,

---

days. It was usual for the Thursday before the Supper to be designated a fast day, with a preparatory service held on the Saturday, and a thanksgiving service held on the Monday following.—P.

as if previous to any consent on my part. The token received with sorrow was now used with joy, and for the first time I sat down at the Lord's table with faith, truly partaking of those signs and seals of the Lord's dying love, for which I often ardently long, since I have been laid aside. This day I have entered upon my eightieth year; it is fifty-nine years since the Lord spoke to me in saving grace and power; and of his gift on that day he has now been saying: "Behold I come quickly, hold that fast which thou hast that no man take thy crown."' (15 June 1888, Annat.)

The great transaction was now completed, and one was enrolled among the followers of the Lamb, who was to follow him with peculiar consistency and ardour through the seventy years of earthly pilgrimage that were still before him.

No sooner has he with the heart believed unto righteousness, than with the mouth he makes confession unto salvation. The following letter from his brother George attests this in an interesting manner:—

Paisley, 9 June 1830.

My Dear Alexr.,

Jane has shown me one of your late letters descriptive of the great transformation that God has so graciously wrought within you, and I do 'rejoice for the consolation,' and blessed be God I can now sympathise in your feelings and participate with you in that joy which is indeed unspeakable and full of glory. Christ has to me also appeared exceedingly precious— yes, precious beyond all conception and altogether lovely. On Sunday last Jane repeated to me the account of God's dealings with her soul: she told me of what his Spirit has been doing for you, and urged me to ask the teaching of the Spirit of Truth, and to apply directly and immediately to the Saviour of sinners. Accordingly God graciously inclined my heart to ply the throne of grace with much earnestness in seeking for an interest in the blood of sprinkling. Continuing to seek, in the confidence that God would hear me, yesterday morning

I found I trusted him whom my soul loveth. While reading the Scriptures, and praying, and meditating on the work of Christ, I was enabled by the grace of God to lay hold on the hope set before us, and a flood of joy burst in upon my soul. Since then I have scarcely known another feeling but joy and gratitude; much of my time has been spent reading the word, and never before did I realise what it is to *rejoice in it as one that findeth great spoil.* Every verse seems to tell of the Saviour, and what was before passed over with indifference is now delighted in beyond expression. Such indeed is the preciousness of this golden treasury that tears of joy run down my cheeks while its unutterable riches are unfolded to my view. Pray for me, my dear Alexr., that Christ may continue to be my All and in All, and write me of your own experience, so that we may provoke unto love and every good work.

Yours, with much affection,

GEORGE MOODY

This brother died in 1839, and as he was closing life he stopped his brother Alexander while repeating a text of Scripture, and asked: 'Are these the exact words of the Bible, for I am dying, and I need the *ipsissima verba?*' And when his brother read them from the book, he said, 'That's enough.' His son, the Rev. Andrew Moody, D.D., is our Church's able and devoted missionary to the Jews in Pest.

All the members of the family seem to have come under the power of religion while still in youth, although the transition from darkness to light was not so striking as in the three cases recorded. The two remaining brothers, Andrew and Robert, both became elders of the church. The latter during a long life exercised an important Christian influence in Bothwell, where he resided, and his second son, the Rev. Campbell N. Moody, is now a missionary in the great island of Formosa. Jessie, the youngest of the family, died in Madeira in 1842. Among her dying utterances she said that she liked very much to think there was nothing between God and her but love; that she was 'wearied of such a finite mind that could not comprehend God'; that she had never looked forward to such a deathbed; she thought there would be peace and joy, but that there would also be doubting, doubting overcome by peace— but it was perfect peace. Enumerating the fruits of the Spirit she said: 'What a glorious thing to have *one* of these fully! What must it be to have them all! but we shall be like him, *like him.*'

During the college vacation of 1827 Alexander and one of his brothers took a long walking tour through Scotland and a portion of England. At an inn on the road to Edinburgh they met two young mechanics returning from worshipping with the Rev. Dr Colquhoun,[8] of Leith, the previous day. They had both become anxious about spiritual things, and not having lighted on any minister who preached the gospel fully in Glasgow (though there were some evangelical preachers there), and having heard that Dr Colquhoun was such a preacher as they sought, they left home every Saturday evening after their work was done (there was no half-holiday then) for Edinburgh, slept all night at this inn half-way, continued their journey on Sabbath morning, arriving in time for forenoon service, and remaining for the afternoon diet; returned in the same manner, sleeping on Sabbath night at the inn, and starting very early began their work at 6 a.m. on Monday! The word of God was precious in these days, and was deeply prized by those who had felt its power.

On their tour they at last reached John o' Groats, and resolved to cross the Pentland Firth to Orkney. The boatmen said the wind was too high, and they must wait a day. They were surprised to find as soon as the sun set the boatmen preparing to set sail, although the wind had risen considerably in the interval. However, the men hurried them off, lighting the beacon signal which summoned a boat from Orkney to meet them in mid-channel. The crossing was

---

[8] John Colquhoun (1748–1827) minister of the New Church in Constitution Street, Leith, was known as one of the ablest exponents of 'Marrow' theology, with its emphasis on the free offer of the gospel.—*P.*

tempestuous, and they were dismayed to find that they had to step or jump from one smack to the other as the waves brought them for a moment together. The crossing was accomplished safely, though not without danger, and the men of the Orkney smack were indignant that their comrades should have brought them out on such a night. Before they left the Caithness crew they learned that the cause of their previous refusal to sail, and then starting when the weather was much worse, was that after sunset they could charge double fare!

In Orkney they were interested in visiting the Standing Stones of Stennis, and other antiquities of the islands. They did not however on this occasion cross to Shetland, which my father visited long afterwards, bringing back to us many curiosities, such as cups made of cocoa-nuts, which were carried by the Gulf Stream from the West Indies, and stranded on these northern shores, where the islanders tastefully carved them; specimens of various rare minerals, etc.; but best of all bringing back two Shetland ponies which for upwards of thirty years proved a most valuable acquisition in our Perthshire summer home at Annat. They were trained by my father, while we got a good many tumbles off their backs in the process. One was named Rona, after a sea-rock which my father described, the only access to which alike for sheep and shepherd was by a cradle swung on ropes at a giddy height over a surging tide. On this occasion he was hospitably entertained by relatives of his own on his mother's side, the family of Dr Edmonston of Unst. Here he saw a full-grown pony so small that it walked like a big dog under the dining-room table, while the natural history tastes of the household were apparent in their live pets and stuffed collections, the fruit of which is seen in the writings of one of the daughters, the well-known authoress, Mrs Saxby.[9]

On finishing their tour in Scotland they crossed the Border, and in Northumberland an incident occurred, often quoted afterwards to illustrate the truth that what seem insuperable barriers in our way are sometimes not removed till we are actually confronted

[9] Jessie Margaret Saxby (1842–1940), folklorist.—P.

20

by them, and threatened with immediate disaster, just as the Jordan was only dried when the priests' feet touched its flood. He had descended the shaft of a coal pit, and after being ushered into a lofty entrance hall lighted by a circular grate suspended from the roof, a miner placed him in a small truck, and giving him a lamp to hold, pushed him rapidly along the low passages. On coming to a small chamber where a man could stand upright, his conductor informed him that there had been a fall of coal in one of the passages, which made him feel that they were not free from danger. He then ran him on to another railed passage, where their lamps revealed the roof, the floor, the walls, all 'stones of darkness, and the shadow of death.' But now there loomed a black wall also right in front, and he saw that it was too late to call to his guide to stop their rapid progress, and in his constrained stooping position he resigned himself to the inevitable collision. To his surprise and delight the moment the truck struck the wall it flew open, and ere he was aware they were through it and rapidly moving on as before. The wall was a wooden door made to open at the slightest touch. 'Often,' he writes, 'since that day when we had trusted ourselves to the Lord Jesus, and wondered why he was leading us on a way that was walled up before us, the dark stone wall has become an open door at the sound of his voice, and we have passed through it rejoicing in him who openeth, and no man shutteth.'

— 3 —

Christian Work While a Student

Something, my God, for thee,
　Something for thee;
That each day's setting sun may bring
　Some penitential offering
That to thy gracious throne may rise,
　Some incense from some sacrifice,
　　Dear Lord, for thee.

—Anon.

AFTER taking the earlier years of his Divinity curriculum in Glasgow, Alexander Moody finished his course in the Theological Hall in Edinburgh, being attracted thither partly by the fame of Dr Chalmers, who was communicating a deep and widespread Evangelical impulse to those who came under his magnetic influence.

Some time before receiving licence as a preacher, the Lord taught him that he was not to delay doing work for him until he had been placed in a settled sphere of labour. One morning his landlady ushered a young man into his room. His visitor frankly told him that he had returned from the West Indies to find peace with God. He knew a young man who had rooms in the house, and had heard him mention that Mr Moody was studying for the ministry. He had therefore called, hoping that he might aid him in his inquiries. He was attending university classes to improve himself, and his friends all thought this was the motive of his spending a winter at home. In opening up his mind he said that first of all he had given up his youthful sins, and began to read the Bible with prayer morning and night. Still not finding peace of conscience he parted with things innocent in themselves, because they engrossed his heart. He had quite a peculiar love for animals, which they reciprocated. If he saw a horse strained in ascending a hill it gave him the acutest pain; dogs would follow him for miles into the country; he had trained his own dogs to carry any article; his pigeons came to him when called by their names; his horses needed no control beyond his voice, and at his bidding were taught to neigh to any friend to whom he wished to speak. These were his idols, enthroned in his heart, and one after another he put them all away, yet the aching void was not filled. At the same time he had the most sincere belief in answer to prayer, and in a watchful Providence. He had been thrice shipwrecked, and once when lying helpless on a plank in the sea, in a thick fog, he had been picked up by a passing ship, as he said, 'like a needle in a hay-stack.'

He had gathered the little blacks on his property into Sabbath classes, and taught them all he knew of the Bible, and of the ways of God. His estate was prospering, and was engrossing all his thoughts, so he resolved to leave it for a time, and come to Edinburgh seeking for inward peace. He had 'ordered aright his conversation,' and now the unsealed lips of this student were to 'show him the salvation of God' (Psa. 50:23). He said that he had received all that he could understand in the Bible, and had let alone what he could not understand. 'What is it that you have let alone in the Bible?' he was asked. 'The new birth, Christ made sin for us, that we might be made the righteousness of God in him, the sovereignty of God's mercy—I know nothing of all these,' he replied. He came saying, 'What lack I yet?' and his new-found friend told him that he lacked everything. When told that his hope of salvation must rest wholly on the righteousness of another, he was quite staggered. He often returned and they walked together, and he was told about free grace, of which he had known nothing. The Spirit opened his heart to receive the truth gradually, till he was translated out of darkness into Christ's marvellous light, and he now grew rapidly in the knowledge of Jesus, and was filled with peace and joy. The spiritual change so quickened his mental faculties as to make his studies far easier, and to bring back to his memory the neglected Latin which he had learned in boyhood. Though he had been before kind to his slaves, he now for the first time wished to see them freed, that they might share his new sense of liberty. Many years after, one Saturday when Mr Moody Stuart was busy in his study, a knock came to the door, followed by the question as the visitor held it half open: 'Is this the man?' and then after a moment's scrutiny: 'It is the man!' He was at once gladly welcomed by the busy minister, and their renewed acquaintance soon showed that in his long absence from Scotland he had not lost his faith or his 'first love.' Long after his death intercourse was resumed with his family.

'On returning to town the following winter,' the autobiography continues, 'expecting to occupy the rooms in which my West Indian friend had called on me, I found them engaged, but the landlady, a clever though not a religious woman, offered to find me a lodging. On my calling again she told me that she had found two suitable rooms in Broughton Place, but knew nothing of the landlady except from her appearance, in which she was sure she could not be mistaken. She was an old woman of seventy or eighty years, but with something quite peculiar in her countenance, such as she had never seen before in any one else. Because there was so much of heaven in her face, she assured me I could not go wrong in taking her rooms without inquiry into her character. It was no common occurrence to hear of one in whom the image of Christ was so visible in her countenance that it could be recognised by a stranger; and I took the rooms with thankfulness.

'In that house the communion of saints was both satisfying and most helpful; and the close of the winter brought with it the grateful recollection that during its course, in conducting family worship, I had never once risen from my knees without a lively sense of the Lord's presence, however dead or cold at the beginning of our devotions. This grace was due to the spirit of prayer in my aged landlady. This mother in Israel, who had for long been full of "love, joy, peace," had shared in her youth with many eminent saints in a lengthened spiritual struggle of intense severity, which she ascribed to want of instruction in the doctrines of grace. When at last she found light in the Lord, her joy was so great that she could not sleep for a whole week; yet so literally was "the joy of the Lord her strength," that although she was then the mother of a young family, with the whole burden of the house, she found herself quite fit without her nightly sleep for all her work through the day. It was a privilege to have been providentially led to the house of this "old disciple with whom we should lodge."

'In one of my walks at this time I had cause to praise the Lord for his "hail and stormy wind" fulfilling the counsels of his love. Being suddenly overtaken by a violent storm of hail and wind, I was driven by main force to turn aside for shelter in an old farmhouse. The house had been divided into labourers' dwellings of one or two rooms with a central passage between them, in which there was most acceptable shelter from the hail. After a little while the question: "Why stand ye here idle?" moved me to knock at the nearest door in the hope of finding some opening for our Lord and Master. In answer to my knock the door was unfastened, but held jealously ajar by a strange figure that forbade all hope of entrance. There was just opening enough to see standing before me the ideal of the Witch of Endor: an old woman, tall, stern, meagre, gaunt, with a white beard such as is rarely seen on a female face. She stood in rigid silence, but as if demanding why I had dared to intrude into her solitude. To prevent her shutting the door in my face, I asked at once: "Will you let me pray with you?" My glad surprise was now more than my disappointment and confusion. Her whole bearing changed in an instant; she exclaimed eagerly, "Pray wi' me,

a miserable sinner!" threw the door wide open for me, and, closing
it again, ran across the room with the agility of youth, placed a
chair for me and another for herself, and before I had got over my
wondering joy was down upon her knees, leaving me to follow her.

'What her history and character had been I did not ask and never
knew. When we got into conversation then and afterwards she baffled me with her acuteness, and often caused me to regret my words
of encouragement by the quickness with which she grasped them as
two-edged swords, and turned them against herself as arguments of
despair. Self-condemnation on account of sin and a deep sense of
her lost state were her leading trains of thought, in which she had
my full sympathy. But this was not relieved by the joy of redemption, and her state, in her own estimation, was lost irrevocably. I
set before her the Lord's free grace and his own words, "Ye will not
come unto me that ye might have life." "Yes," she replied with vehement energy, "because your deeds are evil." After telling her that I
had never found peace with God till I saw my own lost state, that
her case now was the same as mine had been, and that salvation was
as free to her as to me, she replied at once: "Yes, but the word had
ta'en a grip o' you, and it has never ta'en a grip o' me."

'One day after opening to her the grace of the Lord Jesus Christ
very fully, she looked on me very wistfully and said: "Oh, sir, I wish I
had seen you when I was a lassie; but its ower late noo." Thinking to
comfort her I answered, "But there is hope at the eleventh hour." She
caught, as she always did, at any element of darkness in the offered
light, and exclaimed with thrilling and appalling fear, "It is the eleventh hour wi' me!" Then she rose from her seat, drew a large circle on
the floor, and gazed on it as the mouth of the bottomless pit opening
to devour her. This was the lowest despair I saw in her, or have ever
seen in any other. But gradually she listened to the gospel with growing interest and light and hope, till one day on leaving her she said to
my great joy: "Ye'll maybe mak' mair o' me than ye're thinkin'."

'When calling to bid her farewell before leaving town, the closing scene presented a bright and beautiful contrast to the opening

one in the wild fury of the hailstorm. She was no longer shut up in gloom and misery with her jealously closed door, but sitting with one or two neighbours before her house in a bright sunshine, which presented a lively image of the "Sun of righteousness arising with healing in his wings" on one who had long dwelt in darkness and in the shadow of death. Her most welcome and cheering words when I last saw her alone, welcome not for their reference to the writer, but for her own hope of everlasting life, were these: "Maybe I'll be in your croon yet."

'When on a visit to my family in Glasgow, a friend of my eldest sister accosted me before entering church on the Sabbath forenoon and asked me to address her class of thirty girls in the evening. But although in the habit of pressing the gospel on my friends and others, my efforts had been confined to personal intercourse. To any faculty of speech beyond this narrow sphere I was an entire stranger, and all I hoped for in the form of preaching was either by reading or delivering by memory what had been already written, and while ashamed of my own incompetency I could give no other answer but a decided refusal. But throughout the service there ran through my inmost spirit an undercurrent of thought which, without closing the ears to the sermon and the other exercises, maintained a course of its own. If this call was of God, was I willing at all costs to consent to it? Then was it from the Lord or not? It was a shame to any Christian, and much more to one looking forward to the ministry, that there should have been the least hesitation in answering the first question; yet it cost me an agonising struggle before I could answer "Yes". Between the close of the forenoon service at one o'clock and of the afternoon at four, there were three long hours of conflicting and overwhelming thought. After one of the severest conflicts I ever passed through, I came to the conclusion that this might be a call from the Lord, and that it ought not to be refused. At the close of the afternoon service, on meeting the respected lady teacher, I announced to her abruptly, and almost as if submitting to a sentence of death, that I should come to her school in the evening.

'Returning hastily home to think and pray over a suitable subject, I fixed on the parable of the prodigal son with special reference to the words, "When he was yet *a great way off* the father saw him." From the recollection of the "great way off" in which I had found myself on the discovery of my lost condition, I could readily explain to these girls both their natural distance from God and his most tender grace in drawing them to himself in Jesus Christ; but the transference of the thoughts into spoken words was a dark and untried effort. What may have been said in my address I never knew; but to my own consciousness I did not finish a single sentence I had begun, and after about ten minutes quite broke down in confusion. In parting, the teacher in her kindness thanked me cordially for the address, and only regretted that it was so short.

'And now to my own mind the question of addressing others without the written words before me, or committed to memory, was finally settled. Both my own will and my own judgment had been wholly given up, but the Lord had not owned or upheld me, but had left me to stammer through the attempt to my own confusion, and with no possible benefit to any that heard me.

'The conclusion, so clear to me, was completely overturned by a letter from Glasgow a fortnight after to inform me that the Lord had been pleased to use my words for the conversion of two, if not three, of the eldest girls who had heard them. In thankfulness and awe, I knelt down and said: "O Lord, since it pleases thee to use me by making a fool of me, I am willing to be a fool all my days."

Long after (1859), when talking with the Rev. Robert Cowan, then under call to St Leonard's, Perth, he said to him abruptly: 'Would you be willing to be a fool for Christ's sake?' and prayed that he might be made willing.

'Afterwards, in the course of a long ministry, with only a few exceptions, I never either read a sermon or committed one to memory, although for years I wrote them, and the longer I have lived I have attached the more value to most careful preparation for the pulpit, and in most cases either by writing or by well-digested notes. Such preaching is not without its own defects and snares, but if conscientiously exercised it has commonly more power to arrest the attention, to reach the understanding, and to awaken the conscience of the people. For myself, the complete casting of the preacher on the help of the Lord before the sermon, the light and liberty and holy joy when that help is granted, and the humbling sense of deficiency after it, have endeared to me this mode of preaching the everlasting gospel. Yet it was by a read sermon that I was first awakened to my lost state, and every minister must ask to be led into what is best in his own case, and most fitted to profit his hearers.

'When lodging under the roof of the "old disciple" I was beset one morning by a sinful or impious thought which would not leave me. While engaged in prayer the temptation was altogether absent; but so soon as the prayer ended it returned in all its vehemence. This conflict continued throughout the day, and during my solitary meals; it brought me often to my knees, and always with the same result of relief in prayer, and of instant return on rising. It was sorely harassing, for it was last at night and first on awaking in the morning, continuing through the second day. In the afternoon of that day a new reflection presented itself: "This thought is surely not mine—I have no love for it, but an intense hatred, yet can by no effort get rid of it. Every kind of prayer and supplication I have tried, and have pleaded every remembered promise, but only with a temporary effect. Like a man in a leaking boat, as long as he labours in bailing out the water it does not sink, but the water rises faster than before the moment he ceases; so this vehement onset of evil is always waxing stronger, till it has worn me out. All this time I have been resisting it as within myself, but have never yet taken for my relief the promise, 'Resist the devil and he will flee from you.' This evil must be from Satan, and by divine help I embrace this special promise of deliverance." The temptation was gone in an instant; the tempter had fled and taken his poisoned sting with him; ere ever I was aware the thought was away, its poison had lost its power, and the thought itself had completely vanished. In wonder and fullness of delight and gratitude I walked up and down my room as if released from prison.

'In the same year there occurred an instance of Satan's working, not by suggesting evil, but by suggesting other duties that would have hindered present duty. One day a lady put a one-pound note into my hand, asking me to take it to an old woman who had once been nurse in her family, who lived two miles out of town. She was thankful for the gift, and talked most volubly of the kindness of the giver; but on directing her thoughts to the Giver of all good, she answered with a flow of words that seemed to have no heart in them. For some weeks my visits were repeated, but their object was quite baffled by her self-complacent trust in her own moral and religious character. At last in despair of milder dealing I expressed a fear that she was still a stranger to the new birth and to the knowledge of the truth as it is in Jesus. Her hitherto fair talk and unfailing serenity were suddenly transformed into an indignant repudiation of the possibility of her not being a child of God, and she was quite as angry now as she had been plausible before. Her case at last looked all but hopeless, and as if it were only a waste of time to bestow further labour in it, and it must be left in the hand of the Lord.

'After an interval of four or five weeks it came into my mind that I ought to visit this poor woman again, and I set out with no hope of other than a cold reception. When nearly half-way to her house I suddenly remembered a letter that ought to be written, and began seriously to doubt whether it was not a greater duty to return and write it than to persevere in a hopeless visit. Whilst walking slowly in deliberation the duty of returning had begun to seem the weightier of the two, and had nearly turned the scale. Just then there flashed into my mind another reason for going back, and immediately a third reason presented itself, then a fourth, and then a fifth; each pressed more forcibly than the other. But it now occurred to me that if there might be one good reason for returning to town there could not be five or six, and that they must all be the hindrances of Satan to dissuade from this duty. There was no room for doubting now; the divine command was "not to give place to the devil," and my clear path was in an unfaltering determination to persevere.

'It was, however, no easy course, for the arguments for returning poured on the mind as in a shower of hail, and were like to drive me back by main force. It was a solitary part of the road, there was nobody in sight. The mental pressure was so severe that the only resource was in the resolution to stop the flow of my thoughts by running till the midway between home and the object of my visit was fairly passed. This done, the rest of the walk was smooth and pleasant with no more inward urgencies to draw back.

'On opening the door, the old woman's face as she sat on the further side of the room was lighted up with joy and her greeting was music in my ears. "Oh, sir," she called aloud, "I am so glad to see you; I thought you were never coming again." The atmosphere was quite new, for the Lord himself had been showing her what I had failed to teach; she had seen herself a lost sinner, and her eyes were opening to behold the Lamb of God. There was now fellowship in the joy of the Lord, and future visits were only to confirm his own work. The adversary knew too well that one of his captives had been escaping from his grasp in her old age; and as when St Paul would have come to the Thessalonians once and again "Satan hindered"; so he strove on this occasion to hinder my coming by inward suggestions, if it had not pleased the "God of peace to bruise Satan under our feet."'

— 4 —

Holy Island

Dry-shod, o'er sands, twice every day,
  The pilgrims to the shrine find way;
Twice every day, the waves efface
  Of staves and sandall'd feet the trace.
The castle with its battled walls,
  The ancient monastery's halls,
With massive arches, row and row,
  On ponderous columns, short and low.

—*Marmion*

AFTER having received licence from the Presbytery of Glasgow on 5 October 1831, the first call to regular work which Alexander Moody received was in the end of 1832, when he was invited by Mr Buchan of Kelloe, a highly respected elder of the Church of Scotland, to engage in what we now call Home Mission work, in Holy Island, off the coast of Northumberland. In visiting the island in summer Mr Buchan had been impressed with its spiritual wants. Of the place and people the young Scottish probationer knew nothing, but it was his first opening for the work to which he had devoted his life, and he accepted it without hesitation.

The account of his labours may be best given in Mr Moody's own words, except when to save space the narrative requires to be condensed.

'Holy Island is described by Bede as "tossed by great billows night and day," and as a semi-island —

> For with the ebb and flow its style
> Varies from Continent to Isle.

Nature is a loving handmaid to grace, and both at the time and ever since I have looked upon it as of the Lord's singular mercy that he sent me to this lonely island of the sea in the beginning of my work. The Culdees of Iona, in their zealous and successful evangelisation of the north of England in the seventh century, selected Lindisfarne, afterwards called Holy Island, as the centre of their operations. They chose it for its likeness to their own island home in the west, as a fit place for personal devotion, and a secure and convenient centre whence they might go forth to preach on the mainland. Their aim was to make it another Iona. In the process of centuries the venerable ecclesiastical buildings were erected, which are still so grand and imposing.

'Aidan, who came from Iona seventy years after its occupation by Columba, took up his abode in Lindisfarne, and "gathered about him a class of the most promising lads, twelve in number, many of whom were famous in after-life." Of him Bishop Lightfoot says:

> In the simple, wise, sympathetic, large-hearted, saintly Aidan, to whom Northumbria owes its conversion, we have an evangelist of the purest and noblest type. Then commenced those thirty years of earnest evangelic labour, which ended in the submission of England to the gentle yoke of Christ. The Holy Island of Lindisfarne was the true cradle of English Christianity.

Afterwards the bishopric of Lindisfarne was committed to St Cuthbert, whose wide fame overshadowed his predecessor's. The

lustre of his saintliness has been rather obscured by the halo of
fabulous miracles with which it has been encircled, as in the name
of St Cuthbert's beads still given to the fossil entrochites which are
plentiful in the island:—

> And fain St Hilda's nuns would learn,
>   If on a rock by Lindisfarne
> St Cuthbert sits, and toils to frame
>   The sea-born beads that bear his name.

Cuthbert was a man of genuine and singular holiness, with an
extreme love of solitude, reluctantly consenting to be ordained to
the bishopric, yet in his more active years full of loving zeal for the
salvation of others.

'The stretches of dry sand clothed with wiry bent and abounding
in sheltered hollows afforded a rare opportunity for meditation and
prayer, causing the thought to arise irresistibly, "God is here." Into
that wilderness, that unsown land, I was at first led by moonlight,
between walls of water on the right hand and on the left, and in
those sandy hollows it seemed at times as if the glory of the Lord
passed by.

'The distance from Berwick to the village was nearly twelve
miles, and the only inexpensive mode of reaching it was by a very
high-wheeled covered cart, which carried the mail once a week,
every Saturday. It was in the afternoon of a cold winter day in the
end of December that I set out for my new abode; and on account
of a strong east wind the carrier soon asked leave to remove the
canvas covering from his cart, to the great relief of his horse, but
less to the comfort of his solitary passenger. After some miles on
the road we turned down toward the sea, and when the daylight
had already ceased we got fairly into the midst of benty sands
with which I was soon to become familiar in my island home.
By-and-by our carriage stopped, and I suddenly found myself
deserted, in darkness and solitude. Although cloudy it was moonlight, but I had not seen my guide disappear, and could not think

what had become of him. There was no house to be seen, and I sat perched on the motionless cart in the midst of a desert. After the lapse of perhaps half an hour in helpless expectation I began to think what to do if my conductor failed to return; and the only alternatives seemed to be, either to sit all night in the cart, or to make for what looked like a high bank in front, and to the left, which I took for the island. At last came the relief of the loud crack of the carrier's whip, who had doubtless been indulging himself at a public-house in the neighbourhood. "We're most too late," he called with a loud and hasty shout. "Do you see yon that looks high and dark like the land?" (it was what I had mistaken for the island). "Yes." "That's the tide, and it will soon be six feet deep where we are." Then urging on his horse without leaving me either time or inclination to chide his long delay, he drove his high-wheeled cart up to the axle-trees in the water, which looked portentous for the rest of our journey, but it turned out to be only a narrow channel [called the Low] filled by the rising tide, out of which we soon emerged on to the solid sand again.

'The scene had now become singularly weird, mysterious, and grand. Our path was a narrow passage between two seas, whose flowing tides, driven faster by the east wind, were rising rapidly to meet each other on the ground over which we were slowly working our way, and where if we lingered we should soon be immersed beneath the double flood. The height of the dark waters was increased to the eye by the moonlight; and in the centre of so vivid a picture of it we could not fail to recall the passage of Israel through the Red Sea, when "the waters were a wall unto them, on their right hand and on their left."

'When we had fairly passed the sandy waste [three miles] which the sea claimed, and reached the sandy beach of the island, my simple yet witty guide, as if to make up for leaving me so long in the dark, now tried to cheer me by a sudden burst of buoyant eulogy on the brightness and beauty of those sands, "with the ladies walking on them with their parasols in the summer sun." The ludicrousness of the contrast to the present night of bitter cold was amusing for the moment, and on reaching the village the heat of a winter fire enkindled both gladness and gratitude.

'As our mission was only temporary, I avoided all interference with the Episcopal service on the Sabbath morning, which I attended regularly. In the afternoon, with two assistants, I conducted a Sabbath school, composed of nearly all the children in the island, and preached in the schoolhouse in the evening. The people were not unwilling to hear the gospel, and about a month after my arrival the attendance was increased by the sad death of a fine young fisherman, who, when in little or no apparent danger, was carried away from his comrades by a large wave when their boat was not many yards from the shore. His body was never found, and his widowed mother said to me in her grief: "I would wade into the depths of the ocean to find my George." After a time the school was crowded, and so many were left outside that for want of any other resource I divided the congregation into two, and preached at different hours to the men and women separately. We longed for a larger place, and the only one was a commodious granary belonging to the principal farmer, who freely consented to give us the use of it as soon as the grain should be cleared out. But winter had glided into summer, the interest of the people had abated, and the congregation was now too easily held in the school.

'One Tuesday morning I received a message that the granary was now at our disposal and all ready for us; and the kindness which would have so relieved me a month or two earlier only threw me into perplexity. It was impossible to refuse the kind answer to our previous request, and we took steps at once to have the place fitted up with all the benches we had at our command; but it was with a heavy heart, because the fishermen were now all out at sea, and from twelve to twenty of their wives formed the diminished audience on the Wednesday evenings, with the addition of two or three men not engaged in fishing. For this service I was in the habit of preparing very much as for the Sabbath, and on this occasion I felt that I had been specially helped, both in finding my text and in the thoughts to illustrate and enforce it. When the time of service drew near I sat in my room musing sadly over a good text, and what I thought a good sermon, with a hall more than ample for all the island, to be occupied by a few stragglers, only enough to make it look empty. In this desponding mood I was startled by a young fisherman suddenly breaking in upon me in breathless haste. "Oh! sir, come quick," he called; "the whole island's in the granary, it's filled from end to end, and they're all waiting for you." "How is it possible?" I asked in amazement. He hastily explained that the gale which had risen during the day had driven a king's cutter into the harbour, and the mate had sent two of his men to inquire if there was any service that evening, and had come on shore at the head of thirty men, with whom he was now in the granary. The fishermen at sea were also driven home by the gale. The appearance of the blue-jackets landing for such an object took the islanders by surprise, and as they marched in order from one end of the village to the other to reach the granary, the whole people, men, women and children, followed them into it.[1]

'When through the gathered crowd I had reached my own place the sight that presented itself was at once solemnising and inspiriting; many seated in the centre, far more standing behind and around them from end to end of the hall, and ranged immediately in front of me thirty men in naval uniform. In them there was much more than mere customary reverence, for in their leader and in some at least of his men there must have been a sincere thirsting for the living God, and for the word of his testimony, that prompted the inquiry where they might find it. Their reverent listening was fully shared by the whole congregation, and helped me to preach the gospel with liberty, and I trust also in the power of the Holy Ghost.[2]

---

[1] This granary is the building seen to the right of the ruined arch of Lindisfarne Priory in the picture, which thus presents to the eye two contrasted systems of religious worship.—*KMS.*

[2] This incident was published in the *Sunday at Home* for 1883.—*KMS.*

Granary

Lindisfarne Priory on Holy Island, with preaching granary

'A providential and gracious intervention so marked and so cheering was not designed for that night alone, but was followed by an abiding impression and greatly increased attendance that gave us new life and hope.'

Dr Moody Stuart in his diary notes that he had often observed a hidden providence guiding in the choice of texts of sermons. He says: 'In a limited rural parish every man knows his neighbour, and when a sermon without any special reference on the minister's part strikes at any particular sin, the rumour of it is sure to return to him. In the island I often found in the course of the week that the Sabbath text and sermon had been more applicable than I was aware of, as in the following instances:

'In praying and seeking for a text in the earlier days of a memorable week, the painful words, "The devil having now put into the heart of Judas Iscariot to betray him" (John 13:2), constantly recurred, and as constantly I put them away in the search for a more suitable text; but I could find no other, and this text would not leave me. I studied it carefully through the week, but went into the pulpit under the humbling conviction that this was the first text I had ever preached on that was not applicable to a single hearer in my audience. The people however listened with an interest far above my expectation; and their deep attention from first to last, especially in the description of the case of a man betraying Christ by scandalous sin under the cloak of religion, helped me to speak with an energy and effectiveness I had not at all anticipated.

'Next morning I had an unexpected call from one of the oldest of the fishermen, a quiet and friendly old man, who said that he had come to ask who told me about the case I referred to. When I assured him that I did not know what he meant, he replied that most certainly I knew, but the people had sent him to inquire who it was that told me; for they had all been anxious to keep it from me. He confidently asked me if I did not see the whole people turn round and look at the man who, on account of the crowd in the place, had taken an elevated seat on a window sill. To this I replied that I had certainly noticed the people turning round in that part of the sermon, but only supposed that something in the window had attracted their attention. At last he was convinced that I knew nothing, and informed me that one of my people had been guilty of scandalous immorality and that it had given great offence to all the people on account of his high religious profession.' This person afterwards showed signs of true penitence, and came to see Mr Moody after he was settled in Edinburgh.

'One week,' Mr Moody continues, 'I had prepared a sermon on the observance of the Sabbath, without being aware of any desecration of that day except such as is too prevalent everywhere, and I read the passage in the thirteenth chapter of Nehemiah against working, or buying and selling on the Sabbath, without suspecting any special trespasses in these respects. On the Saturday my servant had gone to the butcher to buy a chop for dinner next day, and returned to say that he had none, but had just killed a sheep and would have plenty tomorrow. When she went on the same errand on the Monday she was told that it had all been sold on the previous day, so that many of my hearers in the evening had bought their dinner on the forenoon of that Sabbath. Previously I had not the least idea of such a desecration, and it might seldom have occurred before; but the providential ordering of the sermon was marked on a day when this breach of the Sabbath must have come home to many consciences. The practical fruit of the sermon quickly ripened. On the Saturday afternoons I had been in the habit of taking a meditative walk in a retired part of the island. But soon after preaching on the sanctifying of the Sabbath, in returning home from my evening walk I turned my steps in a direction where the fishermen used to prosecute their labours, for no reason known to myself; and when not far from the village I saw the people all busily engaged in packing their fish which had been laid out to dry. As I passed by, one of the fishermen's wives, a superior woman, who took a leading place among them, and had been one of my most decided opponents, accosted me with a cheerful smile, and said: "Well, sir, you see you're doing some good among us at last." I was glad to hear it, but could not think of what special good she meant, and said in my simplicity: "I don't know how; all I see is that you are packing your fish." Her reply was in a tone of joyful triumph: "This used to be our Sabbath evening's employ"; for hitherto the fish had been packed on the Sabbath to be sent off next morning. Such an occupation of the Lord's day I had never suspected, and was not a little encouraged by this cheering fruit of the singularly-timed sermon on sanctifying the Sabbath.'

Such divine guidance of the preacher was not confined to his early ministry, for Mrs Brown Douglas writes: 'There was a peculiar power in your father, exactly meeting one's needs, in his preaching. We often said coming home, "Mr M. S. might have heard what we were speaking about last night." He seemed so to meet a felt need; I am sure he was directed by the Lord what to say.'

It was hard to convince some of them that they were sinners. Conversing with a fisherman who would not own that he was a sinner the young missionary said: 'I am a sinner.' Then for the first time the man looked up, and fixing his eyes steadfastly on him replied, 'I'm glad I'm not like you.'

"'How do you vex yourself about us?" said a kindly fisherman to me one day when I met him on the road; "we're nothing to you, and you're nothing to us. It can make no difference to you whether we go to heaven or to hell." My distress about himself and his people was both a grief and a puzzle to him. "They nothing to me, and I nothing to them"—the thought was unutterably startling—the people committed to me by the Lord, of whom he had said to me: "Go and speak to this people all the words of this life"! No difference to me whether they were lost or saved! I was bound up in them and could not think of leaving them without seeing their salvation. Beyond the island I could see no horizon in life till my mission there was fulfilled.

'In this little community was one of the best conditioned in outward circumstances of the fishermen's wives, living with her well-cared-for husband in their tidy and comfortable house. Her tall and muscular frame, her vigour of mind and strength of will, with her proud spirit, made her a commanding character in the island. From the first, she had been one of my constant hearers; but in the crisis that followed my sermon on Judas, and a reaction in favour of the delinquent, her previous respect suddenly changed into hatred, and she would gladly have seen me out of the island. After a while, however, she was again amongst our regular hearers, but we had not yet met in conversation. One day in passing along the opposite side of the broad street in which she lived, to my unbounded surprise the tall, high-spirited woman walked across toward me, and in the middle of the street, stretching out both her hands, called aloud in a tremulous and entreating voice: "Tell me anything in a' the world that living cratur' can do to be saved, and I'll do it; for I'm at my wits' end!" As she had no outward trial, it seemed as if nothing but the power of the Holy Ghost could have moved that piteous cry which so recalled that of the Philippian gaoler. Though from that day she continued my steadfast friend, otherwise she seemed to remain for a while the same as before; she could not easily take in the free grace of God in Christ, or receive the kingdom as a little child; but in the end I was persuaded that the Lord opened her ear to hear his own voice, "Come unto me, all ye that labour and are heavy laden, and I will give you rest." Along with others from that island in whom we hope the word of the Lord had taken root we trust to meet with her in the many mansions of our Father's house.'

At this time, however, Mr Moody was sometimes cast down at the apparent want of success in his work. In a letter to Mr Stothert he writes: 'I have been feeling wearied and faint in body, and feel almost beginning to be faint likewise in mind. How humbling it is to discover how much of what we set down for pure faith is mere animal spirit, and when what is natural has been evaporated by the fire of any trial, the residuum of what is spiritual is so small. In the midst of discouragement I would, if possible, wait till there has been some shaking among the dry bones. Although I am ignorant of conversions, I am not without hope that God will yet compel them to hear.' He adds that there had been twenty-two deaths in eleven months, while the average annual mortality was only four or five, and it seemed as if the voice of the word were being seconded by the voice of Providence. This was still more strikingly shown in the visitation of cholera which broke out ere the year closed, and which cut off the stricken community, for about seven weeks, from almost all intercourse with the mainland. When it came, some of the people said: 'It's the preaching that has done this!'

'This sudden outbreak of cholera occurred early in November, 1834, two years after the end of the general visitation in the country, when it passed all along the coast without touching the island. How or whence it came we could form no conception at the time, and never exactly knew; and the deadly epidemic passed nowhere else when it ceased with us. Afterwards we heard that the death of a sailor in a foreign ship in the harbour, who was buried in our churchyard two or three weeks before the outbreak, had been from cholera; this may have been true, but we knew nothing of it at the time. The first startling case in the island was of a fine young fisherman of temperate habits and remarkably hale. He died after thirteen hours, before most of us knew of his illness, and the dark event filled the island with sadness and alarm. A few days later his father was seized, a quiet and decent old man whom we respected and liked. On calling to see him I found him seated in front of the fire, for which he was utterly unfit, and he only lived for a day or two. After assisting his wife to lift him into bed and praying with him, I went straight home to think over our situation; for it was clear now that the deadly disease had begun its course amongst us. The next summons might come to myself, and now first of all I must hear the words, "Be ye also ready"; and if my own life was preserved and I was graciously enabled to be of use to others, it must be by constant visiting of the sick and dying, which would leave me little time for personal preparation if I should be taken away. Before all else I must therefore now commit myself completely to God in prayer for whatever issue; whilst at the same time the preservation of my life was of the utmost importance for the people, because they must otherwise be left helpless in this calamity, with no man in the island to take the burden of their welfare and their lives. In the course of an hour now given to prayer I endeavoured to embrace the gracious promises given us in Psalm 91; and rose from my knees with the full persuasion that the Lord had accepted me both in my dedication of myself to him and in my acceptance of him as my refuge from the noisome pestilence.

'Six weeks later in visiting the last man who died of cholera in the island, when I had opened the door and was about to advance toward his bed, the old and skilful nurse waved me back with both her hands; and not knowing what she meant I took a step or two forward, when she waved still more earnestly. It then occurred to me that the man was gone, and as there was now no room for prayer she was kindly warning me that there was no call for exposing myself to danger by coming near the corpse. Before going forward I stood for an instant to reflect on the new and strange idea that had been set before me. Till this moment the thought had never crossed my mind that I might myself take the sickness with which I was coming constantly in contact, so that the old nurse's kindly fear on my behalf was at first unintelligible. Most exactly to the letter had the words of the promise been graciously fulfilled, "Thou shalt not be afraid for the pestilence that walketh in darkness."

'During all the epidemic, from first to last, I never had better health, and the Lord, who had enabled me to take himself for my refuge, "gave his angels charge over me to keep me, so that the plague did not even come nigh my dwelling" (Psa. 91:9-11).

'Having first gone through this personal transaction with the Lord, my Redeemer, I went out to see what could be done for the people. My kind friend who had given us the use of his granary was the only man in the island who could be of service to us in the crisis, and on him I called immediately. He at once wrote out his will on a slip of paper, asked me to sign it as a witness, and made ready to leave the island. The step was natural even in so kindly a man, for he was not a native of the island, had no personal ties to it, and lived much at the colliery work which he rented near Berwick. But he was on the mainland my efficient and indeed my only help. He sent us from Berwick a most vigorous and intelligent young doctor, a full supply of medicines, two hospital nurses, and a shrewd old man-of-war's man to superintend our soup-kitchen and other operations.

'No people in the world could have been more helpless than most of the islanders now were; for though a few of them had laid past enough to tide over such a strain on their resources, yet the bulk of the fishermen were dependent for their daily bread on their daily labour on the sea. This one source of supply was now suddenly cut off. The people on the coast would not have looked at their fish if they had caught them; they were shut up to dull and absolute idleness, and it was an affecting sight to look at strong men "at the head of the streets standing every man with his hands on his loins" in their forlorn helplessness. Without a supply of food from outside they must have starved, and with only a meagre supply the destroying sweep of the fatal malady would have been dreadful.

'The answer to my letter asking for much-needed assistance was prompt and liberal. The generous Bishop of Durham, in whose diocese the island was, sent me £50. The Earl of Tankerville wrote with six fallow deer, and what was more prized by the islanders, with two fine oxen from his ancient herd of white cattle. But most of the contributions were in sums of £5 and £10. There was thus provided an ample daily supply of substantial soup and bread, with a moderate supply of meat for all who needed.

'Every evening we met in the schoolhouse for prayer. The objects were to pray for the sick and dying, to improve the visitation for spiritual life, and to ask for the preservation of those who were in health. But in a secondary way this gathering together did not hinder but help the people outwardly, for they were encouraged by meeting each other face to face. In this dark calamity the case of ordinary sickness was reversed, when the people in their affectionate sympathy were apt to crowd into the chamber of death. The livid face of the sufferer was itself appalling; and for myself, having seen little of death before, I got so accustomed to it in this darkest form, that afterwards on first witnessing death of an ordinary type, I gazed on it with wonder and almost with admiration. But it was the danger of infection and the dread of death for themselves that kept them aloof from each other, so that a neighbour a few doors off might be dying or dead without their knowing it. One stout woman, who was I trust not without true godliness but through fear of death had been all her lifetime subject to bondage, was so afraid of death that she took ill through fear; and the doctor said there was not illness enough to carry her off, but that she appeared to die through the effects of fear. On the other hand when we were in want of a grave-digger, and all were afraid to undertake the office, a tall, strong fisherman offered to take the unwelcome duty. He seemed boldly to defy death, and in a cheery and dauntless manner went out and in among the sick and dying, telling them there was no fear, bidding them be of good heart. When at last he was taken ill he at once gave himself up for lost, and in twelve hours passed to the great account.'

The strongest man in the island succumbed to the fell disease, whose figure as he lay on the bed of death the young missionary recalled: 'The statue of an ancient warrior seemed to repose before me; there was awful grandeur in the spectacle as he lay motionless, the model of herculean strength.'

'The weather was calm during the first weeks of the epidemic, and the islanders earnestly longed for a gale of wind in the sanguine hope that it might carry it away. The gale came and in full force, but with no mitigation of the virulence of the disease. In the storm a sloop was driven ashore on the opposite coast, but we had no lifeboat and our fishermen were helpless to render any assistance. With sad hearts we stood and witnessed the crew of three men and a boy, having abandoned all other hope, climb the mast of their vessel to which they lashed themselves as their last resource, if so be that it might stand the fury of the waves without being broken in pieces. The scene of Grace Darling's[3] heroic efforts was not far distant, and the height of the billows on that coast had been significantly brought before me, when we saw a large steamer plying to Newcastle cast anchor to save her being driven on the sands and passing quite out of our sight as often as she was in the trough of the wave. Our fishermen looked on the fate of the sloop and her crew as already sealed, yet it stood out the ebb and flow of the tide and got safely away next day; but meanwhile the sight of their helpless distress and danger was doubly affecting to us in the midst of our own calamity. On that day three of our leading fishermen were lying prostrate under the fatal disease—death on the sea and death on the shore.

'Amongst the recoveries the most remarkable case was that of a healthy, industrious and superior woman, the mother of a family, who lay for weeks between life and death. She had sunk so low that the faintest traces of life were scarcely perceptible, as when a mirror was held to her lips with only doubtful symptoms of breath to be discerned. One night the grave-digger called and said to the nurse that he would return in an hour to put her into her coffin; but the old nurse resented this interference and refused the offered help. In the midst of their conversation, as she told me afterwards, the poor sufferer was all the while quite conscious and listened to them arguing as if over her dead body, but was unable to utter a word or to raise a finger as a sign that she was still living.' The family of his kind friend Mr Dods of Belford knew her long afterwards by the soubriquet of 'Resurrection Kate' when she came to sell her fish.

'After she had rallied I inquired with some interest about the pain she had suffered most from when she so completely retained her consciousness yet was so unable to express her wants, and was surprised when she replied that all her other sufferings were as nothing to the dreadful pain of thirst all the time. The thirst she described

<hr>

[3] Grace Darling (1815–42) had taken part in the rescue of mariners from the stricken *Forfarshire*, which ran aground near the Farne Islands in 1838.—*P.*

as so constant and so excruciating that she greatly longed to die to be delivered from it. It gave me a new impression of the sufferings of our blessed Lord, when in the last agonies of the cross he uttered the cry, "I thirst!" as if the manifold other sufferings, the lacerations of the scourge and the torture of the nails, might have been even less severe than this intense pain of thirst.

'With the end of the epidemic my work in the island had likewise come to its end. With the utmost love and longing of which my heart was capable, I had for two whole years, with intense supplication and sanguine hope, asked of the Lord the salvation of the island. Some sheaves, I trust, had been granted to me in mercy, and for these I shall for ever bless the Lord; but without the reaping of a harvest in the body of the people, of which I was both unworthy and unfit to be the instrument.[4] Yet, as with St Paul's fellow passengers in the ship, the Lord was pleased at the end of my two years' labours to give me the lives of my fellow islanders, and to accept of this humbler service at my hands. By the Lord's goodness the deaths did not exceed one in twenty of the population, and if I had not been there it seemed as if half of the inhabitants might have been cut off.

'Being now in need of rest and change I went to visit some friends in Edinburgh. When there I was called to take charge of a mission chapel and district in the parish, where I afterwards laboured for fifty years in the ministry of St Luke's Church. After a few weeks I returned for a time to the island, where Dr Gilly of Norham,[5] so well known for his interest in the Waldenses, kindly came to see me, and invited me to visit him at Durham, of which he was one of the prebendaries. Their official dinners combined modern elegance with certain ancient customs, as the serving of a time-honoured

---

[4] I may state that I paid a short visit to the island in 1886, and got a warm welcome from those who still remembered my father. I met some who told me they had received saving impressions under him in their youth, and others whose parents had got good through him.—*KMS.*

[5] William Stephen Gilly (1789–1855), author of, among other things, *Waldensian Researches during a Second Visit to the Vaudois of Piemont* (1831).—*P.*

omelette, the circulation of the loving cup, and the chanting at the close by a boy from the cathedral choir of a successive part of the 119th Psalm. The daily services of the cathedral and the hospitality of its dignitaries formed a singular contrast to my poor and lonely island home. Yet both were closely bound together, for the stately cathedral owed its origin to the humble island, and the remains of St Cuthbert, after many wanderings, found their last resting-place within the cathedral walls of Durham. A fragment of his coffin, with a piece of the silken robe in which he was buried, was given to me by my kindly host, as if willing to associate me, however remotely and unequally, with the olden times and the early witnesses for Christ in the island.'[6]

---

[6] These fragments remained in the Moody-Stuart (the name is now hyphenated) family until 2007, when they were returned to Durham Cathedral by the widow of George Moody-Stuart, a great-grandson of Alexander Moody Stuart. In 2013 the Anglo-Saxon Laboratory in York, England, forensically examined the fragments and concluded that they were indeed genuine pieces related to the burial of St Cuthbert.—P.

— 5 —

Settled as a Minister in Edinburgh

> There seems in yon city's motion
> A mightier truth for me:
> 'Tis the sound of life's great ocean,
> 'Tis the tides of the human sea.
>
> —*Horatius Bonar*

HOLY ISLAND and Edinburgh are a great contrast. But ministerial experience gained in the sandy hollows of an islet of the North Sea formed a fit training for one who was to pass his ministerial jubilee in the capital of his native land. His case exemplified the saying that 'The best way for a man to get out of a lowly position is to be conspicuously effective in it.'

Early in 1835 Mr Moody began work in Edinburgh, in compliance with an invitation from the kirk session[1] of St George's to assist their recently settled minister, Mr Candlish[2] (afterwards Principal Candlish, D.D.). He preached his first sermon from Luke 20:17, 18—'The stone which the builders rejected, the same is become the head of the corner; whosoever shall fall upon that stone shall be broken.' The

---

[1] 'Kirk session' refers in Scottish Presbyterianism to the minister and elders in a particular congregation.—*P.*

[2] Robert Smith Candlish (1806–73) had become the minister of St George's, one of Edinburgh's most influential congregations, in 1834. After the death of Thomas Chalmers in 1847, Candlish was looked upon as the leading figure in the Free Church.—*P.*

late accomplished Rev. John Mackenzie of Ratho, who on retiring from his charge became an elder in St Luke's, wrote forty years after, that he 'distinctly remembered that sermon, and that it was strongly marked by that unction and evangelical fervour, and high mental culture, which ever since so eminently characterised his ministrations.'

The territorial congregation under St George's, which he was appointed to gather and minister to, met at first in what had been a small Unitarian Chapel in Young Street. This (opened in May 1835) was soon filled to overflowing. Sir John Sinclair, the author of the Statistical Account of Scotland, then upwards of eighty, said to the young pastor: 'I have been looking for a seat, and I find they are all taken; might I have that?' pointing to a stool in front of the precentor's desk. He drew a curtain round it, as he suffered from his eyes, and sat there. Earnest students gathered about him. M'Cheyne[3] hearing him, said: 'I have found the man.' 'To him,' Dr Moody Stuart writes, 'I could not but be drawn in manifold sympathy, and we arranged to meet in my house for an hour of prayer once a week. After some weeks he introduced his friends Horace[4] and Andrew[5] Bonar and Alexander Somerville,[6] with all of whom I now formed a life-long friendship. Of these four friends three have entered into the rest of their Lord;

[3] Robert Murray M'Cheyne (1813–43) studied under Chalmers in Edinburgh, and was from 1836 until his death aged 29 the minister of St Peter's Church, Dundee. See A. Bonar, *Memoir and Remains of R. M. M'Cheyne* (1892; repr. Edinburgh: The Banner of Truth Trust, 2014).—*P.*

[4] Horatius Bonar (1808–89) studied under Chalmers in Edinburgh and was minister of Kelso in the Scottish Borders from 1837 to 1866, thereafter serving as minister of Chalmers Memorial Church, Edinburgh. He was appreciated as a preacher and a hymn-writer. See 'Horatius Bonar and the Love of God in Evangelism', in Iain H. Murray, *A Scottish Christian Heritage* (Edinburgh: The Banner of Truth Trust, 2006), pp. 157-212.—*P.*

[5] Andrew Alexander Bonar (1810–92) was, after studies in Edinburgh, the minister of Collace in Perthshire, and later, in 1856, called to plant a new congregation in Finnieston, Glasgow. See *The Diary and Life of Andrew A. Bonar* (1893; repr. Edinburgh: The Banner of Truth Trust, 2013).—*P.*

[6] Alexander Neil Somerville (1813–89) studied in Edinburgh and was called to Anderston Church, Glasgow, in 1837, where he continued to serve until 1889 (Anderston Free Church after 1843). Somerville was very active in the field of missionary work, and would later travel extensively overseas to conduct evangelistic campaigns.—*P.*

St George's Church in Edinburgh's New Town

(The building is now known as West Register House, and contains
part of the National Records of Scotland.)—*P.*

one taken early yet highly honoured by being fruitful after his death
as well as in his life, the others enabled by grace to keep the faith
through a long course of years, and the one who remains hoping soon
to join them in looking o'er life's finished story':

> Then, Lord, shall we fully know,
>   Not till then, how much we owe![7]

A divinity student who did not sympathise with their evangelical or ecclesiastical views was rather out in his reckoning when, on
being told by a friend that they were meeting for prayer and might
do their opponents some harm, he replied, 'Oh, they're a weakly
set; they'll soon die off'! M'Cheyne's father joined the new congregation, and became its first Session-clerk. Once when Mr Moody
had gone from Holy Island for change and rest to pass a few days in

---

[7] Lines from M'Cheyne's hymn, 'I am debtor'.—*P.*

Roxburghshire, he rode over on Sabbath to the Church of Sprouston, to which his old friend and fellow student, Mr Sym (afterwards of Edinburgh), had been appointed. Having read that morning in the sixth chapter of St Luke, he found that out of its many verses it was the thirty-eighth that clung to his memory, 'Give, and it shall be given unto you,' which seemed to have no relevancy to himself on that day. It recurred to him constantly as he rode along.

On arriving he found that there was a special collection that day for the erection of extension churches in Scotland, in connection with the scheme which Dr Chalmers had originated.[8] As he was not in Scotland, and his salary was the modest one of £50, he thought that this special effort had slight claim upon him, but when the scheme was warmly pressed from the pulpit he felt that had he possessed means he would gladly have brought 'alms to his nation and offerings.' In his pocket were a sovereign and seven or eight shillings. At first a shilling seemed enough to give. Then he mentally increased this to half a crown, then as his morning's text recurred to him he doubled that, and soon added all the silver. At last when the collection was made he gladly put in the sovereign, and would have emptied his pocket but required the change to pay his way home. Fifteen months later, when he found himself territorial missionary in St George's, he got the offer of one of these very *quoad sacra*[9] churches to which he had that day contributed all that he could. As it was his first call to be an ordained minister he did not see that he should refuse it. He felt it his duty to mention this to one of his constant hearers and kindest friends, the widow of the Rev.

[8] Thomas Chalmers became convener of the Church of Scotland's Church Accommodation Committee in 1834, from which point the work of 'church extension' gathered pace, resulting in over 200 new church buildings being erected by means of voluntary contributions.—*P.*

[9] *Quoad sacra* (literally 'in respect of sacred things') parishes had only an ecclesiastical function, and were without civil responsibilities. At this time, Church of Scotland parishes which were *quoad omnia* ('in respect of all things') had such civil responsibilities as poor relief and the provision of education. Rapid urbanization in the first half of the nineteenth century led to many *quoad sacra* parishes being constituted in places where the capacity of the existing parish church was inadequate.—*P.*

Dr Buchanan of the Canongate, and in former days the hostess of [Charles] Simeon of Cambridge, in Edinburgh. She said at once: 'Why should other people get churches, and we not have a church of our own?' As a pre-requisite to the erection of any such charge the General Assembly required subscriptions amounting to £2,000, so he replied: 'It is quite impossible; it would require £2,000.' The good old lady made no reply, but asked him to call next day, and when he came she said: 'The £2,000 will be given you, but on condition that my name shall not be mentioned.' This condition was strictly observed till her death many years after. 'A mature believer in Christ,' Mr Moody Stuart continues, 'and singularly clear in the doctrines of grace, she was exceptionally reticent on her own inward experience, but after communicating an important step like this, she would quietly add: "The Lord told Jacob what he was to do, and you know it is just the same now."'

'After the two thousand pounds were put into my hand for a church of my own, and for the self-same object for which I had given one pound the year before, the forgotten words which had been held at first to be so irrelevant to myself were brought vividly to memory, by the Lord thus returning the gift "into my bosom" twice a thousand-fold; "give, and it shall be given unto you; good measure, pressed down, and shaken together, and running over, shall men give into your bosom."'

On this donation being intimated to the session of St George's, they resolved to promote the erection of a Church Extension Charge, which was called St Luke's. They bought the Unitarian Chapel as a site for a commodious church, and the congregation adhering to Mr Moody more than doubled Mrs Buchanan's gift. During the building they worshipped in a large hall called the Bazaar, in Wemyss Place.

The church in Young Street was opened on 28 May 1837, by Dr Candlish, and Mr Moody was ordained its first minister on 27 July of that year. The Rev. John Sym, then of Greyfriars, delivered the charge to the young minister. Its earnest exhortations (now in my

possession) were amply responded to in the long pastorate then formally begun.

It was no light task for a young preacher to make himself a pulpit
force in the city of Edinburgh at that time. My friend the late Rev.
William Bennet of Moffat has drawn attention to this. 'In trying
to recall the earlier events of Dr Moody Stuart's ministry in Edinburgh, one is strongly impressed with the fact that the power of
the pulpit then manifested in that city was unusually great. There
was, in truth, a very constellation of ability and eloquence. It was
the period of my earlier studies at the university. A usual frequenter
of the old High Church during my winter studies, and thus accustomed to the earnest orthodoxy of Gordon and Buchanan,[10] I
strayed but occasionally into other churches, in which there was a
choice of eminent preachers, among which it must have been difficult to establish a new influence. Candlish was then perhaps at the
height of his brilliant ascendency, while, over a good many studious
minds, the fervid logic of Cunningham[11] exerted permanent authority. Originality in differing forms was conspicuous in the sermons
of Bruce[12] and of Charles Brown.[13] Guthrie[14] was already attracting

[10] James Buchanan (1804–70) became well-known as a preacher first at North
Leith Church, near Edinburgh, and from 1840 as a colleague of Robert Gordon's
at the High Church, Edinburgh. He succeeded Thomas Chalmers as the Free
Church's Professor of Systematic Theology in 1847. His work on *The Doctrine of the
Holy Spirit* is published by the Banner of Truth Trust.—*P.*

[11] William Cunningham (1805–61) became one of the ministers of Trinity College Church, Edinburgh, in 1834. He adhered to the Free Church at the Disruption
and became the Free Church's Professor of Church History in 1845, succeeding
Chalmers as Principal of New College in 1847.—*P.*

[12] John Bruce (1794–1880) first came to Edinburgh as minister of the New
North Church, and in 1837 translated to St Andrew's Church (where the Disruption Assembly took place in May 1843), and after the Disruption continued as
minister of St Andrew's Free Church.—*P.*

[13] Charles J. Brown (1806–84) succeeded John Bruce as minister of the New
North Church, Edinburgh, and continued as the minister of the New North Free
Church congregation after the Disruption. His collection of addresses to theolog-
ical students entitled *The Ministry* is published by the Banner of Truth Trust.—*P.*

[14] Thomas Guthrie (1803–73) came to Edinburgh in 1837 as a minister of Old
Greyfriars Church, and in 1840 was called to the new congregation of St Johns. He
continued as minister of Free St John's after the Disruption. Guthrie was known

crowds in the Old Greyfriars. Chalmers even, and Welsh,[15] had not entirely renounced the functions of the pulpit for those of the chair.

'In such circumstances the success of an unobtrusive stranger was scarcely to be looked for. Yet early and distinctive success did attend the pulpit and congregational labours of Moody Stuart. He soon assembled a flock deeply attached to himself as well as attracted by his ministry, many of whose members possessed important positions in society, along with deep piety—names still associated with his own.

'On several occasions, in days preceding the Disruption,[16] I had the opportunity of hearing the new minister of St Luke's, whose originality of manner and style was, of course, the subject of many and various criticisms. What impressed me, in those days of very imperfect appreciation, in addition to his unusual but solemn and memorable delivery, was the searching skill with which he laid open the secret self-flatteries and errors of the human heart, as manifested in delusion, delay, and false apologies for sin. To some, in conse-

---

as a preacher and a social reformer, pioneering the work of 'ragged schools' in Scotland.—*P.*

[15] David Welsh (1793–1845) occupied from 1831 the Chair of Ecclesiastical History at Edinburgh University. He was a leading member of the Evangelical party in the Church of Scotland, serving as Moderator of the 1842 General Assembly. After the Disruption he served until his death in 1845 as the Free Church's Professor of Church History.—*P.*

[16] The 'Disruption' was one of the most significant events to occur in the religious and political history of nineteenth-century Scotland. Coinciding with a revival of Evangelical religion in the Church of Scotland, the 'Ten Years' Conflict' over the issue of patronage and the 'intrusion' of ministers upon unwilling congregations by patrons (usually landowners) led to a protest on the part of the Non-Intrusionist commissioners (mostly Evangelicals) at the 1843 General Assembly. At the opening of the Assembly on 18 May, almost 200 commissioners (ministers and elders) walked out of the gathering in protest, eventually being joined by many others. In total 474 ministers (out of 1,195) demitted their charges at great personal cost and constituted the 'Church of Scotland, Free' (thereafter adopting the name the Free Church of Scotland), and a large proportion of members left the Established Church for the Free Church. Although Moody Stuart was overseas (see Chapter 6) when the event occurred, he was a strong supporter of the principles at stake, and the St Luke's building had been used for meetings at which the prevailing issues had been deliberated. See Appendix, pp. 407-9, for minutes detailing the involvement of St Luke's in the Disruption.—*P.*

quence, his discourses seemed too generally introspective in character. The events of that stirring time, especially the trying struggle of the church questions, tended to depress the minds and even to affect the health of our more thoughtful or sensitive ministers. The shadow of the approaching Disruption hung over a great part of the Christian community. Deep responsibility was felt in connection with events which seemed to involve something like a revolution. When the crisis came, however, it found Mr Moody Stuart fully equal to its requirements, and also revealed the extent to which his principles and character, in their quiet power, had leavened his own congregation, and also affected many outside of it.

'It is not chiefly because of his length of days and services, or even because of his peculiar gifts and fine mental powers, that he is to be ranked among the eminent men of the Disruption era. His memory will long be preserved by higher and holier associations.'

The congregation which in increased numbers (the roll was 750) was now gathered into St Luke's, was a well-balanced combination of the different classes of society. Before coming to Edinburgh their pastor had laboured among a hardy and intelligent country population, where the women used to read substantial volumes brought in their fishing creels from the Bamborough Library. Now his work was among a similar city population in Rose and Thistle Streets, while a considerable number of the professional classes of the West End joined his church, and a few of the higher classes, such as Lady Harriet Dunlop (aunt of Lord Rosebery) and the Honourable Charlotte and Augusta Mackenzie (daughters of the last Lord Seaforth) attached themselves to his ministry. The latter became his warm friends and devoted aiders in carrying out his schemes of usefulness. Their features and profiles were striking, combining in their contour a certain massive power with cultured grace. Miss Mackenzie suffered from deafness, and as a boy I well remember her venerable figure with snowy hair seated on a chair within the platform close to the preacher, trying to catch with her hearing trumpet every word that fell from his lips. My father used an interleaved Bible, on which in very minute characters he carefully wrote down all the divisions and subdivisions and leading thoughts of his discourse. The earliest of these Bibles was one with massive boards and silver clasps and corners given him by Miss Mackenzie. When this was quite filled with manuscript notes she presented him with another in two volumes with gold clasps and corners, the clasps closing with lock and key, so that no one could pilfer its contents, a needless precaution as the calligraphy was an admirable cipher. This gave rise to many a joke from strangers about the minister keeping the Bible locked. It was my father's habit, at least in the church at Queen Street where the pulpit was a platform, to walk up and down while preaching with his Bible in his hand, indeed occasionally pressed to his heart, while it was opened at each new 'head'. The attitude and actions, if rather unusual, were natural and at the same time impressive, and harmonised well with the appearance of the preacher, now wrapt in thought for a moment, and now urging the words of life upon the attention of his people, as one of his later hearers says, 'with that thoughtful penetrating look of his like a messenger from another world; and when he stopped and leaned over the pulpit, looking down at you with so much interest, you felt that the message had come for *you*, and that he loved your soul personally with a great love. Oh how he pleaded with you with such sincere faithfulness and yet with a charming winsomeness of manner which it was difficult to resist.'

Considering that his voice was weak it would probably have been better, to ensure his being heard well, especially by strangers, if he had not exercised his thinking powers so constantly while he was speaking. On the other hand it sustained the hearer's interest by giving him a sense of the freshness of what was said. A man who once heard him preach in the Wynd Church, Glasgow, said to the Rev. D. MacColl: 'He stood and rubbit his broo, and rubbit his broo, and ilka time he rubbit he brocht something new oot o't.' There was no want of careful premeditation. He spent more time on this than most ministers do on sermons fully written out, but he passed the matter and message again through his own mind as he delivered it to the audience.

Another mark of his pulpit ministrations was their solemnity. The preacher seemed impressed, sometimes almost oppressed, with his position as standing between God and man, and bearing a direct message from the divine Father, Son, and Spirit, to his hearers. He seemed constantly to realise for himself the charge given to Jeremiah: 'Thou shalt go to all that I shall send thee, and whatsoever I command thee thou shalt speak.' One who led the psalmody in St Luke's recalls the solemnity of his short prayer in the vestry before entering the pulpit, a solemnity which impressed itself on the congregation as he ascended the pulpit stairs, and pervaded the whole service. Indeed it was as marked in his own manse on the morning of the Lord's Day, and also on its evening, when some preachers are wont too much to cast off the sense of responsibility that has rested on them during the hours of worship.

A young lady who came from Germany as a teacher in 1846, was taken by a friend on her arrival to hear, on two successive Sabbaths, two of the leading preachers of Edinburgh. But she could not follow them. Being taken on the third Sabbath to hear Mr Moody Stuart, they were told it was a stranger who was to preach, though it turned out not to be so. Miss M. was at once arrested by the appearance of consecration on the countenance of the preacher as he entered the church, and on retiring her friend asked if she understood that sermon any better. 'No,' she replied; 'but if Mr Moody Stuart is like that little minister—he my minister.' 'Why so?' was asked. She explained that it was because when he opened the Psalm-book and the Bible his very handling and opening of them seemed to say, '*These books are not my books; and these hands that hold them are consecrated.*' She felt that he regarded the volumes as entirely of God. On her friend saying, 'Well, after all, that was Mr Moody Stuart!' she went to see him about joining the church. As she knew little English he tried to instruct her in French, and as she was rather agitated, he gave her the text, 'When Ephraim spake trembling, he exalted himself,' and added her name to the roll, where it still stands.

Another aged member of St Luke's tells how the first time she heard Mr Moody Stuart, nearly sixty years ago, she 'experienced such a sacred influence that she was constrained to say in her heart, "Surely we are very near to God!"' Prof. Cooper, D.D., of Glasgow, says that when a student in Aberdeen he had a similar sense of being brought into God's presence when hearing him preach.

Among those who joined St Luke's at its origin were William Stothert, Esq. of Cargen, and Dr James Russell. Mr Stothert had endeavoured to get Mr Moody settled in a church in his own neighbourhood, near Dumfries, and when that was not accomplished, in the providence of God he was brought himself to reside in Edinburgh. 'He was,' writes my father, 'for many years my best friend and most efficient elder, working as diligently as if he had been a city missionary among the members of the church, by whom he was greatly beloved and honoured.' He was a fine type of the county gentleman and soldier, and a fine type of Christian. He acted as session-clerk for many years.

Dr James Russell was unwearied in promoting the spiritual and temporal prosperity of the flock. His sunny smile and kindly words must have often communicated something of their brightness to the more sombre disposition of his attached pastor.

These elders, while eminent men of God, were somewhat old-fashioned in some of their religious opinions. They objected to the use of anything beyond the Psalms in public praise (a view shared by many of the congregation), and had doubts about the expediency of Sabbath Schools, as tending to interfere with family religion, and to lessen the parents' sense of responsibility. Their minister had laboured so diligently in Sabbath School work in Holy Island that he cannot at first have shared this view, but it seems gradually to have influenced his mind to some extent. This was dispelled by practical proof. After meeting one evening with the young people preparing for the communion, the superintendent of the Sabbath School, coming to a meeting of session, found him sitting alone before the session-house fire. 'Turning round,' he says, 'to greet me with his usual beautiful smile, he remarked, "I have been agreeably surprised tonight: on asking the young men and women where they got their first religious impressions, the answer I got from *all* was—'in the Sunday School.' I find I have been mistaken about the school, as I had no idea conversions were so common there as they seem to be." You may imagine the feeling of the superintendent when he got such a testimony.' There were other periods of special blessing in the Sabbath School. About twenty years ago, twelve to eighteen of the senior lads were brought to the Saviour at one time. One of these, who became an engineer in a high post, said to Councillor Brown: 'I have been all round the world, and during all that time my soul has prospered.'

Mr Moody Stuart seldom preached sermons to children, but for very many years he catechised the children every Sabbath forenoon for ten minutes on the sermon. This made the children feel that they were expected to listen to and understand the regular sermon, and they certainly remembered it well. It was rarely that even a subdivision was forgotten. My own experience agrees with that of others who have told me that they still remember sermons thus impressed on their memory. Many adults used to remain in the church till this catechising was over.

Lady Colquhoun of Luss attended his ministry when in town, appreciative references to which are made in her memoir, and with her rich experience of divine grace she wrote to him fully and touchingly on the entire freeness of the gospel offer.

Another prominent elder who joined St Luke's at an early period (1841) was Mr John Macdonald, widely known as the general treasurer of the Free Church. He combined with high Christian character great prudence and sagacity, and his minister relied on his judgment more than on any other. Ordained an elder at an early age, he survived all those who at first held office along with him. It is interesting to observe how in a single congregation the Lord gives helps of various kinds, all exercising an influence on the pastor, who in turn influences them all, his spirit animating and pervading the whole.

It cannot have been very long after his ordination that the Duchess of Gordon,[17] as famed for her playing of Scotch music as the Duchess Jane had been for her beauty, became an attender on his ministry when in Edinburgh. Mr Moody visited Her Grace at Huntly Lodge in 1838, and their friendship continued till her death.

In the year 1839 Mr Moody took some share in the great awakening at Kilsyth, and stated, long after, that one of its most noted results was the recognition by the general Christian community in Scotland of the necessity of the great practical change in the history of a Christian, called conversion. Mr William Burns, the chief instrument in this revival, was by many accounted a fanatic, but my father said that so far was this from being the case, that when the strain upon him was most severe he was observed, in order to retain due calmness in his mind, when driving in the coach from Edinburgh to preach, to be busily engaged in reading one of Aeschylus' Greek plays.

In the autumn of this year, Mr Gow, a hirer of those picturesque Sedan chairs, which were soon after supplanted by cabs, called to ask the minister of St Luke's to marry him, at which the latter seemed much amused, and laughed as he replied that he could not perform the ceremony. Mr Gow was considerably discomposed by his amusement, until he learned later that the reason was that his minister was about to be married himself! Mrs Gow, now for many years a widow, said 'they got Dr Candlish, so they were not badly off.'

His marriage took place on 9 September 1839, to Jessie Stuart, eldest daughter of Kenneth Bruce Stuart, Esq. of Annat, who died

---

[17] Elizabeth Gordon, née Brodie (1794–1864) was born in London and in 1813 married George Gordon, Marquis of Huntly, heir to the dukedom of Gordon. She became distressed by the vice that she found in the high society of which she was a part. Through reading the Bible and books by Robert Leighton and Thomas Erskine of Linlathen, she became an earnest Christian. She subsequently exerted significant spiritual influence amongst her peers, and was a generous supporter of the evangelical cause in Scotland. In 1846 she joined the Free Church, and many of its leaders were her personal friends. Alexander Moody Stuart authored *Life and Letters of Elisabeth, Last Duchess of Gordon*, published in 1865.—P.

in 1832, and whose widow had resided for some time in Heriot Row, Edinburgh. His bride had just completed her eighteenth year, but even then displayed those remarkable qualities, both of head and heart, which characterised her through life. Her father, who was an Indian officer, but was specially distinguished for his linguistic and literary attainments, knowing most of the languages of India, including Persian, as well as those of Europe (of the chief literary works of which he had formed a choice collection), was a man of devout spirit, who loved the ordinances of grace, and left an amiable example of active benevolence. Her grandfather, Lieut.-General Robert Stuart, went out to India when a lad as a cadet in the Company's service, where he greatly distinguished himself as a successful soldier, holding the rank also of Major-General in the Royal Service. General Stuart, retiring from India after long service, early in this century purchased the small estate of Rait, on the braes of the Carse of Gowrie. To keep up the association with an old family estate he entailed it under the name of Annat on his son Kenneth, providing that if a female succeeded, as was the case with our mother, her husband should take the surname of 'Stuart of Annat.' It was on this account that our father added Stuart to his own name.

The bride's mother was a lady, as one who knew her well has said, 'beautiful in character as in countenance.' On the death of her father, Æneas Morrison, she was brought up by two aunts in Perth, who belonged to the 'Glassite' persuasion, and she often told me that it was to their training and the bright example, which the congregation of Glassites or Sandemanians[18] gave of loving provision for any of their communion who were in want, that she owed that remarkable interest in the poor, and delicate kindness towards friends or neighbours who might be the better of a little considerate help, which characterised her through her long and honoured life. Mrs Stuart's home

---

[18] For a summary of the teachings of John Glas (1695–1773) and his son-in-law Robert Sandeman (1718–71), see John Macleod, *Scottish Theology* (1943; repr. Edinburgh: The Banner of Truth Trust, 2015), pp. 194-7.—*P.*

was at Annat Lodge, situated with its beautiful garden on Kinnoull Hill, overlooking the fair city of Perth, sleeping beneath it on the broad-bosomed Tay, with its green Inches and its varied spires, from which the chimes of the bells float softly up the hill. She often denied herself small comforts, such as the use of a carriage even in her old age up the very steep hill to her home, that she might not require to curtail her gifts in charity and to the Redeemer's cause.

For several years the great ecclesiastical controversy which was soon to rend in twain the Church of Scotland had been going on, and though Mr Moody Stuart had no love of controversy, and was not constitutionally peculiarly fitted for it, both his judgment and sympathies went fully with the evangelical party, who were contending at once for the supreme crown rights of Christ as the exalted living head of his church, and for the liberties of the Christian people. The late Dr Elder of Rothesay, one of my father's oldest and most valued friends, in an unpublished autobiography wrote: 'In 1839 the critical circumstances of the Church led to the formation of a ministerial club in Edinburgh, from which I derived much knowledge of church principles, and important preparation for the great conflict and work in prospect. It consisted of men then in their prime, who afterwards became prominent and most influential in the Free Church movement, together with others like myself who, though not fitted to lead, were heartily willing to follow in the path which Providence seemed to be marking out for us. It included (none of them being doctors then) Messrs. [William] Cunningham, [Robert] Candlish, [Thomas] Guthrie, James Buchanan, [James] Begg, C. J. Brown, [William King] Tweedie, [James Julius] Wood, Liddell, [John] Sym, Moody Stuart, [George] Lewis, [Alexander] Gregory, and myself. We met once a month in each other's houses, dined together, and spent the evening in prayer and consultation regarding the state and prospects of the Church. I look back to these meetings with the deepest interest and gratitude, and record my conviction that they formed the most influential agency at the time in guiding and sustaining the great conflict, and bringing it to a successful issue, our leading members being in constant communication with the older men, Drs. Chalmers, Welsh, Gordon, and others, and with laymen like [Alexander] Dunlop[19] and Graham Spiers.'[20]

While such far-reaching ecclesiastical principles were being contended for, as the freedom of church courts from the encroachments of the civil courts, the gospel was now fully preached by godly men in districts that had long been under the darkness and death of that form of preaching called 'Moderatism', in which the doctrines of grace held no clear place, and under which there was no earnest pleading with sinners, or leading anxious ones to Christ's cross as their only refuge. When the seven ministers in Strathbogie who resolved to obey the mandate of the civil judges as to the discharge of their spiritual functions, and to disobey the injunctions of the church courts, were suspended by the Church from their office, Mr Moody Stuart was one of those sent as deputies, along with Drs. Chalmers and Gordon, in 1839, to preach in these parishes, and much blessing accompanied his words. The civil courts first interdicted them from preaching in the churches or schools, to which they bowed, and met the congregations in the open air. Interdicts were next issued by the Court of Session prohibiting them from preaching anywhere in the parishes, in market-place, barn, or field. It was then that these faithful ministers of Christ felt called upon to scorn the interdicts and to preach in

[19] Alexander Colquhoun-Stirling-Murray-Dunlop (1798–1870) was a lawyer and politician who played a prominent role in supporting the Non-Intrusionist cause in the Ten Years' Conflict. Dunlop authored the Claim of Right, adopted by the General Assembly of the Church of Scotland in 1842 to assert the Church's spiritual independence from the state, and would act as legal counsel for the Non-Intrusionists in a number of Court of Session cases—Dunlop represented the Presbytery of Auchterarder in 1838–9 for what would become a test case on the legality of the 'Veto' Act. He was Member of Parliament for Greenock from 1852 to 1868.—*P.*

[20] Robert Cunningham Graham Spiers (1797–1847) was an Edinburgh lawyer who in 1840 became Sheriff of Midlothian. He was an elder of the High Church congregation in Edinburgh, and took a keen interest in the unfolding crisis in the Church of Scotland prior to the Disruption. Having sided with the Free Church of Scotland in 1843, two years later he was appointed convener of the Free Church's sites committee, to deal with the problem of site-refusal for the erection of Free Church buildings.—*P.*

defiance of them. It was not only great, and it might be thought fiery church leaders, but men of the most saintly character, like [Robert Murray] M'Cheyne and Andrew Bonar, as well as MacDonald[21] the great 'Apostle of the North', who acted thus. In a long pastoral letter which Mr Moody Stuart addressed to his flock on this subject, he states that the question is 'religious and spiritual, and that spiritual men alone can fully apprehend its bearings.'

The Duchess of Gordon having carefully studied the question for herself placed her mansion at the disposal of the ministers who came as deputies, and finally became herself an attached member of the Free Church.

While staying at Huntly Lodge in 1841, engaged in preaching the gospel in that district amidst much exposure to weather, Mr Moody Stuart was attacked by a severe form of ministers' sore throat, which entirely deprived him of the power of using his voice, which at its best was a weak one. The physicians indeed feared serious affection of chest supervening, and he was ordered entire rest from all speaking, and prolonged residence in a warm climate. This took him away from Scotland from the autumn of 1841 till the summer of 1843, so that he was not himself a spectator or participator in the stirring events which immediately preceded the Disruption, or in that memorable scene itself.

It was, however, in St Luke's Church that the important Commission of Assembly met on 18 November 1840; and again on 25 August 1841. Here also on 24 May 1842, the overture was subscribed by members of Assembly, which on the 30th was adopted by the Assembly as the Claim of Right.

'Mr Moody Stuart,' as his friend Mr James E. Mathieson writes, 'was the last survivor of the foremost group of the Disruption

---

[21] John MacDonald (1779–1849) was from 1813 the minister of Ferintosh. His evangelistic campaigns in the north of Scotland led to his being called the 'Apostle of the North'. See John Kennedy, *The Apostle of the North* (2nd edn; Inverness: Northern Counties Newspaper and Printing and Publishing Company, 1932); Iain H. Murray, *A Scottish Christian Heritage* (Edinburgh: The Banner of Truth Trust, 2006), pp. 123-56.—*P.*

period who belonged less to the statesmanlike leaders who were the administrators of the Free Church in her early struggles, than to that cluster of pietistic order, who not less than the others attracted to the Free Church all that was best in Scotland in these memorable days, and of whom M'Cheyne was the first to be removed as your father was the last.'

To the same effect Mr A. Taylor Innes[22] of Edinburgh writes of him as 'a man who was the first and earliest of a well-defined and very remarkable school of preaching; who was also its patriarch and survivor; and who, besides being the originator, was himself the most original man not only in that school but, according to my judgment, in the whole Scottish pulpit during the long span of his ministerial career.'

While it is true as stated here that Mr Moody was the originator of the school which contained M'Cheyne, the three brothers Bonar, [Alexander] Somerville, [John] Milne, R. M'Donald, [James] Manson, and James Hamilton, his views and the character of his preaching in some respects differed from theirs. He never adopted the pre-millennial advent view which most of them held,[23] although he considered that Christ might return at any time, since it is said that 'the Son of Man will come at an hour when ye think not': while in the experimental, subjective, and searching character of his preaching he was more allied to the Highland divines such as Dr Kennedy[24] of Dingwall, so that many highlanders used to be attracted to St Luke's.

---

[22] Alexander Taylor Innes (1833–1912) was a lawyer who exercised significant influence in the Free Church of Scotland. That his views were often not in line with those of Moody Stuart, for example on the Establishment Principle and the question of the Free Church's proposed union with the United Presbyterian Church, makes his high estimation of him all the more compelling.—*P.*

[23] For a brief discussion on the dissemination of Pre-millennial ideas at this time, see John Macleod, *Scottish Theology*, pp. 290-92.—*P.*

[24] John Kennedy (1819–84), a highly influential Highland minister and a sought-after preacher. He was ordained and inducted to Dingwall Free Church in 1844, where he served for the entirety of his ministry. He was the biographer of John MacDonald of Ferintosh.—*P.*

— 6 —

Visits to Madeira and Brazil

> What should we do but sing his praise
>   Who led us through the watery maze,
> Unto an isle to us unknown,
>   And yet far kinder than our own;
> Who gave us this eternal spring
>   Which here enamels everything,
> And hung in shades the orange bright,
>   Like golden lamps in a green night?
>
> *—Andrew Marvell*

BEFORE sailing for Madeira Mr Moody Stuart addressed a letter to the elders and members of St Luke's from Greenock on 12 November 1841.

'You scarcely require to be assured,' he wrote, 'that your kind expressions of attachment to your pastor have found in him a full and cordial response. Next to the direct consolations of the Holy Ghost there is nothing of power to comfort and strengthen the heart of a minister in any affliction equal to the sincere sympathy of his people. His love to his people will strike root and grow, even although "the more he loves the less he be loved."[1] But it is one thing to be independent of our people's attachment and quite another to

---

[1] cf. 2 Cor. 12:15.—*P.*

be indifferent to it. That attachment, both in its existence and in its utterance, we cherish as most dear and precious. Our Heavenly Father is at present evidently dealing with us as a congregation. His doings are neither random nor solitary acts, but are regular steps in one continuous path, although that path is often in the sea, and those footsteps therefore not known. In every trial, then, while we walk under it by the guidance of the written word as our only infallible rule, it is our wisdom, with this lamp in our hand, humbly to inquire into the Lord's past dealings with us, if haply these may throw light on the present—being assured that there is a close and singularly beautiful connection, if we will only discern and trace it. On a dark and cloudy day I have wandered over the watery sands from which the sea had just ebbed, and strained my eyes to catch the way-marks that pointed a safe course to the opposite shore (from Holy Island to the mainland) and could discover nothing save a solitary stake that gave no information and only increased the confusion, but the instant I came upon the track itself, so as to direct the eye along it, the whole line to my joyful surprise became visible at once. One moment I saw that single post standing alone, telling me nothing and guiding me nowhere; the next moment at the distance of a few paces there stood ranged both before and behind me a long and distinct and most welcome line of way-marks; and even so it is with the line of Providence that directs the path of the pilgrim through the sandy waste of this dark and cloudy world. A single event, however dark in itself, and doubly dark through our blindness, may become full of light and meaning when viewed in connection with other events of kindred character. In the development of that connection we must sometimes patiently wait for the future, because he who has had the way itself before his eye from eternity may not yet have actually planted with his hand the way-marks for us; but when the particular history has been somewhat developed and more than one guiding post has been fixed, then the wise contemplation of the past may go far to discover the line of Providence.'

Their minister then recalls to them how on successive anniversaries of his ordination they had been visited by startling deaths in the congregation; he reminds them how at the close of his third year as minister he was 'silenced by an unexpected stroke, and preached the following Sabbath a bereaved parent. The removal of an infant that had not outlived a day may be accounted a comparatively light affliction, yet nothing brings a man more sensibly near to death than to see his own offspring laid in the grave, with his own hand to consign part of himself to the dust. The axe that has cut away this branch may next be laid to the root. "The husbandman had come three years seeking fruit."' Now his fourth anniversary came; it was their communion, and the following week his present illness commenced, which was soon to stop his preaching. Perhaps each of these trials had brought some blessing to them and to himself, for 'whom the Lord loves he chastens,' but it was 'a call to them all to bring forth fruit in amount and quality suitable to the soil where the tree was planted, and worthy of the Vinedresser who tends it, and the Husbandman who owns it.'

The infant whose death is here referred to was a daughter who only lived a day, and was buried at South Queensferry (where they were staying in summer quarters in July 1840), in the burying-place of the parish minister. This first-born babe, only opening her eyes upon this earth to close them, sleeps quietly close to the southern wall of the church of that old-world-looking little town with its many red-tiled roofs and quaint gables, almost under the shadow of that greatest achievement of modern engineering science, the Forth Bridge.

As Ralph Erskine sings:—

> Babes, caught away from womb and breast,
>   Have cause to sing above the rest;
> For they have found that happy shore
>   They neither saw nor sought before.

I was born in the summer of 1841, and was taken as an infant with my parents to Madeira, where their second son Andrew was born at the end of 1842.

'On arriving in Madeira,' my father writes, 'the custom-house officers objected to our landing till our packages had been examined, and it seemed as if we might be detained all night in the ship. When we told them that we had letters to the consul it had no effect, but they at once allowed us to go ashore when we said that we had letters to Dr Kalley,[2] and we afterwards learned that he had performed a difficult operation on one of the custom-house officers, which the Portuguese surgeons were afraid to attempt. On looking out for a house we met with further traces of his influence in the unexpected and welcome sight of a large Portuguese Bible on some of the drawing-room tables.

'As I stood one Sabbath at the door of Dr Kalley's house, observing the worshippers as they entered under the inspection of an official who wrote down their names, I was much affected by the sight of a middle-aged man, who had just been released from gaol for his previous attendance at these meetings. He came forward with no apparent hesitation, in the full knowledge that the step involved a return to prison. But instead of the bold front which men of some other nations would have borne after they had made up their minds to proceed, this poor man walked on weeping as he approached and crossed the forbidden threshold, in him a singularly noble act, because it was felt to be at so great a sacrifice. One Sabbath forenoon when the enmity to Dr Kalley had reached its height, and there was no longer any Portuguese service, I went over to his house because there was an apprehension of riotous proceedings. The house was above the town, on a road that led to a church on the top of a hill dedicated to the Virgin Mary, from which it received the designation of 'Mary of the Mount'. In the lower part of the house there was the door to the street, but no windows, so that we were pretty secure except from extreme violence. After a little we heard

---

[2] Robert Reid Kalley (1809–88) was a Scottish physician and missionary who worked predominantly in Portuguese-speaking areas. He was the founder of the Presbyterian Church of Portugal. He went to Brazil in 1854, where he and his wife Sarah founded the Igreja Evangélica Fluminense in Rio de Janeiro.—P.

a loud shouting, and looking out at the drawing-room windows we saw a vociferous company of twenty or thirty men. Their shout was not "Great is Diana of the Ephesians," but "Viva Maria do Monte." Their jumping from the ground and their gesticulations were so violent, and the shouting so loud and fierce, that we were amazed at the unbroken continuance of the scene for the greater part of an hour, and it might have lasted much longer if Dr Kalley had not interrupted it by going out to the rioters, a step from which we earnestly dissuaded him. When matters were drawing to a crisis a friendly official warned him that if he persevered he would be stabbed, to which he returned the noble reply, "Then I shall be the sooner in glory." What alarmed us for his safety was not so much the crowd as their leader. He was an immense man; he had a chest of abnormal breadth, and arms of portentous length, and in times of political trouble was said to have been employed by the Government to get obnoxious men out of the way by squeezing them to death, which made an English gentleman remark that he would like to see him grappling with a bear. When my friend went down, and stood within a yard of this formidable man, shouting and dancing as if he would strangle him, we could not but fear that he might try the length of his arms on the victim within his reach. But Dr Kalley's coolness disarmed both him and his whole company, and after a little they ceased their maddened yells. He then spoke a few quiet and kindly words to them, to which they listened respectfully, and afterwards held out his snuff-box to his opponent as a token of friendship, which was pleasantly responded to, and the two shook hands. The lions changed into lambs went quietly home, and Dr Kalley returned to us to render thanks together to him who had thrown his shield around his faithful servant, and been "a very present help in trouble."'

This 'singularly devoted and singularly honoured' man of God often had audiences of 2,000, many of whom had walked ten or twelve miles over mountains 3,000 feet high. Dr Kalley, as is well known, continued his labours, reaping large success amid much persecution, during which he himself suffered imprisonment for six months, and, escaping with difficulty, ultimately settled 800 of his exile converts in the New World.

Madeira presented Mr Moody Stuart with a wholly new and very attractive scene for his observant mind. He noticed Scripture illustrated before his eyes, as when he watched the gardener irrigating his plots on the hill side, when the water was let on to the channel at the top, by stopping the smaller runnels with his foot, exactly as described in Deuteronomy 11:10 as being practised in Egypt. Or again, his attention was drawn to an express courier, panting in his running, who stooped for a few seconds over a wayside well, without wasting time by kneeling down, and, by a rapid motion of his hand similar to a dog's action with his tongue, tossed up the cooling water in an almost continuous stream into his open mouth. By observing this incident he for the first time understood what was stated of Gideon's 300 chosen warriors, who were selected because 'they lapped of the water with their tongues as a dog lappeth, putting their hand to their mouth, and did not stoop down upon their knees to drink' (Judges 7:5, 6).

Meanwhile ecclesiastical affairs in Scotland were hurrying on to their great crisis, and Mr Stothert, his session-clerk, kept his beloved pastor fully informed both as to these and as to the spiritual state of the congregation, the care of which, during his absence, had been entrusted to the Rev. William C. Burns, afterwards so widely known for his devoted missionary labours in China, and whose sister had been married to Mr Moody Stuart's brother George. A few extracts from Mr Stothert's letters may be given as describing St Luke's at an interesting period, in reply to which the absent minister was able from time to time to address much valued pastoral letters to his distant flock.

Mr Stothert writes: '30 December 1841. The church is filled to the door every Sabbath with a strange medley of ever-varying countenances—Newhaven fishwives, sneering young men, etc.... 18 March 1842. Sabbath desecration completed in 800 or 900 people having been carried out and in last Sabbath on the railway. Burns was at his post at the terminus morning and evening preaching to thousands of the stragglers, besides being with us as usual.' Miss Mackenzie informs me that Lord Mackenzie's coachman heard the preacher's voice at Belmont (Corstorphine Hill), which is one and a quarter miles from the Haymarket. He also preached in Grassmarket and Calton Hill. 'You may easily imagine what your elders have to do when forty-eight are already seeking admission to the Lord's table. (Of these forty-eight the session admitted thirty-seven.) It is comforting to think that some are joining us just because the elders do some duty... John Milne (of Perth) preached on Friday evening and Saturday, and Sabbath morning at railway; served four tables, and preached gloriously in the evening, and concluded on Monday evening after being at Leith. I met three who blessed the Lord that he had sent him to put a new song in their mouth.' Islay Burns succeeded his brother in November 1842. 'Our feast on second Sabbath of February. Somerville takes the Fast day; Milne and M'Cheyne do the rest.'

'Edinburgh, 18 February 1843.

My Dear Friend,

The table is drawn—we are down from the Mount, having again enjoyed one of those short yet blessed preludes of that never-ending supper of the Lamb, for which his wife is making herself ready. Blessed are they that shall be called to *that* Feast! Our way to it may be through fire and water—we may be destitute, afflicted, tormented, yet let us rejoice, inasmuch as we are therein partakers of his sufferings—and *what joy* that may bring to us we cannot tell. *This* we know—that under that or the other personal or relative trouble we have experienced a joy unspeakable—how much more when suffering for Christ when the Spirit of Glory and of God shall rest upon us! The Lord has been giving us another lesson to cease from man, in that M'Cheyne on whom our hearts were set was not permitted to be with us at all.[3] Somerville did his own part on the Fast day. There were several most interesting cases admitted at this time; thirty-six joined by certificate. Many whom I have seen speak of it as a time of great refreshing, but it is so easy to *say* so, and there seems a natural backwardness to say anything else, as tho' no communion season could be profitable that was not refreshing. Alas, a day! if the benefit were restricted to *sense*. O that the Great Master of Assemblies may put fresh power into the means of grace that his children and servants may be prepared for the coming conflict!

Since we had a meeting of Scotland's elders in St Luke's, addressed by Dr Chalmers, we have set ourselves to provide for the worst and several thousand pounds have been subscribed.[4] The ministers and some of us are leaving our houses for moderate rent ones. Candlish and Cunningham have gone into *common* stairs.[5]

O that it might yet be averted! If indeed the Kirk of Scotland could ever be called a vine of God's planting, and who can doubt it?—less now than ever, seeing he is visiting it with the refreshing dews of his Spirit,—what will it be *to leave it*? I cannot divest myself of the conviction that no power on earth should have tempted us to leave it; I suspect Begg, Kirkwood, and those with them were right: we should have preferred to suffer *in it*. What comes of separation? But I must cease.

Ever affectionately yours,

Wm. Stothert.'

The view given in the last paragraph I have heard expressed long after as their mature opinion by several prominent members of St Luke's who were steadfast in their attachment to the Free Church, and it was a view for which much could be advanced, but the course

---

[3] M'Cheyne was sent by the Convocation to preach in Deer and Ellon at this date. He died on 25 March.—*KMS.*

[4] The St Luke's building was the location of several important meetings in connection with the Non-Intrusionist cause in the lead-up to the Disruption. See minutes of the St Luke's kirk session in the Appendix, pp. 407-9.—*P.*

[5] That is, tenements (apartments) which were accessed by a shared central stairwell.—*P.*

of events was otherwise, and the Disruption became inevitable, which Mr Moody Stuart afterwards termed 'one of the noblest sacrifices which the church on earth has ever been privileged to offer to her Head in Heaven.' He, however, always held strongly that it is the duty of the state to acknowledge, protect, and cherish the true church of Christ, and this position, which was that of the Fathers of the Disruption, he felt called upon publicly to defend at a later period.

In May 1843, Mr Moody Stuart sailed from Madeira to Brazil. In crossing the Equator he saw Neptune's fairy car on the ocean (a boat rigged out by the crew), and was duly admitted a subject of his dominion by being soused from head to foot with two bucketfuls of sea water.

In letters to our mother he describes the approach to Rio de Janeiro through the magnificent bay, interspersed with islands, clothed with trees, palms and cocoas, surrounded on all sides by land except at the somewhat narrow entrance, which is unobserved from within, beside which rises a beautiful and very singular hill, about 900 feet high, called the Sugar Loaf. On the opposite side of the bay is the city of Rio, beautifully situated among knolls covered with trees, while in the distance rise the Organ Mountains.

The traveller describes various objects of natural history, *e.g.*, huge spiders with teeth so large as to be made into ladies' ornaments, great centipedes, land crabs, etc. The mules are pictured marching in files, sometimes of nearly fifty, the leader choosing the way by unerring instinct, and the rest following through treacherous bogs, etc., exactly in his footprints.

'Near one of the harbours of Brazil,' he says, 'where slavery has since been happily abolished, I saw a strangely painted ship, with her colour nearly resembling the hue of the ocean beneath her. She was an African slaver, and her hold was said to have been the coffin of 400 human beings, who had been mercilessly suffered to perish by the cruellest of all deaths—the want of water, while 900 survived, and their sale brought a large profit on the voyage.

'In one of the harbours one of the sable daughters of Africa, stolen in her youth from her own sunny home and sold for a slave, followed the footsteps of her mistress (whose child she was carrying on her side in the manner described by Isaiah) into our ship, a Government mail packet, 3,000 miles from our shores, and I remarked to the captain that on reaching England she would be free. 'No,' he replied, 'she is free already. The Queen of England has no slaves; the moment she set her foot on the planks of the ship she was a free woman.' She seemed well treated and happy in her slavery, and it would have been cruel to tell her she might claim her freedom and come with us to England, where she might have died of want. So she returned on shore ignorant of her liberty.' I have heard the narrator forcibly illustrate the case of sinners under the gospel dispensation by this incident, showing that they were ignorant of their dearly purchased freedom, and went back contentedly to their bondage.

'In Brazil,' he said to our General Assembly, 'I saw the fairest scene that I shall look upon till I see the paradise of God above, a valley filled with every tree that is fairest to the eye—lofty palms, tree-ferns with their utmost softness of grace; araucarias, with their perennial spikes of green iron for leaves; bamboos tapering into tall trees, then curving to the earth in grass-like slenderness; climbing plants using the trees like masts for the rigging of ships, and interlacing them with an intricate green rope-work; pitcher plants, whose cups of water you were apt to pour over you by carelessly touching them; flowering shrubs of exquisite beauty; on the right hand and the left, as far onward as the eye could reach, the lofty trees clothed with plants that needed no soil, and hanging the valley for miles with garlands of flowers, with a variety and amplitude of brightness and of beauty that irresistibly constrained the praise, "O God, how manifold are thy works; in wisdom hast thou made them all: the earth is full of thy riches." In wonder and ecstasy I was ready to exclaim, "The eye is satisfied with seeing."

'Still far from human dwellings I turned my horse's head out of the valley at a point where two paths met, and seeing what seemed a guide-post, rode up and read in Portuguese: "Hue and cry! Reward for capture—runaway slave-woman, twenty-three years of age, of such a height, such features, so many scars on the shoulders, each so long and so broad, so many teeth out, such and such mutilations of different parts of the body"—the published fruits of the lash, and of the rage of a brutal master, and it might be of a fiery will writhing against its wrongs. The eye was sickened with seeing, and I turned aside with horror from the blood-red fangs of the serpent at the very gates of paradise. Oh! accursed African slavery, darkest and sorest of human ills! Father of the spirits of all flesh, look down in pity on the untold woes of Africa; hear the groaning of the prisoner, and loose those that are appointed to die!'

His letters after describing the same scene, continue: 'I felt as if I could gladly wander for weeks in those wild woods and admire the works of him who, being so "wonderful in counsel and excellent in working," yet "bore our sins in his own body on the tree"; ours in having made us, ours in having bought us, ours in standing as constantly at God's right hand for us, as he constantly upholds all these things by the word of his power. Today for the first time I saw the hummingbird, shining in the sun with its bright plumage, and flitting rapidly from flower to flower, with its long bill sipping the honey from their deep tubes, in appearance not unlike the long-tailed moth of Madeira. The shrill, prolonged and somewhat melancholy whistle of the monkey we heard occasionally, and the forests often rang with the sound of the "blacksmith," a bird with a very loud and piercing note, exactly resembling the stroke of an anvil, at which it keeps hammering and hammering with prodigious power and perseverance, as if it were trying for its life how many times it could repeat the sound without intermission. Our ride continued through bamboos, cocoas, nut-palms, tree-ferns, with flowers and shrubs and trees without name or number.

'It is scarcely possible not to be struck with the unsearchable wisdom of the Creator, and to feel that the Father of our spirits with whom we have had sweet communion is more wonderful and incomprehensible and more infinitely unlike us than we had at all conceived, and to wonder that such a Being could have stooped to hold intercourse with us, or we have dared to hold intercourse with him: yet are we ourselves above all these other works curiously and wonderfully made!'

That night they had to put up at a small country inn, in the public room of which was a table, with a bench on each side, a swing in the centre suspended from the joists, with two blackguard-looking boys amusing themselves on it. On the benches sat three or four men of idle aspect, thrumming on a guitar. The shutters were by-and-by closed, and a lamp lighted, a Scotch 'cruisie'. Then a tap at the door was followed by the entrance of a man with a bag and a gun, accompanied by a boy. Then they heard horse-hoofs, and a tall black entered, wearing a large, long, heavy, hatchet-like knife called a *fuca*, used for all purposes—cutting brushwood, carving food, and stabbing men when required.

The guide, who was an English schoolmaster in a mountain town, was anxious to leave such suspicious company, but as they had no arms and no conductor in the dark they thought it safer to remain. The supper though ample was far from appetising, but as they had had no food since breakfast they ate it with relish. Salt was never set on the table in Brazil but often bits of it used to be produced after the meal. Mattresses were brought in, but Mr Moody Stuart preferred sleeping on the bare table. The schoolmaster had resolved not to go to bed or close his eyes, and kept his master awake by pouring his fears into his ear (none of the guests knowing English). However at last they were both overpowered by sleep. No evil resulted, and early next morning they started anew on their way. After breakfasting frugally at another country inn, towards evening they missed their way, taking the wrong road, which being at first a 'corduroy' or plank road, with many rotten planks in it, at last in descending a mountain degenerated into something like the bed of a torrent, with huge stones, sometimes rocks, strewn down its course. The sun set and there was no moon, but the traveller's sorrow for the departing day was swallowed up in joy and gratitude to him whose name, 'The Father of Lights,' he says he now prized more, as raising his eyes to heaven he saw the fair Southern Cross and a bright host of stars glittering in the sky.

Every second step in the dark was 'a leap, or slip, or fall, or stumble,' as with his staff he groped his way, dragging his horse after him, and he realised the preciousness of the promise, 'He shall give his angels charge over thee, to keep thee, lest thou dash thy foot against a stone' (Psa. 91:11, 12), which gave him confidence to proceed. One cottage they descried through the trees proved to be deserted; then they saw a light, but were disappointed in thinking it proved the presence of man, for it turned out to be the glow of the firefly. They heard the roar of a stream which at last crossed their path, and gave them a much needed draught of water to quench their unceasing thirst.

They now crossed various streams, and the wanderer was surprised that his boots let in water. In the morning he saw that they were all cut into holes. The fireflies were now very plentiful on the grass, strewn as thick as daisies, and gave them a useful light. He describes them as 'a very common-looking fly. Its light is all its beauty; an earthly fly with a most heavenly light. Is it not so also with us?' After having had to lead their horses for more than three hours down this breakneck path they were able to remount. At length they thankfully came upon an inn. In vain for long they called and knocked at doors and windows.

At last the sleeping host was aroused, and a voice answered from within. But nothing would induce him to give them admittance, as he thought they were robbers and dismissed them with horrible curses. At last they came among scattered huts, and finally to a large village where they found an inn whose landlord on being aroused from his dreams was kindly, and gave the wildered rider his own bed. They had had no food for twelve hours, and no really satisfying meal for thirty-six hours, but he got into bed and there got the only food the house could afford, *viz.*, rusks and gin, which fortunately warded off a chill. Altogether he could not easily forget his descent of the Serra do Soccovao.

From this he continued his tour up the Organ Mountains, the scenery of which he described as very fine.

In his tour to Brazil he had a fellow traveller whom he was told he might find it very difficult to get on with, so he resolved that any quarrel should not arise on his side, and that he would always give him the first choice and take himself what was left. He acted thus in regard to the choice of a berth and several other things, and his companion remarked that Mr Moody Stuart always took what was left, and that it always turned out the best in the end. On starting for a long ride in Brazil with a large party, when the horses they had ordered were brought out he adhered to his rule, and allowed all the others to take their choice, and on this occasion there was none left at all. His companion laughed at him and said: 'Well, you see how you have fared this time by always giving others their choice. You'll be left behind.' On the hotel-keeper coming out to see them off, and asking why he was not mounted, he replied that the groom had said there was no horse for him. The proprietor said: 'Well, there's my own horse which is too good to hire out, but I'll lend you it.' So he got it, and when all the other horses were wearied out it went on with its rider as fresh as ever. So even here he found the benefit of taking what others left.

— 7 —

Minister of Free St Luke's

> Blest by our heavenly Father's hand
> Were thy deep love and tender care,
> Thy ministry and fervent prayer,
> To those who drew
> In crowds around thee in the hour
> Of prayerful waiting hushed and deep,
> Seals of thy true apostleship.
>
> *—Whittier*

RETURNING to Scotland in the end of July 1843, Mr Moody Stuart resumed his interrupted ministry in renewed health and vigour. The Lord had graciously heard the earnest prayers that had ascended from his attached flock on his behalf, and added to his days fifty-five years. Many long remembered the thrill which went through the crowded congregation as he rose and gave out to be sung:—

> I shall not die, but live, and shall
> The works of God discover.
> The Lord hath me chastised sore,
> But not to death giv'n over.—(Psa. 118:17, *Scottish Psalter*).

The Disruption made very little difference in the congregation of St Luke's. All the twelve elders and 98½ per cent of the congregation had left the Establishment, their minister signing the Deed of Demission on his return from abroad, and six years elapsed before they were forced to quit the church which they had themselves built. Nor would their minister's stipend have been affected, but Mr Moody Stuart voluntarily restricted it for a time, until it was assured that the newly organised Sustentation Fund would yield a dividend sufficient for the maintenance of the brethren in country charges. In so doing he was making no greater sacrifice than many others. His attached friends, the Hon. Misses Mackenzie, gave up their carriage, sold their family plate, and economised in various ways, to the extent, a relative writes, of 'enduring hardness like soldiers in a campaign.' Those who had in many cases to surrender family ties and friendships for Christ's sake, did not hesitate freely to sacrifice their possessions at the call of conscience.

Mr Moody Stuart notes: 'A remarkable sermon was preached before the Assembly of 1844 by my friend Dr Charles Brown, which made a great impression. It was followed by heart-searching and quickening meetings of presbyteries for spiritual conference, and in our own Session records there is often a very full and affecting account of meetings for humiliation and prayer after that Assembly.' A little later: 'The Session resolve to make conscience of closet work, and of a closer intimacy with God therein.' An old member of St Luke's recalls that at this date her minister addressed the prayer meeting from Psalm 25:4, 5, and asked them all earnestly to pray that they might be taught God's way for blessing them, adding, 'I believe some here think there's no need; I have more hope of such than of those who know their need, and will not pray for it.' 'I was among the needy,' she added, 'and had great fear of losing the blessing.'

At this time Mr Moody Stuart's preaching, always subjective, and dealing with individual experience, was considered by some of his congregation to be of too searching and introspective a character. Their views on this point were so decided that in the year 1845 several esteemed elders resolved to resign. This must have been a great trial to the minister, but in such circumstances it is often best that 'every man should be fully persuaded in his own mind.' Mr Moody Stuart held that no minister should preach to his people truths of the power of which he has not had personal experience. But he went further than this, and felt it necessary to have a *present* experience of the power of the truth which formed the substance of his message. This gives great force to a ministry, but it is obvious that if this be rigidly adhered to, it will tend unduly to make the present religious experience of the pastor the standard to which that of his congregation must be conformed, and with a congregation of any size this is not desirable, nor indeed possible.

As has already been indicated, the state of his health and the crisis in church matters had no doubt tended to depress his spirits, both physically and spiritually, for the physical state affects the religious emotions through the subtle interconnection of the two parts of man's nature. Between himself and those who left his ministry at this time there continued to subsist the most cordial esteem. I have heard on good authority that one of these elders on his death-bed years after, found great comfort from recalling his former pastor's sermons, and the same was the case with the wife of another in such a marked degree that her widowed husband, then an old man, rejoined St Luke's, and was readmitted as an elder. The friend already quoted writes regarding this time: 'Some had sparks of their own kindling extinguished, myself among them.' Meanwhile the Lord did not cease to own his servant's message.

A lady who, though not a member, used to attend the prayer meeting in St Luke's, asked a young married friend to come with her and hear Mr Moody Stuart, who was 'said to be preaching more law than gospel.' She came, and was so much impressed that she with her husband joined the church. One day during the sermon she was overpowered by a sense of her lost state; the question arose in her heart: 'Must I perish?' She then thought she saw the Saviour hanging on the cross, and seemed to hear the words, *This death was for you!* In the pew, she placed all her trust on this crucified Redeemer,

and she and her husband were long eminent for Christian usefulness in a wide sphere. No doubt the preaching did not always end
in conversion. Duncan Matheson, the widely known evangelist,
then a thoughtless youth working in Edinburgh, 'yet felt,' writes his
biographer, 'that he must needs sit under the most faithful minister
he can find, and accordingly goes to hear Mr Moody Stuart. No
sooner is he seated than a lady enters the same pew, and leaning her
head on the bookboard engages in silent prayer. Matheson is self-
condemned. His conscience upbraids him for his prayerlessness. He
is now at the preacher's mercy, and he goes away saying to himself:
"I cannot bear this; if I am to come here I must be converted."
He resolved to return to that church no more.' But before long by
various instrumentalities he was brought to Christ, and became a
warm life-long friend of the minister whose preaching he formerly
could not stand.

If the freeness of the gospel was not made so prominent in his
preaching as afterwards it became, it would be a great mistake to
suppose it was absent. The Rev. T. Grant of Tain has told me that
about this time, he, then a boy, was awakened to spiritual concern,
and he had heard so much about Mr Moody Stuart that he thought
if he could hear him it would do him good. Learning that he was
to preach in Huntly he went from Keith, but arrived late and found
a crowd outside the place of meeting who could not get in. With
the ardour of youth he determined to press his way in, hoping to
find some vacant corner, and when at last he got in he found an
empty space in front of the preacher, where he established himself
just as the speaker with his finger on his forehead gave out his text,
'*Yet there is room.*' The sermon made a deep and helpful impression
upon him, and he realised from it that there was room in the Kingdom of Christ for all who would press into it.

We give a few extracts from this sermon from notes taken by a
hearer when it was preached as the concluding address at a communion about that date: 'The feast is not closed; the door is not shut
yet; the supper is not done: if you go out quickly, another company

may be brought in. Go out and tell those that are farthest off to come: those in the lanes and closes, tell them there is room. There is great guilt resting on us because while we are willing enough that those who choose should come in, we are not willing to go forth to those who need to be compelled to come in. It is sometimes hard to compel; it needs faith in the living God. I do not think our consciences are awake to the command, "Compel them to come in." The command is that you use such arguments and entreaties that men shall be constrained to come in. It implies that you go to those who are exceedingly averse to come, and also that those who are averse may be made willing, and be constrained by God's servants. If Jesus says to you at the table, "Go, compel them to come in!" you may not say, "No; I will sit at Jesus' feet, and hearken to his word." You are ready to say, "We must get more of Christ first," but this is the way to get more of Christ; this tries our faith, our love to God and man. But you may say, "Men will say, What right have you to judge my case?" It may be they are more ready to be drawn to the feast than you think. But how hard it is to tell an old story, and to tell it as if it were new! But it is not hard to tell what we have newly seen. We cannot refrain from telling that. And it is because we are so little in the inner room ourselves that we cannot tell men, "Yet there is room." If we were fresh in the grace of God; if we saw the heart of Christ that there is room there, we could not but go out and compel men to come in. There is none but can go to some one. If you are not willing to be contradicted, gainsaid, despised, in asking men to be reconciled to God, you are not fit for the kingdom of heaven. If we had in us any freshness of the love of Christ, and if we were taking that love forth till it reached the hearts of men, it would be very hard for them to refuse it. There is room in the compassion of God, but not in our frozen hearts.'

Addressing those still outside, even though they had sat at the table, the preacher went on to say: 'Dear friends, bone of our bone, flesh of our flesh, you must come into the kingdom of our Lord Jesus Christ. You must come in quickly (1) because it is so evil where you are, and will be so wretched and ruinous to all eternity. You must not remain another day where you are; it is the city of destruction, and you will be destroyed body and soul together if you remain in it. (2) Because it is so good to be within; it is so safe, and so sweet: because within there is righteousness, and peace, and joy, and pardon, and dominion over sin, and the love of God shed abroad in the heart; because there is as good a place for you if you come in as for any there. Every one that has gone in has found a ring that fitted him exactly, shoes made for him, and the best robe ready for him. You must come in because these are waiting for you. (3) Because the King of kings invites you, a perishing sinner, by name; and such an invitation is a command. What a slight if you refuse! What infamy by which you shall be marked for ever! (4) Because the Lord says, "Come!" and he makes willing in the day of his power. We doubt not there are those present, now without, who must come in, because all that the Father giveth shall come.'

May the entreaty prove as availing with some who read it, as with some who heard it, for surely, 'He being dead, yet speaketh.'

The Rev. A. C. Fullarton of Glasgow, who joined St Luke's in 1846, writes: 'There was then a spirit of great tenderness manifest in the congregation. Your father was lecturing that winter on the eleventh chapter of Hebrews; Abraham leaving his country and his kindred at the command of God, going forth not knowing whither he went; Isaac allowing himself to be bound and laid on the altar as a sacrifice, etc. It was a style of preaching adapted to the time. Self-sacrifice was required on a large scale. The ministers had been called to self-sacrifice by the Disruption. The people were called to self-sacrifice for the building of churches, manses, and schools throughout the land. And as if that were not enough, God in his providence during that winter permitted the potato disease to carry away the principal sustenance of the people both in the Highlands and in Ireland, and left them depending on the charity of the Lowlands. The congregation of Free St Luke's responded to the appeal from the pulpit with marked liberality, the poorer members doing their part equally with the wealthier, and it showed that men and women of faith truly love their God and their fellow men more than they love their money.

'Two things in your father's preaching particularly impressed me: *viz.*, his earnestness and his originality. Divine truth was brought direct to the consciences of his hearers, and pressed home by incident and illustration till men were made to feel that they were face to face with God, and had to decide either to embrace Christ and become new creatures, or else to make up their minds to live the life of unconverted persons, knowing themselves to be such. With regard to his originality, I never heard your father preach without carrying away with me some fresh views of divine truth, either in its bearing on spiritual experience, or on the relation of one truth to another, or in something fresh out of the original Hebrew or Greek; such as I was not likely to hear in any other place.'

It was at this period that Dr John Duncan, Professor of Hebrew in the New College (Rabbi Duncan), became an elder, and was long one of the spiritual factors and forces in St Luke's. A man of great learning, a noted linguist, an acute thinker, and a profound theologian, he combined with these qualities a high-toned spirituality of mind, a childlike simplicity, great tenderness of conscience, and deep humility. His opinion was highly valued by his minister on all the knottiest points of theology as well as in cases of conscience; while he in turn said of his minister that 'he knew not a greater master in spiritual analysis.'

A volume of reminiscences of this great divine was written by Mr Moody Stuart,[1] of which Dr Marcus Dods wrote in a critical review, that 'they were moulded by the hand of a master into a likeness which must rank among the half-dozen masterpieces of literary portrait-painting which our country boasts. Mr Moody Stuart handles his difficult subject with the ease of old and familiar acquaintance; with the grace, tact, and insight of a keen, cultivated, and sympathetic critic; with the self-concealment and delicacy of a gentleman.

[1] A. Moody Stuart, *The Life of John Duncan* (1872; repr. Edinburgh: The Banner of Truth Trust, 1991).—*P.*

He justly observes that Dr Duncan had genius, a gift which requires to be shared for its right delineation; but this, which he intends as a modest disclaimer of the requisite ability to do full justice to his subject, will seem, by the adequacy of his work, to have unintentionally become a well-founded claim to that order of genius which is needed in a biographer.'

Another prominent member who was attracted to St Luke's about this time from the Episcopal Communion[2] was Miss Marianne Robertson. She was a deeply experienced Christian of the same school in divinity as Dr Duncan. To her manuscript notes of sermons left behind her at her death I am indebted for much of the matter of her minister's discourses contained in this volume.

It was characteristic of St Luke's that so many pencils were always kept going while the minister was preaching. Indeed near the manse pew the rapid running of the pencil over the paper was distinctly audible in various directions; and these were guided by very competent hands, moved by heads and hearts that were themselves able to instruct others. In some cases such notes were carefully transcribed and lent to friends who were invalided to read in their retirement; occasionally they were sent abroad to those who had once been fellow-worshippers, and who valued sermons by their old pastor.

An English clergyman stationed abroad, said that during a year when he sat in St Luke's he had taken copious notes of the sermons, which he preached over again to his distant flock, but each discourse had so much matter in it that his one year's notes had lasted him for three years! Even the boys and girls were encouraged to write down at least the text with its divisions and sub-divisions, so that in this church there was no risk of the preaching falling into a subordinate place. Indeed the importance and wide and lasting influence of 'preaching' is one of the outstanding lessons to be drawn from Dr Moody Stuart's ministry.

It must not be supposed, however, that the congregation, while comprising many devout and reflective Christians, was lacking in

[2] That is, from the Scottish Episcopal Church.—P.

those who engaged in the more practical efforts that are so characteristic of the present type of active Christian workers.

Miss Flynn, who must have joined about this time, was one of the very first to work among our soldiers. She walked from her house near Stockbridge up to the Castle, where she regularly read and prayed with the young soldiers, especially visiting those who were sick, and in this way she exercised a most beneficial influence over the men of various regiments. I remember the deep interest she took in them, and their gratitude to her when the troops in the Castle left for the Crimea, and also for India after the mutiny.

Peter Jackson, the converted cabman, who sat for fifty-five years in St Luke's, and 'whose face,' one says, 'as he listened to his minister's preaching, was a study,' was impelled by his fervid spirit to commend his Master in season and out of season to all whose ear and eye he could arrest. Many a quiet word for Christ did he drop in the ear of his 'fares'. In 1869 he wrote to me: 'It was not till Sabbath last that from the same dear lips that I first heard the voice of the Beloved, he shewed me that it was on my cross he was crucified, even mine. Yes, he made it his, and now (O wonderful!), through his grace I am journeying on to sit down with him upon his throne.'

All these and others were persons of mature Christian experience, whose souls were fed from Sabbath to Sabbath by the deeply spiritual ministrations of their pastor, and they carried the influence and the echoes of the Sabbath sermons to the ears and hearts of many to whom the preacher could gain no access. Such workers, along with several of the elders of St Luke's, began a territorial mission in Holyrood in 1844, which was energetically wrought by the congregation till it was formed into a regular charge in 1849. Upwards of a dozen ladies visited the district assiduously, and held small meetings, and the congregation employed earnest missionaries in it, *viz.*, Mr George Bain (afterwards of Pitcaple, who with his admirable wife became our lifelong friends), and Messrs. M'Gregor, Johnstone, and James Bennet, Congregational missionary, whose labours were much blessed. The Duchess of Gordon built the Holyrood school in connection with the mission, which was furnished with devoted teachers; and the young ladies of Miss Banks' Seminary in Moray Place, among whom there had been a remarkable work of grace, went down and held meetings with the children once a week. Thus St Luke's, itself originally a territorial charge, became the parent of another similar congregation. The new church was opened by Mr Moody Stuart in February, 1850. Its minister, the Rev. William Balfour, came to be his earnest coadjutor, ably defending the old faith and principles of the Free Church.

Mr Moody Stuart had not the physical strength to enable him to undertake any amount of that outside aggressive work which so many of our active territorial ministers achieve with marked success. Indeed the large amount of time which he always devoted to preparation for the pulpit would alone have made this impossible. But while carrying this on mainly through voluntary and approved helpers, and also latterly through ministerial assistants, part of whose duty it was to conduct services and visit regularly in the mission district of Thistle Street, etc., attached to the church, he did not altogether omit this work personally.

An instructive incident occurred in the early period of his ministry. There were twenty-one public-houses in the mission district, and he resolved in his annual visitation to devote a considerable time to each, trying to convince the publicans of the evil they were doing, and to press the claims of eternal realities. He did this, but went home much discouraged, and said to himself: 'The Bible says, "In all labour there is profit," but labour in public-houses must be an exception.' Next year, in going round the district he went to none of them, feeling he had done what he could. One woman stood at the door of a large public-house, and begged him to come in, but he told her he could not pray in her house; that he had shown them the year before what he considered they should do and it had no effect, and he would not go in. The third year he was making his usual round, and was surprised to see no barrels or sign of public-house where this large one used to be, so he went in and asked how this was. The woman replied: 'I could not stand what you said last time, that you could not pray in my house; so I said to my husband, "We must make a change," and we have given up the trade.' Another woman who had a smaller public-house also met him at the door, and said: 'I've taken your advice, and have begun to keep a dairy,' and a third had done the same. So he said: 'The Bible is right even as regards public-houses—in *all* labour there is profit.'

While not always able to get through the regular visitation of the congregation so systematically or rapidly as he desired, no minister was more attentive in visiting the sick and dying among his flock. He took a very great burden of such cases, praying not only with them in the chamber of sickness, but at his own family altar as if they had been members of his own household. Numerous testimonies have reached me as to the value which sick and suffering ones, and the members of their families, attached to his visits, and the benefit derived from them. One writes: 'In my long illness years ago, I always felt after a visit from him as though he left my dark bedroom flooded with sunlight.' Many domestic servants attended St Luke's, and their minister when unable to visit them all personally, used to invite them to tea, after which at worship they were addressed by himself, and one or more of the elders. Many of this class were noted both for grace and for liberality, contributing handsome sums to church collections and missions.

In his dealing with young persons preparing for the communion he was very thorough and faithful; but it was a mistake to suppose he was severe or extreme in his personal examination. A lady (Mrs Macdonald) writes to me that she came to St Luke's in 1846, the very period when some charged him with undue strictness. 'With fear and trembling I went to speak to him, before the October communion, but I found him so gentle and kind, and withal so faithful, I never had any fear in going to see him after that. In all our joys and sorrows we found him the loving, kind sympathiser. It was sorrow that called out the depths of his sympathy, and I can never forget how in one very deep distress his prayers comforted and soothed as if oil were poured down my troubled breast.'

Another honoured Christian lady, who joined St Luke's about the same date, gives me this account of her first interview with him: 'How impressive for a young woman of twenty-five (who had already been a communicant) was her first meeting with the faithful pastor, when he led her into his study, spoke of sin and the wonders of redeeming love, and after some time of conversation expressed himself to this effect: "A high natural state is very like a low spiritual state. I don't know in which you are, but the Holy Spirit is evidently working" (then holding forward one finger); "there is a line that must be passed."' On her leaving Edinburgh two years after, he took leave, saying, 'Moving from place to place, you will need much grace.' Returning long after in later life, she attached herself to his ministry and became one of his main supports. Once visiting her in sickness, on her lamenting being set aside, the tone of voice was never forgotten with which he said: 'Oh, oh, it is not what we do, but what we are!' Again on her remarking, 'What a mine of wealth the Bible is, and we can only scratch the top!' he replied, 'Yes; but how much there is in one scratch!'

A minister of the Church of Scotland, who has faithfully served his Master abroad as well as at home, told me that when he went as a young communicant at a much earlier date than the above, on being asked a number of questions, he felt quite overcome, broke into tears, and could answer nothing. In this case the minister was intimately acquainted with the candidate, and knew that it was no mere passing emotion; so without saying more, he just warmly pressed his hand, and slipped a 'token' into it. Such cases show that however searching his personal dealings often were, they were mingled with great tenderness.

Many of the letters sent to me speak of the bond of affection which united him and his people as being unusually strong.

At this period, as throughout his whole ministry, Mr Moody Stuart's services were much prized at sacramental occasions in localities far from his home, such as Glasgow, Rothesay, Perth, Aberdeen and

Huntly. Such preaching engagements often involved long journeys and exposure, especially when there were no railways in the north of Scotland. I remember his telling us on his return from one of these visits to Huntly, that the coach-and-four by which he was travelling (the 'Defiance', I think) had been overturned, but providentially without any serious results. He was sitting near the driver when one of the reins broke, and the spirited team bolted. The experienced driver, knowing that they were rapidly nearing a dangerous part of the road, where a serious disaster was inevitable for coach and passengers, turning round, said: 'Gentlemen, I can't save you from an upset, but I'll upset you as easy as I can.' Then as they were being whirled past a steep grassy bank, by a dexterous jerk of the sound rein he brought down his team and overturned the coach against the slope. So well was it managed that beyond a few scratches from the broken windows no one received any injury.

These communion services were often signally blessed, not only to God's children, but to the awakening and conversion of the unsaved. A picturesque account may be given from his own pen of such a communion at Huntly in July 1847.[3] Many strangers had gathered; some from twenty, some from fifty miles. The church not being large enough to contain the assembly it was arranged that they should convene within the walls of the ruined castle. A few of the Duke of Gordon's old military tents were pitched to shelter the communion elements and the infirm. Describing the scene he writes:—

> 'Then did we worship in that fane [temple, shrine]
>   By God to mankind given;
> Whose lamp is the meridian sun,
>   And all the stars of heaven.
>
> Whose roof is the cerulean sky,
>   Whose floor the earth so fair;
> Whose walls are vast immensity—
>   All nature worships there.

[3] See A. Moody Stuart, *Life and Letters of Elisabeth, Last Duchess of Gordon* (London: James Nisbet & Co., 1865), pp. 329-33.—*P.*

The long communion tables covered with white, and surrounded with benches for the communicants, occupied the centre, and round about during the 'action' sermon[4] the crowd was closely seated on the grass. Some men stood outside but drew gradually nearer as the service proceeded, and their hearts softened. One young country woman with rosy cheeks and colourful attire had taken an elevated seat on a heap of ruins, evidently intending to be merely a spectator. But by-and-by her wandering gaze became fixed; her lofty head bent slowly down, and ere the services were closed she had hid her face to conceal her fast-flowing tears. The old wives in their snow-white caps came from their seats on the grass to take their places at the table, their widowed lady among them, the men following with backward and reverent air. The most of the people who were not partaking of the Supper likewise rose, standing compact like a living wall around the communicants with deepest reverence. As the bread and the wine were blessed and divided among the guests, the lofty heavens appeared to open clear to where the Great High Priest stands at the Father's right hand, and the blessing seemed to descend even sensibly upon the worshippers below. As the blue sky in the heavens above met and kissed the green earth beneath, so the unseen above the heavens was revealed by the Spirit to the opened hearts of many.'

On 1 March 1849, minister and kirk session of St Luke's received notice from the kirk session of St George's Parish to quit their church, which they left at once, and worshipped in Queen Street Hall, while they were engaged in building a new church in Queen Street. The congregation was thus called upon twice to build a large church in twelve years. The action of resuming[5] these Chapels of

---

[4] In traditional Scottish communion seasons (which lasted several days), the 'action sermon' was the sermon preached at the communion service itself—the term comes from the Latin for 'thanksgiving', *grattarum actio*. For a fuller description of such a communion service, see John Macleod, *Scottish Theology* (1943, repr. Edinburgh: The Banner of Truth Trust, 2015), pp. 100-101.—*P.*
[5] That is, taking back.—*P.*

Ease[6] which had been practically built entirely by congregations that had now left the Establishment, was felt to be even a greater hardship than was involved in the Disruption itself, all the more so that it took place after the heat of the recent conflict had had time to cool down. Before proceeding however with the ministry in Queen Street it will be needful in the next chapter to give an account of an important visit paid to Ireland during the great famine.

[6] At the end of the eighteenth century the General Assembly of the Church of Scotland legislated for the creation of 'chapels of ease' to cater for the requirements of growing populations, particularly in urban industrial areas. Thomas Chalmers' 'church extension' drive in the 1830s (see above, p. 54) greatly increased the number of these chapels, many of them self-funded by congregations which subsequently adhered to the Free Church at the Disruption, as was the case with St Luke's. A House of Lords decision in 1849 returned these chapels to the possession of the Established Church, which led to the requirement for St Luke's to vacate their building.—*P.*

— 8 —

Visit to Ireland During the Famine

Erin! thy silent tear shall never cease,
Erin! thy languid smile ne'er shall increase,
Till, like the rainbow's light,
Thy various tints unite,
And form in Heaven's sight
One arch of peace!

—*Thomas Moore*

THE tears of Ireland never fell in fuller flood than when the calamitous years of 1846–7 had changed her languid national life into national desolation and death, forming a loud call for the kindling of a new gospel light in her darkest districts, and the cherishing of it until it should span her shores with the covenant bow of peace.

The potato blight of 1846, which deprived the people of the west of Ireland of their main sustenance, caused that country to be visited by the horrors of famine that lasted over more than one year, and by the scourge of fever which immediately followed it.

The Free Church General Assembly, although its hands were full with building churches and manses, as well as with collecting for the support of its now disendowed ministers, felt itself called upon to do what it could, not only in aiding the efforts that were

99

made to relieve the temporal distress of the Irish people, but to assist their Presbyterian brethren in the sister island in ministering to the spiritual wants of their Roman Catholic neighbours.

It was recognised that the terrible calamities they were suffering might open their hearts to embrace the gospel of Jesus Christ. They accordingly sent out deputies to visit the darkest districts of Ireland, which were also those which had suffered most from the famine, to preach the gospel and report upon the condition of the people. Mr Macnaughton was sent to Galway; Messrs. Wm. Arnot, Andrew Bonar, and Moody Stuart to Mayo and Roscommon. We give in his own words the experiences and impressions of the last of the scenes which he witnessed, and the sorrows which fell on the land fifty years ago. This visit to Ireland occupied the autumn months of 1847. Had the Protestant churches of Great Britain entered more generally into the work of evangelising Ireland and continued in it more perseveringly, the troubled history of the island during the succeeding half-century might have worn a widely different aspect.

'The still legible records of the past,' the deputy wrote, 'were saddening. You might visit the house of a minister of the gospel, and be shown the kitchen where the infants died in their mother's arms while they were wailing for food, and hear the servant tell how, when they opened the door in the morning, they used to find lifeless corpses in the porch; while the family, incessantly engaged in relieving others, perhaps tasted nothing themselves till the afternoon—pursued into every chamber of the house with piercing cries, by men who were unwilling to go away and die, and having had food prepared seven separate times, and as often consumed, before their own children had broken their fast. When questioned in reference to their own prospects, the people had nothing to say of this expedient or that, but returned the brief unvaried answer, "The Lord is merciful."

'While you stood in the midst of a graveyard, far from any church, every foot of it filled with graves, and every grave covered with stones, you might suddenly awake to the reflection that the wooden coffin, and the deep narrow pit, and the heavy stone slab that cover our dead, are not for decency merely, but for use; for these rude and motley stones over each body are not memorials of the deceased, but are here to prevent the uncoffined corpse from being torn up out of its shallow bed and devoured by the famishing dogs. For the same reason you hear of a lone widow interred beneath the hearth of her now tenantless cabin. In Currawn Achill the people showed us the place where, three weeks before, they had buried in the bog the corpse of a poor lad who had died of hunger. A little further on the same road we passed a gravel-pit, in which had been found, a month before, the remains of a young woman, who had died of want in similar circumstances—a friendless stranger. The body was discovered by the peasants who carried it a short distance and buried it, in like manner, under the turf, where the stranger girl and the poor wandering boy lay buried (alas, as the event proved all too ineffectually!) in the same wide field of heath. I also saw for myself a dead man lying unburied on the side of the highway on the spot where he fell five days previously, the body covered with straw, his head still sheltered by the hat which the living had worn. Burial had been delayed for the inquest, and it seemed as if nobody would now touch the decomposing corpse.

'We gladly turn for a moment from these harrowing scenes to admire the manifold wisdom of God and his abounding mercy in the midst of judgment. When I had finished the previous paragraph, before commencing to write of this unhappy pair hastened to an untimely grave, the hour had arrived which I had appointed for conversing with applicants for communion. It was equally refreshing and surprising for me to find amongst them a young Irish girl, whom that same awful famine had driven from her native land— who, after enduring many hardships, had experienced in her new country the cravings of another hunger than she had ever felt in her own—even hunger for eternal life, and was now asking to be permitted to eat bread at the Lord's table. Her prompt and brief reply to the inquiry why she sought admission to the sacred feast evinced at once intelligence and desire, "That I may see more of Jesus."

'When you have passed through a town, and all around you is shrouded in midnight darkness, you are attracted by a light, not brilliant, indeed, yet sufficient to show long ranges of tents covering a field—it is the lamp of those who watch by night over the sleepless fever patients shining dimly through the canvas. On the solitary road, far from towns or hospital tents, the coach-lamps reveal in the midst of the green grass some spot burned black and covered with lighted embers—they are the ashes of the couch on which had slept the night before some sick and weary family whom the people of the neighbouring cottage could not shelter for dread of infection, but for whom they had strewed a bed of straw on the wayside, and burned it after they had gone. But far more frequent than the fever-tent or the fever-couch is the fever-hut—a rude hovel on the road-side, formed usually of walls of turf, three or four feet high, with one side left open for entrance, and roofed with the same material, or perhaps without any roof save the hedge under which it lies. Such a hut sometimes contains a large family, sometimes a wretched solitary female; and, in one instance which I saw, a single little girl, who had lived there for weeks, and had often been compelled to share the bread and milk, which some kind neighbour gave, with the neighbouring dogs, which came regularly to claim their portion, and, when they could, to seize the whole.

'The first fever-hut I chanced to meet with was in respect of shelter, and indeed in all other respects, by far the best that I observed; it was fashioned with sticks sloping up against the wall of a field, covered with straw, and serving at once for roof and walls; the door was an opening, perhaps nearly three feet in height, in this slanting roof, and protected by a piece of old rug.

'That the habitation of any human being was there no stranger would have suspected; and it was certainly one of the most pleasing incidents that occurred in Ireland to see Her Majesty's mail draw up before this humble hovel.

'The shout of the coachman met with no response, and it was not till he had made his whip serve as a knocker at the rug that covered the entrance that the cloth was drawn aside, and the bright eyes of five or six children were seen glancing through the dwelling. The oldest girl came out alone, and if it were not that a Scotchman, who is cautious of using superlatives at home, is disposed to drop them altogether after visiting Ireland, I should say that this was one of the most affecting sights I have ever witnessed. She was a girl of fourteen, interesting, but sorrowful, spiritless, and sadly emaciated.

'She looked naked rather than clothed, for she had not an article of dress but a piece of old blanket thrown over her shoulders, that did not half cover her, and the alms that were given her she received thankfully, but without eagerness, as one dejected and stupefied. Although the coach passed regularly, she had never begged from it till the day before, when she came out, entreated the driver to stop, and craved help to bury her mother, who had died the preceding day.

'That unhappy mother was travelling toward some kindlier home with her young and helpless family when she was arrested by the children taking fever. It was far from any town, and she reared her little hut by the roadside to nurse them. The sickness spread from one to another through the little group, and detained them five or six weeks, till they were all recovering, when the mother, having watched her little ones into returning health, was seized with the same malady. It was too much for her exhausted frame—she sank under it and died, saving her children's lives at the sacrifice of her own, and leaving them to weep over her dead body in a miserable kennel, scarcely sufficient to contain them all. But the Father of the fatherless did not forsake them. The coachman's compassion was moved, and by setting the example himself, he induced the passengers to contribute as much as might serve for the funeral. He did the same the second day with equal success, endeavouring to feed and clothe the orphans, and, if possible, have them removed. Forty miles farther on the road he showed me another fatherless family, whom he had rescued from death by similar means, and was daily nourishing into health and vigour; and I was afterwards informed that, during the winter, he was supposed to have spent most of his gratuities in similar deeds of charity. In a land of such poverty and suffering it is refreshing to witness such humanity, and so successful in its humble efforts.'

Their tour was not wholly devoid of some spice of danger, for preaching at one place till after dark, 'in driving along a solitary part of the road,' the deputy writes, 'between nine and ten o'clock we came suddenly on four men, who blew a horn as soon as we appeared, divided into pairs to await our approach, and planting themselves two and two on each side of the car, fixed their eyes intently on us as we passed. The horn with its subdued tone, as if meant to be heard only within a measured distance, is used in Ireland by evil-doers as a sign to their accomplices, and was therefore also a signal for the smack of our carman's whip, setting our horse at full speed, so that we soon cleared sufficient ground to be free from all risk of others starting upon us from the fields. The fears of my companions were confirmed on our arrival at the inn, where we learned in their own expression that "there was not a worse spot on Irish ground." Why the men abstained from their design we could only surmise, but we were engaged in the Lord's service, and were at the time solemnly conversing on his great salvation, and he remembered his promise, "Thou shalt not be afraid for the terror by night," and we knelt down together and gave him thanks.

'We proceeded to Tullylin on Sabbath morning; the schoolhouse was filled with a hundred and fifty, including many children. Before sermon, which fell to me as my share of the work, Mr Brannigan catechised the children, prayed, and read a chapter in Irish. Just as the prayer was closing there was a great sensation throughout the meeting—it was reported that the priest had come. The children and young women, trembling and pale with fright, rushed to all the doors. I found it for a moment impossible to resist the sympathy of fear painted on so many young faces. It was a false alarm, though not quite groundless; it was only the priest's horse that had arrived, mounted by the parish clerk—a large horse with a little hunch-backed rider.

'This was observed by a woman who stood beside me at a window, and who did not want for a dash of Irish readiness. In the midst of the confusion she called out to the scholars: "Children, what are you frightened for?—it's only the little clerk." And then by way of diverting them more effectually from their fears, she turned to him and called through the window: "Tam, come in." He galloped after some of the children who had made their escape at the first rush, then returned and dismounted, stationed himself in the doorway, and took out his pocket-book and pencil to write down the names of the wandering flock.

'When I began to preach he stood outside, where he remained all the time, and heard the sermon—Who can tell with what effect, for he was very civil withal? The congregation were solemn and attentive, but excited and easily disturbed—every noise alarming them, and every horse that passed attracting their watchful eyes. The children, mostly boys, who went out at first, had returned before the close of the meeting; and I could not dismiss them till it had been intimated that I would preach there again the following day. Once dismissed, the congregation was soon scattered—the girls running along the roads, and scampering over the fields as if they had been hunted.

'On our return to Tullylin yesterday we were glad to find a con-gregation both larger than before, and enabled to listen without distraction or fear, being emboldened by what had happened. After sermon we were informed that the priest had come, and were requested to protect the children. This time it was neither priest's horse, nor priest's clerk, nor priest's curate, but the very priest him-self, or rather a very priest—for he did not belong to that parish—who had no doubt been watching till we departed. He was a big, stout man, and was said to be one of the most vigorous of their number. His attire was neat, but singular and picturesque—his stockings appearing at the knee, so as to leave a broad band of white in the black dress. He went in pursuit of some young women who were passing through a field to escape, but stopped when he called them. We saw him shaking his staff with great violence while he addressed them, then hastening back to the school. [From the deputy's account the priest's staff and whip were used pretty freely to maintain his spiritual authority.] The school-mistress, who had lately been one of his people, received him civilly, bidding him welcome, at which he took great offence, and left the house, exclaiming, "Bad luck to you!"—an expression which was very sore both to the family and to the people about, and made them very indignant. The priest was told of our presence and requested to remain; but he was now busily effecting his retreat, so as not to suffer us to close with him. First one and then another of the people followed him, anxious to embrace the opportunity of speaking their mind, while he was equally eager to get out his word to them, but bent at the same time on avoiding us. He thus kept up a sharp retreating fire, turning round on his pursuers, speaking fast and loud, with violent action, and, as the people said, "shaking like a bulrush," then retreating and turning again. His voice was very audible to us, though we made out none of his words; but we understood that he had cursed in Irish the man who had given me his horse; and we heard him answer with warmth that a priest ought to bless and not to curse.

'The priest now walked along the high road, quite alone in the midst of his own people, without a single individual to countenance him, while we were surrounded and accompanied by a group of Roman Catholics.

'The Lord grant grace to Ireland both to disown her false priests, and to acknowledge and embrace the great High Priest, the one Mediator between God and man.

'Yesterday afternoon I preached again at Tullylin, where the priest encountered, or rather shunned to encounter us, ten days ago; and we found that he had now mustered greater strength and did not decline an interview. The school is situated not far from the chapel, and, being near the borders of the parish, is attended by many of the children of the next parish, and is "convenient" to the dwellings of both parish priests. One of these seems to be a quiet, reasonable sort of a man, and is said to be fonder of hunting hares in the fields than of chasing poor children out of the schools. The other is fierce and boisterous.

'They both returned while I was preaching from the 110th Psalm, on Jesus Christ, the only priest; and nothing in the whole proceedings surprised me so much as the change which ten days had produced on the feelings of the people. At first the sight of the priest's horse on the road had caused the greatest trepidation and confusion; and now we had two priests, with their clerk and their greyhounds, all inside the house, yet there was no commotion or appearance of alarm, but rather of curiosity.

'It was a novel scene, in the middle of divine service, to have a big blustering priest bouncing into the congregation, wheeling round and round, with red face and rolling eyes, and bawling out furiously: "I am a Deist! I am an infidel! I am a pagan priest!—I deny revelation!" He never once stated that he took up this position for the sake of argument (which was evidently his design, with a view to claiming for his Church superiority to Scripture), and never attempted to draw any argument from it in his own favour and against us, but persevered with his noisy vociferations. We told him that if he came in his own character as a priest of the Church of Rome we would reason with him; but finding that I could make nothing of him, I charged him severely with the sin and folly of his conduct, a mode of address which seemed to take him by surprise, and have some effect, for he offered no reply, and became rather more manageable afterwards.

'His second position was the denial of the present existence of the word of God, on the ground that every copy of the Bible had been burned.

'In the course of this discussion Mr Brannigan reminded him that the Apostle Peter, to whom he deferred so much, declares that the word of God liveth and abideth for ever; and a respectable female, thinking that we questioned what could not be denied, stepped forward and said, "With your leave, the Bible was burned; for the priests have burned it often."

'The last topic discussed was a text of the Bible. The priest, meaning to quote against us the passage in 2 Peter, respecting unlearned and unstable men wresting the Scriptures to their own destruction, gave it incorrectly—although, to do him justice, he certainly had it in substance—and Mr Brannigan replied that there was no such passage in Peter. "Then it is in Second Peter." "No." "Then it is in James"; which Mr Brannigan denied, at the same time offering him the Bible. "Then it is in the Second Epistle of James." "There is no Second Epistle of James." "Has your Bible no Second Epistle of James? You see what a Bible you have got that wants the Second Epistle of James."'

At this juncture Mr Brannigan told a friend that Mr Moody Stuart cut the knot at a stroke. Giving the Bible a slap with his open palm, he said with vehemence, 'Sir! your own Church believes this to be the word of God!' The priest fell back as if shot. The people were delighted, as Mr Brannigan said that he had shown himself no longer 'the meek Moody Stuart, but a lion,' and they spoke of him afterwards as 'the great little soldier.'

On his return Dr Moody Stuart presented his report to the Assembly's Commission in November 1847, and also published a vivid narrative of what he had seen of the temporal and spiritual needs of the country in a booklet, *Ireland Open to the Gospel*. In both of these he depicted the religious darkness of the country in trenchant terms which many, in this era of hyper-sensitive religious charity, would brand as 'narrow' and harsh. They were only clear statements of facts, and of the recognised Protestant position, which the present anti-ritualist agitation in England proves to be more deeply entrenched in the judgment and hearts of our people than was at all supposed.

Dr Moody Stuart took a gloomy view of the future, and expected, in accordance with his interpretation of prophetic Scripture, that

Popery would regain ascendency and oppressive power in Britain to the extent of silencing the public gospel testimony, though only for a very brief period, indicated by the 'slaying of the witnesses.' While he urged that the spiritual darkness of Ireland should be dispelled by diffusing gospel light, he held that Romanism, as a political power, subversive of civil and religious liberty, must be combated by legislative measures. A friend who heard him at a meeting held in Edinburgh against the papal aggressions recalls his uttering in prayer the exclamation, 'O God, we have no Protestant statesman!' Holding these views, he was one of those who strongly opposed our Church's resolution to accept Government grants for education concurrently with Papists. His position coincided, in resisting the indiscriminate endowment of truth and error, practically with that of many 'voluntaries', while again he objected as strongly to the extreme voluntary[1] view that the state must not protect or favour the true religion of Jesus Christ.

The Free Church undertook no separate mission in Ireland, but sent collections in money to assist the Irish Presbyterian Church (whose deputies to the Church of Scotland had in May 1843, followed the Free Church to Tanfield Hall, recognising it as the true Church of Scotland) in overtaking the work. Robert Johnstone, 'a Nathanael,' and Mr Malcolm M'Gregor, a very godly man, both connected with Free St Luke's congregation, were left to labour; the former being supported as catechist by St Luke's, the latter (afterwards settled as Free Church minister at Gartly) by the Free Synod of Aberdeen.

Protestant schools were also established in the Wild West by the Misses Pringle of Edinburgh, which did much good, and by Miss

---

[1] Voluntaryism held that churches should be financially supported voluntarily by their members, rather than accepting endowment from the state (as was the case in the established Church of Scotland). The Free Church, despite separating from the Establishment in 1843, continued to hold to the principle of establishment, a view which Moody Stuart strenuously defended during the discussions around the Free Church's proposed union with the United Presbyterian Church in the 1860s and 70s. See pp. 183-5, below.—*P.*

Banks in County Kerry, where a colporteur is still maintained in memory of her; while Dr Hamilton Magee was appointed by the Irish Synod in 1848 to carry on evangelistic operations, a history of which he is now engaged in preparing.

When in the island of Achill during this tour our Scottish deputy saw the finest lunar rainbow he ever beheld, wearing not its usual ghostly hue, but having the full complement of colours, and was reminded by it of the covenant of grace, which shall assure to Ireland, under the prayers and efforts of God's enlightened children, even a brighter future than that sighed for by Thomas Moore in the stanza which opens this chapter, because its 'arch of peace' rests on a still surer foundation.

— 9 —

Sabbaths in St Luke's, Queen Street

> God's chosen servant—kindling hearts grown cold,
>   Raising dead souls to life. Cast in the mould
> Of ancient prophet, breathing words of flame,
>   He told heaven's judgments; yet his heart was filled
> With sweet compassion for the sick, and poor,
>   And heavy laden. Countless souls were thrilled
> With divine impulse, as he told that tale
>   Which to transform the earth shall yet prevail.
>
> *—Frank Millar*

FOR the site of the new church several houses were purchased, adjoining No. 43 Queen Street, which was already the manse, the house in which Lady Nairne, authoress of 'The Land o' the Leal,' etc., had resided. On their back greens a handsome and spacious place of worship was erected, which was opened by Dr Candlish on 27 June 1852. The plans were drawn to contain a congregation of 1,000, but Canonmills Hall, in which the Free Assembly had met since its memorable exodus from St Andrew's Church, having been sold, and it being necessary ere long to provide another meeting-place, at the request of the Assembly additional accommodation was provided for 1,500 in all. The extra seats were shut off by movable panels, both in area and galleries, from the regular church. The Assembly afterwards

The façade of 43 Queen Street is all that remains of the Free St Luke's building, the main body of which has long since been demolished. A health club, still accessed through the original church entrance, now occupies the central Edinburgh site.—P.

Queen Street, Edinburgh, in the nineteenth century
The street's appearance remains largely the same in the twenty-first century.—P.

having decided to build a hall for its own meetings close to the New
College, St Luke's Deacons' Court never claimed the guarantee which
the Assembly had given for the extra expense, and in God's good
providence the church from its large size and central situation became
the favourite resort of the great revival preachers.

To meet the cost of this building the plan was adopted of supple-
menting the original subscriptions by making a special collection for
it every Lord's Day for upwards of a year, Mr Stothert putting £10
weekly into the plate, and every one following his example according to their means. It made a large demand upon the liberality of
the people, but the debt was wiped off in about fifteen months. One
lady (Miss Mackenzie) gave a capital sum of £2,000 to the fund, but
the interest on this was destined otherwise for a long term of years.
Even the poor gave liberally.

The beautifully carved oaken pillars of the pulpit canopy and
reading desk were executed by Mr James Bennett, a most devoted

Christian man, much respected as congregational missionary, and presented by him to the church. His diary shews how remarkably earnest and skilful he was in dealing with souls in his visiting the people.

It was about the time of the opening of this church that Mr Francis Brown Douglas, advocate, joined it. A man conversant with public affairs, and widely esteemed in the city of Edinburgh, of which he became Lord Provost, he was an outstanding follower of the divine Master, glad to take the lowly place of teaching in the Sabbath School, which he superintended, even during the period when his time and strength were taxed by the public duties and functions which fall to the Chief Magistrate. Another prominent elder who joined later was Mr James Cunningham, W.S., whose handsome figure and features emphasised the practical testimony by which he adorned the gospel of Jesus Christ. The interest which he took in his valuable collections of autographs, letters of Robert Burns, and specimens of natural history, was always kept in due subordination to his deep interest in Christ's kingdom. Godly, laborious, and prudent elders are one of the best gifts of our ascended Saviour to any congregation of his saints. These and other office-bearers equally devoted were attached to their minister by close bonds of mutual esteem and affection, which along with the spiritual help they felt they derived from his preaching, prayer and example, prevented any friction from arising between them, even when they might not fully agree with him on all public church questions.

In St Luke's, as in other churches, it was often a stranger's tones that were used to bring life to a listener, but sometimes a hearer who had long sat in the pew unsaved was brought to Christ by the pastor's message coming to the heart with new power.

A lady, who had long sat under his ministry, came after the service and said, with joy and gratitude, '*I have heard the gospel today!* When the people began to cough I could have put my hand upon their mouths, and said to them: "Oh, don't cough any more till I have heard the gospel!"' It was only then that under the Spirit's power, 'faith came by hearing.'

In old St Luke's Mr Moody Stuart had lectured through the Book of Proverbs, and as he said had never ventured for twenty years to take a text from Canticles when his friend M'Cheyne was preaching, with his own singular sweetness, from this wonderful book. Soon after entering the new church he began to expound the Song of Solomon consecutively, displaying wonderful spiritual insight and penetration, as well as learning in the study of all authorities on the subject. Lecturing and exposition was a field in which he excelled, and he made the deepest book in Scripture most interesting and attractive even to boys and girls, who answered his catechising on it with great exactness. These lectures were published as a commentary, and of it Dr James Hamilton wrote: 'My dear friend, *exegisti monumentum.* Your book will now be the comment on the Song, and the effort to exalt the name that is above every name, will to all that love that name endear your own. It is a delightful combination of your own independent meditations, and of curious and interesting collections from the wide field of authorship.' While Spurgeon said of it: 'We do not know where to find a book (on Canticles) of equal value in all respects. This admirable author has poetry in his soul, and, beyond that, a heart like that of Rutherford, fired with love to the altogether Lovely One.' Some twenty years later (1875) he lectured through Job, 'lectures,' one who heard them says, 'which live in one's memory. Many a time have I read Job through from beginning to end—he made one love it—and every chapter and almost every verse seems still alive with the poetry and insight of these beautiful expositions.' Another writes that many of the texts of his sermons, 'always seem to *stand out* in one's Bible. One felt he could with truth say, "We speak that we do know, and testify that which we have seen." With him nothing was hearsay—all was such real, deep, heartfelt, personal experience.'

Mr Moody Stuart had a peculiarly happy way of opening up his text, in its divisions and subdivisions, which presented the whole subject to the audience in an exhaustive manner, and at the same time impressed themselves readily upon the memory. An aged

Christian tells me that she can recall most of the last sermon she heard from his lips forty-five years ago, on 'Revive thy work in the midst of the years!' His illustrations were almost always drawn from his own observation of nature, or his experience of men.

His valued colleague, Dr Cunningham, has written: 'The interest of the devout listener is soon enchained by the luminous fullness with which some verse hitherto almost unnoticed flashes out from its neglected place in Scripture, or two texts are suddenly brought together so as to yield a spark which kindles thought and feeling with strange power. Again the imagination is quickened to vigorous and delighted exercise by some bold stroke of fancy, or unexpected poetical conception. Presently there is an appeal to the conscience; sin is not spared; or a description of some phase of religious experience lays bare the heart's inmost thoughts. In every discourse a place is found for the cross of Christ, and for the loving declaration of the glorious largeness of that divine mercy which is high as heaven, or the words of reconciliation are pressed home by direct question and personal entreaty, well fitted to win the ear and subdue the heart.'

Mr [James] Durran, the junior colleague [from 1892] in St Luke's, who had never heard him preach, writes that he 'can well believe from his own observation the statement of a leading minister of our Church that few preachers of the time have influenced others so profoundly as Dr Moody Stuart influenced those whom he won over'; and speaks of him as in some of his published work 'standing forth as a personality instinct with spiritual genius.'

Mr J. Howie Boyd of Carlisle, who acted as missionary assistant in St Luke's, recalls his impressions there after the lapse of twenty-five years: 'There were days of grace, times of refreshing in the sanctuary, continued through many years. One day would be a season of unwonted solemnity and power. The psalms, the prayer, the Scripture lesson, the text, all pointed to the searching of the inner nature, close dealing with the conscience, the secret heart unveiled, sin tracked to its last hiding-place in the darkest cavern of the soul. The word of God is living, sharp, piercing, unsparing.

What awe on the spirit! What stillness, what fear, what self-loathing! The last day has come—the day of judgment, some may feel; and who can restrain the cry, "God be merciful to me, a sinner"? But the sweet word of grace, of forgiveness, of healing, is heard, "Your sins and your iniquities will I remember no more." With trembling joy you leave the house of God. Another day the gate is opened wide, and sinners pressed to enter in. The joyful sound is heard, Christ is preached in all his fullness. Can any one be unimpressed? Can any one go away unsaved? What waves of tenderness pass over the soul! This is none other than the house of God. This is the gate of heaven.'

Communion services in St Luke's seemed to possess a peculiar sacredness. They were looked forward to with earnest desire and expectation of blessing, and were diligently prepared for. From the beginning of the week before a sacramental Sabbath Dr Moody Stuart turned the thoughts of all at family worship to the approaching holy ordinance, reading generally in the gospel of John from chapter 12 onwards. He strove to excite in the hearts of all his household a sense that a special blessing might and should be received at such a time, and that its amount would largely depend on earnest and careful preparation for it. In leading the household in prayer, the acknowledgment of sin, and the pleading for divine blessing, were fuller and more importunate than usual. The conversations at table with the ministers assisting were most interesting and profitable, even to the younger members of the family.

Mrs [Anne] Cousin[1] writes that such occasions were 'times to be remembered. There was something remarkable in his manner even when distributing the tokens. In recent days I have heard one say that it was only on meeting his look of solemnity and searching power that the significance of the act was realised. It seemed as if he had a present awing sense of his responsibility in

---

[1] The authoress of 'The Sands of Time are Sinking,' and other favourite hymns.—KMS.

admitting guests to his Lord's feast. At these seasons there was an atmosphere diffused which the gathering of the prayerful and expectant people and their beloved pastor combined to create, as if the Lord were in very deed remembering his promise, "I will be in the midst of them."

An aged lady of ninety-six tells me that she was so struck by their solemnity, that though belonging to another congregation she frequently communicated in St Luke's. She was impressed by the deep silence,[2] and by seeing the minister sometimes following the elders as they passed with the consecrated elements down the passages, and handed them to those seated at the tables, absorbed in earnest silent prayer for the communicants. A Hungarian divinity student seeing a tear roll down the pastor's cheek as he dispensed the sacred symbols, was overwhelmingly struck by the thought, 'If such a man so feels, why am I so insensible?'

The Rev. Robert Cowan of Elgin, in the beautiful sketch he contributed, of his attached friend, to the *Free Church Monthly,*[3] wrote: 'Especially on communion Sabbaths did his excellences appear. To apply a remark he quotes about Dr Duncan, "The man was at his best then, and a wonderful best it was." The word was good, the gracious influence was still better. One felt the beauty of holiness, and realised what it is to sit in the heavenlies. He himself seemed often to be filled with a holy joy. Those who had seen it could understand a remark he made when presiding at the first Conference communion at Perth, that he "would wish for himself nothing better for the remainder of his life than just to be permitted to go about breaking the bread and offering the cup."' Taken in connection with this, it was touching for those surrounding his dying couch to hear him giving parts of 'table' addresses of great beauty.

---

[2] Mr Gladstone [four times Prime Minister between 1868 and 1894] has said that the simplicity and silence of a Scottish communion are as impressive as the most elaborate ritual.—*KMS.*

[3] See Appendix. pp. 439-48.—*P.*

He kept up the old Scottish custom of 'fencing' the tables, but it was as much to encourage the timid as to warn the presumptuous. Memory cherishes such scenes in a life-enduring photograph. We still seem to see him dispense the sacred elements—

> He breaks the bread, he pours the wine—in fervent prayer they
> bend,
> That the Holy Spirit in his power may on their feast descend;
> Then silently, from hand to hand, the bread and wine are passed,
> Till all have owned their dying Lord, from the first unto the last.[4]

After the tables he gave a short concluding address. One recalls his saying, 'If you have not eaten, eat! If you have, eat yet more! The Lord looks at the table; he says, "I am sorry that they took so little—that so much is left. I meant them to take all. They took a little, and were glad of it; but, oh, what a pity they did not take more!"'

At the close of a sacramental season he was often filled with happiness and holy joy, and once remarked to a brother that he could sympathise with King David when he 'danced before the ark.'

Some of his sermons were specially blessed to the awakening and conversion of souls. But it was by no means always those that seemed most suited to convince and convert that were used for this end by the divine Spirit. A woman once came to him in deep spiritual distress, and weeping bitterly. After pointing her to the sinners' Saviour, he said, 'What was the means of awakening you to your lost state?' 'It was your sermon last Sabbath,' she replied. 'The forenoon one, of course,' he remarked. 'No, sir,' she said; 'it was the afternoon one.' 'That is very strange,' he said, 'for it was all for Christians; there was not a word in it for you.' 'Oh, that was just it,' she answered; 'I saw it was all for Christians, and I felt there was not a word in it for me, and that made me see that I was not a true Christian.'

Sometimes the word that was blessed to a hearer was not connected with the theme of the discourse. Having preached on 'Rejoice

---

[4] Lines from a poem entitled 'John Knox Administering the Sacrament at Calder House', which appeared in *The Drawing Room Table Book* (London: George Virtue, 1849).—*P.*

in the Lord alway,' a woman came to him afterwards, thanking him for his sermon, which, she said, had been very helpful to her. He asked what was the message that had been so helpful. She said: 'It was a text you quoted.' 'Well, what was it?' 'It was, "Blessed are they that mourn."'

Dr Moody Stuart placed great reliance on the simple word of God, as the power of God alike for salvation, and comfort, and guidance. When persons came to him in distress or perplexity, he frequently did little more than give them a text, and then engage in prayer for them. But he had such a quick discernment of the state of the inquirer, and after a little talk selected a text so suitable, that in numerous cases it brought immediate light to the troubled spirit. Various persons have told me this very emphatically. One recalls having gone to consult him as to what he should do, at a time when he was suffering much trouble from the action of some persons opposed to him. His minister said, 'Well now, Mr——, have you considered the text, "When a man's ways please the Lord, he maketh even his enemies to be at peace with him"?' The applicant said that both the implied reproof and encouragement of that text proved a remarkable help to him, and were just what he needed.

The New Year's addresses formed a characteristic and much appreciated feature of his pulpit work. Delivered regularly through a long course of years, they were always fresh, always helpful for the year then opening. The thoughts were not so elaborated as in his ordinary discourses, and the style was simpler, and perhaps on this account proved all the more attractive.

In his preaching, as in all his ministerial work and his personal religion, great prominence was given to the work of the Holy Spirit. This was not only felt to be deepest, but was also uppermost and foremost in his whole religious life. He ever realised for himself his absolute need of the presence and power of the Holy Spirit to make the word of God, whether read or preached, effectual, and he let others see clearly that he realised this. In every service he prayed for the breathings of God's Spirit. 'Awake, O north wind; and come, thou south; and blow upon my garden that the spices thereof may flow out.' Or in New Testament words he prayed that the Spirit might come from heaven as a rushing mighty wind, and fill all the house where they were sitting, or that the ascended Saviour would breathe upon them and say, 'Receive ye the Holy Ghost!'

In his discourses he gave a clear and full place to the doctrine of the Holy Spirit, and his part in the economy of redemption, but he did not consider that in order to honour the Spirit of God every sermon should have something said directly about his work, for I have heard him say that the Spirit is often greatly honoured by a simple declaration of the work of the Son, as man's Redeemer, for he is said to take of the things of Christ, rather than of his own things, and shew them unto us. Still one always felt that he was having regard to the place and office of the Holy Ghost, as Convincer, Enlightener, Renewer, Sanctifier and Comforter.

In the service of the sanctuary it was sometimes a word of explanation of the psalm or the chapter, which he usually annotated, that brought light and help to the soul. A member of his flock who joined in 1846 tells me that once when she was in the deepest distress, aggravated by the reflection that it was her own fault, she derived the greatest comfort from her minister as he gave out the psalm:—

> For he despised not, nor abhorred
> The afflicted's misery,

adding twice over 'though they brought it on themselves.' An old elder of St Luke's, who looked up to its minister as his spiritual father, said that on the Sabbath mornings he used to bound across the Meadows to Queen Street, saying to himself—

> I joyed, when to the house of God,
> Go up, they said to me! (Psa. 122:1, *Scottish Psalter*)

that he felt just like a bee returning for a fresh supply of honey from the flower, and was never disappointed in getting what he sought, if not in the sermon, then in the chapter commented on, or in the prayers offered.

It must not be supposed, from these instances, that the interviews of hearers with the preacher were without exception of the nature of thanking him for good received. Dr Duncan, while often thanking him, occasionally made some brotherly criticism. Once I remember his saying: 'Mr Stuart, you said today that the divine Son left his Father's bosom, and came into our world. When the Son came into our world, he *came out from* the bosom of the Father, but he never left it; he remained there always.' My father at once acquiesced in the correction, and the Rabbi said: 'I corrected Dr Thomas Guthrie for the use of the same expression, but the next time I heard him he slipped into it again'; so sensitive was Dr Duncan's ear to the slightest theological inaccuracy. Of a different character was the criticism of a lady who came and said: 'Sir, you do not preach enough about humility,' adding, what rather blunted her remonstrance, 'Humility's my forte!'

It was his custom to declare very fully 'the whole counsel of God,' not confining himself to a few favourite topics; and his practice of 'lecturing' once a day in regular course, through a book of Scripture, or a series of Scripture characters or subjects, helped to give great variety to his discourses. At the same time there were certain cardinal subjects which were specially dear to him, and on which he delighted to expatiate in preaching and to exemplify in his life. I should select repentance, prayerfulness, assurance of forgiveness, and faith as the religious emotions in which he most delighted. Any one reading the diary of his closing years will see how constantly he exercised the grace of repentance.

Dr Moody[5] writes from Pest that a Hungarian student was much struck when he heard Dr Moody Stuart offer David's prayer, evidently with self-application, 'Wash me, wash me, and I shall be whiter than the snow'; and he asked Miss Buchanan, 'How is it that that good and perfect man prays thus?' He never forgot her reply,

[5] Andrew Moody, the nephew of Alexander Moody Stuart.—*P.*

'The nearer one is to the sun, the more does one discover one's defects and spots.'

To the subject of prayerfulness I have thought it right to assign a whole chapter of this memoir. Of God's pardoning grace he said: 'Every new sense of forgiveness comes as a glad surprise.' His diary is the offering of a forgiven heart. His faith in Jesus and in the word of God was very simple and very strong. It was a single faith in the Living and Written Word, which he would not divide into two faiths. With the whole force and with every fibre of his nature he believed in Christ as revealed only in the word, and in the word itself which reveals him. It was this which made him so jealous of any attempts to dissociate these two. While not overlooking any of the attributes of God it was the *grace of God* in Christ towards sinners that was his absorbing theme, and it was in their connection with this and in the bright light of grace that he exhibited the other attributes. But it was in setting forth Jesus Christ as the Saviour that he specially delighted and excelled. He did not care much for 'doctrinal Christology,' and disliked dissecting the two natures of Christ in the fashion of a theological anatomist; but he delighted to portray and commend the living Christ in his divine majesty, his infinite love, his eternal loveliness, and his human beauty and attractiveness. The latter I have never heard so effectively portrayed as by my father, forming all the more an entrancing portrait because one saw in every feature the glory of the divinity behind it, within it, and streaming forth from it. One heard and saw perfect humanity beautifully depicted, but it was in a way that had the same effect on the listener as the sight of the features and hearing the utterances of the dying Redeemer had upon the Roman officer, constraining the exclamation, 'Truly this man is the Son of God!'

Few have been able to draw more life-like portraits of the Redeemer, or to add with more truth to their description, 'This is my Beloved, and this is my Friend!' And in reproducing before his hearers' mental vision the Christ of the inspired prophets and evangelists, he sought (and surely to a large extent succeeded in his effort) to say 'Behold the Lamb of God,' in such a manner that those who heard him speak should straightway follow Jesus, and walk in holy fellowship with him. He pictured him so truly and so winningly that those who beheld and followed him should be constrained to open their whole hearts to receive and embrace him, that Christ might be formed in them the hope of glory, and his image and life be reproduced in their lives as well as in his own.

We subjoin one or two specimens of addresses from notes by hearers:—

Social Meeting Address

Grow in grace (2 Pet. 3:18)

"'Lord, give us grace to know our need of grace; give us grace to pray for grace; give us grace to receive grace; and when we have grace give us grace to use it,' was the blessing before meat asked by a poor wayfarer, about a century ago, over a meal set before him by the loving hand of charity. Paul has sometimes been called the apostle of faith, John the apostle of love, Peter the apostle of hope. Hope is founded on grace and rooted in it; "God according to his abundant mercy hath begotten us again unto a lively hope." "Hope to the end for the grace that is to be brought unto you at the revelation of Jesus Christ" (1 Peter 1:13).

'Grace will not force and growth will not force, but through grace we grow in grace, and the daily food of grace is the "sincere milk of the word, that we may grow thereby." Growth is freshness, hopefulness, beauty; "they shall revive as the corn, and grow as the vine." The dew of heaven gives the growth, and the growth again attracts the dew; "I will be as the dew unto Israel; he shall grow as the lily and cast forth his roots as Lebanon"; "To him that hath shall be given, and he shall have more." Our growth in grace is pleasant to the Husbandman; but if any man draw back, he saith, "My soul shall have no pleasure in him." It is profitable to others, for we "provoke one another to love and to good works"; it is interesting to ourselves, intensely interesting, with an ever new surprise of joy, when our faith "groweth exceedingly," "increasing with the increase of God." But when grace ceases to grow it is "like corn blasted before it is grown up," a withered, repulsive sight; and then the soul is always filled with a noxious growth. "I went by the field of the slothful, and lo! it was all grown over." But what a dismal growth!—"all grown over with thorns and thistles."

'The farmer tells you that nothing prevents or checks the growth of weeds in his field like a good crop of wheat, and nothing so keeps down or destroys the growth of manifold evil in the heart as growth in grace, and in the knowledge of our Lord and Saviour Jesus Christ.

> Against myself I bear record
> That hence my bondage flows,
> When I neglect to serve my Lord
> I'm left to serve my foes.

'One word more, and it is a marvellous word, "that we may grow up into him in all things." It is a miracle of grace that we who were once "dead" in sins should be called and enabled to grow up into Christ at all, to grow up into him in anything, even the least. But what an object of holy ambition is set before us, dear friends, when we are called to grow up into him in all things, having nothing in which we are not growing up, in union and in likeness to our Lord Jesus Christ. Therefore let us every one "as new-born babes, desire the sincere milk of the word, that we may grow thereby, if so be that we have tasted that the Lord is gracious."'

Address to Young Communicants on 31 January 1886

'"Speak to the children of Israel, that they go forward," was the Lord's command to Moses at the Red Sea after the first Passover; and after this Passover the Lord is saying again, "Speak to the children of Israel, that they go forward."

'Forward, notwithstanding all that is behind you, all your past life with all its sins and all its accusations; forward, notwithstanding all that is before you, with all its difficulties, its Red Seas, and its sandy deserts between you and the Land of Promise.

'Forward, by the necessity of your condition, for the vows of the Lord are upon you, and "if any man draw back, my soul shall have no pleasure in him"; forward by the glory of your calling to an "inheritance incorruptible, undefiled," "eternal in the heavens." Forward in the path of duty, of every commanded duty, and especially of a neglected duty; forward in the faith of supernatural help, in the new strength now received from the King at the King's own table.

'Forward from where you now are; forward from where you have ever yet been. Forward within the veil that has been "rent from top to bottom"; into your closet, into the tabernacle of the Lord, into its court, within its veil, into the holiest of all through the blood of the Lamb; forward outwardly into open confession of the Lord, into fellowship with his saints, into testimony to his grace. Forward into the fullness of Christ, for out of his fullness you have received, and, if ever so little, it has come from a full and overflowing fountain; forward from weak faith to strong, from little petitions to great, till you have opened your mouth wide and he has filled it. Forward, because in lagging behind you are sure to keep others back, and in advancing you cannot fail to help others forward.

'Forward from good purposes to good actions, for many of our good intentions never come forward into fruit. Forward in love for all the children of God, and into yearning pity for the lost that are near and that are far off. Forward to the "well of Bethlehem by the gate" and drink of its living water. Forward to "the tower of David" to be clad in the whole armour of God, that you may stand in the evil day, and have your feet shod with the preparation of the gospel of peace, that it may be said of you, "How beautiful are the feet of him that bringeth good tidings of good, that publisheth salvation."'

— 10 —

Drops and Showers
of Blessing

Then grant, O Lord, mine earliest latest prayer,
That some fold in thy pasture be my care;
Where from all tumult, all ambition free,
Save that of winning many souls to thee,
I may, unnoticed, pass my tranquil days,
And lead my flock in wisdom's pleasant ways;
And meet in bliss, when every trial's o'er,
The ransomed flock I loved so well before!

—Rev. R. Swan (St Monans)

THE following jotting in an old notebook made by Mr
Moody Stuart in 1855 was quoted by him in a sermon on
Deuteronomy 8:2, 3, 16,—'Thou shalt remember all the
way which the Lord thy God led thee,' preached on 31 May 1885,
the jubilee of his settlement in Edinburgh. He calls it a fragmentary
record which he came upon accidentally, and had no remembrance
of having written:—

'...The one thing I care for is the salvation of the lost, the gathering in of God's elect to the glory of Christ, the Redeemer. It has
long seemed to me that the only way in which I could do any good
in the world was in the salvation of souls. Having no capacity for

benefiting others by literature, or by other means for which other men are competent, I have foregone the pleasure of books for myself, except in so far as is necessary to keep the mind from stagnating, in the earnest hope that by giving myself with any energy I have to one thing, I might by the blessing of God save some, and I have felt this the more on account of the expected shortness of my life.[1] If I miss this end I do not miss heaven or Christ, or the company of the redeemed above, I do not lose for myself profitable training of chastening to bring about conformity to the will of God as most of all, but I lose my work on earth, all I have attempted to do for the good of others. I have embarked my all in this endeavour, and if this barque does not reach the shore, I have nothing, except that I have always this, "Lord, remember me when thou comest into thy kingdom."'

In that retrospective discourse he goes on to say that soon after this they had tokens of encouragement. There was desire in God's children for the conversion of souls, and a great desire on the part of sinners to come to Christ. There were very earnest meetings for prayer, not only in the Session but among the people, and in one case the Session records how thankful they were that the hall had been nearly filled for a week at 7.30 a.m. in the winter mornings, as well as afternoon meetings in the church. He mentions that over thirty persons brought certificates from ten different denominations outside the Free Church. Six months later, on returning from the country, he noted that in six weeks he had conversed with more than fifty inquirers. The convictions of some had been very deep, and the joy of deliverance had been very great. He felt like the friend of the Bridegroom rejoicing greatly because of the Bridegroom's voice.

'It was then,' he said, 'that among others a stranger came to me whom I found to be very intelligent in her Bible and in the doctrines

---

[1] Like his friend Dr A. A. Bonar, he was often under the impression that his life was to be a short one, an impression entirely mistaken in both these eminent ministers.—*KMS.*

of grace, and after conversing with her I thought I could give her no further instruction and began to speak on the text, "Jesus Christ came into the world to save sinners," and prayed with her. After prayer she left without saying a word, but I noticed that the tears were coming down her cheeks. She came back a week afterwards, beaming with joy, and I said to her, "Why did you weep so much the other day?" She said, "I wept for joy when I saw that Jesus came to save sinners." I answered, "But you knew that quite well when you spoke to me!" She said, "No." "What then did you think?" She answered, "I always thought that Jesus Christ came to save *saints*, and when I saw that he came to save *sinners*, I wept for joy." And I and you also would all this day weep together for joy if we did fully know that Jesus Christ came into the world to save sinners.'

Then there is a further record concerning this work of the Lord so begun: 'I seek to give myself more unreservedly to it, and to be willing, if the Lord wills, to send others, that I might be nothing, and that others should reap the sheaves for which I have been long labouring.'

A year after that, Mr Brownlow North[2] came to Edinburgh with an introduction to my father, in March 1857, and received from him a hearty welcome, with the use of his church for the following Lord's Day evening. The pulpit and church were never given to lay preachers during the regular hours of divine service, though Mr North got these after he was, chiefly through Mr Moody Stuart's efforts, officially recognised by the General Assembly in May 1859. My father in the forenoon read Acts 9:20-29 (the first preaching of the converted Saul of Tarsus), with the remark, 'How soon God can make a preacher!' a remark amply verified by the results immediately seen, not only in the dense crowds that filled passages and pulpit stairs, but in the numbers who were awakened to anxiety about eternal things, and who were brought to walk in newness of

---

[2] For an account of the life and ministry of Brownlow North, see K. Moody Stuart, *Brownlow North: His Life and Work* (1878; repr. Edinburgh: The Banner of Truth Trust, 2020).—P.

life through Mr North's earnest and eloquent pressing of the divine message on conscience and heart.

Next year (1858) there was associated with him in this work Mr Hay Macdowall Grant of Arndilly, that fine specimen of a Scottish laird, whose plain and earnest exhibition of the gospel way of salvation was even more largely blessed among the families of St Luke's than the fervid appeals of Mr North. He grudged neither time nor toil in private dealings with souls. One day he said to me, 'Who is Jessie Veitch? I have just been conversing with some young women in anxiety, and on asking one, "Who spoke to you about your soul?" she answered, "Jessie Veitch." The next also said "Jessie Veitch", and a third the same. Now, who is Jessie Veitch?' It was explained that she was a city Bible-woman, who also did a great deal voluntarily in St Luke's, of which she was a member. She was a devoted and experienced Christian, who prayed much, and no doubt the showers of blessing that were now descending were owing partly to her prayers, and those of like spirit with her.

While the gospel message was being thus earnestly proclaimed and eagerly received in Edinburgh and in the North of Scotland, the remarkable Irish revival broke out in the spring of 1859. It seemed to be the offspring of the great revival of 1858 in America, with which country Ireland then as now had many close connections. Mr Moody Stuart now paid a second visit to Ireland to witness for himself the intense hungering for the bread of life of which we heard, and to assist the overpressed ministers of Ulster in dispensing this living bread to the eager people. On his return the reports which he and other brethren from Scotland furnished of what they had seen of this phenomenal movement were eagerly listened to. His opinion coincided with that of his brethren, that it was a genuine and very remarkable work of grace; that the strange physical phenomenon of persons being suddenly 'struck down' and continuing prostrate for a longer or shorter time, though very common was by no means uniformly present; that there were many cases of persons so struck down who gave no evidence of true conversion, and that many truly converted had not been the subject of these strange manifestations.

The opinion thus formed was borne out by the test of time. On the whole the results were as permanent as the temporary impression was deep. When I happened to be in Belfast some twenty-five years after, a stranger, who did not sympathise with such things, asked Dr Williamson, in whose house we were dining, whether he could point to any really good effect of it, to which he replied that multitudes of persons living in intemperance and other vices were entirely reformed, that many family feuds were composed, and debts paid, and that there was a marked improvement in the moral and religious tone of society. His guest acknowledged that these were good fruits. The Rev. Jonathan Simpson of Portrush told me two years ago, that during the last forty years the greater number of triumphant Christian death-beds which he had been privileged to witness had been those of persons brought to Christ during that awakening.

The testimony of our Scotch ministers borne to what they had seen and heard tended greatly to extend the awakening already begun in Scotland. St Luke's became a centre for evangelistic work in the New Town of Edinburgh. North and Grant continued their labours from time to time, and others were associated with them, such as Mr Reginald Radcliffe, the simplicity of whose faith in God and in the power of prayer was so largely blessed wherever he went. It was beautiful to see these great evangelists on whose lips thousands were hanging, drinking in the word preached by the pastor of St Luke's, and the humility with which they welcomed any occasional slight correction of doctrinal statement which he suggested, and their anxiety so to deliver their message, as not to offend the most critical ear. They sought and obtained new power for the word, and a new forth-putting of the Lord's right hand, but none of them desired or needed any new doctrine. Mr Richard Weaver also addressed great crowds in St Luke's at this time.

Being desirous of ascertaining how far the impressions made at such revival services had proved abiding, I called recently on a lady whose husband, the late Mr A. Jenkinson, had been much associated with them in dealing with anxious inquirers. In reply she said, 'A lady called on me a few days ago who had come from England to attend the death-bed of a friend here. She came to me straight from the chamber of death where she and two other ladies had been engaging in prayer, and she remarked, "We three who were kneeling round that open coffin, and our friend whose cold clay was laid out within it, were all brought to Christ thirty-five years ago in St Luke's, at revival services conducted by Mr Richard Weaver."'

Calling on another friend, on my alluding to the same point he handed me from the mantel-piece a New Year's card just come from New Zealand, with the words, 'I ever bless God for salvation in Free St Luke's in 1859.' The writer, Mr A. R. Falconer, has long worked as a successful missionary to seamen in Port Chalmers.

Such testimonies, got almost accidentally, combined with the results of one's own observation, speak volumes for the permanence of such work when prudently conducted in dependence on the divine Spirit.

St Luke's Church was also the scene of fruitful revival services by Bishop Taylor, the American evangelist, and the Rev. H. Grattan Guinness. Mr D. L. Moody also conducted services there at a later period, but his centre of operations was in the Free Assembly Hall and the Corn Exchange, and owing to this fact, while Mr Moody Stuart rejoiced in the wonderful blessing attending his ministry, he was not able to be so fully associated with it.

We must return, however, from efforts carried on in St Luke's, under the pastor's surveillance, to his own labours.

While his ripe Christian experience and his exact theological knowledge were eminently useful in guiding these honoured evangelists, they in turn exercised a very beneficial influence upon him. I can clearly recall that his preaching at this period became distinctly less introspective, and that while he had always preached a free salvation, the gospel invitations and appeals which fell from his lips now became more full and free and touchingly persuasive. M'Cheyne's counsel 'for every look at yourself take ten looks at Christ' now became his rule when pleading with men for God, and it continued so to the close of his public ministry. His wonderful power of analysing the human heart, in its motives and inner workings, was not disused, but it was now employed as an aid to persuading his hearers to embrace the Saviour, presenting him not only as portrayed on the apostolic or prophetic page, but also as known, trusted and loved by himself. Seldom has the gospel message been more freely and persuasively preached. A stranger, comparing him with a minister whom she valued, said, 'Mr —— shows me the way [of salvation], but Dr Moody Stuart comes down where I am, and seems to give me his hand over it.'

In the end of 1859 a remarkable revival took place in the fishing village of Ferryden, near Montrose. The respected minister, Dr Mitchell,[3] was thankful to get assistance from brethren capable of rendering it, and Mr Moody Stuart was one of the first to throw himself into the work there, and the weeks of his visit were memorable ones. This awakening he refers to in the following letter to Dr J. H. Wilson[4]—

'Montrose, 28 November 1859.

'There is now nothing whatever exciting here, but I never was in a place where I had such a sense of the Spirit both in preaching and in conversing with the people. There is a large number of awakened persons not yet brought to Christ, and I fear some in whom the awakening is subsiding without conversion.

'You will be thankful if you come. There are few things for which I feel more grateful. You will find it very quickening to your own soul; all is quite calm.'

---

[3] Hugh Mitchell (1822–94) was ordained in 1848 as the minister of Craig and Ferryden, Forfarshire, where he served for the rest of his life.—*P.*

[4] James Hood Wilson (1829–1903) was ordained in 1854 as the first minister of Fountainbridge Free Church in Edinburgh, which, similarly to Moody Stuart's charge of St Luke's two decades earlier, was planted by the Free St George's congregation. Wilson shared with Moody Stuart in the work of the Free Church's Jewish mission.—*P.*

Dr Wilson describes this movement thus: 'The fishermen are a fine body of men, and their relations to each other in their work, and by intermarriage, are so close that when one was affected others were also. The awakening, especially among the men, was very deep and widespread, and their sense of sin was often overwhelming. This gave a character of thoroughness to the whole work, and when at length light came, the people came out on the side of Christ brightly and boldly. There were many remarkable cases of conversion which have stood the test of time and have borne beautiful fruit. The consistent life and active Christian work of some, and the dying testimony of others, during the forty years that have since elapsed, have set it in the forefront of the religious movements that have taken place in Scotland within the last half-century. Mr Moody Stuart, along with others, did much to give it a right direction. Mrs and Miss Arkley of Inchbrayock threw their house open and made it a home for the brethren who came to assist, where inquirers had free access to them, and they went out and in among the people with almost daily ingathering.' Mr Moody Stuart preached a sermon from Zechariah 14:7, on 'The one day's work of the Lord,' which made a deep impression, and was published by request.

From his experience, and his deep interest in such revival movements, his services were naturally in request from many quarters, but the limits of his strength, and the constant claims of a city charge, prevented him from acceding to these to any great extent. The work of grace in the north of Scotland was both extensive and deep, and Huntly might be said to be the centre of it. The late Rev. Dr Williamson, afterwards of Belfast, who had been settled there in 1855, was a means of wide blessing not only in Huntly (where the ground had been prepared by the prayers of the Duchess of Gordon, and the spiritual ministrations of Principal Rainy,[5]

---

[5] Robert Rainy (1826–1906) was ordained at Huntly in 1851 and translated to the Free High Church in Edinburgh in 1854. In 1862 he was elected to the Chair of Church History in New College (then belonging to the Free Church) and succeeded Robert S. Candlish as Principal in 1874. He became the dominant leader in the Free Church, but was of a different school to Alexander Moody Stuart—Rainy

who began his ministry there), but over the whole north-east of Scotland.

When Dr Moody Stuart was preaching in Huntly on a 'fast day' about the year 1860, a young woman went to speak to him along with some others as an anxious inquirer, to whom thirty years later he wrote the letter addressed to Mrs M'Connachie, printed in chapter fifteen. In Huntly also, in 1859, a matronly woman said to Mr Moody Stuart: 'I had long been seeking a distant Christ, and was passing by Christ who was close beside me'; and her experience, he remarked, was that of many others. He wrote: 'At that time there came by the Spirit a quick perception of the nearness and freeness of saving grace. The presence of the Lord seemed to be diffused all around so as to draw a quick response to his voice even from the dead in sins, gloriously fulfilling the words, "The hour now is, when the dead shall hear the voice of the Son of God, and they that hear shall live." One day an elderly gentleman, whom I sometimes met in Queen Street, accosted me with the remark, "This world is quite changed since I knew it; in my youth my sisters had to hide their Bibles, and now every one you meet speaks about salvation."

'An old Highland minister said of a time of revival that during it they were "like men walking on ice," they had to be so watchful over every word and thought not to slip, and so grieve the Holy Spirit, who was working amongst them and resting over them in his love. And if we pray for an awakening there must be the same care, for the least sin, or what might not be sin in all circumstances, may grieve the Holy Spirit, and it may be difficult to recover his presence again.'

He prayed much both in public and in the family for seasons of revival, and constantly stirred up others to pray and labour for this, being fully aware of the general apathy in regard to it. Still his expectation of spiritual blessing in a congregation or a locality did

---

was, according to Principal John Macleod, the 'leader of the party of change.' See John Macleod, *Scottish Theology* (1943; repr. Edinburgh: The Banner of Truth Trust, 2015), pp. 99, 329-31; and Iain H. Murray, *A Scottish Christian Heritage* (Edinburgh: The Banner of Truth Trust, 2006), pp. 367-92.—*P.*

not depend upon the coming of a general revival in the land. His own view in regard to this was in full harmony with that expressed in a note to him from Dr Andrew Bonar in August 1880, from Mull: 'In this island, where we are at present sojourning, we often see yachts and vessels trying to cross the Sound of Mull, or sail up it, but they find there is scarcely a breath of wind, and so they wait, and tack, and watch, and try again. Are not we in this case? The breathing of the Spirit among us is so faint and low. Yet I see sometimes all at once the wind rises, a favourable breeze springs up. Why may we not look for this in our Church? "Call on me and I will answer thee."' 'Come, O Breath, from the four winds of heaven, come!' was a favourite petition of my father's alike in public and in private.

— II —

Convener of the
Jewish Mission Committee

Oh, weep for those that wept by Babel's stream,
Whose shrine is desolate, whose land's a dream!
And where shall Israel lave their bleeding feet?
And when shall Sion's song again rise sweet?
And Judah's melody once more rejoice
The hearts that leaped before its heavenly voice?

IT was natural that Scottish Christians should take a special
interest in the conversion of the Jews to the acceptance of Jesus,
the world's Saviour, as their own Messiah. Our Scottish love for
the Old Testament Scriptures is a close bond of connection between
us; and some characteristics of the Jewish race are akin to our own,
such as their intense love of their own land combined with an adapt-
ability for settling in all lands and making money in them. In our
Directory for Worship we are instructed to 'pray for the propagation
of the gospel to all nations, for the conversion of the Jews and the
fullness of the Gentiles, the fall of Antichrist, and the hastening of
the second coming of our Lord.' Mere New Testament Christians
rarely take any special interest in the conversion of the Jews. Our
simplicity of worship, our Presbyterian government, our love of the
Sabbath, are all national elements that give us a nearer approach to

them, and make it peculiarly fit for us to cast ourselves with interest into the cause of their conversion. Still the Church of Scotland had made no efforts for the conversion of Israel when, writes Dr Moody Stuart, 'in 1838 the Hon. Mrs Smith of Dunesk, daughter of Henry Erskine, the celebrated lawyer and wit, said to me: "Take these 100 guineas for the Church of Scotland's Mission to the Jews." "But," I replied, "there is no such mission, and no prospect of it for many years to come. It has never been even proposed in any of our church courts." "Well, lodge this money in the bank till the Lord has need of it for that mission." There was less faith,' he continues, 'in the receiver than in the giver, but I took it to the bank, and the banker said it looked strange to open an account for an object which had not even a prospective existence. "But," he quietly added, "we never refuse money."'

When a year or two later the Church, in God's providence, was led to inaugurate this mission, he drew the deposit which had been dedicated in such beautiful faith. The very year after this the Church, though in the thick of her conflict with the civil courts, sent out a mission of inquiry into the state of the Jews in Palestine, which issued in the establishing of our mission in Buda-Pest and other great cities of the continent. In 1873 the same lady, on finishing her course of ninety years, left to the Free Church the sum of over £600 for a mission to the Jews in Palestine. This sum lay in the bank also unclaimed for twelve years, and it rejoiced the heart of the then aged convener when in 1885 the Free Church established a mission at Tiberias and Safed on the Sea of Galilee, and was able to claim the sum destined in faith to this special work. The faith that inspired the heart of this devout Christian lady animated also the hearts of the convener and committee at home, and of the missionaries abroad, and has sustained them in their difficult labours to the present day.

Much earnest effort was expended by our devoted missionaries, the Rev. Daniel Edward at Jassy and Breslau, Dr John Duncan, Dr Robert Smith, Mr Koenig, and now Dr Andrew Moody at Buda-Pest, Dr Schwartz at Amsterdam, Dr Alexander Thomson, Mr Allen and Mr Tomory at Constantinople, and others of like spirit, in seeking Israel's conversion. Dr Thomson of Constantinople, one of the earliest of these missionaries, wrote to me shortly before his death last winter: 'The Convener's official letters to me were all extremely brief, but perhaps there was not one that did not contain a hint or a distinct reference to the necessity of keeping in touch with the Lord Jesus for light, hope and strength.' The only survivor of this worthy band, the Rev. John Wingate, now in his ninety-first year, writes in affectionate terms of the benefit the missionaries received from Dr Moody Stuart, and of 'his warm heart, on which they all knew they could safely rely for sympathy and help.' Fruit that has proved good and lasting has resulted from their efforts, and this sowing, if continued in the same faith and zeal, will yet yield an ample harvest that will make us ashamed of all our despondency that sometimes weighs upon the hearts, though it is never suffered to paralyse the pleading lips or busy hands of the mission workers.

Among the earliest fruits of this mission was Israel Saphir, a learned and influential Jew, who attended Dr Duncan's services in Pest (chiefly to learn English), accompanied by his son Adolph, a boy of twelve. The truth penetrated both their minds, neither speaking to the other about it, when one morning Adolph asked his father to allow him to ask the blessing at breakfast, and greatly to the consternation of the family poured out an earnest short prayer in the name of Jesus Christ. The result was that the whole family of six were baptised together. The boy grew to be the well-known minister, Dr Adolph Saphir of London.[1] Another early convert of the mission was Dr Alfred Edersheim, who by his *Life of Christ* and other works has done almost as much as Dr Saphir to enrich the modern religious literature of England. So great was the interest of the Jewish inquirers at this time that Dr John Duncan said they read together the Epistles of Paul as eagerly as if they were letters delivered by the morning post.

During the long period of forty-two years, after his appointment to succeed Dr Keith in 1847, Dr Moody Stuart continued in his post

---

[1] See Memoir of Dr A. Saphir (Shaw & Co.).—*KMS*.

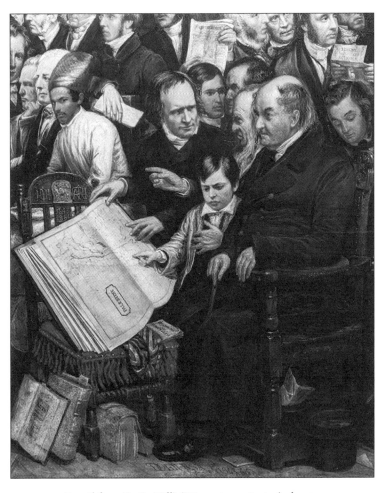

Detail from D. O. Hill's 'Disruption painting', showing those involved in mission to the Jews

L-R: Dr Alexander Keith (holding map of Palestine), Prof. Marcus Sachs, Alexander Moody Stuart, Prof. John 'Rabbi' Duncan, Prof. Alexander Black (in chair). The small boy is Adolph Saphir.

Neither Moody Stuart nor Duncan were actually present for the first General Assembly of the Free Church of Scotland, but Hill included them, along with other absent figures, as those who had significantly contributed to the Free Church's coming into existence and subsequent development. The painting is displayed in the Presbytery Hall within the Free Church of Scotland offices, Edinburgh.—*P.*

of Convener of the Jewish Committee (with a brief interval), having during the last five years Dr J. Hood Wilson associated with him as joint-convener. In this work he had the aid successively of Mr J. G. Wood, W.S., Rev. Walter Wood, Mr Francis Brown-Douglas, advocate, and the Rev. Wm. Affleck, who during many years acted as honorary secretaries with exemplary zeal and efficiency. His annual addresses made the Jewish evening of the General Assembly an important event, and were looked forward to with more than ordinary interest. In the passages quoted in this chapter from these annual addresses and appeals, what is merely of temporary importance is omitted, and it is hoped that what here meets the reader's eye may have the effect not only of showing the views of the subject of this memoir on a branch of his Master's work which largely occupied his thoughts and time, but also of kindling and cherishing in the hearts of those who never heard him, an intelligent interest and desire for the conversion of the Jewish race scattered through so many lands. It may be best to transcribe the passages without distracting the eye by inserting the date of each.[2]

'The first prayer the Jew is taught to lisp in infancy and the last words he utters in death are, "Hear, O Israel, the Lord thy God is One GOD." They are among his first words in the morning, and the last at night. In his creed he declares, "I believe with a perfect faith that the Creator is One God (blessed is he), and that there is no unity like unto him... I believe with a perfect faith that the law of Moses will never be changed." What a tremendous barrier there is in such a nation, and to the tenderest consciences the greatest barrier, to acknowledging and worshipping Jesus Christ! Even among Protestants there is this barrier to the Jews becoming Christians; but living mostly in the midst of Popery, the everlasting command must ever sound in their ears, "Thou shalt have no other gods before me," when they see the Virgin Mary worshipped as a goddess and the churches full of graven images.'

---

[2] Two sample addresses from the years 1869 and 1882, together with a lecture delivered in 1839, have been provided in the appendix to this edition, pp. 411-37.—*P.*

Again he says: 'It is a striking fact that as the cross of Calvary is the recognised centre of the whole Christian world, so the day of atonement, which foreshadowed the great expiation on the cross, is recognised by the Jews as the grand centre of the Hebrew religion. Yet in their strange darkness they now set aside all that constitutes atonement, either in type or in substance, and attribute the whole efficacy of the day to their own repentance and their own prayers. In their leading organ in this country they expressly deny all atonement in these words: "The dominant [the Christian] religion has invented a scheme according to which this object was attained by the surrender to the divine wrath as a sin offering of the highest for the low, the innocent for the guilty, the everlasting for the evanescent, the immaculate for the impure, the Creator for the creature; the indispensable condition attached being, not the performance of meritorious acts and deeds of virtue to obliterate the memory of past wrongs and iniquities, but faith in merits in which the offender can have no part, and an atonement in which he had no share." Such an atonement they say they will not accept.'

Then he would strive to arouse interest in that chosen race by pointing to the terrible persecutions they had suffered in every Christian land. Almost each recurring year, alas! could furnish him with a new instance of this. Now they were massacred in Roumania, now banished from Russia; the populace was excited against them by anti-Semitic riots, now in Berlin, now in Paris. It is said that Israel is the only people which treasures up the memories of her calamities and keeps their anniversaries. But he delighted to show how through all the terrible ordeal of a protracted dying without being slain, the nation had clung to its faith in the true God and in his revelation.

'The Jews were more religious than any nation on the face of the earth. How lightly religion rested on the Greek and Roman in comparison! With other nations it was *a part* of their life, but with the Jews it was *the chief object*; it was not national games that engrossed their thoughts, but great religious festivals. Their national history is in the Books of Exodus, Judges, etc.; their national laws are in the words of Moses, the man of God; their national proverbs are those of Solomon; their philosophy is in Job and Ecclesiastes; their poetry is in the prophecies of Isaiah; their national songs are the Psalms of David. This specialty has still left its deep stamp on the national character. The words of the Lord to be written on the lintels and the door-posts, and to be as frontlets between the eyes, are now but the dead letter; but that letter is branded deeply into the national character. I was told that of 900 African slaves whom I saw in the hold of a slave-ship in Brazil, not one would object to learn the creed and Lord's Prayer and be baptised before being sold up the country. Imagine 1,000 *Jews* dealt with in such a manner! For nearly 2,000 years they have been fined, banished, tortured, killed for the sake of their religion, and have submitted to it all rather than renounce the faith of their fathers. And as you would convert 10,000 sons of Ham into nominal Christians sooner than a conscientious son of Abraham, so also for the true conversion of Israel there must be, as compared with the heathen, either an extraordinary work of the Spirit of God, or else a far longer time in the use of ordinary means. Our answer therefore to those who reproach us with taking so long in the conversion of the Jews is, that in the nature of things it cannot be, in the first instance, a rapid work, and that we did not expect that the conversion of Israel would be short and easy.

'But how does the case stand after all? Have we been long seeking the salvation of Israel? It is now eighteen centuries since Jerusalem was destroyed and Israel scattered. In the seventeenth century it is recorded of the Rev. Mr Blackerby, an eminent minister in Suffolk, that "he was one of the first that convinced men in those parts of God's intent to convert the nation of the Jews. Divers ministers much opposed that opinion at first, but were at last, by his discourses, fully satisfied and really persuaded of the truth of it." And it is less than a century since earnest effort was commenced in Britain for their conversion by the establishment of the London Society for the conversion of the Jews in 1809; and their cause was taken up by the Church of Scotland only in 1841.'

To illustrate how hard the heart of the Jew is, he described a visit he had paid to a large diamond factory in the Jewish quarter of Amsterdam with all its workmen Jews.

'The work is so extensive that the diamond trade in connection with it is said to give subsistence to about 10,000 Jews. Their knives are diamond chisels, and as hard emery powder, which polishes the agate and the sapphire, is too soft for their purpose, it gives place to diamond dust. The diamond alone cuts the diamond. But they showed us, among their treasures, one stone which there is no other stone in the world hard enough to cut, and which therefore lies there useless. The first thought was to plead for oneself to have the heart of stone taken away; the second was to remember that the heart of the Jew is compared not merely to stone, but to the diamond described as the "adamant harder than flint."

'But again, what was this adamant of adamants to look upon— this diamond harder than all the diamonds of the earth? The Lord said to his prophet, "Go, get a potter's earthen bottle, and break the bottle in their sight, and say, So will I break this people as a potter's vessel, because they have forsaken me." That adamant stone is believed to be of exquisite lustre and of immense value if any man could bring forth its hidden beauty. But meanwhile it is so like Jeremiah's broken piece of an earthen bottle that not one man in 50,000 would stoop to pick it up from the street. It is very like the broken stopper of a bottle of coarse green glass, and surely this stone presents a lively image of that people in whose charge it rests. Yet the same Lord God who charges them with making their hearts adamant, changing the image, said, "The Lord their God shall save them, and they shall be as the gems of a crown", "a crown of glory in the hand of the Lord, and a royal diadem in the hand of thy God."'

The heart of the Jews, so hard towards Christ, had yet many soft points towards religion and home which gave hope regarding them. He mentioned that a Jewish preacher in addressing boys leaving school for holidays had said: 'You leave your books, your Euclid and Virgil, but never forget your prayers and your Bible. Your problems will not suffer by a vacation, but *religion cannot wait*.' In a similar sermon to girls the preacher said: 'Man's home is the world, but woman's world is the home. In the home every harsh expression should be hushed, and no act should be done that we should fear to perform in the Almighty's presence in the synagogue; for of the home it may specially be said, "Surely God is in this place."'

Again the Convener pointed out that the Jews are one of the great permanent races of men, so that the results of labour among them will be enduring and not like that expended on an American tribe now extinct, with no survivor able to read the Bible that was translated for it; that the Jews also are in all lands, so that missionary work among them touches the world everywhere, and if they were once converted, they would with their ardent religious zeal, and their constitution acclimatised to every zone, prove the most effective agents for the conversion of the world. He often pointed also to their rapid rise in financial, literary, political and social influence in all the great modern nations, which indeed is the cause of the exasperation against them so easily excited, so that a German paper drew attention to the fact that at a coroner's inquest which its columns reported, the police superintendent present was a Jew, the doctor called in was a Jew, the coroner was a Jew, the corpse alone, it added with grim humour, was a German! Again he showed how the Jews still recognise their place as the custodiers of the oracles of God. They themselves write today:—

'With the Jew the conception of the Deity is primarily a product of revelation. He believes that the Deity has revealed himself externally to the prophets of his people. Reason and moral sentiment may confirm him in this conviction, but they did not originate it. It originated in authority. The Jew is a heaven-appointed custodian of the most precious jewel intrusted by God to man; and this office lays upon him special obligations from which he cannot arbitrarily withdraw without deserting the post assigned to him by Providence. It is Providence itself, not man, that makes the Jew.'

'The Jew with all his faults and sins has been a faithful guardian of the written oracles of God; and for this we owe the nation a lasting debt of gratitude. If they are once enlightened on the fulfilment of the Old Testament in the New, the Jews, who claim an absolute divine authority for the Bible, will bring a singular accession of strength to the church in her conflict with the rationalism and unbelief of the world, which will amply repay all our efforts for their conversion.

'It is ever to be remembered that into all great works for the salvation of souls there enter two elements: the one is the effort of the church for the salvation of the lost; the other is the ripening of God's gracious purpose toward them. The effort of the church is valuable chiefly on this account, that it is a token of the ripening of Jehovah's purpose of grace. If it were possible for the church to neglect the Jews for one hundred years, I believe it would postpone the coming of the kingdom for one hundred years. Our love to the heathen, or our love to the Jew, is but a sweet drop in the salt ocean: it sinks, is lost, and where is it? Nay, every moving of your heart, every moving of my heart, every moving of the church's heart is but a drop from the great ocean of the heart of God. It is not we that love lost men, but the great Almighty God; and those drops oozing through our hard hearts are the sure token that the deep ocean of hidden divine love has begun to rise, and, once swelling up, it will burst every barrier, and all the guilt and all the enmity of Israel will be but a drop in the ocean in that day when he will cast all their sins into the depths of the sea.

'The intensest love on record, except only the love of Christ, was toward Israel—blind, dead, cast off—in the heart of Paul, who declared that he could wish himself "accursed from Christ" on their behalf. He had said the moment before, in the full assurance of faith, that nothing could separate him from the love of Christ, and then he solemnly declares that if it were possible, if it were lawful, and if it would save Israel, he would for their sakes consent to become a curse instead of Israel, even as Christ had become a curse instead of

Paul. Love could not possibly go further; and I believe that neither before nor since, in all the human family, has love ever gone so far as in the heart of this Jew for the Jews. Now this love was no more natural to Paul than to us; it was wrought in him, as he says himself, by the Holy Ghost: it was the mind of Christ in Paul; it was the mind of Christ towards Israel, the very same as at this day.'

The Convener used to animate the hope of the Assembly by reminding the fathers and brethren that if the number of baptisms reported annually was often small, they had 700 Jewish children year after year in their schools, who knew as much about Jesus as our own children, and whose hearts are evidently receiving the love as well as the knowledge of the truth. In support of this he reported that 'when the teacher asked for an example in grammar of the conditional mood, one girl replied with earnest face, "I would rejoice if I did not sin so much"; another, "I would be glad if God would manifest himself"; another asked, "Will we, when we are in bliss, see the marks of the wounds in Jesus' hands?"'

'These children, taught in their various tongues by their parents to curse the crucified One, were now taught in large numbers in our Mission Schools in German, Magyar, Italian, French, Hebrew and English, to know and love him, and it was a striking thing that they were attracted more by the sad story of the cross than by the hope of their King coming in glory. They were learning to look upon him whom their fathers had pierced, and to mourn for him. When the teacher, explaining the words, "I love them that love me," asked, "Who are they that truly love the Lord Jesus?" one Jewish maiden replied, "Please, teacher, I love him," a confession which visibly affected her companions as well as her teacher.' He told how one of the old pupils, calling to purchase a Bible, said, 'Of course we have one Bible, but my sister is very ill and will not part with it; she sits up in her bed and reads it constantly, and so I have come for another.' This girl's younger sister of eleven had called on a neighbouring Roman Catholic girl who had come to live next door, but was treated with disdain because they were Christians and she a

Jewess. But the children met in the court, and the Roman Catholic mother overheard the young Jewess repeating to her daughter one of the gospel stories she had heard in school. She then came forward and said, 'Come in, my dear girl, you know more of the Christian religion than I do myself.' The sequel was that every evening she went and entertained the family with her gospel stories, and asked leave to bring her companion with her to school.

The operations of the Jewish Mission which Dr Moody Stuart so successfully guided during most of its history are very extensive. One thousand five hundred Jewish children are receiving Christian as well as secular instruction, of which the Jewish authorities in Buda-Pest last winter wrote, in warning the parents against sending their children, that 'the doctrines taught impress themselves so deeply that neither the most zealous religious [Jewish] teachers, nor devout parents at home are able any more to efface them.' Close upon 10,000 Jews were treated either medically or surgically at Constantinople last year. At Safed there were 600 Jewish patients (implying thousands of consultations), and at Tiberias upwards of 10,000 consultations by Jews. The gospel of Jesus is read and explained to all the patients.

The needed funds for all this enterprise flowed in steadily, sometimes from outside our Church, and in curious ways. I remember that for several years in succession a draft was received for a substantial amount, the letter, bearing an English postmark, signed 'Dolittle, Negligent & Co.' The last time the letter came from the Channel Islands signed 'Careless Dolittle'. It may have been a tender conscience that made the donor thus style himself an 'unprofitable servant,' and the Convener could not learn whether he had died or lost his means when his gifts ceased. Whatever his opinion of himself he seemed to be faithful to his trust. Domestic servants often sent in really handsome donations to this favourite mission. Meanwhile the Convener said, 'We are privileged to sow the seed of the gospel, and the Lord in his own time will ripen the harvest. The day is surely hastening on when it shall be said of all the scattered nation: "Who are these that fly as a cloud, and as the doves to their windows?"'

Again he said: 'It was while looking with infinite pity on Israel, "scattered abroad as sheep having no shepherd," that our blessed Lord spoke those memorable words, rendered so vividly in our oldest English Bible: "Soothly there is much ripe corn, but few workmen: therefore pray ye the Lord of the ripe corn that he send workmen into his ripe corn" (Matt. 9:37, 38).

'In the first half of the great parable that teaches the restoration both of the individual soul and of Jew and Gentile unto God, the Father himself welcomes us back, as the younger and prodigal son; and in the second half the same Father persuades our elder brother, who will not come in because the fullness of the Father's house has been bestowed on us. But the servants first tell him of the family joy in which they are sharing; and it is after their failure that the Father himself entreats and prevails. But if, as our Lord's servants, we shall refuse or delay to deal with our elder brother because the Father has not come forth to him while standing without, as he came forth to us when afar off, our guilty indifference tends to postpone the day of final blessing, because the dealing between the servants and the elder brother must precede the Father's own entreaty. The servants speak with the elder brother, and they report to the Father that they cannot persuade him; and when we shall have done both of these, entreating our brother to come in, and then entreating the Father to persuade him, both Jew and Gentile will hear the words of wondrous joy: "Son, thou art ever with me, and all that I have is thine. It was meet that we should make merry, and be glad: for this thy brother was dead and is alive again: and was lost, and is found." So in the quaint old lines—

> The Gentiles once got to the height of sin,
>   And fullness of the savèd come to sight,
> Their elder brother Jew will straight come in,
>   And mourn for that he had no sooner right:

Their coming in will be the Gentiles' light,
Nor till that time will sun again be bright.'

The Convener, however, thought it quite likely that in the fulfilment of the divine purpose the Jews might be restored to their own
land before their conversion as a nation.

In the beautifully illuminated address presented by the Edinburgh Presbytery on the occasion of Dr Moody Stuart's jubilee,
they say: 'One special service in connection with which your name
will ever be remembered with love and admiration by all friends of
missions, is in connection with the Jewish Committee, alike as its
Convener and by the speeches with which from year to year you so
powerfully and pathetically advocated the claims of Israel on the
church's regard, and the place of Israel in the purposes of God. That
that race, beloved for the fathers' sake, has so large a place in our
Church's liberality, and so warm a place in its heart, is due in no
small measure to your advocacy and instrumentality; and it will be
a memory fragrant still to the Church of a new century that some of
the saintliest names of Disruption times form a garland around the
cause of Jewish conversion planted there by the hand of the King of
the Jews himself.'

A congratulatory address in similar terms was sent to him by the
Jews' Conversion Committee on occasion of his diamond jubilee
in 1897. In returning his thanks to Dr Cunningham, Dr Moody
Stuart refers to it as 'a cheering cordial in my old age from the God
of Abraham who is their God and mine, and who of his own free
grace is pleased to enrol us as Abraham's seed, and heirs according
to the promise.' He always asked that the Jews should be remembered in family and private prayers on Friday evening and Saturday
morning, which is their weekly Sabbath, and very specially on their
Day of Atonement, the changing date of which is published in the
leading newspapers, and on which he presided annually at a large
meeting for prayer for Israel's conversion. Nor did his interest in
the conversion of Israel ever flag in warmth. As I sat in his little

sitting-room at Ellerslie, Crieff, when we were watching his closing days, my eye often rested on the text that hung prominently on the wall: 'To the Jew first.' To the end of life he felt daily the obligation laid on Christians by their ascended Lord, 'Go to my brethren,' and he continued to be fascinated by the truth expressed in Herder's words, which he often quoted, 'Israel's still incompleted guidance is the grandest poem of all time.' George Herbert's lines on the Jews were great favourites with him:—

> Poor nation, whose sweet sap and juice,
> Our scions have purloined, and left you dry;
> O that my prayer; mine, alas!—
> O that some angel might a trumpet sound,
> At which the church, falling upon her face,
> Should cry so loud until that trump were drowned,
> And, by that cry, of her dear Lord obtain
> That your sweet sap might come again!

— 12 —

Visits to Hungary and Bohemia

Land of the Magyar, old heroic land!
As 'freedom's vanguard' oft thy sons would stand:
Oh now may pristine love return to thee,
With truth in Christ that maketh doubly free!
                                                —*W. Bennet*

IN the summer of 1862 Mr Moody Stuart was appointed, along with Dr Duncan, by the Jews Conversion Committee to visit the Free Church mission stations at Breslau and Buda-Pest. A friend having kindly put it in my power to accompany them, I was only too glad to do so. We crossed the North Sea from Leith to Hamburg, where the deputies visited Dr Craig, the esteemed missionary to the Jews from the Irish Presbyterian Church, who accompanied us as far as Vienna.

At Breslau the deputies were much interested in the work of their Church's devoted representative, the late Rev. Daniel Edward, who laboured as zealously and successfully among the German population as the Jewish. A German congregation was established under his pastorate, where the full gospel was proclaimed in a city whose pulpits were blighted with Rationalism, whose members were earnest in seeking the salvation of Israel. The need of such preaching was shown in an incident Mr Edward gave us. One of the town ministers having come to a house to conduct the funeral service of a little girl whose parents were distracted with grief, the father said to him: 'I suppose you have no doubt that the body of our darling will be raised again, and that I was right in comforting her mother with this assurance?' To this their pastor only replied by a too significant shrug of his shoulders! No wonder that the old definite gospel of pardon through Christ's death, resurrection of the body and reunion in glory soon attracted a congregation. Mr Edward's daughters became their father's earnest helpers, Miss Edward having great success in teaching a large class of lads. The Scottish Sabbath would have been a boon to Breslau's busy toilers. We were told that the empty state of the churches was due to the fact that only persons of means could afford to set apart the day for worship, when all work was proceeding as usual, and the six days' wage would not suffice to maintain a family.

Mr Edward accompanied us to Hungary, and as he along with our other missionaries had been expelled from the Austrian empire in 1848, he thought it advisable that we should post by a quiet road instead of going by train across the frontier, where possibly his history might have been inquired into, as the passport system was then very rigidly enforced. The roads by which we traversed Silesia reminded us of Scotland, except that they were bordered with fruit-trees, the cherries, which were then ripe, hanging most temptingly over our heads. We passed two old settlements of the Moravian Brethren, with the beautifully significant names, 'Free-Grace' and 'Grace-Town'. The blessing of heaven appeared to rest upon these communities planted in the midst of their widely extending orchards.

At one small town near the frontier which we reached in the afternoon in rather a famished condition, Dr Craig, who ordered dinner, returned to tell us that they had no butcher meat in the inn, but had eggs, and were going to make us a pancake. I objected that one pancake could never satisfy four hungry people. He said he thought their pancakes were larger than ours, so after demur we compromised the matter by ordering one for each. At last the first was brought in with the announcement that the rest were following, and a large savoury omelet was set on the table, the size of a small pillow! We begged them to consume the other three themselves, and the flavour of garlic was so strong that except for the sauce of hunger we would have declined the small portion we managed to eat.

At one halt, while the horses were resting, we went to see a famous herd of white cows belonging to an Austrian archduke, which my father was interested in, and much admired. There were eighty in one beautifully kept byre, in ten rows, the end stall of each row containing a magnificent bull with black tips to horns and tail and a sprinkling of black spots on the shoulders.

In Bohemia we were struck to notice the interest aroused among our fellow passengers in the train whenever we happened in conversation to mention the name of John Huss. My father, sitting opposite an aged lady, referred to Huss in English, of which she did not understand one word, and in a moment her old eye was lighted up as if by an electric spark, and drawing herself up to standing height she exclaimed with intense emotion, 'Huss, Huss!'

From Vienna, where we learned something of the Bible Society's work, we sailed down the Danube to Buda-Pest, admiring the vast expanses of grain on either side of the lordly river, and watching sometimes rows of huge horned heads stretching out from the bank, for the cattle to escape the heat, which was intense, had waded into the yellow flood until only the heads of those furthest in appeared above the water. Dr Duncan conversed with the Hungarian gentlemen on board in Latin, which they all spoke fluently, as although he could read Magyar, having learned it when a missionary to the Jews in Pest, he had forgotten how to speak it. The Hungarians said his Latin was so beautiful that they were ashamed of their own. As we passed the Hungarian frontier he took off his hat with a loud '*viva*' of salutation to the Hungarian colours. The ship's officers now changed their costume for the Hungarian dress, and a soldier on board warned the Scottish ministers that it would not do for them to go ashore at Pest with tall silk hats, the badge of the Austrians. My Balmoral bonnet was *en règle*, but Dr Duncan went bareheaded to the hotel where the party provided themselves with low felts.

'Four cities,' Dr Moody Stuart said in our Assembly, 'have sometimes been named as conspicuous for beauty of situation and appearance—Naples, Edinburgh, Constantinople and Buda-Pest. With its old and new town Buda-Pest bears some resemblance to Edinburgh; but instead of the North Loch dried up into gardens is the noble Danube rolling between the two cities. The Danube is their ocean; and in figures of speech, where we speak of the sea, they use the Danube instead. On the Pest side of the river there are modern buildings like our own; on the other side stand the rock and the castle and the old city of Buda, with beautiful hills beyond like our Pentlands. In passing from the one to the other the transition is striking. Suppose Princes Street opposite the Castle, with twice the breadth of the gardens, filled with a deep and rapid river. The Danube was formerly crossed by a bridge of boats, and the rock beyond was ascended by a winding road. But now you cross this river of 1,200 feet by a magnificent chain bridge,[1] reckoned one of the wonders of Europe, and then by a tunnel through the hill you go right into the heart of the old city. It is as if you passed by an iron bridge across Princes Street Gardens, and then by a tunnel through the Castle rock into the Grassmarket. So in Pest, from modern palace-like buildings facing the river you cross into old Buda, and you seem in a moment to be transferred a thousand years back, and thousands of miles away—all is now so Eastern and so old. Instead of the excessive uniformity of the view,

---

[1] The Széchenyi Chain Bridge was designed by the Englishman W. Tierney Clark (1783–1852) and the resident engineer was a Scot, Adam Clark (1811–66, becoming well-known and respected as Clark Ádám in Hungary). Building commenced in 1839, and a number of Scots went to Hungary to work as skilled labourers on the bridge project. John 'Rabbi' Duncan became their unofficial chaplain after he arrived in the city in 1841. The bridge was completed in 1849, and after being blown up by the retreating German army during the Siege of Budapest in 1945, was rebuilt and opened again in 1949. For more on the Scottish mission to Jews in Budapest, see John S. Ross, *Time for Favour: Scottish Missions to the Jews 1838–1852* (Stoke-on-Trent: Tentmaker Publications, 2011), pp. 229-39.—*P.*

every man has built his house after his own mind, yet all after an old-world model—churches, synagogues, mosque-like buildings, baths, with rows of one and two-storeyed houses in long succession. We entered one of the synagogues where a lad most politely showed us everything he thought interesting. We offered him a gratuity, but nothing would induce him to take it because it was Saturday afternoon. Their Sabbath was not yet over, and he would make no gain, even from strangers, on their holy day.'

The city of Pest has a population of 500,000, of which nearly one fourth are Jews. A week was spent by the deputies in Pest inspecting the mission and arranging with Pastor Torok, the esteemed Superintendent, or Presbyterian Bishop, who did much for this mission, and for its affiliation with the Reformed Church of Hungary so as to secure protection. In taking supper at his house one was struck with the servants' duty being merely to carry in the viands, while the daughters rose from the table, out of respect for their guests, and handed round the dishes to each. Buda-Pest was endeared to the Free Church as being the place where her deputy, Dr Keith, on returning from the Mission of Inquiry to the Jews in Palestine in 1839 was nursed into life by the pious Archduchess Maria Dorothea of Hungary (mother of the present Queen of the Belgians) after he was thought to be dead, who also nursed into life this Scottish Mission to the Jews.

One important result of this mission was the establishment by Dr Duncan and my father of a scheme for raising bursaries in Scotland to bring over to Edinburgh a certain number of Hungarian divinity students each winter to study in our Divinity Hall. Of the Hungarian Reformed Church Dr Duncan had said: 'The Magyars will die for their Calvinism; I wish I could add that they will live it.' Evangelical life was at a sadly low ebb. The result of this wisely planned and executed scheme for bursaries was that many of their best students, seeing warm spiritual life in Edinburgh, and hearing the gospel fully preached to heart and conscience, were entirely changed, and carried the new life back with them to the parishes in which by-and-by they were settled, and in some cases to the colleges where they have become professors.

Dr Balogh, who was soon appointed Professor of Church History in Debreczin, has kindly written to me sending some extracts from his diary, from which I have only space to make a few selections:

'I was deeply moved on hearing of the departure of your father, this saintly pastor. My impression on leaving your country was that the Apostles have been of such a nature as your father.

'(March, 1865.) As a candidate for the ministry I went to see at first Rev. Mr Moody Stuart, Convener of the Committee (on Bursaries). The pious soul received me with utmost cordiality, and expressed joy at being able to speak with a Hungarian co-believer, and heard with great interest what I told about our college. After two hours' conversation before starting he offered a fervent prayer. The living example is like the living fountain: it gives life to a permanent river. When calling and real inmost mind are linked with godliness, this acquires a charming shape. Today (26th March, '65) I observed, yea, and nearer, the soul of this extremely pious man, whom I must hold an example of first rank among the representatives of piety whom I ever saw. A truer servant of the Redeemer cannot be imagined than he, the Pastor of Free St Luke's.

'I entered this spacious church: a seat was offered to me among the elders, beside the good Macdonald. I pitied the preacher's feeble voice, and remarked to myself, if he possessed the sound of Spurgeon (whom I had heard in London), Rev. Mr Moody could conquer half a world by his lively, charming manner. The text was Psalm 133:1, and in the afternoon 2 Kings 25:1-30. Moody spoke always fluently and by heart. The great effect lay in this also. We may be kings before our Lord, and may change the darkness of prison if we reflect the sanctity of the splendour of our great King. He sketched with heavenly sentiment the kingdom of God, this fundamental subject of Jesus' teaching. I went home as feeling a new heart in me.'

The acquaintance he thus formed with the Hungarian student bursars made my father's name known and loved in many

Hungarian manses. A copy of a Hungarian periodical (*The Christian*) for November 1898, has reached me. It is edited by Pastor Szalay, and its leading article, headed 'Dr Moody Stuart,' is surrounded by a deep black border. This is followed by a sermon of his on Matthew 7:14.[2] I sent for a translation of the strange Magyar columns from which I give a few extracts:

'That most distinguished minister of the Free Church of Scotland, the warmest, best friend of the Hungarians, the kindest, best friend of the Hungarian students, Dr Moody Stuart, is no more among the living. Although the departed had reached the age of ninety, nevertheless his death has filled with sorrowful emotion the heart of his friends and the church of the living God. Why? Dr Moody Stuart was one of those Scottish Evangelical preachers who from the year 1840 and onward by their preaching and their praying filled the Scottish church with new life. Of these men Dr Somerville who preached in various places in Hungary was also one. These saintly ministers were united in one company by the power of the Holy Spirit, and began to study the question how religious revival is to be brought into the church.' The editor states that Dr Moody Stuart ascribed the work of revival to the Holy Spirit, who shows us the things of Christ, and enables us to receive him. He mentions that the revived life of Scotland reached their land through the Bursary Scheme, and adds: 'the hearts of increasing numbers among us are now moved by the love of Jesus. And how this man of God cared for these students in Edinburgh! He was to them a true father, brother, friend, teacher and leader to a holy life. I shall never forget the kind, condescending, gracious manner in which he conversed with us, and the clear, pure gospel instruction which he imparted to us, and the kind hospitality with which he seated us at his table. And here I confess, what perhaps I did not even say to himself, that one of his sermons, of which the text was: "Narrow is the way which leadeth unto life" (Matt. 7:14),

---

[2] This sermon, which was greatly blessed in Strathbogie in 1839, is the first in the volume of sermons, *The Path of the Redeemed* (Edinburgh: MacNiven & Wallace, 1893).—KMS.

opened my eyes, and was by the grace of God the means of making me one of the men who walk in the narrow way. Blessed be thou, my spiritual father, good teacher! May the earth rest lightly on thee! And do thou, O gracious God, grant that the spirit of thy truly devoted servant may be in a double measure mine! Amen.'

Dr Somerville of Glasgow, whose apostolic fervour carried him in advanced years over a great part of the world, preaching to large audiences the unsearchable riches of Christ, translated from his eloquent lips into the language of each people, on returning from Hungary in 1888, wrote to my father: 'I frequently heard grateful reference to you on the part of those who are now ministers in Hungary, and had spent a session or two in Edinburgh. A great many of these young men attended Free St Luke's. A professor said that after being benefited by M. St Hilaire in Paris it was when he came to Edinburgh that he "tumbled into the gospel," and he said this was under your ministry.'

The Reformed Church of Hungary, thus widely influenced by Dr Moody Stuart, is the largest Presbyterian Church in the world outside of America, containing 2,000 congregations and 2,000,000 adherents. We returned home by Vienna, Innsbruck in the Tyrol, and Munich.

'In Munich,' my father writes, 'on turning from a narrow street into a crowded thoroughfare, the sight that first arrested me was a flock of three- or four-score sheep passing along, a singular picture of quietness and confidence, through all the bustle of the multitudinous throng and traffic, with no shepherd following to take care of them. After looking round on every side for the absent shepherd I saw straight in front of them an old man, whose years might answer to the number of his flock, walking quietly "before them." This position he never left for a moment, nor moved from side to side, but he looked constantly and carefully to make sure that all the flock were following him. At the same time he seemed to call them by name, for if any one straggled to the right or the left, and he turned his eyes in its direction, it ran instantly towards him. His voice I could not hear through the noise, but his sheep seemed to hear it as the only voice in all the throng that reached their ears. It was a beautiful sight and most helpful lesson, for even so the ransomed of the Lord to whom he calls "Fear not, little flock!" are passing quietly through this thronging world hearing his voice, and following him, and not hearing the voice of strangers that call to them from every side.'

From Bavaria our homeward route lay through Stuttgart, Mayence [Mainz] and the Rhine, which seemed a small river after the majestic volume of the Danube.

Visit to Bohemia

From Hungary let us pass to Bohemia, which was visited by Dr Moody Stuart in 1869 in company with his attached friend and co-presbyter, Dr J. H. Wilson of Barclay Church. The Protestant Church in Bohemia was much older than that of Hungary, and had come through a more fiery ordeal. It was also weaker in numbers, and much poorer, so that it stood still more in need of help and sympathy from strong churches. It is interesting to observe how it was the concern of the Free Church for the Jewish population of both these countries that brought her into contact with the native Protestant churches, and led to a marked reviving of their spiritual life and influence. The Bohemian Church in its origin and history was closely associated with our own. Jerome of Prague returned from a visit to England in 1400 A.D., bringing with him the writings of John Wycliffe. These were the means of unfolding the truth to him, and to his coadjutor and brother-martyr, John Huss, who preached 'like an incarnate conscience.' Anne, the wife of Richard II of England, was a Bohemian princess, and became a disciple of Wycliffe, and on her death the ladies of her court also brought back with them to Bohemia many of the English reformer's writings.

Bohemia repaid her debt to our own island. One of her sons, Paul Craw, was sent to preach in Scotland, and was burned at the stake in St Andrews in 1432, before Scotland had produced any native martyr.

It was therefore only fitting that now after four centuries Scotland should do a little towards returning to Bohemian Protestants the good service they had rendered her of old. Dr Moody Stuart writes:[3] 'In Prague I walked down alone to the scene of martyrdom in the large square of the Grosser Ring, where the scaffold covered with black was erected, on which forty-seven Bohemian noblemen and leading citizens sealed their faith with their blood on 21 June 1621.'

The great contest of the Bohemian Protestants, from the death of Huss to this martyrdom, had been for the use of the communion cup which the Romanists denied to the laity. In Bohemia the symbol of the cup takes the place of the cross as the symbol of their faith, setting forth and sealing the precious blood shed for sinners, at once the atonement and sustenance of the soul.

The Scottish ministers were deeply interested to see the sacred symbol of the cup carved in stone on the walls of the churches, and the Bible and the cup carved in wood as the chief ornaments of the pulpits. The 'Cup' met the eye over the door of the Protestant schools and on the tombstones of the dead. Their warriors carried the silver communion chalice with them in the field, whence the ministers dispensed the sacramental wine to the soldiers fighting for faith and civil rights.

My father got a model of a silver cup dug up from one of their old battlefields.[4] Of it he said: 'Blessed Cup, filled with the blood of the one, great, only Martyr! How sweet is every drop of its sacred wine! How cherished every word that encircles it! "The Book" and "The Cup", sweet union of the noblest objects on earth! "The Book" dear to Scotland, the Book and the Cup dear to Bohemia; but the Cup dear also to Scotland in her sweet communions in the recesses of the mountains, when its silent circling round the worshippers was followed by a song of triumphant praise which the fear of the lurking foe could not hush. May the Book and the Cup unite these

[3] See his *Visit to the Land of Huss* (Edinburgh: James Nisbet, 1870).—*KMS.*
[4] A photograph of this cup is given beside that of the Kuttenberg Martyrs' Church. [See p. 164.]—*KMS.*

two lands in bonds of brotherhood in this hour, when Bohemia, trodden under foot for centuries, is rising again out of the martyrs' grave, and asks our hands to help to loose the grave-clothes.'

In driving through the country their attention was directed to some large mounds of stones, the heaped-up diggings of a silver mine. In these mines thousands of the slaughtered saints of God sleep till the earth shall give up her dead.

'The year 1421 is marked by a dark line of the blood of the followers of Huss. In that single year this one town of Kuttenberg, dug about for its treasures of silver ore, witnessed the unparalleled spectacle of a whole army of martyrs dragged as felons to the shafts of these old mines, to one 1,700, to another 1,308, and to the third 1,321. Men of wealth and rank together with men rich only in faith, and devout women not a few, convicted of no sin, but charged with reading the Book of Life and drinking the Cup of Salvation, numbering in all 4,329, were cast headlong into the yawning pits. In that day when the Lord shall make up his jewels those mines of martyrs' dust will be more precious far than the silver lodes they have replaced; and by the grace of God I resolved before I died to see, in that town of 16,000 souls, a church of living men once more on the face of the earth above that great congregation sleeping in Jesus.' This church, which Mr Karafiat says might appropriately be called *Dr Moody Stuart's Memorial Church*, was built, as one of the fruits of this visit to Bohemia. A good congregation of 490 baptised members was gathered under a godly pastor, M. Victor Szalatnay, who writes to me: 'We have to thank Dr Moody Stuart, next to the Lord God, that we could build a church and form a self-sustaining congregation. We could not have done this except through his help, and help out of Scotland. When we heard of the death of our friend and benefactor, we were deeply grieved. His memory will never be forgotten by all who knew him, especially by those who knew him in Kuttenberg.'

After the decease of Dr Moody Stuart a desire was expressed to raise a memorial tribute to his memory. A circular letter was drawn

Kuttenberg Martyrs' Church (or, 'Dr Moody Stuart's Memorial Church'). The photograph was taken especially for the first edition of this memoir. Inset: *The replica cup.*

up by the Rev. Prof. W. G. Blaikie, D.D., a warm friend of Bohemia as well as of Dr Moody Stuart, in which he stated that it was desired that the memorial should be 'of a kind to harmonise with the great object of his life, and that it was deeply impressed upon some of his friends that nothing would have been dearer to himself than the clearance of the remaining debt from the church at Kuttenberg, for the erection of which he longed with such tender emotion, and also to provide for the pressing need for a cemetery' in connection with it. It is touching to be told by Dr Cunningham, who signed this appeal when it was issued, that 'it was probably the last contribution of Dr Blaikie's accomplished and ever-busy pen to the diffusion of the gospel on earth, for between its preparation and publication the hour came in which it has pleased the Lord to call his servant to his rest and reward.'

The kirk session of this church in Kuttenberg have resolved to erect a memorial tablet with the following inscription:—

IN MEMORIAM
ALEXANDRI MOODY STUART, D.D.
EDINBURGENSIS, PRÆCLARI VERBI DEI
MINISTRI, PATRIÆ ECCLESIÆQUE NOSTRÆ
AMICISSIMI.

Translation:
TO THE MEMORY OF
ALEXANDER MOODY STUART, D.D.,
OF EDINBURGH,
A DISTINGUISHED MINISTER OF THE WORD OF GOD,
TRUEST FRIEND
OF OUR COUNTRY AND OUR CHURCH.

An interesting link between his earliest and later labours is furnished by a note received enclosing a subscription to this memorial, 'in grateful remembrance of the morning prayers Dr Moody Stuart conducted in the school Mrs M. attended 64 years ago.'

'A large meeting of pastors,' writes Dr Hood Wilson, 'from different parts of the country was held at our hotel in Prague, where Dr Moody Stuart's earnest and suggestive address bearing on the weighty responsibilities of the Christian ministry produced a deep impression. We held a meeting in a village where no one could be found who knew English and Czech (the language of the country), so addresses and prayers in English were translated sentence by sentence into German, by one who only knew English and German, and these were repeated in Czech, by one who only knew Czech and German. It seemed a slow and cumbrous process, but the people were deeply interested and impressed, and Dr Moody Stuart remarked to me that he never was more conscious of the presence and power of the Holy Spirit.' Similar meetings were held in various places.

Bursaries of £50 were offered to Bohemian students, as well as to those from Hungary: the same blessed results followed, and the struggling Protestant Church has been greatly heartened and strengthened by the sympathy and aid of Scottish Christians.

Pastor Karafiat, in a letter from Prague, dated 20 October 1898, says: 'Dr Moody Stuart will ever have a chapter in the Reformed church history of Bohemia and Moravia. Since his visit thirty years ago two or three students or probationers have studied yearly in Edinburgh, being in a sense altogether the guests of St Luke's, where also they regularly worshipped. With that visit there begins a new phase in our church history. There is here a section of men who mind spiritual things a good deal more than others do, and nearly all of them have been in Scotland, *and the personal influence of Dr Moody Stuart* was for them of the greatest importance. Several of his writings are in the hands of our ministers who can read English, and your father's book, *The Three Marys*, is in the hands of many of our peasants, as it has been translated into Bohemian, and published by our Tract Society. [My father was much gratified when he received a copy of this work of his printed in the strange Czech language.] When last August our papers reported Dr Moody Stuart's departure, very many of my countrymen remembered him lovingly, and sadly as well. Your father was a man to whom the fear of the Lord was the beginning of divinity, and for whom, without a closer walk with God in Enoch's fashion, there is no progress in theology.'

Surely others will, with the subject of this memoir, esteem it a privilege to be the Lord's 'remembrancers' and fellow workers towards bringing in the long-delayed answer to the prayer which ascended from multitudes in that pre-eminently martyr-land, who were led to the place of execution singing Psalm 44:22, 23:—

> Yea, for thy sake we're kill'd all day,
> Counted as slaughter-sheep.
> Rise, Lord, cast us not ever off;
> Awake, why dost thou sleep?

IN MEMORIAM
ALEXANDRI MOODY STUART D.D.,
EDINBURGENSIS PRÆCLARI V.D MINISTRI
PATRIÆ ECCLESIÆQUE NOSTRÆ
AMICISSIMI.

*Kuttenberg is now known under its original Czech name of Kutná Hora.
The memorial to Alexander Moody Stuart (depicted above) remains
in what is now the meeting place of Kutná Hora Evangelical Church.
In 1918 the Evangelical Reformed Church merged with the Evangelical
Lutheran Church in Moravia and Bohemia to form
the Evangelical Church of Czech Brethren.—P.*

Alexander Moody Stuart in middle age

— 13 —

Summers at Annat

How pleasant was the morning ray!
　　How fleeting was its shine!
The joys, that seem o' yesterday,
　　Are the joys o' langsyne!
Has friendship lost the power to charm?
　　Can age its tie untwine?
Is yet the grasp o' love as warm
　　As it was langsyne?

　　　　　　　　　—*Charles Spence (of Rait)*

IT is time now to say something of the home life of the subject of this memoir. While the manse at 43 Queen Street was our endeared home, hallowed by the recollections of many joys and some sorrows, still as it had more points of connection with the work in the church which it adjoined, the home life may as suitably be depicted in connection with Annat, which was our usual summer home. Besides, the period spent happily here in autumn brought into play some of our father's qualities which could not find scope for exercise in the heart of a great city. When the tension of constant work is relaxed in the summer holiday the bow springs back to its natural position; the man is exhibited in his native character, without the presence of his usual surroundings which have a constraining as well as a valuable formative influence. His surroundings at Annat were wholly different from those in Edinburgh, and the rest and change of scene enjoyed here fitted him for resuming with fresh strength and zeal the hard work of a city minister's life while at the same time he never demitted the functions of his sacred office, but used to preach the Word on Sabbath evenings in the little village chapel with as much interest and care as in his Edinburgh pulpit.

The village of Rait is situated on the southern slope of the Sidlaw Hills, the Braes of the Carse of Gowrie, in the county of Perth, midway between Perth and Dundee. When General Stuart acquired the estate of Rait he secured as gardener Archibald Gorrie, a very superior man of high Christian character, who remained in charge of the place till his death fifty years after. In his old age he said to me he had no desire to outlive his power of acquiring knowledge. He became widely known through Scotland as a botanist and as a propagator of new and valuable varieties of fruits and grains. The Annat barley is still in request among farmers, and a beautiful plum which he called the 'Annat Gage', but which was brought into the market as Lawson's golden gage, became a favourite variety. When Mr Gorrie was established at Annat there was very little wood on it, the whole policy being laid out and planted by him. General Stuart had plans drawn up for the erection of a mansion house, but these were never carried out. He had however laid out a large garden, with lofty brick walls, where both climate and soil being peculiarly favourable, very fine fruit is grown, including pears of the finer sorts, all varieties of plums, along with apricots, nectarines, peaches and figs. While the climate has not the mildness of the west coast nor its freedom from frost, so that the more delicate shrubs which grow on our western coasts, such as myrtles and hydrangeas, would not grow at Annat, its greater amount of sun peculiarly fits it to develop fruits, and also some of the rarer pines. It even occasionally ripens the mulberry and the walnut. Mr Gorrie imparted his love of arboriculture to our father, who delighted to add, from time to time, to the fine collection of firs, cedars, and cypresses.

Our father built a cottage on a beautiful site, and this being added to afterwards, while still retaining its cottage form, and roof thatched with the long reeds from the Tay, formed a very pleasant and commodious, and certainly a very picturesque, family residence. The house was planned by himself, and the dining-room was panelled and roofed with timber grown on Annat—oak, chestnut, walnut and plane, after a model that had struck his fancy in England. The view from the front windows which face the south-east is very extensive and striking. Standing some 200 feet above the level of the Carse of Gowrie, this fertile plain lies spread before the eye, bounded in front by the Norman Law and other hills of Fife, six miles distant, which interpose a barrier to the ample waters of the Tay, often lit up by a sheen which seems to double their volume. Against this range of hills the village of Errol stands prominent on the top of a ridge, with the tower of its beautiful church reflecting brilliantly the morning and afternoon sun, while nearer lie the rich grain fields of one of Scotland's most productive areas, bounded by deep and wide ditches called 'pows,' which carry the water from the hill burns and the drainage of the clay lands down to the estuary of the Tay. The rotation of crops causes the fields to present to the eye the appearance of the whole Carse being covered with a carpet of varied tints of green, and in autumn of yellow and brown, which stretches away on the eastward to the city of Dundee, conspicuous in the distance by its spires and chimney stalks. Even beyond it the old castle of Broughty Ferry, fifteen miles off, is discernible to a sharp eye, while the still more distant sandhills and lighthouses of Barry are more easily visible from their reflecting the sunlight. The long iron viaduct of the Tay Bridge, connecting the ancient kingdom of Fife with Forfarshire and the north of Scotland, is prominently in view, while the various stately mansions and substantial farm-houses, situated generally on heights called 'Inches,' still rise like islands out of the sea of grain and grass, as formerly, when they got their names, they rose out of the inland sea which the estuary of the Tay must then have formed. Certainly one main current of the river once flowed along the base of the braes on which Annat is situated, six miles north of its present channel, as iron boat-rings have been found stapled into the rock at Fingask, while some knolls in Annat policy bear the name of 'Fiery Knowes,' which was supposed to be a corruption of 'Ferry Knowes.' The Raith Hill close by bears an ancient moat supposed to have been used as a place of council or of justice (rath), while the glen of Rait is commanded by the Hill of Baal, a reputed site of the ancient fire-worship of our forefathers. Thence their fires could be viewed over a vast extent of country, embracing not only the Carse of Gowrie and the Fife Lomonds, but the whole of Strathmore to the north, bounded by the magnificent barrier of the Grampians, with the unique cone of Schiehallion as its central peak. It was across this great strath that Malcolm's warriors were said to have marched from Dunkeld (seen to the north), carrying the boughs which they cut from the wood of Birnam, twelve miles to Macbeth's castle of Dunsinane (seen to the east), thus fulfilling the prediction that the castle would not be taken till Birnam Wood marched against it.

At the foot of Dunsinane Hill lies the village of Collace, which was Dr Andrew Bonar's first charge,[1] and whence he used often to ride over to preach on Sabbath evenings in the village of Rait with tones of tenderness and heart of love. The small church (a cottage turned by Mrs Moody Stuart at the Disruption into a place of worship)[2] was also favoured by the ministrations of other eminent men

---

[1] For details of Andrew Bonar's ministry in Collace, see *The Diary and Life of Andrew A. Bonar* (1893; repr. Edinburgh: The Banner of Truth Trust, 2015).—*P.*

[2] This primitive church has recently been replaced by a modern hall kindly presented by Mrs Armitstead, Castle Huntly.

Peter Ferguson, the deacon who stood at 'the plate' of the old chapel, and who, when the sermon was drawing to a close, lighted the candles for the last psalm in the late autumn evenings, was a superior man. He had reminiscences of King George IV's visit to Edinburgh in 1822, where, as a young man, he was attracted by the high wages offered—a guinea a day—to make dress suits for the royal festivities. On this occasion George IV was struck with admiration of three sisters

of God now gone to their reward. So that if the old proverb is still at all applicable, that 'the Carse has three wants—rain in summer, sun in winter, and the grace of God all the year round'—it is not for lack of means of grace. There on the Sabbath evenings we listened to the glorious gospel message faithfully delivered in the quaint phrases of Mr Joseph Wilson, the memorable sermons of Professor Bannerman, the earnest teaching of Mr Greig (father of the present head of the MacAll Mission in France), and the lucid diction of Dr Grierson, whose sacrifice of so much at the Disruption for conscience' sake was itself a sermon. So benevolent was his aspect that I remember once a feathered songster which had strayed in through the open church door at Errol, after flying in a scared manner hither and thither for an hour over the heads of the worshippers, at last utterly wearied, fled to the patriarchal minister for rest and clung to his bosom, while he gently placed his hands over it and gave it to one of his sons to carry out into the open heaven again. As years flowed on others, younger men, succeeded these, as they were called to their rest, and such were not confined to the Free Church, but the neighbouring United Presbyterian and Established ministers were associated with them.

To these services many came from a distance. A large contingent used often to drive over from Glendoick, the hospitable mansion of the late Laurence Craigie, Esq., whose family, Major and the Misses Craigie were among our parents' warmest friends, and to whose generous support the Free Church in the district has been largely indebted. The manse family used also to come over from Free Kinfauns, one of whom writes: 'Your father is associated with all my sweetest and holiest memories; and yet who am I to say so? There are such a multitude who will be telling you this, but not all

---

(cousins of our grandmother, Mrs Stuart)—Misses Lee—whose beauty was sung by the poet Campbell. The king presented a rose to the youngest, who married the Rev. C. C. Stewart of Scone Free Church, seven miles from Rait. She retained her grace of figure and features, delicacy of complexion and lovely smile, to the close of life.—*KMS*.

of them have the associations with the dear old church at Rait, and the wonderful services that seemed to bring us so near to heaven. You all, those here and those away from earth, come so close to my heart when I let my mind go back to these old days.' It is the feeling here expressed that led me to prefix to this chapter two stanzas from a song by the late Charles Spence, a mason in Rait, whose genius found expression both in his sculptures and his poems.[3] Such recollections lead one naturally to the family tomb in Kilspindie. To this hamlet our Scottish patriot, Sir William Wallace, was, as Blind Harry sang, taken as a boy, for safety, when his father having refused allegiance to Edward,

> His modyr fled with him frae Ellerslie,
> Till, Gowrie past, he dwelt in Kilspindie;

from which he was sent to attend school in Dundee. Two centuries later Kilspindie was the property of Archibald Douglas, High Treasurer of Scotland under James V, one of the heroes of the Lady of the Lake and of Scotch Ballads:—

> Archie Kilspindie, my ain Grey-Steel,
> Kilspindie who was aye trusty and leal.

In its peaceful churchyard about half a mile from Annat, on a rock overhanging the stream and under the shade of old elms, repose the ashes of many of those who were loved and loving. Besides General Stuart and our grandfather, there were buried here our mother's sister Robina, who was married to the Rev. John Milne of Free St Leonard's, Perth, and Eliza, her youngest sister; while Mary, who was married to the Rev. Napoleon Roussel, a distinguished French preacher and author, survived our mother and was laid beside her husband in Geneva. Their tombstone bears the true record: 'These all died in faith.' Their mother, Mrs Stuart of Annat, 'a most devoted and exemplary Christian lady, died in 1873. The doubts which with characteristic humility she sometimes expressed regarding her own

[3] A volume of his songs is now printed by Young & Co., Watergate, Perth.—*KMS.*

interest in Christ, while others could only see in her a most attractive example of the spirit of the Master she so well served and loved, were all dispelled on her death-bed.' Like the ancient patriarchs, ere departing she left a special blessing to each member of the family. 'He has been a faithful God to me,' she said, 'and I can testify that not one thing has failed of all the good things which the Lord my God spoke since I was left a widow with my fatherless children.' In answer to some inquiries about her suffering, she replied: 'I am perfectly happy. He maketh my heart to rejoice: for sixty years I've served him. I'll soon be among my own people.'

Our brother Andrew and sister Margaret also rest here. Andrew's tall manly figure and fine features were the fitting frame of a noble nature further beautified by divine grace. He had longed to be a minister of Christ, and when in the Divinity Hall he used to go down with other young men to help Christian work in Cowgatehead, in co-operation with Dr Thomas Smith, a work that was aided for many years by St Luke's. There he sat by a child ill with fever to let the mother go out for a little to a religious meeting. In speaking there on the street he was struck by a stone, and by unduly raising his voice to overpower the shouts of a big Irishman he seemed to injure his chest. He derived no benefit from a visit to Madeira, his birthplace, and died in September 1866. In a letter from Funchal he wrote: 'I had given myself to the work of the ministry sincerely and unreservedly. I was willing to suffer any privations and to spend and be spent in it; but I was not willing to give it up. I did not count it among the *all* things to be counted loss for the excellency of the knowledge of Christ. The two things had become to me inseparable; loving Christ and serving him in the ministry. God has, I trust, enabled me to look contentedly forward to the future with the possibility of never being permitted to proclaim publicly the gospel of his Son.' A beautiful address by him on *The Christian Race* was published as one of the monthly 'Pink Tracts.'

Margaret, the eldest of our sisters, died in 1880. Like Andrew, she thought very little of self, and much of others, and in her divine grace was specially characterised by humility. Seventeen years after her death one of her friends, who had been impressed by her thoughtfulness in helping others, opened a small Convalescent Home in Juniper Green which she has called after her—'Stuart Cottage'—and a medallion likeness of her is fitted into the overmantel of the sitting-room, with an inscription and the text: 'I thank my God upon every remembrance of you.'

When visiting towards the close of his life the resting-place of our dead, which then contained the dust of one nearer and dearer to him than all, our father pointed to a little bird that had flown in through the iron bars on the roof of the tomb, and was singing among the varied ferns and lily-of-the-valley that keep the built-in plot green, as a symbol of the joy of life in the midst of death. About the same time (1894) another lesson was suggested to him by 'a singularly beautiful greenfinch, which,' he writes in his diary, 'I saw entangled in the net spread over the strawberries to protect them from thrushes and blackbirds. The net was sorely twisted about it, and it stoutly resisted my attempts to relieve it, which at last I did by breaking the net, and how joyously it then soared away and escaped! Even so has the Lord today broken Satan's snare for me and set me free with holy liberty.

> Our soul's escapèd, as a bird
> Out of the fowler's snare;
> The snare asunder broken is,
> And we escapèd are (Psa. 124:7, *Scottish Psalter*).

'The beautiful bird that was caught in the net yesterday was bound and entangled with it more than I could have thought possible, and it took the cutting of many strings to relieve it, and it has brought to me these two thoughts: First, how utterly helpless we are in ourselves to break "the snare of the devil" in which we have been taken, and how the strong arm of the Lord can set us free; next, that what we may have thought only a passing entanglement of Satan belongs to the whole network of his wiles, and that when the Lord

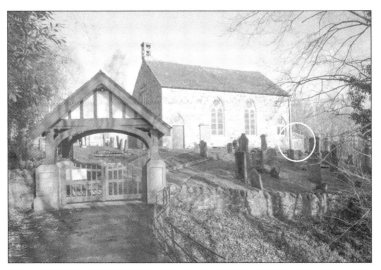

Kilspindie Church and churchyard—The family tomb of the Stuarts of Annat can be seen immediately to the right of the church building.—P.

The Stuart family tomb at Kilspindie. The long rectangular plaque commemorates the tomb's restoration in 2007 by Sir Mark Moody-Stuart, great-grandson of Alexander Moody Stuart.—P.

breaks the present snare, he at the same time cuts through all his wiles, past and present.'

Although he never evinced any taste either for singing or music, his ear was so appreciative of musical tones that he could distinguish all our singing birds by their notes, and knew the hours of the early morning by having observed at what hour each of our warblers began his song.

Of the same garden he writes: 'Two or three days ago on the garden-seat I recalled the forenoon, fifty-five years ago, when M'Cheyne[4] and Andrew Bonar sat with me there in holy meditation, and, I think, in prayer together; and the thought was very pleasing to me that at that same hour they might also be recalling our hallowed converse in the earthly garden and expecting me, though greatly less worthy, soon to join them in the heavenly paradise.'

In front of the dining-room window stood a large Swedish juniper, and in certain states of the atmosphere a fire might be seen burning briskly in the midst of the bush—the reflection of that in the room. One of the family, knowing his father's deep reverence of spirit, was almost surprised to hear him say, as he gazed at it one day: *Nec tamen consumebatur* ('Yet the bush was not burnt'). On thinking it over, he wondered whether his father suggested as the interpretation of the text that the fire Moses saw was the reflection of the glory of God. 'In passing through the lobby,' writes Dr Moody Stuart, 'I was arrested by what I thought was a withered

---

[4] The note-book containing the last sermons of Robert Murray M'Cheyne, in his own careful and clear handwriting, were given me as a memorial of him. The first sermon is on 'Lot's Choice,' dated 9 November 1842. The last, written just before his fatal illness, is on the 'Eternal Inheritance' (Heb. 9:15). Among the closing words in the concluding application are: 3. 'The amazing love of Christ to the called'; of which he writes: 'We can only glance at it now, we shall gaze into it through all eternity'. 4. 'The peace of believing: "Comfort ye, comfort ye, my people." Your past sins are borne and done away. God is pacified for all you have done against him.' With these last words of this good servant—

'Closed was his day,
And the hand that had written it
Laid it away.'—*KMS*.

Annat Cottage

evergreen among the shrubs at the back of the house, which I supposed must have been killed by the severe winter frost, and was
only now showing its fatal injury. But on taking my eye-glass I saw
with surprise that it was a red flowering currant rapidly bursting
into blossom, and that the plant was not clothed with the withered
foliage of death but with the luxuriance and beauty of life. Then I
trustfully and joyfully asked: Has my soul, so covered with dead
works, been stripped by the Lord of its old raiment and clothed
with the robe of righteousness and the garments of salvation in my
loving and beloved Saviour Jesus Christ?'

From our father's having no aptitude for business, the management of the estate (always an anxious matter with a small property)
fell too heavily upon our mother, but this did not arise at all from
his considering such cares or pleasures inconsistent with his high
ideal of a Christian life; it was merely that he had neither the taste
nor faculty for it. While not a great walker (we used to say that his
early pedestrian tour had cured him of that), he was fond of driving,
and managed with dexterity his spirited pair of ponies. One of the
avenues which he had laid out had rather sharp turns, and guests

were sometimes alarmed at the rate at which he drove downhill. Even such an experienced whip as Mr North when staying with us said: 'Moody Stuart, you'll take that turn at that pace once too often'; but he forgot that the teams he had been accustomed to drive were of a very different weight from these Shetlanders, and that not to speak of their sureness of foot, his host's hand was quite able to hold them up had they stumbled. He was also fond of swimming, and as there was no river or lake to swim in, he got an open-air swimming bath dug out, and paved with brick, which was stocked with trout from the Rait Burn to keep it free from insects. Surrounded with a thick evergreen hedge and fed by a spring, its water was only too cold to admit of most persons staying in it for any time with pleasure or even safety, but our father seemed never to be chilled by his daily plunge and swim. When lawn tennis came in, though already in old age, he set himself to learn it, and when considerably over seventy he might be seen with his coat off playing it most enthusiastically with his family.

He took an occasional share in parochial business, at meetings of heritors, and was chairman of the School Board. He also took an intelligent interest in the state of agriculture, and while not caring so much for the garden, had decided aptitude and skill in the planting and management of trees.

Reading was one of his favourite pursuits, and those who conversed with him were often surprised at the wide range of his information, and at his accurate acquaintance with all the philosophical and political, as well as the theological and religious, movements of the day. He liked to meet persons of good conversational powers who were thoroughly conversant with any important and interesting subject, and when thus brought into full play his own conversation was sparkling and racy, as well as informing. 'When he stayed in the house with us,' a friend writes, 'he was a delightful companion, so well up in natural history, and interested in puzzles and other things that amused the children. I often wished that we had seen more of him in this way.'

While he as well as our beloved mother made their home a very bright and happy one by their intelligent interest in all our pursuits, the readers of this memoir will see that he acted fully up to the remark which Professor Blaikie, who was for over fifty years his co-presbyter, recalls his having made to him when Dr Moody Stuart called on him, in 1845, after his marriage, that 'a minister's house should always be marked by a savour of Christ.'

One who was for years in his service at Annat writes: 'In all his walk and conversation I never observed him to be out of character as an ambassador of Christ. I do not think any one could be long in his presence without feeling much of the very atmosphere of heaven. He truly had the divine stamp of a man who could say: "God, before whom I stand." He appeared so calm in midst of trouble. Humility, patience and good temper were marked features in his character.'

It can be said without fear of contradiction that his character and conduct at home were in fullest harmony with his preaching. He emphatically wore the ornament of a meek and quiet spirit along with the white flower of a blameless life, and while he did not hold or teach the doctrine of perfection, the members of his family and household who knew him most intimately would be the first to testify that they never knew any one who more nearly attained it; while yet his motto ever was: 'Not as though I had already attained, either were already perfect, but I press on.' When asked once to define self-denial, he replied: 'To act towards self as Peter did towards his Lord, when he said, "I know not the man"': and few could have exemplified this definition more beautifully than he did in his whole life.

Occasionally our holidays were spent in other districts of Scotland. Two summers successively (1863–4) we passed in Inverness-shire, where we stayed in the old house of Corrimony, placed at our father's disposal by the proprietor, the late Thomas Ogilvie, Esq.[5] The schoolhouse where Mr Moody Stuart used to preach on

[5] Mr Ogilvie was a cousin of Mr Gladstone, whom he used to call 'William

Sabbaths had packed audiences, as even Gaelic-speaking people could follow his plain style, with its emphatic repetitions. We walked to divine service past a very perfect Druid altar, whose stone slab still bore the holes into which the blood of human sacrifices had once been drained, and its contrast with the great New Testament self-sacrifice of Calvary, where One died for all, was impressively exhibited, while we heard from the lips of one who had drunk in its meaning the glorious revelation that 'God is love.'

The people at the head of Glenurquhart were rather primitive. A son of a shepherd, who lived some miles over the moor, was dying of consumption. My brother Andrew and I used to visit him, and on entering the cottage one day I was startled to see a black coffin laid in the doorway. On coming in, I said to the mother that I was sorry I had not heard of his being worse, or I would have called again sooner. She said: oh, he was just much the same! and when my eyes recovered from the outside glare I saw that this was the case, and we were able to read and pray together as before. On going out I asked his mother what the coffin was here for, and she explained that as her husband had to go to Inverness, at any rate, he had just brought back a coffin with him, which lay in the passage till required.

A suffering, bedridden woman whom our mother used to visit replied to an inquiry she made as to where her pain was, that it was 'in her *east* side.' Scotch people are twitted with liking to fix their bearings by the points of the compass, but surely this national idiosyncrasy has seldom been carried to such an extent! The neighbouring farmer's wife, Mrs Blake, who came from Tweedside, had interesting recollections of Sir Walter Scott's youth, who as a boy, nearly eighty years before, used to come to her dairy for a glass of milk.

Ewart,' and whose later career he forecast accurately from his intimacy with him as a play-fellow when they were boys. He was a very accomplished man, and was the originator of the 'Corrimony' wire fences now so widely adopted.—*KMS*.

— 14 —

Ecclesiastical Work and Honours

And yet a banner thou hast given
To those who thee do fear;
That it by them, because of truth,
Displayed may appear.

—*Psalm 60:4 (Scottish Psalter)*

THE scope of this memoir, and the limited space available, preclude its embracing anything like a history of two important church questions in which Dr Moody Stuart took a leading part. The first of these was the union negotiations between the Free and United Presbyterian churches, which extended over ten years from 1863 to 1873. Twenty-five years have elapsed since this controversy was brought to a close, and fresh negotiations between the two churches on a new basis are now pending, and it was considered, both by himself and his family, that it would be very unwise at his great age, and in the enfeebled state of his health, that he should study this subject afresh, in its new aspects. It would have involved an examination into how far the opinions of either or both of the negotiating bodies had become modified during the last quarter of a century, as well as the precise terms of the new basis of union. He made it a point to go very thoroughly into any subject which he felt bound to examine, and threw himself with the whole force and ardour of his nature into the side which his judgment led him to espouse. Clearly, for one bordering upon ninety years to have studied anew all the bearings of this question, would have been to put a strain upon his physical constitution which it could not have borne, and would have disturbed that calm which the Christian desires to enjoy to the full in the closing years of a long and active life. It is fitting that the enjoyment of the eternal rest should have as its prelude, 'resting for a while apart' even in this world's 'desert place.'

In the Union controversy Mr Moody Stuart gave his thoughtful and influential support to those who opposed the carrying out of the union at that time, and did so at a very considerable sacrifice of his own feelings, as he found his judgment on this opposed to that of Principal Candlish, to whom he was very warmly attached on personal as well as public grounds. He felt afraid that by entering into the proposed union the Free Church would have to surrender her full testimony to one of the 'crown rights' of the Redeemer—his headship over the nation, which is the complement of that for which she had so nobly contended at the Disruption—his headship over the church.

On this matter he ably supported the views advocated by Drs. Begg, Julius Wood, Kennedy and William Balfour. One line in which he did great service was by thoroughly expounding the views of the Westminster divines on this subject as embodied in the Confession of Faith, and vindicating them from false interpretations. He showed that the place they assigned to the civil magistrate did not involve any Erastian interference with the spiritual independence of the church, although they stated that in certain circumstances the magistrate should summon an ecclesiastical synod to settle ecclesiastical questions. He proved that the power assigned in that whole symbol to the magistrate to 'take order that unity and peace be preserved in the church,' 'that all blasphemies and heresies be suppressed, all corruptions and abuses in worship and disciplinc be prevented or reformed, and all the ordinances of God duly settled, administered and observed,' denied to him the liberty of effecting these ends by the power of the sword. The only measures he was to take were to summon a synod, and to be present to see that they used only the keys of Christ's kingdom, which he had specially entrusted to them, and did not usurp civil power, which the same divine authority had assigned to the magistrate; while in duly settled kirks synods, whose members should be freely delegated by the churches,[1] should convene by their own intrinsic power derived from Christ, as often as was needful.

While considering the question of public endowment of the Church as quite distinct from, and very subordinate to, that of the public 'recognition' or 'establishment' by the magistrate, he did not unduly exalt even this latter, as some of its advocates do, for not very long ago he quoted to me with approval a remark of Professor Gibson, one of the strongest supporters of Establishment in our Assembly. During the heat of the contest, when a speaker alluded to the 'doctrine of Church Establishment, so ably defended by Dr Gibson,' the latter at once corrected him, saying, 'I never called it a *doctrine*: it is simply a church *principle*: Church Establishment is not a doctrine, and Voluntaryism is not a heresy.' In consequence of the strong opposition made by a large portion of the Free Church the negotiations for uniting these two churches were broken off in 1871, and arrangements were simply made in 1873 for closer relations between them.

Dr Moody Stuart earnestly desired that the three Presbyterian churches of Scotland should be united in one church, and to the close of his life considered that every effort should be made to achieve this. He was strongly opposed to the agitation for disestablishment carried on in the courts of the Free Church.

Mr Moody Stuart published his *Exposition of the Song of Solomon* in 1857, *The Three Marys* in 1862, *Capernaum* in 1863, *The Life of*

---

[1] It is one of those curious anomalies brought about by the march of events, that the most conscientious opponents of the disestablishment of the Church may find themselves forced to advocate this, if the only alternative offered to them should be the indiscriminate endowment of truth and error; while many who oppose establishment on the simple ground of religious equality, may in this case be found supporting it.—*KMS.*

Elizabeth, Last Duchess of Gordon in 1865, and *Recollections of Dr John Duncan* in 1872, to some of which reference has already been made. In the spring of 1875 the University of Edinburgh conferred upon him the degree of Doctor of Divinity, in recognition of the prominent position which he had so long occupied in the city, and of his having enriched the religious literature of the country by so many valuable works.

In the same year he was cordially and unanimously elected Moderator of the General Assembly of the Free Church of Scotland. When doubting as to his ability to undertake the onerous duties, Isaiah 61:10 came to him as a word from his Lord: 'Fear thou not; for I am with thee: I will strengthen thee; yea, I will help thee'; while he was also cheered, as well as amused, by a kindly message from his own former beadle, Alexander Stocks, who was now Assembly Officer, that he was 'to be sure not to decline, for he would do everything to make it quite easy for him!'

Dr Stewart of Leghorn, in nominating Dr Moody Stuart as his successor, introduced his name as that 'of a minister well known to the church at large, one who was so highly respected by all parties on account of his high Christian character and attainments.' He eulogised his work in the various positions which he had filled, and spoke warmly of his thirty-eight years' pastorate of St Luke's. 'During the long period of his ministry, there was no spiritual awakening which has taken place in Scotland with which his name has not been associated.' He referred to the notable contributions—theological, expository, and biographical—which he had found time, amid all his ministerial occupation, to make to religious literature; and said that that court would recognise that a stronger claim than all these was his having discharged lovingly, laboriously, and prayerfully the office of Convener of the Assembly's Jewish Committee for twenty-three years, and his efforts on behalf of the Protestant churches of Hungary and Bohemia, on which a great blessing had rested.

It has been said of him that 'when called to special service he always reached a high ideal, and that he attained this in the opening and closing addresses which he delivered from the Moderator's chair.' The subjects of these respectively were 'Recent Awakenings' and 'Higher Holiness.' They were immediately published as a pamphlet, which ran through several editions. Whatever he did was done with the utmost care, and done well. He threw all his ability into work which is often done carelessly, even by great men, because its interest and influence seem likely to be temporary. Pamphlets generally fall into rapid oblivion, perhaps without any great loss to the community, but some of Dr Moody Stuart's best work was given to the public in pamphlet form. That readers appreciated the quality of the work is shown not only by the demand for them at the time they were issued, but by the fact that so many of them have been carefully preserved by their possessors as valued treasures. This was true of these addresses.

After going over the list of the honoured names of ministers and elders removed from the Church during the previous year, he took occasion to speak a few words on the future state. 'Augustine and other fathers were surely right,' he said, 'in their idea that our bearing the image of Jesus Christ includes the likeness of apparent age, and that childhood will be brought up, and old age brought back to the likeness of the mature and perfect yet youthful manhood in which Jesus died and rose again. For however beautiful the hoary head is on earth, it is the ripe fruit of decay, and infancy with all its loveliness would cease to be attractive if it did not grow both in wisdom and in stature. It has been said acutely that "the oldest angel in heaven looks the youngest," or, in other words, is the brightest and looks the freshest, as if most newly fashioned by the hand of his Creator. Sin was never young, was never new, and never can be new. Sin was tarnishing, defilement, corruption, oldness from first to last, and in all its changing forms is corrupt and old for ever. But as in the new covenant and the new heart, that never become old, so in the new heavens and the new earth, the Lord Jesus makes all things new and incapable of growing old. And as he has himself the dew of youth for ever, so, doubtless, his redeemed will grow in beauty, in freshness and in dew-like youthfulness, while in their spirits, and in their bodies illuminated by their spirits, they become ever more nearly conformed to his transcendently glorious image, yet each retaining his own individuality, with his own new name, which no man knoweth save he that receiveth it. What a joyful conclave that will be of all the just, the holy, the true, the pure, the brave, the loving and the good, who have lived on this earth, and each not the image of another, but bearing the personal stamp impressed on him on earth, by his first birth in nature, and his second birth in grace, by his country, his family, his education, his history, his mercies, his trials, his falls, his recoveries, his tears, his songs, his life in Christ, his death in the Lord.'

His counsels given in this address on the conducting and following up of revival movements were felt to be weighty and valuable, as coming from one who had had such large and varied experience of them. He urged a deep sense of the need of conversion, reminded his brethren that if men are to be awakened from spiritual slumber they must be aroused, it may be somewhat roughly, so as to startle them with a sense of their danger. They must avoid encouraging to an excessive confidence in their own salvation those who may be merely under hopeful impressions; and there was great danger of taking at once too much notice of real or supposed cases of conversion. As regards doctrines to be taught at such times, they should teach that the letter of the gospel is powerless without the agency of the Holy Spirit; and while the doctrine of the divine sovereignty should not be pressed to the front, neither should it be omitted, else the young convert will be greatly troubled when he meets it for the first time in his own experience. They should press 'the fear of the Lord,' of which the elder M'Crie had said that it is the only recorded element in the worship of the angels, and of which Bunyan had said that he wished that the key of Man-soul was always in the keeping of Godly Fear.

In his closing address from the Moderator's chair, an equally important subject was dealt with, and he exhorted his brethren to aim at the attainment of higher personal holiness. On this topic he warned them against so dividing between the old and new natures in the person of the believer as to lead him to think lightly of sinfulness of the flesh, because of holiness of the spirit; against making such a distinction between the will and the emotions as to say that if the will is right we need not be distressed for wrong emotions; against reducing the divine standard of holiness to a measure of man's own. He reminded them of Dr Owen's weighty words, that 'he who contends against indwelling sin will find it to be present and powerful, as he who swims against the stream feels the strength of the current to which he is insensible who is floating down with it.' He said that while 'joy in the Holy Ghost' belongs to the highest holiness, godly sorrow for sin pertains to it also; that this holiness is attained by faith, because we are sanctified by grace; but not by faith alone, but by faith conjoined with intensity of prayer, by unreserved dedication of ourselves to God in Christ, and by attention to the details of holy living; and that hope and fear are true New Testament motives for holiness, being made even more emphatic by Jesus Christ than by Moses.

The sermon with which he opened the Assembly in 1876 was a striking one—published at the request of a large number of leading ministers—on 'Jesus Christ, the Bond of the Holy Universe'; and it is reprinted in the volume of his sermons, *The Path of the Redeemed*.[2]

On 22 June 1876, the Rev. J. G. Cunningham, Lochwinnoch, was happily settled as Dr Moody Stuart's colleague, thus furnishing him with the aid which he now required both in the pulpit and pastoral oversight of the congregation. His colleague, to whom he became warmly attached, was a man whose scholarly acquirements and wide culture were never obtruded in his proclamation of his Master's message, and who was in fullest sympathy with Dr Moody Stuart's views of divine grace.

The second great church controversy, in which Dr Moody Stuart was called in providence to take a leading part, was that which arose

---

[2] A. Moody Stuart, *The Path of the Redeemed: Sermons Preached in Free St Luke's Church, Edinburgh* (Edinburgh: MacNiven & Wallace, 1893).—*P.*

on the publication of the views of the late Professor Robertson Smith in regard to the genuineness and authenticity of the books of Moses and other portions of the Old Testament. He studied this whole question with great care, and came to the conclusion that these views were erroneous in fact and dangerous in their tendency, and should not be allowed to be taught in our theological halls to candidates for the holy ministry. This controversy, while not so protracted as the earlier one, was quite as acute, and Dr Moody Stuart deemed it to be more fundamental in its character, as in his judgment the position of Professor Robertson Smith and his supporters in their logical consequences threatened the very foundations of the faith. He indeed gladly acknowledged that many who held even extreme positions on the side of the new, or as its advocates styled it the 'higher' criticism, retained their faith in the divine word, as well as in the great doctrines of grace, but in his view their attitude was not consistent, and the ultimate result of holding their premises he considered must be the weakening of this faith to an extent which, whether greater or less, was fraught with grave peril.

The newer criticism, as is well known, regards the Pentateuch not as the work of Moses, but as the composition of a variety of authors extending to a late date in Jewish history, assigning to Moses the authorship only of a comparatively small portion. On this theory the first five books of Scripture form a collection of sections and sentences drawn from many far separated sources, carefully pieced together so as to form a whole.[3] This position was defended by the argument that the Confession of Faith says nothing about the authorship or date of the various books of Scripture, stating only that they all possess divine inspiration. The question then arose, Was this point one of first-rate importance? Dr Moody Stuart was convinced that it was. Had these books

[3] Strangely enough, a 'mosaic' is the word which best expresses the critics' view of the nature of the Mosaic writings; but we need hardly guard our readers against the mistake of a not very learned supporter of this theory, who claimed the sanction of antiquity for it, being under the impression that the term 'mosaic' was derived from Moses instead of from the Temple of the *Muses*!—KMS.

been anonymous, like some books of Scripture, different views might have allowably been entertained as to their authorship; but all of them, except the first, claim over and over again that the words were spoken, the ordinances of worship instituted and the laws promulgated by Moses personally, while the new critics taught that many of these laws and ordinances of worship were not instituted till ages after the death of Israel's great lawgiver. Their being issued under the name of Moses they held to be a device or fiction, in accordance with a supposed literary usage of the time, to secure for them the highest sanction. The theory that these authors 'personated' Moses, Dr Moody Stuart regarded as inconsistent with their being divinely inspired. In the volume which he published on this subject, *The Bible True to Itself*, which contained the substance of the speeches he made on this important subject in the church courts, carefully put into one connected treatise covering the entire ground of controversy, he shows that this theory reverses the whole current of religious history as presented to us in the Old Testament, being framed by its originators on the Continent to suit their view that the Old Testament religion had grown up by a process of orderly natural evolution. It implied, further, that the theory of inspiration held by its supporters covered the use by the inspired writers of expedients of a very questionable moral character. It demanded the admission of errors in Holy Scripture in matters of fact and history; and since Jesus Christ himself attributes these writings to Moses and others to David, which this criticism denies to them, it involved a very low view of the Saviour's supreme authority as a divine teacher. At the same time these teachers presented Christ, as contrasted with the Scriptures, as the object of faith. 'In these days,' Dr Moody Stuart writes in his diary, 'many good and able men count it a great discovery and a grand principle that the authority on which we are to trust is not the Bible but Christ, and so they have no scruple in making the Bible one of the least trustworthy of all books; yet we know nothing of Christ except what we read in the

Bible, and when it is discredited men can have no Christ except by their own conception. The authority of both is supreme. We have both or we have neither.'

In vindicating the church's historical position in regard to the Pentateuch, he pointed out that the finding in the Temple in the reign of Josiah, by Hilkiah the high priest, of the book which is called 'The Book of the Law of the Lord given by Moses' (2 Chron. 34:14), does not imply that the Book of Deuteronomy was then for the first time published to the Jews, as the critics assert, for a statute which is only inscribed in this book (Deut. 24:16) is quoted (in 2 Kings 14:6) as having 200 years before Josiah's time guided the conduct of King Amaziah in not slaying the children of his father's murderers.

In regard to Israel's Service of Song, he argues that the constant ascription of the origin of vocal and instrumental praise in the Temple not to Moses, but to David, proves that no prophet, priest, or king was invested with authority to issue new religious ordinances in the name of Moses. Also that the absence of any allusion in Deuteronomy to any Service of Song proves that it was written before the time of King David, and not in the late reign of Josiah, with the view, as the critics allege, of bringing down the institutions of Israel to that date. If this were the case Deuteronomy must have included the institution of praise.

Again he shows that Deuteronomy interweaves through its entire laws the edict for the extermination of the Canaanites (chaps 7, 9, 20, 31); that the issuing of such an edict not when these races were in open warfare with the Jews and leading them away from Jehovah by their foul and bloody idolatries, as was the case when Moses issued it, but after they had been living for centuries as peaceful citizens among them, protected by law, would have been an order for the treacherous massacre of tens or hundreds of thousands of their confiding and helpless subjects, repugnant as much to the character of Moses as to that of Christ. Yet such a treacherous massacre, comparable to that of St Bartholomew, must have been the design of the author of Deuteronomy if it were written in the days of Josiah or later, an idea, 'contrary to all righteousness, all covenant keeping, all humanity.' We cannot go further into this important subject, but readers who may wish to study it more fully are referred to the volume, *The Bible True to Itself*.[4]

The amount of ingenuity and learning displayed by the advocates of the new views was very great; though one is tempted to think they might have made as good a case against, say, the historical truth of the debate on this subject in the General Assembly of 1881, when the tide turned in favour of the old views, from the fact that the first name on the list of those supporting the mosaic authorship is that of *Adam*, and the last that of *Moses Winning*! It might be averred that such suspicious names proved that the debate and vote were a fabrication!

In some cases the arguments of this book did not receive the justice of being carefully studied. I took it down from the bookcase of a brother minister, whose library was of a markedly broad-church character, wondering how it had got on his shelves, and on opening found that it had been presented to him, and that no single page was cut[5] except the title! Others, however, prized it more highly. A Free Church minister of an important charge wrote to the author: 'The part of your volume which had been issued in pamphlet form had found its way into my waste-paper basket, but in clearing out it attracted my attention, and I read it with great delight. I write to express my gratitude for the profit I have derived from your book. I write as one who did doubt; my doubts are now gone. I had great difficulty in connection with the Pentateuch and the latter part of Isaiah. I seem to have none now.'

The eminent theologian, Professor Godet wrote:—

Neuchâtel, 21 Feb. 1885.

Dear Sir,

I am much obliged to you for the work which you have had

---

[4] A. Moody Stuart, *The Bible True to Itself: A Treatise on the Historical Truth of the Old Testament* (London: James Nisbet, 1884).—*P.*

[5] The older method of book production often required the reader to cut pages at their edges in order to separate them.—*P.*

the goodness to send to me. I have already found in it many things which have greatly interested and seriously instructed me. The church of Christ could not with impunity lose her confidence in the Pentateuch, which is the foundation of the Scriptures, and I am amazed at the want of anxiety with which I see many Christian theologians viewing this critical school which undermines this foundation with such alarming success. But it is not *enough* to anathematise them. We must have more reason on our side than they. And here is the difficulty. Theology is called to an entirely new effort. And it appears to me, so far as I have already given a first reading to your work, that there is there a study well fitted to cause reflection alike to those who regard the question with entire placidity, and those who believe it has been solved by what is called the Modern School. May God grant great success to your labour so serious, so profound, above all among your young divines!

Yours, very devoted in a common faith,

F. GODET

In a long letter the late Canon Liddon wrote:—

3 Amen Court,
St Paul's, 19 Aug. 1885.

My Dear Sir,

I am very much obliged to you for your book. I need not say how thankfully I rejoice at every effort in this direction, and should like to add, if it is not impertinent in me to do so, that you seem to me to have succeeded remarkably in combining the results of critical study with such recognition of the conditions of being generally understood, as alone can make a book generally useful. In particular, I have read with great pleasure what you say about the hypothesis of a second Isaiah.

... The odd thing about both Wellhausen and Professor R. Smith is, that they seem to think that the religious sanctions and uses of the Bible will survive if these theories of its 'growth' should be accepted. But older rationalists[6] were less able to blind their eyes to the necessary effect of arranging the contents of Scripture on an *a priori* theory that nothing could be accepted as history which could not be naturally accounted for. …

I pray God to enable you to continue labours which are so much needed in our day.

Pray believe me to be,

Yours very faithfully and obliged,

H. P. LIDDON

Professor Stanley Leathes, D.D., wrote: 'In some of your answers to Robertson Smith it seems to me that your argument is simply conclusive, and personally I have to thank you for very valuable help.'

Letters of cordial appreciation of this volume came also from such well-known English exegetes as Dr Joseph Angus, Canon Faussett and Dean Plumptre, and from Dr Green and Dr Howard Crosbie of the United States.[7]

Nor was an appreciative estimate of his work confined wholly to those who agreed with his views. Dr Robertson Nicoll, while not accepting his conclusions, writes: 'I may say that I think Dr Moody Stuart deserves great credit for being almost the only one of Dr Robertson Smith's opponents who made a serious and sustained effort to understand precisely the ground on which the new criticism was defended, and to reply to it.'

Sir William Mackinnon, Bart., interested himself in circulating this volume among theological students and others. It was translated into Dutch by Mr Schill, of the Hague, to try to counteract in some degree the mischief wrought in Holland by Professor Kuenen, the originator of this school.

---

[6] The Scottish school, however, remained evangelical in doctrine while adopting the historical theories of Wellhausen.—*KMS.*

[7] Mr C. H. Spurgeon, in conveying warm thanks for a copy, wrote: 'I love the love of saints, for it is an outflow of the love of Christ. May the best of blessings drop upon you as the latter rain! We shall meet at the dawn.'—*KMS.*

While in his latest diary regret is recorded by Dr Moody Stuart that he had sometimes expressed himself with undue warmth,[8] his views remained unaltered, and as all his friends knew how deeply concerned he continued till the close of life to be in the rise, development and issues of this question, the compiler has felt he would not be giving a fair presentation of him if this subject had been passed over in this memoir in a more cursory manner.

The year 1885 was the jubilee of Dr Moody Stuart's ministerial work in Edinburgh, and his congregation with many other friends resolved to celebrate it by the presentation of his portrait. This was executed by Mr Hole, and is a very successful likeness, the subject being drawn as descending the pulpit stair after the benediction, with that preoccupied and thoughtful expression which was characteristic of him at such times. The donors of the portrait met in the Presbytery Hall on 18 November 1885; Dr Burns, of Kirkliston, opening the meeting with prayer. Principal Brown, of Aberdeen, Moderator of the Assembly, presided, and delivered a touching address. He was followed by Dr Somerville, Dr Elder, Mr T. Stothert, etc.

A second meeting, presided over by his colleague, Dr Cunningham, was held in the evening, at which Dr Moody Stuart reviewed the Lord's dealings with the congregation during fifty years, and said that of those who were members in 1835, he had reason to believe that he alone was left. An illuminated address was presented to Mr Macdonald on completing the jubilee of his eldership, and special reference was made to the lamented decease of Mr Brown Douglas. This full-length portrait now hangs in the Moncrieff Hall, off the Free Assembly Hall, and a replica was presented to Mrs Moody Stuart.[9]

In 1887, which was the jubilee of his ordination, gratifying addresses of congratulation, couched in very appreciative terms,

---

[8] When he heard of Professor Robertson Smith being seriously ill, he included his case among those whom he remembered in his prayers.—*KMS.*

[9] This full-length painting now appears to be lost, along with the replica. A monochrome engraving of the painting appears on p. 198.—*P.*

were presented to him by his own Presbytery of Edinburgh, and by the Jewish Committee.

On this occasion a donation of £10 was sent to him for the Jewish Mission from 'a friend who, remembering 1837, wishes this to be her thank-offering for the Queen's jubilee[10] and Dr Moody Stuart's.' The donor was not a member of St Luke's, but had got spiritual good in the 'Bazaar' fifty years before.

The following lines are from a sonnet on his jubilee by one of his flock, Miss J. M. Gillies:—

> The summer day, with song and fragrance sweet,
> With radiant sun and zephyr wind, has died
> Into the rest of eve.
>   … So let it sleep.
> And wouldst thou, loving and beloved, recall
> Thy manhood's strength, with its pure noble grace?
> Ah! no. The brightest day has ne'er the fall
> Of noble sunset that illumes thy face;
>   To others thou hast been a sun so bright:
>   To thee, at evening time may there be light!

---

[10] 1887 was the year of Queen Victoria's golden jubilee.—*P.*

*Engraving of the painting presented on the occasion of Dr Moody Stuart's
fifty years as a minister in Edinburgh, 1887.*

— 15 —

The Correspondent[1]

So mused I silently, as o'er and o'er
I turned the wrinkled pages lying round,
The well-worn relics of long-buried years,
Which rise to life again in every page;
Brief memories of love, and grief, and peace,
With glimpses of still unforgotten scenes;—
Faces and names of former days are here.

—*Horatius Bonar*

Letter to a Young Lady before her Marriage

Edinburgh, 12 March 1856.

My Dear Miss Bethune,

I was greatly obliged by Sir John communicating the interesting intelligence concerning yourself.[2] I am much delighted, my dear friend, at the prospect before you, because I understand that it is a union in the Lord. It is good to learn in whatever state we are therewith to be content, and therein to glorify God, and it is impossible for us to know the position in which we may best secure our chief end of glorifying and enjoying

---

[1] Portions of these letters that are personal are omitted.—*KMS.*

[2] Written to Lady Anne Campbell (sister of the late Earl of Lindsay) on the announcement of her approaching marriage to John T. Campbell, Esq.—*KMS.*

him. At the same time the most *eventful* life *providentially* has in it much fitness to be also the most eventful and fruitful in the history of grace in our souls. In your present position you are indeed united both to Christ and to the body of Christ on the earth, but you are at the same time a certain free spectator of the history of the human family. You are now in the providence of God to be united not to the world but to the human family, and partaker of its interests, bound up with its joys and sorrows, and sharer in the manifold providential events by which it is tried, helped, hindered. It is a *great* change, greater in this respect than you can at present conceive, but through grace it is a *good* change, fitting you to learn more good, to receive more good, and to do more good.

Only, my dear friend, remember this, *it needs more grace.* The amount of grace that is sufficient for single life is not sufficient for married life, and what seemed a fair amount of grace in the daughter and sister seems often to evaporate and disappear in the wife and mother. But the Lord will give more grace, and with more grace there is unquestionably more ample opportunity both for its exercise and its influence.

* * *

We have had in our congregation more awakening and conversion than for many years past. There were some most interesting cases, perhaps toward thirty in all, in the beginning of winter. Oh that it were renewed and increased! Mrs Moody Stuart joins me in kindest regards and best wishes.

Yours, with sincerest regard,

A. MOODY STUART

Counsel to a Preacher

Brownlow North, Esq.

13 August 1859.

My Dear Brother,

I trust the Lord is still helping you in Ireland, and that he will grant you such a baptism as will make you a great blessing on your return to Scotland. How little man is! How the Lord can work mightily with the weakest instruments, or with next to none (for with absolutely none he rarely works); how he uses us for his glory, and for his glory uses us not! We think as if he could not do without us, he sets us quickly aside; we think that nothing can be done by us even through him, and then he takes the worm to thrash the mountains.

Our communion roll in March was 610. At our July communion it was 718, and I do think the greater part of the increase, partly young persons and partly members from other churches, consisted of souls added to the Lord. … Oh may he empty all of us of ourselves, and fill us with his Spirit. May we forget ourselves and remember the Lord!

The Lord keep you continually!

Ever affectionately yours,

A. Moody Stuart

On the Illness of an Infant

4 February 1860.

My Dear Mrs Brown Douglas,

I sympathise most sincerely with your husband and yourself in your severe trial, and I pray that the Lord may soon remove it and give you a song of praise. The way I always take in such cases is to look steadfastly at it in its most terrible issue, as what the Lord threatens; then to bow down beneath this as what we can't avert, and what *we* deserve, especially in the case of an infant, where the trial is for us rather than for the child; then to plead as earnestly as if the life of the child depended on our prayer, and on nothing else whatever—as if our prayer were its life and our silence its death.

Oh what answers the Lord gives us when so enabled to pray, and what entrance into the heart of his love, and how blessed the result whatever it may be! It is a great encouragement to remember that if the Lord purposes to give much grace to the child, it is one of the ways he often takes to draw out much prayer on its behalf.

* * *

It seems strange, but somehow we cannot often get or keep such nearness to him when all goes smoothly as when we are chastened and tried. What the Ferryden fisherman said to me is often true of us all—he complained of coldness and deadness since his conversion, but added, 'Yet when a cross comes, Christ is always uppermost.' How often we need a cross to make Christ fully and gloriously uppermost! I trust and pray that you may both find it so abundantly in your present trial.

The blessed truth that 'whom the Lord loveth he chasteneth' extends in his purposes of mercy far beyond our present consciousness of benefit. With us all, and much more with children, he *prepares blessing*, and he sends chastening to plough and harrow the heart to receive it, in a manner most mysterious to us, but very evident in the end.

Ever affectionately yours,

A. Moody Stuart

On the Death of a Father

Rait, 22 August 1870.

My Dear Miss Sprot,

I am deeply grieved to see the account of your sad bereavement. The heart knoweth its own bitterness and scarcely any other can enter into it. But there is One who knows it all, and in every case there is true consolation in referring all our thoughts to him—in saying, 'Lord, I am not sufficient to think anything of myself, what wilt thou have me to think?' I have found this an unspeakable relief in sorrow, because you doubt the consolations which others suggest and which your own mind clings to, but when you have first referred all to the Lord himself you have the persuasion that these are the thoughts which he would have you think and the consolations which come from himself. Jesus Christ is the nearest and dearest of all, and he remains. 'When my father and my mother forsake me, the Lord will take me up.' The soldier David leaves himself in that case in the Lord's own hands to be taken up by him as a little child in his own arms; and not merely asking the Lord to take him up, but confessing that he will take him up; and his words are given to us to be made ours and if we make them ours they will not fail us. Christ Jesus has borne all *our* sorrows, and he chastens us now that we may enter into *his* sufferings and have fellowship with him in his sorrow for us. What an honour to be taken thus into his friendship, and how lovingly should we kiss the rod that makes us partakers with him! With much sorrow for you and your trial,

Ever affectionately yours,

A. MOODY STUART

To a Young Lady drawing near Death

Edinburgh, 24 Oct. 1876.

My Dear Miss Shepherd,[3]

I have received your kind message, and desire to sympathise with you in your weakness and suffering. 'How many are thy thoughts which are to usward! I am poor and needy but the Lord thinketh on me.' His works are known to him from the

[3] Daughter of the late Captain Shepherd of Kirkville.—*KMS*.

beginning, and he has ordered all your way. His work is perfect, even as regards us, both in wisdom and in love, and he will perfect that which concerneth us. How blessed it will be afterwards when we shall see what a beautiful piece of workmanship he will have made out of our poor selves to the praise of his grace! Yet the one great good is this—if we have been brought to sing 'Worthy is the Lamb!' That song is always true, and it will never fail in life, or death, or before the great White Throne. May the Lord himself bless you, and keep you, and cause his face to shine on you, and give you the peace that passeth understanding, and may the everlasting arms be underneath you.

Believe me, very affectionately yours,

A. Moody Stuart

When the writer of this note was called himself to pass through the Dark Valley some twenty years later, the text which he sent his friend, as suitable for a deathbed, and for entering heaven with, 'Worthy is the Lamb that was slain,' was constantly on his own lips. Miss Shepherd's sister has told me that they found the note under her pillow after her death, and that they can never forget the heavenly light that illuminated her face as she passed away with the words of the text thus sent her on her lips.

To a Wife watching her Husband's Deathbed

Bank House, Lossiemouth,

10 December 1887.

My Dear Mrs McConnachie,

It is a great disappointment to me to be deprived of seeing your dear husband again and bidding him a last farewell on earth in the earnest hope of meeting again at the marriage supper of the Lamb. When the hour comes may the Lord Jesus say to him, 'I will come and receive you to myself.' It is not death that comes to take him but his Redeemer from death, saying, 'Today *thou* shalt be with *me* in Paradise. Come with me from Lebanon, my spouse; from the lions' dens, from the mountains of the leopards.' He appoints the way, the place, the hour, for 'precious in the sight of the Lord is the death of his saints.' These words have often been a comfort to myself: 'Hope to the end for the grace that is to be brought unto you at the revelation of Jesus Christ'; it is not merely the glory for which we feel unfit, but the abundant *grace* that is to be given to us among 'the spirits of the just made perfect.'

When we sat together at the Lord's Supper I little thought the words were to be fulfilled so soon, 'Ye do show the Lord's death till he come.'

Yours, in much sympathy and affection,

A. Moody Stuart

Letter to his Brother in Weak Health

Lossiemouth, 10 January 1888.

My Very Dear Robert,

I was very sorry to hear that you are so poorly, and trust that the Lord may strengthen you as the spring approaches. These words have often run in my mind in connection with leaving the manse: 'In my Father's house are many mansions.' One afternoon here, a little before sunset, I had been looking at a fine rainbow, and just as it was disappearing I was startled with the sight of a magnificent mansion in another part of the same cloud. At first I supposed that, like the rainbow, it belonged entirely to the cloud. It was by far the most singular and, I think, the most beautiful sight I have ever seen. After recovering from my surprise and looking at it more closely, I saw it was the reflection of a villa on a cliff near us, but greatly magnified and covering a large section of the heavens. The house was as distinct as any house on the earth, with windows and roof and chimneys, with a higher centre and lower wings, and fringed with bushes at the sides. It always brings back to me the blessed hope: 'In my Father's house there are many mansions.'

Your affectionate brother,

A. MOODY STUART

To Miss M. Robertson when Seriously Ill

Annat, Errol, 20 April 1889.

My Dear Miss Marianne,

I am grieved to hear that you are so ill, for though I knew you were poorly I was not aware that the illness was so serious. May the Lord graciously restore you, if it is his blessed will,—if otherwise, 'may an entrance be ministered to you abundantly into the everlasting kingdom of our Lord and Saviour Jesus Christ.' For myself I have just been dwelling on the words, of which I would affectionately remind you, 'Having loved his own which were in the world he loved them *unto the end*' and on the wondrous proof he immediately gave them of his love by washing their feet. When our end draws near he comes to us graciously to bestow a special washing from all the sins of the whole course of our life. These indeed are more than the hairs of our head, but he loves to wash them all away, and to give us a new song to him that loved us and washed us in his own blood. He delights to make us white as snow, and his atoning blood is infinitely more cleansing than sin is defiling; and he clothes us in his own spotless raiment that we may 'walk with him in white' in the many mansions of our Father's House.

* * *

Ever yours in the love of Christ,

A. MOODY STUART

To One Drawing near the End of Life (Miss Janet Robertson)

3 The University,

Glasgow, 20 January 1891.

My Very Dear Friend,

I am very sorry to hear of your great weakness, and would affectionately remind you of the words of our Lord Jesus spoken to Paul, but *written* for me and for *you*: 'My grace is sufficient for thee, for my strength is made perfect in *weakness*.' Our weakness is allotted to us by our Lord that 'the power of Christ may rest upon us.'

The Good Shepherd who laid down his life for the sheep takes a special care of the weak in the flock. One day, in looking out of my window in Queen Street, I saw a large flock of sheep in the street, and a shepherd with his sheep is always an attractive sight.

To my surprise, the whole flock stopped for a good while opposite the church, but I soon saw the reason when I looked at the shepherd and saw that he had a lamb in his arms, which seemed to have fallen down on the way; and he left the ninety and nine and was binding up the wounds of this weakest of all the flock. Even so, my dear sister in Christ, the Good Shepherd is thinking of you, and carefully tending you, and saying to yourself: '*My* strength is made perfect in (your) weakness.'

*   *   *

I am, ever affectionately yours,

A. MOODY STUART

In the following short note the writer touches on an aspect of heaven of which he often spoke, *viz.*, its 'home-like' character. He used to say that with the presence of his Lord, whom the Christian knows, as well as loves, better than any other, and that of so many of those he loved on earth, the child of God would not have any feeling of 'strangeness' in entering the unseen world.

Answering a Letter of Sympathy

Annat, Errol, 29 May 1891.

My Very Dear Miss Cook,

Accept my most cordial thanks for your sympathy and very kind letter. Your loving remembrance of my dear wife is very soothing and gratifying to me. The blank is very great, but the promise very sure: 'I will not leave you comfortless, I will come to you.' For me, it cannot be long till I likewise shall be called 'to be present (to be at home) with the Lord.' What a hope it is, that we shall there be at once *'at home'* as we have never been till then. Meanwhile may it be given to me to say, that 'to me to live is Christ and to die is gain!'

* * *

Yours, very affectionately,

A. MOODY STUART

To Mrs John Milne, when Drawing near Death

Annat, Errol, 4 May 1892.

My Very Dear Sister,

We are both now experiencing the truth of our Lord's words, 'When thou wast young thou girdedst thyself, and walkedst whether thou wouldest,' and how different it is when we are old and inwardly helpless. We are thrown back on our whole past life, our own past sins and present sinfulness, but far more on our Lord's past grace and present exceeding mercy. When the conflict is sorest we must still thankfully say, 'By the grace of God I am what I am,' and however humbled for our sins we must not dishonour our God by denying his own grace. Both of us are compassed about with a great cloud of *witnesses*, and we may well view with *patience* the rest of our race that is so nearly ended, 'for now is our salvation nearer than when we believed'; and when our Lord fulfils his word, 'I will come again and receive you to *myself*' it will seem as if we have never known salvation when compared with 'the grace that is to be brought to us at the revelation of Jesus Christ.' Let me send you two texts on which I am constantly falling back for myself: 'Jesus Christ came into the world to save sinners, of whom I am chief,' and 'Go thy way till the end be, for thou shalt rest and stand *in thy lot* at the end of the days.'

Ever yours, in most affectionate love,

A. Moody Stuart

Letter on the Death of a Mother

Annat, 7 May 1892.

My Dear Miss Mure,[4]

Accept my sincere sympathy with yourself and your sister in your great bereavement, in which you have my earnest prayer that in your earthly desolation your heavenly Father may be very near to you both. In committing the beloved remains to the grave you will 'go forth weeping bearing precious seed' in the assurance that the 'body is still united unto Christ,' and that what you 'sow in weakness he will raise in power, and what you sow in dishonour he will raise in glory.'

My dear friends, in now drawing near to Jesus, the Mediator of the New Covenant, you are coming to one more of 'the spirits of the just made perfect,' and in running 'the race set before you, looking unto Jesus,' you are compassed about with a great cloud of witnesses, amongst whom you have other dear ones gone before, and one more now added to the joyful company.

With much sympathy to you both,

Ever yours affectionately,

A. Moody Stuart

---

[4] Written on the death of Mrs Mure Macredie, of Perceton, widow of P. B. Mure Macredie, Esq., an influential Disruption elder. Their eldest son, the late Thomas M. Mure, advocate, was a noble Christian character. He was in great measure the originator of the Miners' Mission of the Free Church.—*KMS.*

On the Remembrance of Sin in Heaven

Annat, 10 June 1892.

My Dear Miss Sprot,

I entirely agree with you on the remembrance of sin in heaven. When God remembers our sin no more, he does not cease to know that we have sinned, but in his own mercy, through the blood of the Lamb, he loves and delights in the redeemed as much as if they had never sinned, and *much more*. And we will love much because we are forgiven much. We would regret not to remember, because we shall so rejoice and so glorify Christ in washing us whiter than snow.

In an article some years ago, one of our Professors, holding rightly that we must remember our sins although they are quite forgiven, finds difficulty in seeing how the recollection of sin that has injured others eternally can fail to make us unhappy, and says that happiness is not our chief good but holiness. This would be the case if sin were only forgiven, and not atoned for to the glory of God more than if we had never sinned. It is expressly written that there will be no more sorrow, and if the remembrance of sin could make us unhappy when we increase in holiness for ever, there would be an everlasting increase of misery. But thanks be to God there will be everlasting joy to us in him who 'loved us and washed us in his own blood.'

Adam can never forget his sin, but we all believe that the remembrance of it in heaven does not lessen his everlasting peace.

Ever yours affectionately,

A. MOODY STUART

At each New Year, and also on the recurrence of our communion seasons, my father used always to write showing his watchful interest in the spiritual welfare of my flock. I insert one of these notes, but indeed on their sacramental occasions he was much in prayer for any congregation with which he had any special associations.

New Year's Good Wishes

3 The University,
Glasgow, December, 1894.

My Dearest Kenneth,

For the opening of another year I have been thinking of this promise for you, 'Yet will I gather others to him beside those that are gathered—with great mercies will I gather thee.' It is good to enter on the year with faith and lively hope for the Lord's work among your people, and to embrace the promise, 'Open thy mouth wide and I will fill it.' It is the Lord's will that we should be enlarged and the people saved through the ministry of his own word, and the supply of his grace.

* * *

May the Lord richly grant to yourself and your dear wife[5] and each of your four children a very good New Year 'Full with the blessing of the Lord.' For myself I sometimes think of the Lord's words, 'The year of my redeemed,' and I pray that the coming year may be such a year to you all, and to yourself in the Lord's own work.

* * *

Ever your loving father,

A. MOODY STUART

Letter on Providential Direction

29 December 1896.

A happy New Year! is a very welcome greeting to you at present, for you are hoping that in the Lord's goodness it will be one of the happiest years of life both to yourself and to your

[5] Susan, youngest daughter of the late George Lyon Walker, Esq., of Garemount, Dumbartonshire.—*KMS.*

betrothed, and I pray that the Lord may grant it to you both in all things even beyond your expectation. '*Casting all* your care on him'; even in the *least* that concerns you, how good it is to know that if you are looking to him 'the hairs of your head are all numbered.' When you are covenanting to give yourselves to each other may you be graciously helped to yield yourselves daily to the Lord in the 'New Covenant,' which he desires and loves to make with you both, and to keep with you continually, giving himself you as your portion, and receiving you to himself as his.

* * *

I am glad to learn that you are committing yourself and your way into the hands of God, and to the disposal of his holy will. After we have done so he often tries us by keeping us *waiting*, to test if our submission is sincere, and to train us to patience, till patience have her *perfect* work. 'Commit thy way unto the Lord, trust also in him, and he will bring it to pass.' He often teaches us, 'My ways are not your ways, nor my thoughts your thoughts,' on very purpose that he may also say to us, 'I know the thoughts that I think toward you, saith the Lord, thoughts of peace and not of evil, to give you an expected end.' May he who openeth, and no man shutteth, and shutteth and no man openeth, prepare all your way! 'God is faithful who will with the temptation' (the trial) make a way to escape (literally *the* outgate), provided by himself when he allowed or ordered the trial. 'Though it tarry *wait* for it.' With him it is no after-thought but arranged in his purpose. Everything is to commit yourself as a helpless child into our heavenly Father's hand. And may the Lord grant you his saving and providing blessing and give to you a new song for all his mercies for the life that now is, and for the life to come.

Your ever affectionate,

A. MOODY STUART

The reference in the following note to the Lord's making up in a case of sickness for exclusion from the sanctuary by his nearness to the soul, is beautifully illustrated in the writer's own experience about this time, in Chapter 19, where his diary shows that this nearness of the Lord was to him a wondrous and brilliant reality.

To a Friend in Sickness

3 The University,
Glasgow, 28 January 1898.

My Dear Miss Buchanan,

I am grieved to hear that you are still laid aside, and I pray that your health may soon be restored by him who giveth strength to the weak in his own good time. 'He doeth all things well,' and it is in mercy and fatherly love that he chastens us. He can more than make up to us the want of outward means by his blessed nearness to our souls, and by the gift of his peace that passeth all understanding.

There is no exhausting of the fullness and manifold fitness of the promise, 'My grace is sufficient for thee, for my strength is made perfect in weakness.' Because he loves to reveal to us the all-sufficiency of his strength he takes away our strength, and eye hath not seen what he hath prepared for them that wait for him.

'The Lord bless thee and keep thee; the Lord make his face to shine on thee and give thee peace!'

Yours in much esteem and affection,

A. Moody Stuart

Letter to an old Assistant (the Rev. J. Howie Boyd, Carlisle)

Ellerslie, Crieff, 13 June 1898.

My Dear Friend,

I rejoice to know that the Lord himself has been upholding

you during these many years since we parted company. Truly a faithful God is our God, and through all our provocations he still delights to pardon and to bless us; and I pray that our gracious Lord may be in the midst of you by his free Spirit, reviving your soul and granting you a fresh start in the race set before you, looking unto Jesus, at the same time gathering to himself a new flock out of the many who are still outside in all our congregations.

My own eighty-ninth birthday falls on the 15th, the day after tomorrow, when, if the Lord will, I shall enter on my ninetieth year; a long life, with many sins and declensions, yet graciously strengthened to cleave to the Lord Jesus, who in his wondrous mercy has loved me and washed me from my sins in his own blood. Blessed be his name for ever and ever.

Yours in sincerest affection,

A. MOODY STUART

— 16 —

A Man of Prayer

Since then these three wait on thy throne,
   Ease, Power, and Love—I value Prayer so,
That were I to leave all but one,
   Wealth, fame, endowments, virtues all should go;
   I and dear Prayer would together dwell,
   And quickly gain for each inch lost an ell.

—George Herbert

D R Moody Stuart was pre-eminently a man of prayer. He assiduously cultivated private prayer. His prayers in the family were no mere formal acts of worship; they were very solemn, very earnest, realising the presence of the great God, and making others realise it also; yet in their pleadings, they almost amounted to a holy familiarity with God. In these prayers he almost always addressed his Maker by the Scriptural and endearing name of 'Father,' 'O Father!' 'Holy Father,' 'Heavenly Father'; and certainly he manifested filial trust and confidence in approaching him, and in leading others to the throne of grace. The American church standards give 'pleading' as a special part of prayer (omitted in other directories of worship). 'Pleading' was very characteristic of the prayers of this man of God. He often seemed to wrestle in prayer, like Jacob at Peniel, saying, 'I will not let thee go, except thou bless

215

me.' This was manifest also in his prayers in public, from which some worshippers said that they derived more spiritual help even than from his sermons. Of him it might truly be said that he prayed 'without ceasing'; that he 'prayed always, with all prayer and supplication in the Spirit, watching thereunto with all perseverance.' He felt that nothing was too small for him to bring to his God in prayer, and that nothing was too great for him to ask in Jesus' name.

Principal Rainy has told me that on one of my father's visits to Huntly, Mr Duncan Matheson had taken him round to see some aged Christian people, and that among others he engaged in prayer with one old woman who had a good deal of 'character', and who after each of his petitions interjected some ejaculation of assent, or comment. When my father at last asked that the Hearer of prayer would according to his promise give us *all things*, she exclaimed: '*All things*, na, that wad be a lift!' Her remark was not more characteristic of Scottish caution, even in religion, than the petition itself was of him who offered it. For while no one was more specific in the matter of his petitions than he, he also kept his eye always fixed on the largeness of the promises, and the power of God to fulfil them above all that we ask or think.

He often seemed to look for answers to prayer at once, and a favourite text of his was Isaiah 65:24: 'Before they call I will answer, and while they are yet speaking I will hear.' I remember well that when he and my uncle Mr Milne (whose ministry both in Perth and Calcutta was so largely blessed) had arranged in 1860 for the first of those religious gatherings which developed into the Perth Christian Conference, the latter came down to Annat to join in prayer along with my father that the divine blessing might be vouchsafed, and especially to supplicate that the weather might be favourable.

The meetings, which were to begin next morning, were to be held on the South Inch, and for several days it had been raining heavily, and there seemed no hope of any change of weather. Very earnestly did these two devoted servants of God, with the family assembled around them in our dining-room, pray that the rains might be restrained. After prayer my father walked forward to the large window, which commands a prospect of over twelve miles, and raising his eye-glass to view the sky, he exclaimed in a tone of disappointment and surprise: 'Oh, it's worse than ever!' Mr Milne smiled and said: 'Moody's impulsive,' and added 'now we'll wait and see.' In this instance the character of the two men seemed to be reversed. Mr Milne then drove back to Perth to complete the arrangements.

When beginning this memoir I met a minister of the Established Church, who has now retired from a useful ministry abroad, who told me that the last time he saw or heard my father was about forty years ago, when in travelling from the North, and having a detention in Perth, he went out and saw a large crowd on the Inch, and had the pleasure of listening to an address by my father. On my asking what sort of a day it was, he replied: 'It was a very fine day.' The morning had broken in bright sunshine, and no rain fell to interrupt any of the services.

Recalling my father's long connection with these Conferences the Earl of Moray writes: 'His addresses at the forenoon meetings, usually on some aspect of the Christian life, were characterised by freshness, power, and spirituality; while his remarks at the afternoon meetings on some branch of Christian work at home or abroad, and partaking more of a conversation, indicated his inner life as one of nearness to Christ and devotion to his Master. To his advanced age he adorned and enforced the gospel, and during one's life one can look to his example and walk before his fellow men.'

But while there was often holy urgency and importunity in his pleading, there was no lack of submission to the divine will, or of patience when his request was deferred, or in some cases denied. He sought to practise patience like that of Job as well as to commend it to others, of which he said, 'it was not the patience of indifference—no man ever felt bereavement more keenly than Job did; it was not the patience of stupidity—his was one of the greatest intellects that has been in the world. And it was not the patience of timidity—he said, 'I brake the jaws of the wicked and plucked the spoil out of his teeth.' It was the patience of submission to the holy sovereignty of God, of knowing that God could do no wrong, that God is good, and that everything that comes from his hand must be good. Grand old hero, formed by God's own hand! How blessed to be a man when a man through grace is capable of such patience as that!'

But if he was urgent and importunate in praying for temporal blessings for those dear to him, much more than for himself, he was still more urgent and importunate in his supplications for spiritual blessings both for himself and others. Delay in granting these did seem sometimes to affect him with a holy impatience. It was with him, as he said of Job, 'When there was the continued hiding of God's face, that Job's spirit could not endure. For God was far more to him than all else, than all others. That light of God's presence, that secret of God's covenant, that shining of Jehovah's face, of these he sighed, "Oh that I knew where I might find him! He hideth himself that I cannot see him!" Then he cried, "Why died I not from the womb if I am to die without God? Why was I born when I have lost my God?"'

And if in prayer his longing after God expressed itself in the psalmist's words, 'My soul waiteth for the Lord, more than they that watch for the morning,' when the morning did begin to arise, when there was the least faint streak of dawn in the heavens, he took it as a token of the sure coming of the sun. 'When Elijah's little cloud of blessing, no bigger than a man's hand, comes, it is God's little cloud in answer to prayer. All is in it, for God is in it, and it cannot go away and disappear till from that small beginning the heavens are black with clouds, and there is an abundant rain. So it is to every one who waits on God.'

In his Holy Island ministry he says of his hours of prayer, 'Sometimes when I was occupied during the day, the holy certainty of meeting the Most High God in the evening would come upon me with a sense of awe; partly stirring up from its hidden depths the aversion of the carnal mind, which is enmity against God, yet more sensibly affecting the natural shrinking of flesh and blood from entering quite into the unseen, and holding intimate yet awful converse with the Father of spirits. But once entered upon, this converse was as full of heavenly joy as of holy awe, and without the least disturbing element.'

At this period he records a remarkable case relating to access to God in prayer. He had asked a Christian ploughman, who settled in the island during his own stay there, to meet with him once a week in prayer. 'He was in the prime of youthful manhood; his fine countenance stamped with the double impression of meditation and intelligence, yet blooming with the glow of ruddy health, the fruit of constant outdoor labour. One summer evening, the moment the hour allotted to prayer was ended, he went home without uttering a word. He appeared unwell, his face had sunk, the bright hue of his cheek was pallid; he looked as a strong man ready to faint, but bearing up against some physical distress that all but overmastered him. Partly from his haste, and partly from his obvious aversion to speak, we parted without exchanging words.

'The second day following, I hailed him at some distance in the fields to inquire for his health. "You seemed unwell when we parted the night before last; were you sick?" "Oh, no." "Were you in distress of mind?" "No." "What then?" Slowly and reluctantly he replied: "When we were on our knees I was so filled with a sense of the love of God, that the joy was too much for me; it was all that I was able to bear, and it was with a struggle that I did not sink under it." The fact itself was obvious, although to me it had not excited the least suspicion of the cause. The joy of this divine love had remained with him all the night, and, though less intensely, throughout the next day and the night following. For myself, it was singularly refreshing to witness the presence and power of the Holy Ghost manifested in a manner so remarkable; and not under any moving address, but while two of us were quietly engaged in reading the word of God and in prayer. It was a gracious out-flowing of the love of the Lord Jesus making his servant "sick of love.'"

He derived great help from the sympathy of others uniting with him in prayer, and felt conscious of a mysterious action of one heart upon another when both are attuned to the same notes in this holy exercise. He frequently gave it as his experience that when engaged in private devotion on the morning of Good Friday, forgetful of its being the sacred anniversary (from these days not being observed in Scotland), he was conscious of unusual help and enlargement in prayer, which he could not account for until he discovered that it was one of those days on which the church of Christ throughout the world is presenting more petitions or thanksgivings at the throne of grace than on any other.

A remarkable instance bearing on this he gives in his *Recollections of Dr John Duncan*. He writes: 'All who are in the habit of leading in social prayer know how sensibly the petitions of the speaker are influenced by the spirits of those who silently aid in the exercise, and how real and practical in this relation is that "communion of saints" in which we believe. We had been on terms of intimate friendship when Dr Duncan was a minister at Glasgow, but at this time he never attended my church, not even once to my knowledge. This summer (1845) he had passed in Pest, and from my connection with our Jewish committee I believed, as certainly as if I had known, that he had not returned to Scotland. In church, one Sabbath in the morning prayer, I became gradually, but at length clearly and definitely, conscious that my thoughts and words were flowing in a channel that was not indeed alien to my intentions, but was distinctly different from any previous conceptions of my own. The impulse of a sensible force seemed increasingly to move me onward, but after a time one petition after another filled me with wonder. As they came up in succession I thought at last, "How is it that I am praying today in this manner? These thoughts are not my own thoughts, and the words that clothe them are words I never used before, nor thought of using. They are Dr John Duncan's; it seems as if he were praying in me, for both the ideas and the language are his and not mine. He must be here, yet he never comes to this church; and he cannot be here, for he is in Hungary." Bewildered how it could be, but confident that he was in the church, I bent over the pulpit as soon as I had finished the prayer, and saw him close under me in the session seat. Dr Duncan had entered the church after the commencement of the service, and in the exercise of his spirit there had surely been more than a merely passive following of the supplications that were pouring themselves through my lips. At the close of the service I found him "full of faith and of the Holy Ghost," and under a more powerful and subduing impression than I had ever seen him before. He had arrived in town, I believe, the previous evening and had come to live nearer my church. As soon as we were in the session house he said with deep emotion, "I could not help coming to this church this morning. It seemed to me that the Spirit was here, and that he drew me irresistibly to this place."' Many definite answers to prayer were received by Dr Moody Stuart. One family incident may be given. When we were boys at the Edinburgh Academy, one winter Saturday, Andrew and another brother had gone to skate, and instead of going to Duddingston Loch, our usual resort, had gone to the small Loch of Dunsappie on Arthur's Seat, on which from its higher elevation they expected the ice to be stronger. The authorities also had intimated that they had drained off some feet of the water, so as to make it safe. The skaters here were almost all young boys, and the ice had not formed with sufficient strength over the springs, which arose in holes much deeper than was supposed. These dangerous spots were not marked and there was no boat, ladder, or ropes provided. All that day my father had a strong impression that his boys were in danger, and was engaged constantly in prayer for them. Opening his study door whenever a bell rang, to see if they had returned, and much disappointed when he never heard their voices in the lobby, he returned always to pray. This was quite unusual, as we had been constantly at the lochs on skating holidays, and were never in any real danger. At last a bell rang and he heard their longed-for voices, and on asking if they were all well, they called upstairs, 'Yes; but a boy has been drowned.' The ice over a spring, not marked, had given way beneath him. Only one or two adult skaters were on the loch, one of these plunged in to try to rescue him, but could do nothing with the breaking and floating ice, and was at last himself rescued with difficulty by those on the loch grasping each other's hands, so as to form a chain extending from the shallow water to near the spot, and he managed to struggle till he grasped the last outstretched hand. What is remarkable is that Andrew said that he felt an almost irresistible impulse to plunge in, not reflecting that he would only have been another victim, and was restrained by feeling something like a strong hand pressing him back.

On one occasion at Rait, he writes in his diary (1895): 'There has been a long continuance of drought which has been becoming serious, withering the pastures and injuring the crops. This forenoon the heat was greater than ever, under a cloudless sky. I had a sense of guilt in not having prayed more earnestly for rain, and now it seemed further off than ever. This set me to seek "the effectual fervent prayer that availeth much," and I pleaded with much earnestness, remembering that even for temporal blessings there is only good in intense supplication if it is with childlike submission to the will of God, and if we resign not only the object prayed for but likewise the prayer itself to the will of our heavenly Father. I quite hoped that in due time, it might be after a day or two, and more prayer, there might be an answer, but to my surprise and thanksgiving, since four in the afternoon there has come a copious rain with a magnificent thunderstorm, the God of glory thundering and his voice upon the waters. The thunder has not yet ceased, and the rain has come in such an uncommon downpour, mingled with very large hailstones, that already it must have brought a great refreshing to the dry earth. O for another such shower on the souls of many, and the God of heaven who sendeth rain upon the earth desireth much more to pour out his Spirit upon us, and is '*waiting* to be *gracious*' till he is entreated by us.'

The clerk of the Kilspindie School Board recollects that once during Dr Moody Stuart's chairmanship he was engaged with him after their meeting in adjusting the minutes, when they found it very difficult to choose the proper terms to express exactly the understanding the meeting had come to. After working at it for some time the chairman said, 'We had better pray for direction.' After he had done so, the proper words at once suggested themselves, and fell into order without any more trouble.

It was his regular habit thus to take every perplexity to the Lord in prayer, whether it was small or great. He never read or studied the divine word in the family, or I believe in private, without lifting up his heart and voice in prayer for a blessing on it. One day in his last illness, when he seemed to be unconscious, I opened the Bible and began to read a few verses aloud, when he suddenly said, 'Oh don't begin to read without prayer!' This is one of many instances that prove that persons may be able to hear and follow words of Scripture, or supplication, when to all appearance they are quite unconscious and irresponsive.

Three directions that he gave for prayer were:—

1. Pray *till* you pray.
2. Pray till you are conscious of being heard.
3. Pray till you receive an answer.

Wherever he was he loved to associate himself with praying people, and to unite with them in presenting their common petitions at the throne of grace. We have already noticed the weekly prayer meeting of students at his house in Edinburgh in 1836; also the frequent meetings of his Session simply for prayer.

For many years a prayer meeting of ministerial brethren was held in Free St Luke's manse each alternate Monday morning. One of those who attended it some time after its commencement, the Rev. J. Morgan of Viewforth, speaks of it as having proved 'a great spiritual force.' He writes: 'The study in 43 Queen Street was familiar and almost sacred. I can vividly recall that quiet face, with its firm, square brow and strong-set mouth and chin, both hands grasping his thick well-worn interleaved Bible. His plaintive winsome voice in prayer and intercession was most impressive. To some of us these Monday forenoon meetings for devotion, conference and study of the word, were unspeakably precious and profitable, and are a dear remembrance still.'

I have a minute of this Prayer Union, drawn up by Dr R. G. Balfour, of their meeting on 10 February 1867, in which interesting accounts were given of revival movements going on in Tullibody, Torphichen, Larbert and Dunipace. Earnest prayer was offered for all these places, and for the congregations of those present, and suggestions were made as to the mode of preaching most likely to be blessed to effect this end, and the most approved methods of conducting such spiritual movements. Increased prayerfulness on the part of the ministers and congregations was specially recommended, and it was suggested that ministers might exchange pulpits occasionally with the express purpose of preaching to the unconverted.

Dr J. H. Wilson says that 'several movements resulted from this hour of prayer which bore precious fruit.' Besides ministers of Mr Moody Stuart's own standing in the Church, e.g., Drs. C. J. Brown and Robert McDonald, it was attended, in addition to those mentioned above, by such younger men as Dr Oswald Dykes, Mr Kelman, Mr Alexander Mackenzie, etc.

With regard to the duty of prayerfulness on the part of ministers, and its relation to the effective conducting of public prayer in the sanctuary, Dr Moody Stuart said in addressing a conference of ministerial brethren: 'The impressibleness of our people on the Sabbath depends much on prayer through the week; and their praying for us and for themselves depends much on our praying for them. And then on the Sabbath how much hangs, not merely on the words that are spoken, but on the spirit in which we preach and pray. Especially in extemporary prayer, we are in constant danger of sinking into a formality perhaps more lifeless than if we were using a form; a formality which we must all have detected in ourselves, by falling into the groove of the same words for want of fresh life within. Or if in such a state we make an effort at the moment toward real prayer, the prayer is constrained and laboured, instead of the spontaneous utterance of our thoughts. When the mouth speaks out of the abundance of the heart, out of spiritual desire, spiritual sorrow, or spiritual joy, what conciseness, what tenderness, what power is in the supplication, taking the people along with us in all our petitions, or else making them to feel their own lack of the spirit of grace. This one ordinance in our church of public prayer without a form of words, shuts us all up to a very peculiar necessity of becoming and continuing to be men of prayer; shuts us up under the pressure of a severe penalty, resting on ourselves and on our people week by week, as the sure consequence of our failure.'

Frequently Dr Moody Stuart was asked to write the 'Call to Prayer' before the meeting of the General Assembly, and none joined in such prayer more heartily, or took a greater burden of it, than the writer of the appeal.

In one of the circulars of the Mildmay Prayer Union for Israel, he urged his believing brethren to 'give their God no rest till he made Jerusalem a praise in the earth,' reminding them that the prayer 'Father, forgive them, for they know not what they do,' still ascends continually from Calvary into the ears of the Most High.

In his latest years of retirement he was joint honorary president with Lord Kinnaird of the Carse of Gowrie Prayer Union, which embraced ministers and elders of all denominations, who met monthly for prayer. The weekly prayer meeting he regarded as the most important part of the congregational machinery. He always prepared most carefully for it. A poor woman once remarked, 'He comes into the prayer meeting and sits down like a little prince!'

Another writes: 'His prayers when he visited our house were things to be remembered for their apt appropriateness, and their bringing you into the presence of Christ.' Prayer was to him a second nature. It might be truly said of him in Montgomery's words, that prayer was 'his vital breath, his native air, his watchword at the gates of death—he entered heaven with prayer.' While always valuing skilled medical advice (such as that of our kind family physicians and friends, Professor Miller and Dr John Moir), most unweariedly did he betake himself to prayer in every case of sickness in the family, and many recoveries of his loved ones were granted to his importunate intercessions. Mrs Kalley mentions that Dr Kalley was restored from a critical illness in Madeira, after my father and others had met to pray that the physician might be guided aright, the next remedy that he tried proving successful.

Even as young children we had the greatest confidence in the value of our father's prayers for our recovery when sick. This must have impressed other children also, as was the case with a boy in Rait, who on recovering from a severe illness, answered a friend who said, 'Well, the doctor has managed to make you well again,' replied, 'Na, it was Dr Moody Stuart's prayer made me well.'

Through all his life it could be truly said of him that like the apostles he 'gave himself continually to prayer.' Many letters have come from friends stating that before they parted from him after a call he always joined with them in prayer. When any of his family started on a journey his last farewell was a loving commendatory prayer, and it was noticed by them that none of those thus commended to the divine protection ever encountered the smallest accident of any kind in their journeys.

One of his assistants writes: 'He was a man of prayer. If we were engaged in any work in his study and it did not progress as desired he stopped for prayer. All his work, and specially his difficulties, were brought to God in prayer. If money were wanted for some religious work he made it a matter of special prayer. Some of the incidents, which now I could not trust my memory to recall accurately, reminded me of incidents in the life of George Müller. One however came under my own observation. He called to pray with a woman who had begun business but had not succeeded. He prayed very earnestly with her for success in the venture that had caused her so much anxiety. He was hardly out of the house before an order arrived, as she herself said, in answer to prayer, which proved to be the beginning of a very successful business.'

It may be suitable to close this chapter with notes of a communion table address given in April 1855, dealing with the subject of importunity in prayer. It is based on the parable of the friend at midnight asking for three loaves (Luke 11:8).

'Jesus Christ is the Bread of Life; this spiritual bread is the most abundant of all things (John 10:10), the freest of all things (Isaiah 55:1), but the rarest of all things in actual possession, and the reason is, "We have not, because we ask not" (James 4:2). Jesus tells us to ask, but he teaches us also how we should ask, and loves to place the petitioner in the most unfavourable circumstances, that others may be assured likewise that they shall obtain if they ask.

'The first thing in prayer is a *sense of need*: a need which is *entire* and *ascertained*. The supplicant must first *know that he has nothing*, but is poor and needy. He must be sure of this, and make it a settled point, and not merely suspect it. There is a great difference between suspected and ascertained want. Many say they have little if anything good, but they don't want to be sure of it and so never cry for the bread of life. The supplicant's need must be *urgent*, requiring immediate assistance whether for himself or for others. Christ puts a case in which the man requiring bread could not wait till tomorrow. The need must be felt to be *irremediable otherwise*. Neither shop nor market was open at midnight, and the man had nothing to set before his guests, and he was shut up to go to his friend as his only resource.

'Next, *the supplicant must have confidence in Christ as being willing to grant his request*. This is supposed to be a very common belief, but if this belief were to come athwart you it would be a new thing to you. It has run current among you that Jesus Christ has bread to give, but is it a reality to you? Sometimes men are ready to say, Christ *can* give, but he has no will. Oh, what blasphemy! How amazing that God hath endured his people when they have brought up such an evil report against him!

'Oh, dear brethren, it is this that hinders prayer, and success in prayer, when we say, "He has no mind to give us what we ask." Next, *perseverance in asking* is needful. *The first knock has obtained nothing;* it seems to have produced no result, but the man continues knocking. *Many knocks have produced no effect,* but these knocks have troubled the possessor of the bread, and have brought out the secret, not that he has no bread, or objects to bestow it, but that he is not willing to be troubled at present. The petitioner is unwilling to trouble his friend, but he is still more unwilling to go home and tell his guest that he must starve; so he determines that he must knock, for he cannot do without it, and for his importunity he gets it. Even so with our Father in heaven. We begin to be ashamed of asking the same thing over and over again; but then there is the great want; and the feeling, "I cannot go without it," leads to perseverance, and this obtains it in the end. The difficulty becomes the greater, the longer we continue knocking; for if we are not to go without it, we must make louder and more continual knocking. I must either go away, and give it up, or seek with such vehemence as must obtain it, as if a greater effort than ever were needed and must be made. And it must be so with us, seeing how dreadful it is to perish. I cannot perish! Or in interceding for others, "How can I bear to see the destruction of my people? Therefore let me seek until I find." Jesus says, "Every one that asketh receiveth." Never was there a case to the contrary. Thousands of cases there have been when men have knocked and got nothing and gone away; but there never was a case of a man who *sought to the end* and did not get.

'Then, *the bread is supplied, and in great abundance.* He gives "as many as he needeth." This importunate petitioner never lessens his request because of the denial, and it is great wisdom in spiritual things not to lessen our requests because of the delay. We should not diminish the request, but increase the importunity. *There will be no counting of the loaves.* There is bread enough in our Father's house and to spare; and, oh, there is want enough! Though God tarry, have large desires and expectations, but these come to nothing unless there be large faith and large requests. Let us, dear friends, ask much of our God, and keep asking much, because when he arises he will give an abundance.'

— 17 —

Memorable Sayings

May all the grain thou sowest take root,
And all that roots bear perfect fruit,
And may the fruit be reaped by thee,
    Abundantly,
Or here, or in eternity!

T HESE sentences are extracted from notes of sermons, jottings and recollections of various hearers, but the selection is difficult in such a wide and fruitful field, and might have been increased manifold had space permitted.

* * *

Self-elation never comes with present joy in the Lord, for his presence is humbling and hallowing.

Self-emptying exalts Christ, and Christ exalted humbles self.

Christ's thought of me is not the same as my own thought of myself. Oh what is it of my past? and what for my eternal future?

If Christ is in us the hope of glory, the angels who wait on him, will also wait on him dwelling in us, and wait on us dwelling in him.

If there is anything I can affirm without hesitation or abatement it is, 'Oh how I love thy law!'

Who can understand 'Thou hast redeemed us to God by thy blood'? I have long believed it, but am still at the mere outskirts of knowing and receiving it.

'In the last days men shall be lovers of their own selves' is the darkest brand of the ungodly. Oh that it may be quite effaced from me in little things which may have been neglected, as well as in great things in which I may have rejoiced in gracious victory!

The maxim in law, *de minimis non curat lex* (law does not take charge of things minute), is reversed in the divine life, *de minimis curat Deus* (God takes charge of the smallest things).

In every thing greater or less the Lord has taught me, 'Thou has destroyed thyself,' yet in everything great or little he has said to me, 'But in me is thine help.'

All things are little in the universe compared with Good and Evil, Sin and Holiness.

There is nothing more dangerous to man or woman than to know, and not to do.

Adam said, 'My will,' and he took it. God's Son lived and died in the world and said, 'Not my will!'

Paul does not say that 'Demas gained the world,' but that 'he loved it.' I think no one ever asked, 'Did he get the world?'

Demas was tempted and fell: Luke was no doubt equally tempted and tried, and he got the crown of glory. Paul in the many mansions above is saying, 'Luke is with me: Demas forsook me.'

God loves to give the desires of the heart even here when he has subdued the heart, but in heaven he will give you literally all you desire. Just as he has given to Jesus 'all that his heart could crave,' so will he give to all that are his.

God has said, 'Open thy mouth wide, and I will fill it,' but he has nowhere said, 'Half open thy mouth and I will half fill it.'

The cross is a place for me; the cradle also is a place for me. He could not give us the Babe in Bethlehem to take in our arms except his arms were to be stretched on the cross.

Christ's death was not simply the putting down of the evil power; it was the triumph of truth and goodness.

We must come *down* to the cross of Christ; if we had to come *up* to it, it would be impossible.

'Father, forgive them!' He cried; and will it not come from you, 'Father, forgive me'?

'Kiss the Son lest he be angry!' He is only angry because he is not accepted.

We are accepted in the Beloved as if we had never displeased God at all.

It would be the utmost misery if it were possible for a man to be received into God's presence and to continue a sinful man.

In the law of Moses the sheep died for the shepherd; in the law of Jesus the Shepherd died for the sheep.

He gave his life for the sheep because the Shepherd was good, not because the sheep were good.

Wherever there is a seeking soul there is a seeking Saviour.

The same One who says, 'I am the Door,' will say, 'The door is shut.'

A brief life it seemed to man, those thirty-three years—it was the longest life the world ever knew; it was Eternity writing itself in Time.

The briefest record of a life of grace is that of the thief on the cross, but in that brief time the Lord led him a long way from his own height to the utmost lowness—to confess that he was guilty before God.

In the end all will depend not on my thinking of Christ, but on Christ's thinking on me; and all through it remains from first to last, 'Herein is love, not that we loved him, but that he loved us.'

'The peace of God that passeth all understanding, keeping the heart and mind in Jesus Christ,' sounds strange at first, for what passes our understanding is apt to disturb our peace, but in this case its amazing abundance only increases the inward calm.

Before thou goest to feed my sheep, answer this question, 'Dost thou love me?'

With me it is not the fear of being shut out of Christ's paradise, but the shame of being taken in that overawes me.

If I might sullenly refuse to receive for myself the free joy of his salvation, I cannot refuse to my Lord the joy of his soul's travail for my redemption.

In God's earth without God!

Every place and every time is full of God. Yesterday morning I awoke in the midst of God, and was ashamed and saddened to reflect that I had so often not been alive to his blessed presence around me and within me.

Without the sacrifice, Christ's name would never have been 'Ointment poured forth,' for all the unction would have been his own, and not ours.

The savour of Christ's sacrifice has ascended to the Father for us, and the exquisite odour of the anointing for his burial[1] has filled the highest heavens, to the gladdening of all the angels, filled the many mansions of the Father's house above, filled every house of God on earth, and all the dwellings of Jacob, and will fill the universe to all eternity.

The martyrs on the scaffold have praised God for the shining sun; but in the day of our Lord's distress there was no shining sun. When sin and curse were made to rest on Christ, it was that he might go with them into a land where no man was

---

[1] Dr Moody Stuart took the anointing in Bethany to be typical of Jesus' being anointed with the Holy Spirit both as priest and sacrifice.—*KMS*.

[referring to the scapegoat]. God was away, the very innocent creatures were away.

There is not one humble heart in all the world that the High God is not dwelling in.

If you are lost, you need no change in you to fit you for hell.

There is not such a thing as a soul believing in Christ and being lost.

Oh that I could continuously delight to receive the mercy which it is always a delight to thee to bestow!

You are as much under the eye of God at this moment as you will be before the Judgment-seat.

Is the kingdom of heaven highest with you? If not, it is not yours.

The Apostle says, 'Let your speech be *seasoned* with salt'; he does not say, 'Let it be all salt'!

There is many a man who will never consent to come to the gospel-feast who would not for any consideration give up the privilege of the invitation.

We often see Christians who may be called lop-sided. They are developed on one side of their character but not on another, but the Apostle tells us to grow up into him in all things.

The Psalmist says, 'Look down from heaven.' Are none of you saying 'Do not look down'?

How much well ordered speech there is in prayer, and how little prayer!

How the heart pours itself out to God when we know that he is bowing down to hear our petitions!

Christ hath honoured God more than sin hath dishonoured him.

Sin is not so defiling as the blood of Jesus Christ is cleansing. It makes a greater whiteness than Adam had before he fell.

Your great sins are little compared with God's great mercies.

I would be much richer than I am, if I only knew how poor I am.

'There is no night there.' … Probably the sweetest songs we shall sing there will be the rehearsal of the songs we have sung in the night here.

What a great day it was when Jesus said, 'I am the vine and ye are the branches'—not you are invited to be, but *you are.*

How glad every one of us is that it is not a man that judges us. We could not trust any man to *justify* us.

'The word of God is quick and powerful and piercing'; it makes a sharp cut but a clean one, not like a man's rebuke, which sometimes makes a ragged cut like a piece of rusty iron.

He did not come to break the prison down by mere strength of arm, but he said, 'I have got the keys.'

To all eternity there is reference to the Blood. Nothing else will make me clean. It is all-sufficient.

Every one has his own place, and every one has his own work in his own place.

Have you taken your cross? Did you take it yesterday? 'I have no cross,' you say. Maybe there was a cross that you did not take up.

The salvation of the Jews is an undeveloped mystery: yet there is nothing more certain in the Scriptures than the conversion of the Jews.

As a nation they were taken captive into Babylon; as a nation they were restored; and as a nation they crucified Jesus. The most national of nations. A nation without a king. And surely the time is drawing near when the veil shall be taken away from them as a nation.

A great part of the Psalms consists in knocking: 'Be not silent unto me,' 'I wait for God'. ... It is knocking at his gate.

Each man thinketh that he hath a way. ... Christ comes to you and says, '*I* am the Way.'

He brings us into difficulty that he may help us out of it, and that we may know our own helplessness.

In some way or other we are *masters* of ourselves, and it is a sad discovery to a man when he finds that he that sins is a *servant* to sin.

Christ does not say, 'Be filled with the Spirit!' without giving the Spirit.

Believe that you receive the Holy Spirit and you have him! [Recalled after sixty-three years by a hearer, who at first rejecting it, in later life found it most helpful.]

The besetting sin of believers is unbelief.

We never can face saying, 'I am lost,' till we say, 'The Son of Man came to seek and to save that which was lost.'

It was with the blood of the Man at God's right hand that the mercy-seat was sprinkled. Even this Man, however pure and gentle, could have done nothing for us without the blood.

In the ship when crossing to the Gadarenes there was infinitely more strength in the little boat than in all the billows, though stirred by the Prince of the Power of the Air. There was strength enough in the Lord if he would stir himself up (Psa. 80:2).

'Let my soul live and it shall praise thee!' What a sight a living man is! He is a mighty power round about, a power with God.

How many have never realised the power of God's salvation! Save the lost! Save the saved! Give *new* salvation!

Paul having made the announcement, 'This is a faithful saying, and worthy of all acceptation, that Jesus Christ came into the world to save sinners,' hastens to place himself at the head of the list of sinners, and writes down, 'Of whom I am the first.'

When we wait for the Lord we not only tarry the Lord's leisure, but we tarry with wistful longing for his presence and help. In like manner when the Lord waits to be gracious unto us, he tarries with longing desire to grant us the health of his countenance and the joy of his salvation (Isa. 30:18).

The soul convinced of its own guilt cannot bear to be looked on by God's eye above, cannot bear to be looked on by human eyes around, cannot bear to be looked on by its own eye within. 'Look not upon me!'

We shall scarcely know ourselves when we are without fault before the throne of God.

'The midst thereof being paved with love.' Love is the midst and the heart of the whole covenant of redemption.

If you are not receiving Christ you are rejecting Christ.

'That we might know the things that are freely given to us of God'; i.e., that we might know the *grace* of God, and that the things of God are of grace.

If Christ is any way admitted he must be all in all, and through all, and over all, and instead of all—the first and the last, the foundation and the head of the corner.

His work is perfect: there is in it no lack and no excess; we need it all and we need no more, for 'I,' saith he, 'have finished the work.'

How many are willing that Christ should be something, but few will consent that Christ should be everything!

Be lowly and broken in heart, and then you shall not fall and be broken on Christ. The lowly cannot fall, for they are on the earth already; the prostrate cannot stumble; the weak and the childlike will not dash themselves against the rock of offence.

You are children of light. Whensoever the love of your heart waxes cold, the light of your eye will wax dim.

Oh what could we do without Peter and David and Thomas! What hope could we have? But they were saved from their sins—so we shall be too.

This world is the outer field in which the stones are hewn and the work prepared, and various and curious and wonderfully wise are the means by which the great Artificer is making ready his chosen ones. The dead stone he is quickening into life by the resistless energy of his Holy Spirit, and the living stone, which is still rough and unformed, he is by the same Spirit, as by the gentle and continual dropping of living water, polishing into shape and seemliness.

Dead one, you do not know that Jesus is calling you. When Jesus came to call Lazarus out of death, Lazarus, for whose sake Jesus had come, was the only one who did not know that the Lord was there. Yet the dead heard the voice of the Son of Man, and hearing it he lived.

I would not give much for the assurance of some people. It just means, 'I believe that I was converted at such a time.' If your assurance is not founded on a present fellowship with the Son and with the Father it is little worth.

Christ and self cannot live in the same man. If self lives in us, Christ cannot; if Christ lives in us, self is crucified.

'Wilt thou be made whole?' Jesus requires nothing and accepts nothing at your hands. The pleasure of healing you is all he asks.

The man whom the king honours with his commission may not be the man who seems to us to be nearest to the work, but he is the man who is nearest to the king.

Some people think there are fifteen virgins instead of ten—the wise, the foolish, and those who are neither: but the Lord says there were only ten.

The wise virgins could have given light, but they could not give oil.

When we pass one of life's waymarks we are reminded that our time has risen in value, as every commodity does when it grows scarcer.

Be like a Christian, many say, and you will become one, when it is plain we must first be Christians, and then we shall be Christian-like.

Christ is *the* door to God, with no other door *beside* it, *before* it, or *after* it. There is *no outer door to Christ.* How amazed I was when I found there was not a door to *him.* There is *no inner door* after Christ, for 'This is the Gate of God.'

Oh if it were said today, 'The Books are closed,' what a rush would there be that our names might be written in them!

Christ took the cross as his throne; and that throne was transferred to heaven. 'I saw in the midst of the throne a Lamb as it had been slain'—the throne of God for ever.

Jesus Christ is the golden knot that binds into one the universe of holy beings.

In him, mind and matter, spirit and body, Creator and creature, God and man are united in one Person for ever: our sins and our selves seemed to be one, but he took them from us, and through his unspeakable loneliness and desertion he unites us for ever to himself, to his Father, and to each other.

The Holy Spirit who dwells in the Father and the Son, and who forms the mysterious link of their union and communion, is the same by whom we are united to Christ and to each other. [At Perth Conference, 1867.]

Sinners are not first separated from sin, and then united to Christ, but are united to Christ, and by the act of union are separated from sin.

Some think themselves too good to come to Christ, and some think themselves too bad, and between the two Christ loses his glory.

It is by the *foolishness of preaching*, not by *foolish preaching*, that 'it hath pleased God to save them that believe.'

A preacher must be 'a new sharp threshing instrument *having teeth*' (Isa. 41:15). Your sermons must *have teeth* if they are to do good. [Remark addressed to a young preacher in the session-house, whose sermon he thought not fitted to 'take hold' of the hearers.]

A cleaner or smoother part of the broad way is not the narrow path that leadeth unto life.

The whole narrow way is a series of mountains that rise up continually before you in your path, and that are levelled continually to faith in Jesus Christ.

It is the mustard seed of faith on the one hand, and the great mountain on the other, and the trial is whether the mountain shall bury the mustard seed, or the mustard seed cast the mountain into the sea. Which of the two shall it be with you?

The great aim of every man should be so to run from this time forward that when you come to die there shall be a happy retrospect looking back, and a happy prospect looking forward.

When you see no spot in me, and I see no spot in you, and God himself sees no spot in us, surely it will become us daily to sing louder and louder, 'Worthy is the Lamb that hath washed us!'

Surely we should make much of ourselves when the Father makes so much of us. I do not mean lifting up ourselves; but what a high calling is ours!

Suppose a criminal could be redeemed by ten talents, and 100 talents were paid down, he would be rich as well as ransomed. [Referring to the atonement.]

'In all their affliction he was afflicted.' Is not the salt wave sweeter for having broken first on Jesus?

'Whom the Lord loveth he chasteneth': love is first, chastening second—not worse, but second best.

Men often speak of faith as if it were the easiest thing in the world: of all things in the world it is the most difficult. It is impossible to man; it is the gift of God.

Heaven is light and no darkness: hell is darkness and no light: earth is mingled light and darkness: it was darkness, but the true light now shines in Jesus Christ.

The light often comes gradually into the soul: but all the light you will have to all eternity is here in Christ Jesus, and you are as welcome to it in this hour as you will be to all eternity.

To 'abide in Christ' is living by faith on his broken body and shed blood, and keeping his commandments.

When I first awoke out of death it was in the light of the Lord's finished work and sacrifice, and when I awake out of the grave it will be the very same.

What a blessing to be the Lord's servant for ever! he accepts of your service through all eternity.

Oh that the eternal smile of the Lord may rest upon you and me!

* * *

— 18 —

Influence on Ministers and Others

> He, armed himself in panoply complete
> Of heavenly temper, furnishes with arms
> Bright as his own, and trains, by every rule
> Of holy discipline, to glorious war
> The sacramental host of God's elect.
>
> —*William Cowper*

D R Moody Stuart's influence on those who in their turn were influential in Christ's church was a marked feature of his ministry. The Edinburgh Presbytery, in the minute which they drew up expressing their sense of the loss sustained through his removal, refer to this in these terms: 'His saintly character, his power in expounding Scripture and in illustrating and applying evangelical truth, and his skill in dealing with individual souls, made his church a great centre of Christian influence. Many who afterwards came to occupy important positions in the service of Christ at home and in the mission-field received their first religious impressions, or had their spiritual life stimulated or helped, under his ministry.' Various important instances of this have already appeared in these pages, and a few more are now presented to the reader.

A perusal of the frequent letters of the Duchess of Gordon to Mr Moody Stuart proves that he powerfully influenced the spiritual life of one who in her turn influenced many others. We give one of these:—

The Lodge,
Huntly, 27 March 1862.

My Dear Mr Moody Stuart,

I delayed writing to you from day to day waiting the arrival of the *Wellingtonia*, which appeared two days ago quite safe and in excellent condition. I am very much obliged and shall hope to be reminded by it of the 'green fir tree in whom our fruit is found.' Your letter was most timely and acceptable, as your letters always are to me. I do often find it difficult to believe that the Holy One can love me, and wonder why he does so load me with benefits when I feel so cold and careless, and so much deserve chastisement and require rousing; but he is faithful as well as holy and loving, and truly I may, if any one in the world can, say, 'He doeth all things well'. … I do most cordially agree with you in the sense of need for more faith. It is so difficult to realise that it is not from any good in ourselves that we may hope for answers to our prayers, but that all good is treasured up in Christ; and when we find nothing but evil and coldness, even when acknowledging most unmerited goodness, I cannot help wondering if the prayers of such a creature can be heard. The church at Ellon was quite filled on the market day, at three or four o'clock. I dare say Captain Trotter has made known his wish for prayer every Thursday in May, June, and July, for him and Mr Blackwood, who are to speak in Willis' Rooms to the upper classes.

With kindest regards to you and Mrs Moody Stuart, I am always, with affectionate gratitude, yours most truly,

E. GORDON

Another Christian lady, who has through her hymns and sacred poems brought guidance and comfort to many, Mrs Cousin, the

The Duchess of Gordon

authoress of 'The Sands of Time are Sinking,' etc., came early under the influence of Dr Moody Stuart, which she thus describes:—

> My recollections of Dr Moody Stuart and his unique minis-
> try date from long ago (1844). In my early days I was irresistibly
> attracted to his preaching, and took every opportunity of hear-
> ing him from time to time during a period of many years, little
> dreaming then that his ministry would come to be so much in
> later days to me and mine. In thinking over the characteristics
> of those discourses, it would be difficult to determine whether
> the exceeding sinfulness of sin or the surpassing love of the Sav-
> iour was exhibited with the more marvellous power. Perhaps it
> might be said that the keynote of his preaching was to be found
> in Romans 5:20, 21. The spiritual intensity which pervaded all
> his utterances was not to be described, and left its ineffaceable
> stamp on the soul. His delivery possessed a strange impressive-
> ness which was due not only to its singular individuality, but

still more to the awfulness and solemnity of the truths among which he was continually dwelling. Many strangers found their way as visitors to St Luke's, drawn by the power and spiritual beauty with which the gospel was there proclaimed. The characteristic feature to be remarked in those discourses was that there was always some memorable thought which might be carried away as a possession to become part of the spiritual being for ever after.[1]

No Scottish preacher of our day exercises a wider spiritual influence than Dr Alexander Whyte[2] of Edinburgh, and the following letter, addressed to me, bearing date 12 October 1898, shows how he was himself influenced in his student days by Dr Moody Stuart:—

As often as I on occasions say, 'Bless the Lord, O my soul, and forget not all his benefits,' I set it down as one of his great benefits to me, that red-letter day to me, when your father took me for his missionary. My duties embraced a little local mission work and the congregational prayer meeting occasionally, but my main duty was to go to the country on certain Sabbaths and supply for those friends of your father who came in from time to time to St Luke's, to allow him to go to the country for rest. When at home on Sabbaths I worshipped one half the day in St Luke's and the other half in St George's. And I used to insist with my companions at the New College that I enjoyed the best combination of preaching within the four seas. Dr Candlish's preaching was as different from your father's preaching as it could well be: but both preachers were simply the very best in their own kind. I need not describe your father's preaching to you; and I could not describe it to any one who had not sat under it. It was spiritual, if ever preaching was. It was scholarly

[1] Some instances quoted by Mrs Cousin are included in chapter 17.—*KMS*.
[2] Alexander Whyte (1836–1921) succeeded Robert Candlish as minister of Free St George's, and in 1909 was appointed Principal of New College. Whilst training for ministry at New College between 1862 and 1866, Whyte had served as assistant, or 'missionary', under Moody Stuart at Free St Luke's.—*P*.

of the best kind. It was very refined: there is no other word I can think of for it. It was original, with all his reading. It was of an exquisite spirituality, in Edwards' sense of spirituality. And it was steeped through and through with a Shepard-like and a Samuel Rutherford-like sensibility to sin, and an unceasing suffering, like all saintly men, from sin. What 'action' sermons we used to have in St Luke's. I shall ever remember one on the text, 'That Cup.' It was a text for a communion morning, and for your father on a communion morning. And did he not make a text of it! The mystical depth, the rich inwardness, the overpowering solemnity, the passion, the rapture of that sermon I shall never forget. I see your father over thirty-four years as he walked about the pulpit floor that morning with his pocket Bible in his hand, and with his rich mind and deep heart welling up over all his week's preparation, and making it all so fresh, so spontaneous, so contagious, so soul-quickening to us all. I see Dr Duncan, now laughing, now weeping, all the time, and all the rest of us in the same state of mind. *Unique* is the word, unique and alone, supreme in his pulpit kind; with no fellow; with no one to come second to him. And then his pure, flawless Christian character. His walk and conversation always of a true Christian gentleman. His noble courtesy to his young missionary—a courtesy so deep in his noble heart that it altered not one whit amid all our altered relationship in after life. A scholar: a student all his days: a preacher in the savour and strength of his quality, quite worthy to be ranked with Shepard and Rutherford themselves; and a holy man if I ever knew one. You are singularly happy, dear Kenneth, to have had such a father, and to bear in the Church your father loved so much and served so well, his greatly beloved and greatly honoured name.

Besides many regular members of St Luke's who became honoured ministers of Christ, like Malcolm M'Gregor of Gartly, Walter Davidson of Perth, Thomas Stothert of Lumphanan, and his brother Richard, missionary in Bombay, D. W. Kennedy of Perth, etc., considerable numbers of divinity students used to attend his church during the college session. The Rev. Robert Cowan of Elgin, who, as a personal and family friend of long standing, contributed to the *Free Church Monthly* of October 1898,[3] the lifelike biographical sketch which appeared there, and to which we have already been indebted in this memoir, worshipped often as a student in St Luke's. He thus describes the impressions made upon him:—

As Dr Moody Stuart entered the pulpit, one felt the man before he opened his lips; there was an atmosphere of prayer and of heaven about him. The voice, though not strong, and somewhat high-set and plaintive in its tones, was clear and penetrating, and effective to express every shade of thought and feeling. The theology was that of the Reformers and Puritans, but taken in at first hand from the word, absorbed into his own life, and touched with his own individuality. The great characteristic of his style, both in writing and speaking, was expressiveness—the right word and phrase found to body forth the thought; and the great characteristic of his message was the life that was in it, and the way it fitted in to the spiritual life in others. Students hearing him for the first time sometimes thought of him only as a good man saying simple things, but they quickly discovered the subtle thinker, the profound theologian, and the master in spiritual pathology. The preaching always dealt closely with experience and the heart, finding out the hearer, and often surprising him with the diagnosis of his particular case, and the tender and healing touch on his hidden sore. John Milne said, 'My brother Moody has an intricate mind,' and this was illustrated in the way his word wound itself into all the sinuosities of the inner experience. Carnal hearers might find little in the message, but to seekers, and to Christians in doubt or darkness, it was medicine and balm, and living souls found in it the very nutriment their life needed. As a student who sat some time in his church says, 'It was a spectacle to see the eager wistfulness of the hearers, watching for

[3] See Appendix for Robert Cowan's tribute in full.—*P.*

every word, and drinking it in.' The word as preached by him, though searching, was always singularly cheering and encouraging; the secret being that he had got down for himself to the bedrock of the sinner's foundation in the grace of God in Christ, was always dwelling there, and felt quite sure of the entire sufficiency of this for others, whatever their cases might be.

The Rev. C. Bannatyne[4] of Coulter, one of his student-missionaries, writes:

> His mode of speaking about divine things always made me think of him as one who in a very literal sense lived, and moved, and had his being in the presence of those spiritual realities very much as others do in regard to the objects of this world. Although this is a truism in regard to the life of faith, yet there are only a few who in a manner all their own impress the fact on the mind of another. Through the whole of my intercourse with Dr Moody Stuart I was deeply impressed by the truth of a remark made by the late Mr Burton Alexander, that his wonderful intellectual power was apt to be lost sight of by some because of his great spirituality, and I cannot but very gratefully recall when he had elicited one's opinion upon some doctrinal point, and approved of what was said, how careful he was to put the matter from another aspect, so that it might be thoroughly understood and looked at all round.

With regard to his dealing with students, etc., while his own views were strongly Calvinistic, not only did he work in loving harmony with ministers of other churches holding divergent views,

---

[4] Colin Archibald Bannatyne (1849–1920) was ordained minister of Coulter, Lanarkshire, in 1876. In 1900, he and others declined to enter the union of the Free Church with the United Presbyterian Church. It is his name which appears on the legal case *Bannatyne v. Overtoun,* the final appeal of which to the House of Lords resulted in the entirety of the property and funds of the pre-1900 Free Church being allocated to the minority continuing Free Church. A Royal Commission was subsequently set up to more appropriately distribute the assets between the two bodies.—*P.*

but he entered sympathetically and prudently into the position of those who felt difficulties on doctrinal points, and often succeeded in removing these. When I was elected a deacon in my father's congregation in 1861, I felt difficulty in signing the Confession of Faith, especially on the point of particular atonement. With regard to this point, he wrote:—

Edinburgh, 13 February 1861.

My Dear Kenneth,

I pray God to direct you about the diaconate; only if you can sign the Confession I have no doubt your difficulties will cease much more readily by accepting than by declining, which tends to keep the questions before the mind, and hinders their natural and gradual solution by a deeper acquaintance with the word of God. If you do it, I have no fear of you regretting, or being worried after. Do you believe that 'Christ laid down his life for the sheep,' and 'loved the church and gave himself for it,' in *any* special sense? that he laid down his life for Peter in *any* sense more than he laid it down for Pilate? Then if you do (as you must if you believe the Bible) you may freely sign in my judgment. It is not at all necessary that you sign a Confession with a cordial admiration of all the way it is put. I have that very much now, but had not when I signed as a probationer. ...

I am, ever your affectionate father,

A. MOODY STUART

A year or two earlier (1859) I had great difficulties about the whole doctrine of the divine election, and thought it wise to consult my father about these. On my explaining to him that I was perplexed by the doctrine of an *eternal and immutable decree* of election he set this doctrine before me in a new light, by what has always seemed to me a very telling piece of reasoning. He said, 'Have you looked at Romans 9:14, 15. "Is there unrighteousness with God? God forbid! for he saith to Moses, I will have mercy on whom I will have mercy: and I will have compassion on whom I will have compassion."' I replied that that could not help me, as it stated the doctrine in its most uncompromising form. 'Well,' he replied, 'I have taken it because it does so, and because it is the kernel of Paul's long argument on this doctrine in Romans 9, 10, 11. But it once removed my difficulties, and should do the same with yours. You will allow that we are taught here that God's will in the present is perfectly free and uncontrolled. *He is, therefore, not bound or fettered by any past decree.* Of whatever nature that decree is, spoken of in our Confession and in Scripture, it is merely one aspect of the *present* will of God, which acts in eternity, and therefore is called *eternal* rather than temporal. But there is no *past* in it: it is *present.*' Having thus eliminated the idea of a *past* resolution, he said, 'You are left face to face only with God's present will, the will of One whom you can pray to, and plead with and reason with. He himself invites you to do so; and is his present will against any returning sinner? Where is that will revealed? In Scripture. Is there anything in that will so revealed fitted to cause you trouble? Does God not solemnly declare, "I have no pleasure in the death of the wicked, but that the wicked turn from his way and live"? (Ezek. 33:11) and Christ says, 'Him that cometh unto me I will in no wise cast out" (John 6:37).' My difficulties were all dispersed by his lucid exposition of the text that had been a special stumbling-block.

Both in private dealing and public preaching my father followed the plan of bringing his hearers up to his own position by putting himself first in theirs, and starting from their standpoint, he let them feel that he understood them, and never stopped short of making them at least fully comprehend what he wished to convey to them.

A rather amusing instance of this occurred with a respected member of my own congregation. She is now in her ninety-fifth year, but her memory and mental powers have remained good. In speaking of my father she said to me that she used to enjoy his preaching when he came to Moffat, and that she often recalled his last sermon on 'Thy word is a light to my path,' in which he compared the promises contained in Scripture to the lucifer matches lying in a match-box, which give no light until they are struck and used; and that in the same way we must use each promise before it will give us any light; that lying within the boards of the Bible they are as void of illumination as the dark-tipped matches in their box. His aged hearer, who was then some years over eighty, found much help from the illustration, but told me that what greatly pleased her was his making it so plain. She said that he just used the homely word 'spunks' instead of matches! I heard the sermon, and feel quite sure that he did not, but he made the meaning so clear to her, that she imagined he used the name by which they were commonly known in her youth!

The Rev. D. W. Kennedy of Perth, who was brought up under Dr Moody Stuart's ministry, and acted for a time as student-missionary, writes:—

> At certain times his heart, as was to be expected, went out in special prayer for the conversion of his hearers. He aimed at nothing short of this. At those times the sermon was prepared with this full in view, and when preached there was no mistaking the object of the preacher. On one occasion he held an 'after meeting' at the close of the regular service, when a large number remained and were addressed by him as he stood at the precentor's table. He told me that he had great faith in getting people to confess themselves anxious, and allowing themselves to be addressed as such, even though he got no nearer to them personally. He often asked anxious ones to speak with him in the vestry or in his house. It was in response to such an invitation that I went to speak with him. I was struck with the difference between his conversation and that of others. He did not seem to be anxious to bring mere peace to the mind. My impression is that his chief concern was with the soul's decision for God, not mere comfort. This intense desire for the conversion of his people was not merely at times of general revival, but when so far as outside influences were concerned nothing very special could be expected. On one occasion, after special prayer and special appeal to his people, he expressed surprise that no one had responded to his invitation to

come and speak with him. In reply I told him I had met one who had been brought to decision through that sermon, and probably others had got good though they had not told him. This led him to speak of past experiences. He said that on one occasion after preaching he felt so convinced that God was using the word in the awakening of men that he went straight to his study to arrange the chairs for the convenience of inquirers. Inquirers did come and filled them all.

His helpful influence was often exerted upon strangers who have been used to influence many for good. This letter from the authoress of the hymn, 'The Old, Old Story,' illustrates what I mean:—

Tunbridge Wells, 10 March 1867.

Dear Mr Stuart,

According to your kind permission my two little books travel to you with this. 'The Old, Old Story' is in its fortieth thousand now, though first published on New Year's Day this year. It just shows how many hearts are *aching and longing for* that *Jesus*, of whom with *no* 'wisdom of words' this 'Story' tells. It is nothing new, and yet *so* new. So marvellously fresh and refreshing, however poorly and simply told.

In illness especially, I have implored to be told about 'Jesus and his love,' as though I knew nothing. No Name like that! no Love like that! From first to last truly he—Jesus himself—is the Bread of Life. You—or rather Christ in you—did me good—real good—the other day, and I want to thank you as well as him.

Some minds, however far above us be their *full harmonies,* are yet so fashioned—we feel it instinctively—as to suit our own tone of mind in a peculiar way, and yours, if I may say it without apparent presumption, *suited* mine, so that what you said found an echo in my innermost life. …

Very truly yours,

KATE HANKEY

The Rev. Dundas L. Erskine, now missionary to the Zulus, writes in September 1898:

> Two days ago I heard of the death of Dr Moody Stuart. The last time we met in Glasgow he stood and lifted his hand, almost placing it on my head, and prayed for me as you know only such as he could. I shall ever be grateful that I listened to the closing years of his ministry. Many a time I went out of St Luke's made glad by the thought that grace was so much greater than sin. … The secret taught me of coming to Christ every morning as a sinner has been more than I can express.

Testimonies might also be given from those who only knew him in his old age, after his retirement from public duty. The Rev. M. D. M'Gillivray of Broughty Ferry, formerly of Kinfauns, writes:—

> I have many happy memories of pleasant intercourse with your father at Annat. He was a delightful companion, his conversation being at once that of a saint and a man of genius. To me he was unaffectedly kind, and I feel that with him has passed away one who influenced me more than any one else, except, perhaps, my old minister, Dr Horatius Bonar. Well, the giants are falling fast, and the Church is the poorer for their removal, but God fulfils himself in many ways, and can work by smaller men as he worked by bigger men.

At ministerial and other Christian conferences his addresses to his brethren in the ministry and to other Christian workers were always much valued, for he spoke as one who had much experience of the minds of men and of the mind of Christ. An address which he gave in 1865 at a ministerial conference on the Spiritual Condition and Influence of the Ministry was issued as a tract, and reprinted in 1880, and, I believe, has been much blessed. At the request of the late Dr Boyd of St Andrews a number of copies were sent to him by its author, and were presented by Principal Tulloch to the divinity students of St Mary's College. The subject is so important, and its writer was one so well qualified to deal with it, that I think it right to embody the address here with slight curtailment, as it is now out of print.

The Spiritual Condition of the Ministry and its Influence on the People

It is almost overwhelming for a minister to consider the *likeness* of the people to the priest, to see his own image reflected on them for good or for evil, himself multiplied a hundred-fold. No doubt you may see a member, an elder, a deacon, a precentor, or doorkeeper in a church, sitting for twenty years under a ministry of a very marked character, without a single feature transferred from the pulpit to the pew; and over many of his hearers, the most faithful pastor must often complain, 'I have laboured in vain, and spent my strength for nought.' But, on the other hand, the minister is very commonly reflected in many of his people, and his cast of thought is frequently exaggerated in its reappearance among them.

For example, in Brainerd's converts among the Red Indians, his doctrines and his own experience were brought out in a depth of humiliation beyond what he had himself preached; yet the natural fruit of his preaching, and still more of his spiritual experience. There is no reason to doubt that a similar process is taking place, to a greater or less extent, in all our congregations, and that our people are imbibing both our doctrine and our spirit; our earnestness, our humility, our love, our faith, our repentance, our joy, our prayerfulness; or our sloth, our self-sufficiency, our narrow-mindedness, our worldliness; our heavenliness, our lively hope, our spiritual insight, or our blindness to the unseen and the future, to God, to Christ, to heaven, to hell, and the value of the souls of men.

Independently of preaching, and even of personal intercourse, *our spiritual state* tells continually upon our people. In our preaching it is often what is within us, in the hidden thought of our own hearts, that influences our hearers more than the mere words that are flowing from our lips.

But to be more specific, it is *freshness* of spirit that tells more on people than any other mental condition. Freshness of desire, of faith, of hope, of repentance, of love, seems to have far greater moving power than the amount of actual spiritual attainment. A minister's attainment appears to produce no effect on his people in comparison with his *progress*. The greatest of all effects has sometimes been produced by a preacher awakened and inquiring; directing his people toward a Saviour still only sought for by himself, and at length finding him along with them. Freshness or reality is that which is most of all influential for good in the ministry.

Freshness of spirit has its origin and daily maintenance in *personal intercourse* with the living God. To stand in Jehovah's secret conclave or council, 'to hear and mark his words,' to get them there fresh for ourselves, and so to carry them fresh to the people, is the great condition of ministerial success. Other things we may have, or lacking them we may be losers by the want; but this is essential to life, and for it everything else must give place. Whatever time it takes, we must have this intercourse with our Master. 'Behold, I am against the prophets, saith the Lord, that steal my words every one from his neighbour. I have not sent these prophets, yet they ran. I sent them not, nor commanded them: therefore they shall not profit this people at all' (Jer. 23:30-32). No doubt this prompt running seems to save time and labour. We have not found God, Christ, the Spirit, for ourselves; but we have the words of the Lord, and we may run with these at once to the people. But our Lord brands these as 'stolen' words, even when they are his own, but heard only at second hand by us; and denounces the hasty self-sent messenger as wholly profitless to the people.

Immediately connected with freshness of spirit or the 'dew of youth,' there is another spiritual element of incalculable power in preaching; that is, *faith*. There is no gift more valuable for the ministry than faith in God that he will not let his word return to him void. But besides that faith in the promise of God, which we should all cherish habitually in preaching the gospel, there is another development of faith of a subtler and rarer character, yet undoubtedly the mightiest element of all in the success of the word. This faith is most rare and precious, hard to find, not easy to retain, and difficult to describe; yet wonderfully simple to the soul to which it is given, and marvellously communicative in its effect on the souls of others. Under any powerful work of the Spirit in a neighbourhood it is often habitual or abiding in the heart, and the man who is thus 'full of faith and of the Holy Ghost' seems to be enabled to carry this faith with him to other places, and to be used to kindle the fire of divine love where all was dark and frozen before.

I have conversed about it with some of the most thoughtful and successful Irish ministers after their Great Revival was past. They said that during that whole period, as compared with the previous years of their ministry, the chief and most characteristic difference consisted in a faith which they had never known before, and which they could not command or recall afterwards, but which was then simple and abiding in their own hearts, and in their daily ministrations to the souls of others. They believed, and therefore spoke; they spoke and believed that God would own their words, and that their preaching would by the Spirit work conviction, enlightening and salvation; and they were not disappointed. Daily believing thus, daily they were not put to shame; for the Lord himself confirmed the word daily with signs following.

The soul of every child of the kingdom ought always to be in some right state towards God; if not of joy for his presence, yet of grief for his absence; if not of victory, yet of true conflict; if not of cleaving to the Lord with purpose of heart, yet of distress for cleaving to the dust. Our hearts ought always to be right towards God. Adequate time given to the word of God and prayer will usually suffice for the righting of the heart. It may not soon effect its restoration, but it will commonly obtain at least this blessed issue, 'My desire is toward thee, and to the remembrance of thy holiness.' A passing desire will not suffice, for the sluggard desireth and hath not; a brief effort may bring only a transient amendment; the ordinary exercises of devotion may end, and leave the spirit as lifeless as when they began. In that case we cannot always resolve with Robert M'Cheyne, on a particular occasion, 'I cannot begin my work, for I have not yet seen the face of my God'; for the work may be such that we must enter upon it, however ill prepared. But we may often follow his example; our work may often lie over till we have seen the face of our God, and be both faster and better done through the holy delay and the divine help; and to a spirit resolved to 'seek first his kingdom and righteousness' the delay occasioned by the search will commonly be very brief. In a minister's daily walk with God one unwatchful hour may involve great loss to himself, which, if not soon repaired, may entail a serious injury to his people.

There must for a lengthened ministry be spiritual *growth*, and therefore spiritual *variety*. If there is the same man in the pulpit, with the same people in the pews for many years, there is a great risk of his rehearsing the same thoughts to unimpressed listeners. Now, while reading and study and other means are necessary to variety, and largely conducive to it, there is nothing so helpful as personal spiritual growth, because there is no such sameness as the sameness of death. Life is variety; death is sameness.

A minister should also seek indefatigably to be an *example* to his people, and ought therefore to aim at being the holiest man in his congregation; the meekest, the lowliest, the kindest, the most joyful, most watchful, most prayerful, the strongest in faith, the liveliest in hope, the highest above self, the nearest to God and to heaven, the purest or the least spotted image of our Lord Jesus Christ. Our falling almost infinitely short of this standard, is no reason why it should not be our earnest and constant aim. The sight of many members of our flock before us in the race will not fill us with grief, but with joy; yet we ought to grieve deeply for our own lagging behind them. Perhaps ministers, while far from being the least, are not commonly the most spiritual in their churches. Now, certainly, on every account a minister ought to be the holiest man in his congregation. His spiritual life is of ten times more importance than that of any other member in his church; and his calling and position are far more favourable to holiness than any other vocation. His calling shuts him up, more than any other, to the daily and weekly need of divine help, and grace is promised and given according to need; given, that is, to faith apprehending both the need and the promise. He is tempted by Satan as no other member of his church is tempted, and stronger temptation, if resisted, ensures more abundant grace; he is prayed for by his people as no other member is prayed for; and above all, he who walks amid the golden candlesticks holds him more than any other as a star in his own right hand.

Blessed be God the highest specimens of saints have been ministers of the gospel in all ages of the church, and it was their being great among the saints that rendered them great in the ministry. Moses and Elijah, John and Paul, were quite as eminent among the saints of God as among the ministers of his word. But so amongst intellectual and studious men were Augustine, Owen, Edwards, and hundreds of others, higher as saints in the kingdom than as preachers of the gospel; and probably nearer to God and liker to Christ than any of their hearers. So likewise with working pastors of parishes, with Newtons and Venns in England, with Calders in the Highlands and Bostons in the Lowlands of Scotland, and with men like M'Cheyne in our own day; they were eminent in the ministry, chiefly because they were eminent in grace; and they could, with Paul, say truly to their people, 'Be ye followers of me, even as I also am of Christ.'

Clearly this is not the exceptional, but the normal state of the gospel ministry; yet we seem to be too often contented with a sadly lower state. The Father is glorified by our bearing much fruit; but there is light never to be neglected thrown on the nature of the fruit and the manner of the fruit-bearing by the accompanying words, 'He that abideth in me, and I in him, the same bringeth forth much fruit.'

In another important address,[5] delivered to his ministerial brethren from the Moderator's Chair of the General Assembly of 1875, he said: 'When a student under Dr Chalmers an elder said to me, "You ministers should have more of the infinite in your sermons." Showing me two family portraits by eminent painters, he said, "That is by an artist; this by a genius. In the one you have the whole before you but nothing beyond; in the other the lines run off into infinity. You will never reach the people by teaching us as if you knew it all, and giving us our lesson as if we were children. If you wish to move us, you must make us feel that you see more than you are able to express, and that you think and know that there is an infinite height and depth beyond what you see. But you go to the brim of the great ocean, you dip your tumbler into it, you set it down before us, and you tell us, 'That's the ocean.'" This elder said truly that this is the weakest of all preaching. And in these days of a ready-made and glib evangelism, when the speaker keeps repeating that it is all so plain and no darkness or difficulty in it, as if there were no unfathomed depth in the heart of man, and no infinite depth in the mind of God, the thought will sometimes arise: That is the sparkling water in your glass; but what of the great ocean? We must both go ourselves to the ocean and lead our people there; we must for ourselves and with them learn to say, "Such knowledge is too wonderful for me."'

Regarding the character of the influence exerted by Dr Moody Stuart upon his contemporaries, the Edinburgh Free Presbytery in the address presented to him on the occasion of his diamond jubilee in 1897 record their judgment that 'few were honoured to wield an influence so profound and far-reaching.'

[5] The address entitled 'Higher Holiness'. See Appendix, pp. 342-65.—P.

— 19 —

Devotional Diary Extracts
(1894–98)

> Mine eyes did timeously prevent
> The watches of the night,
> That in thy word with careful mind
> Then meditate I might.
>
> *—Psalm 119:148 (Scottish Psalter)*

TWENTY years before beginning this diary (practically the only one which he kept during his long life), Dr Moody Stuart wrote: 'The frank interchange of private confidence on the fears, the struggles, the hopes, the victories in our great life-work here that prepare us for the next and chief portion of our history, may be rendered a hundred-fold more fruitful by the private thoughts being made known to a wider circle, who are thus admitted into the bonds of hidden friendship.'

In harmony, therefore, with Dr Moody Stuart's own judgment, and, indeed, in accordance with his own desire, some extracts (which we regret the space at our disposal obliges us to restrict in number) are given to our readers in the hope that they may prove helpful to others in promoting their spiritual life. The diary is not continuous but has considerable intervals. On this account, and to secure variety, the extracts given are not always in chronological sequence.

'Behold my hands and my feet.'

During the night I usually awake every hour and a half or two hours, when I strike a light and stand to read a few verses of the Bible, which seldom fail to bring delight and quickening, with food for meditation and prayer when resting again. Last night after my first sleep I read the words of Christ, 'Behold my hands and my feet, that it is I myself: handle me, and see,' and had a very helpful musing on them. How I love the words of our Lord Jesus! It is hearing himself, and is surely next to seeing him. What will it be to handle for ourselves and to kiss those blessed feet, with the print of the nails that fastened him to the cross for our redemption and resurrection! Are we indeed to see him face to face, and to have our vile bodies fashioned like to his glorious body! What will it be to hear our Lord Jesus, who has so often spoken to us through the veil, then say to each one of us, 'Behold, it is I myself'! Would that I had testified more fully and more lovingly of the grace of Jesus Christ in 'enduring the cross and despising the shame' for us so worthless and so vile, that he might present us to himself for ever without spot or wrinkle. How men would be captivated if they knew what a Saviour he is, who left his Father's glory and took hands and feet to himself that in them he might be nailed to the cross on Calvary, a spectacle to angels and to men, and that he might say to all the world, 'Behold my hands and my feet. Look unto me, and be ye saved, all the ends of the earth.'

Arrangement of Occupation

On Sabbath night I endeavoured to yield myself entirely to the Lord for guidance in my way, which now is only, or mainly, the guidance of my thoughts. This morning I could joyfully say, 'Our fellowship is with the Father and with his Son Jesus Christ'; and I cannot say that any day passes without this fellowship enjoyed more or less fully; and my thoughts have for the most part been occupied with cherishing this fellowship, and next to this with a review of my past life, partly to give thanks for 'the words on which he has caused me to hope,' and partly to confess my sins, both for their cleansing and for the removal of the old roots remaining. My inquiry was, Is this devotion to seeking God first, and my own sanctification next, the best occupation of my days, now that I can do no outward work, or should I give less time to personal waiting on God and on his word, and more time to praying for the church and the world? I pray daily for my children and children's children, and for many weeks have been praying much for my daughter-in-law in Dundee, whose life is ebbing away, and for my daughter in Edinburgh, laid up with protracted sickness. I pray daily for Israel through the world and for our missions to them, for India, Africa, China, South and North America, for my old flock, for this neighbourhood [Rait], for various causes in Christian effort, and for special friends, but these prayers do not occupy the bulk of my time. Almost every night, without any formal intention, on resting in bed I find myself repeating (usually in the metre) the words of the 63rd Psalm, 'O God, thou art my God—my soul thirsteth for thee—to see thy power and thy glory,' and then the 73rd Psalm, from verse 23, 'Nevertheless, thou shalt guide me with thy counsel and afterward receive me to glory.' In the morning I read two or three psalms and one or two chapters of the Bible. In the course of the day, along with much of the Bible, which is *everything* to me, I read various books besides periodicals; at present I am going through the New Testament with Bengel, at different times of the day. On Sabbath night I asked the Lord if, on the whole, this is the best distribution of my time and thoughts, and am still asking counsel. However sadly true it has sometimes been, yet on the whole the Lord has not said of me, 'They would none of my counsel and despised all my reproof,' for I have loved the 'reproof' of the word and the Spirit.

The Saving Words of the Bible

My present aim is for a more intimate acquaintance and more constant walk with our wondrous Saviour Jesus Christ, and nothing is so helpful for this as the very words of the Bible. How precious and how clasping is the divine narrative of every word spoken, every work done, every suffering borne by our altogether lovely and loving Lord; every incident in his life and in his death so winding him into us and our souls into him. Oh that I could walk with him, and speak with him, and listen to him, and follow him every hour. He is willing for this and desiring it, and may I be more willing and more full of trust in his love and grace, and more thankfully assured of the infinite and continual cleansing of his blood. 'This man receiveth sinners and eateth with them,' not *although* they are but *because* they are sinners. How good it is to understand that we don't need to be *not sinners* to receive Christ Jesus. What a holy harmony there is between our heart and conscience and our only and all-sufficient Saviour, when we cease pretending to be what we are not, and take our own character as helpless sinners, and accept the great truth that 'Christ Jesus came into the world to save sinners'; 'humbling ourselves to walk with God' (Micah 6:8, margin), and the Holy One dwelling with him that is willingly 'poor and of a contrite spirit'—the simple mystery of grace, so plain and so omnipotent to all the babes. May I be among the least of the little ones to magnify the only Great and only Good One.

The Resurrection of the Dead

I have been reading and trying to receive our Lord's words, 'I am the resurrection and the life; he that believeth in me, though he were dead, yet shall he live,' and recalling my own conscious death sixty-four years ago, when he called and quickened me into life that was marvellous and inconceivable. All other miracles are little beside this, for which I thank and praise him anew this day, for his own 'good work begun in me,' which I am persuaded he will perform unto the end. In the weakness of age and gradual bodily decay we think more of the coming resurrection, when this body 'sown in corruption shall be raised in incorruption,' like a seed of wheat cast into the earth and springing up in freshness and beauty. With what hallowed gladness shall we rise when we hear his voice calling us from the grave, and when with wonder and joyful shame we see ourselves clothed in immortal beauty after the likeness of the Lord's glorious body.

Longing for the Love of Christ

I have been asking a better grasp of Christ's personal love to me, or rather a fuller revealing of himself to me. I doubt it not—I believe it—but I long to know that love which passeth knowledge. 'As the Father hath loved me, so have I loved you, continue ye in my love,' i.e., my love to you. The mystics rejoice in this love, yet sometimes overlook the divine righteousness, the grace reigning through righteousness, the loving us and washing us in his own blood. This, indeed, I have believed in, in his dying, the just for the unjust, and in all that such a death involves; but I long for a more full and direct apprehension of the *love* that was the source of the sacrifice, and to say, 'We have known and believed the love.' Many years ago Lady Lucy Smith said to me, after an expression of her own unworthiness, '*But oh how loved!*' and I thought this was more than my own spontaneous utterance at the moment might have been.

Rutherford writes: 'Every day we may see some new thing in Christ; his love hath neither brim nor bottom. A few drops from this ocean of love would more than fill our hearts, and we should be constrained to say, "My cup runneth over."'

Attractive Nearness of Christ

In prayer last night I was brought graciously nearer to the Lord Jesus than usual, and was ashamed to meet with him as if eye to eye, and to hear him say, 'I will come again and receive you to myself.' Lord, who am I that thou shouldst look upon a worm of the dust? and 'have I also looked on him that seeth me?' It was a most solemn anticipation, both awful and joyful, of the day when we shall see him face to face.

In the watches of the night, apart from present asking, 'Jesus himself drew near.' It was not that I remembered him upon my bed, but he remembered me, and 'manifested himself' not 'in another form' yet differently from ever before, very attractively and winningly. I trust earnestly that both these revealings of himself may be 'earnests' not only of the eternal future above, but of further disclosures on earth.

The Reproof of the Spirit and the Accusation of Mere Conscience

Today I have been thinking over and deeply feeling the almost incredible difference in the retrospect of life, between its sins and faults when thrust into the mind by the unsanctifying and bitter accusings of Satan and of the natural conscience, and when brought home by the words of Christ and the healing convictions of the Holy Spirit. How I love the reproof of the Spirit and the rebuke of the Redeemer, which are far keener and deeper than all other; yet not for death but for life, not for upbraiding, but for cure and everlasting consolation.

'Ashamed and confounded for all that thou hast done, when I am pacified toward thee for all.' A new and clearer sight of all the evils and all the neglects of the past is quickly followed or accompanied by a fuller and more satisfying sight and sense, both of the complete and abounding satisfaction for all our sins on the cross, and of the tender mercy of the loving God in giving the Sacrifice and in revealing it to our souls. Today it has been a great relief and joy to see that, when we do not reject but thankfully receive the reproofs of the Spirit, we may justly bid defiance to our own inward and to Satanic upbraidings, because 'in him all who believe are justified from all things.' Apart from Christ crucified, all condemn us—Satan, ourselves, every one that we have ever known. But with the sprinkling of the blood of the Lamb on our conscience we are whiter than snow, so that God himself seeth no spot.

Songs in the Night

Last night before falling asleep I lay awake a long time, but had delight and communion in going over some of our Scotch metrical Psalms—27th, 32nd, 51st, 130th, 100th, 63rd, and the last verses of the 73rd. What a refreshing and enlightening these and other psalms are, and in the night watches I find them more helpful in the metre, because more easily remembered, and much more helpful than hymns, chiefly because the soul can rest on them as the word of God; though I frequently add that choicest of hymns, 'Rock of Ages,' and also 'Just as I am.'

Today I have been exploring once and again that ever memorable transaction in the end of the seventh of St Luke, and seeking, and in some measure receiving for myself, the captivating truth that to whom much is forgiven the same loveth much. I trust that Christ has with his own lips been speaking to me the much forgiveness, and constraining the free return of loving much.

The New Wine at the Marriage of the Lamb

In my old church the sacramental cup is drunk today at the supper of espousal, and it is to be drunk new at the marriage supper of the Lamb. Christ is now unseen by the guests with whom he sups; but then we shall be privileged to see him face to face when he sups with us and we with him. But the great consolation is that the heavenly supper, like the earthly, however altered and new, will still be the commemoration of his death for the forgiveness of all our sins, no longer indeed of present sinfulness, but of all our sins from our birth till our death throughout this earthly life. When the *new* wine sealing the blood of the Lamb, shed for the remission of sin, fills every cup at that High Table of the Lord, and fills my cup, I feel humbly emboldened to take my place at that table; and when he 'drinks it new' with every guest, to hear him say to me also, the last and the least, 'Drink ye all of it.'

Earthly Self Unknown in Heaven

'The grace that is to be brought unto you at the revelation of Jesus Christ,' in 1 Peter 1:13, I now find is translated literally by Alford, 'the grace that *is being brought unto you*,' representing it as already on the way to meet us. What an impulse this gives to lively hope, and a prompt girding of our loins to meet our coming Lord by the assurance that this ocean of eternal grace is not only remaining for us in heaven but is even now flowing down upon the earth to refresh us with its welcome stream!

This morning a humbling sense of my sinful self-love, with its incessant intrusion into every sphere of thought and work, was followed by a singularly bright view of its entire extinction in heaven, first of all in me and likewise in the whole multitude of the redeemed. In the bright company which no man can number, out of all kindreds and tribes and tongues, that darkest brand on earth of 'men who are lovers of their own selves' shall not be seen stamped on a single forehead. The love that 'seeketh not her own' will have unqualified and full possession of every heart, and of mine also through abounding grace. A noble world it will be of men once sunk in the depths of self-righteousness and self-seeking, but ransomed by him who 'pleased not himself,' each of us rejoicing for ever in that love which 'envieth not and vaunteth not itself, thinketh no evil, and seeketh not her own.' Every one of us will know every other's inmost soul, will trust every other, and help the happiness of every other, and all love will be swallowed up in the song of everlasting gratitude 'to him who loved us and who washed us in his own blood.'

Three Lines in Life

In reviewing a long life I have been retracing the two great lines, or rather perhaps three, that have marked it throughout, *viz.*:—

1. The black line of my own will and way and walk; distorted by wanderings, by stumblings, by manifold offences; by self-seeking, by back-going; full of sin and shame and self-destruction.

2. The bright red line of the Lord's way with me; of long-suffering, of correcting, of leading, of restoring; of loving-kindness, of truth, of omnipotent deliverances; of enlargement and gladness in the ministry of the word by the Holy Ghost; of providential guidance in things both great and little, and specially in the leading events of life; of gracious remembrances; of victory over the world, the flesh, and the devil; of the lively hope of everlasting life.

3. A third line, it may be called, of my own way through grace; not only of what he has himself done for me and in me, but of what I have been enabled to be and to do by grace; a very chequered and unequal line, still on the whole counting

all things loss for the excellency of the knowledge of Jesus Christ; and rejoicing in 'being kept by the power of God through faith unto salvation.'

Loss and Gain in Cessation from Work

This morning, before breakfast, whilst reading in course the fourth of John, I was reminded of the mediæval lines:—

> *Recordare, Jesu pie,*
> > *Quod sum causa tuae viae,*
> *Ne me perdas illo die.*

> *Quaerens me sedisti lassus,*
> > *Redemisti crucem passus,*
> *Tantus labor non sit cassus.*

> *Rex tremendae majestatis,*
> > *Qui salvandos salvas gratis,*
> *Salva me, Fons pietatis.*

[Which may be thus literally rendered:—

> Loving Lord, recall, I pray,
> > How I caused thy weary way!
> Lose me not on that great day!

> Tired thou sat'st when me thou soughtest,
> > By thy cross my freedom boughtest,
> Ne'er in vain such task thou wroughtest.

> King of dreadful majesty,
> > Saving heirs of mercy free,
> Fount of kindness, save thou me!]

Lord Jesus, am I the cause of thy long journey to this earth and through it? Wast thou seeking me in sitting wearied by the well, and was I in thine heart on thy cross of awful anguish?

I see that outward work is profitable for spiritual health, whilst its distractions demand very careful watching. The freedom from work gives both time and help for fuller communion with the Lord Jesus and with the Father of our spirits, but through our deceitful hearts and the wiles of our great Adversary it gives place also for spiritual languor, and for useless and hurtful thoughts. Lord, in the multitude of thy tender mercies I beseech thee to renew a right spirit within me hour by hour.

Not unto us, Lord!

'Father, I will that they whom thou hast given me be with me where I am (Lord, hasten it in thy time), that they may behold my glory.' I wonder much what that glory will be and what our 'beholding' of it. I should like to be hid when I see it, yet he is 'to be admired in all them that believe'—not they to be admired, but himself to be admired in them. If my Lord will be seen in greater beauty when his grace is seen in saving me, then I consent to be seen, that he may be admired in me, though the last and the least. One saved sinner brought out and a song of praise to the Lamb over him; then another, and a new and louder song; then another—then at length it comes to me, with a greater surprise and still louder song, 'Worthy is the Lamb that was slain.' 'Not unto us, Lord, not unto us.'

Pastoral Failings

Awoke with an overpowering sense of the Lord's goodness to me a sinner, and half weeping with thankfulness for his wondrous mercy in forgiving my sins, so many and so great. My thoughts were, in the words of Jacob's prayer, 'O God, I am not worthy of the least of all the mercy and of all the truth thou hast showed to thy servant.'

But after a good while the review of past mercy brought back the remembrance of past sins, and specially of pastoral neglects.

I remembered that my friend Andrew Gray (of Perth) burst into tears when with some of his brethren, and exclaimed, 'A minister's sins are so aggravated!' and the thought of my own pastoral sins, and many other sins besides, threw me deep down; and as I had begun with Jacob's confession, I had now to take up his wrestling prayer, with the bitter remembrance of his name and I of mine, and to plead for a new blessing. The Lord in his boundless grace did not refuse, and I trust that the words were made good even to me, 'And he blessed him there.'

In the midst of our work we confess our sins with the resolution of amendment through grace, but when life is passed we have no opportunity except in the cleansing of the heart. But I find a great consolation in the thought that all our sins against men, of neglect or otherwise, have been chiefly against God, that he is living and accessible to us though they are not, and that if he, with whom alone now we have to do, shall forgive and cleanse us, it is more and better than if we were forgiven by all against whom we have sinned in any way.

Joy Abounding by Suffering

After laying myself down to rest, though not to sleep, the night before last, the Lord was pleased to visit me with his own presence and peace in a way that was new to me, putting quite 'a new song' into my mouth. For weeks I have been suffering, and for a time I thought the discomfort had quite left me, but it returned again more sharply. I had sometimes prayed for sleep; but not being satisfied that it was the Lord's will to grant it, but rather to make the want an exercise of patience, I had that evening only asked, and had been much helped in asking, a full gift of the Holy Spirit. After lying down the distress became such that nothing could counteract it except the joy of the Holy Ghost, and this was granted to me in much abundance, yet without the slightest alleviation of the suffering. The joy was so great that I could quite rejoice in the pain, with no desire for its removal. Hour after hour the incessant bodily irritation and the peace that passeth understanding, without the slightest mental irritation, flowed rapidly through me like two competing streams, but with the inward gladness so exceeding and triumphant that I was more than content with the suffering, that seemed to be a helpful handmaid to the joy. Comparing little things with great, or rather the least with the greatest, I could now quite understand what had seemed inexplicable to me—how the martyrs could rejoice in their sufferings; and was reminded of the case of a young woman, a member of my church, who, when laid up in the infirmary, assured me with a smile that her joy in the Lord was so great as far to exceed her pain, which the doctors said must have been singularly severe.

Answered Prayer

I have been sadly vexed by being providentially kept from seeing my sick daughter by the great severity of the weather and my own weakness; and I have been in bed till this hour (3 p.m.) with rather a sharp cold. My daughter has now less suffering and much peace and quietness, with no desire for any lengthening of her days. Her rest and quietness in the Lord, more specially for the last two or three weeks, have given us unmingled thankfulness. 'His lovingkindness is better than life,' and this is far, far more to me than if I had the gratification of seeing her. All our prayers have been answered in the very best way, and I can bless the Lord on her account without any drawback whatever. 'He hath done all things well.' Her minister (Dr Whyte of St George's) wrote that she has come forth 'as gold tried in the furnace.'

Joy at Our Reception into Heaven

Have been thinking today with reference both to our dear deceased in the Lord [Mrs Watt], and to my own departure to be with Christ, that as there is joy in heaven over the lost soul's recovery, there will be a second outburst of joy when the ransomed wanderer is finally brought home above. The Lord Jesus then brings the sheep that had been lost to his own home above, and will surely say to the gathered angels and to the sympathising spirits of the just, 'Rejoice with me, for I have found my sheep which was lost.' A lost one saved by grace, and by grace alone, is a wonder to itself and a new song to the Lamb that was slain. The glorious scene foretold in the 45th Psalm will be fulfilled with a constant renewal in heaven:—

> They shall be brought with gladness great,
> And mirth on ev'ry side,
> Into the palace of the King,
> And there they shall abide (Psa. 45:15, *Scottish Psalter*).

When the Lord Jesus entered Paradise with the redeemed penitent from the cross, with what a shout of joy would he call to the expecting angels and to the ransomed throng, 'Rejoice with me, for I have found my sheep which was lost,' and so of each lost one brought home for ever.

Christ's Promised Presence in the Jordan

Yesterday afternoon the Lord Jesus came to me with unwonted nearness, and spoke to my soul with exquisite sweetness and persuasive power: 'When thou passest through the waters I will be with thee, and through the rivers, they shall not overflow thee.' His words brought no trouble but exceeding calmness and joy. Were they an intimation to be ready for his coming? Afterwards I answered, 'Lord if it be thou, bid me to come unto thee on the water.' In the evening at family worship we read in course the ever-memorable words, 'Verily, I say unto thee, today thou shalt be with me in Paradise.' How I love that dying penitent and claim him for a brother, and think to look for him among the first whom I hope to meet in Paradise. But what a worm am I to be there! When thinking of it early this morning it seemed to me that when they saw me sitting at the feet of Jesus all of them did marvel—yet I am humbly 'looking for the mercy of our Lord Jesus Christ unto eternal life.'

The Darkest Sin Whiter than Snow

A thought has occurred to me that is new to myself and may require sifting. David prays 'Wash me *throughly* from mine iniquity,' or, as Calvin takes it, 'many times,' even as the leper was to be sprinkled with hyssop seven times, and he adds, 'Sprinkle me with hyssop and I shall be whiter than snow.' These words have suggested the thought that the washing of a great sin many times in the blood of the Lamb may transform the dark stain into a more perfect whiteness than the rest of the robe in which the ransomed sinner stands before the great white throne, whilst the whole garment shares the benefit of the repeated sprinkling. The Lord Jesus stands clothed in raiment 'white as the light,' with a whiteness divine and unapproachable, to which the redeemed are growing in likeness through eternity. Their robes are all spotlessly white, yet with various lustre, as one star differs from another star in glory. Now if the dark stain of a grievous sin has through grace awakened a deeper repentance and been oftener brought to the blood of the covenant for a more thorough cleansing, may not that darkest spot be transformed into a brighter whiteness than the rest of the robe, yet without the least abruptness, and the whole quite harmonious. What a consolation to think of the *possibility*, and what a soothing to David and *to us,* if while our sin will never be cast up for a reproach, its abundant forgiveness, with its manifold cleansing and transforming, will bear the highest testimony of all to the precious blood of the Lamb. 'Lord, now lettest thou thy servant depart in peace.'

David's sin may be held to be the worst recorded in all the Bible in the life of any child of God; and if the countless pardons and consolations that have gathered around the Lord's wondrous grace to him in the gift of the 51st Psalm, should move any inquirer in the world to come to look for a trace of the deep blood-red stain that gave occasion to the great confession, the answer would be, '*That* is it that has been so thoroughly washed in the blood of the Lamb, and is now so matchlessly white'—'whiter than snow.'

'*Though he slay me, yet will I trust in him.*'

Yesterday, from morning till past midnight, I had a sad and to me quite singular experience in a deep and dark desertion without any conscious cause on my part. At intervals from time to time I had soothing rest in Christ and peace with God, as at family prayers in the evening, and more than once and again through the day; but the greater part of the Sabbath was clouded by a dark withdrawal of the face of God, not through want of watchfulness or the intrusion of idle thoughts, but thinking of nothing except, 'Verily, thou art a God that hidest thyself.' The words were often with me, 'Who is among you that feareth the Lord, that walketh in darkness and hath no light, let him trust in the name of the Lord and stay upon his God,' and my prayer was, 'O Lord, hear; O Lord, forgive; O Lord, hearken and do; defer not for thine own sake, O my God.' Job's confession, 'Though he slay me, yet will I trust in him,' was always returning to my lips. Many years ago I had carefully studied the verse, and satisfied myself that our authorised translation (with which the R.V.[1] agrees) was right,[2] and I concluded that there were no sufficient grounds

[1] Revised Version, a British revision of the Authorized Version (King James Version), of which the New Testament was completed in 1881 and the Old Testament in 1885.—P.

[2] The translation in our English Bible appears to have been the accepted meaning of the words by Jews and Christians from an ancient date, and the difficulty in the Hebrew is removed by Tremellius and Junius, and by Le Clerc, by the translation, 'If he slay me shall I not hope?' (*Si occidat me, annon sperabo?*)—AMS.

for the opinion of an eminent critic, who calls it 'an inspired mistranslation.' Now in extreme darkness it was exactly my own state, both in the sense of God's severe rebuke, and in the response of faith 'yet will I trust in him.' Before lying down to rest I had some help in prayer, but with an immediate return of the painful sense of death, and after midnight I struck a light to read Job's words, and then to ponder them in sadness as my own.

But as soon as I awoke in the morning I began to repeat the 23rd Psalm, and was amazed and delighted when I found that the Lord was giving it all to myself from first to last, restoring my soul for his own sake. The prolonged trouble of soul has weakened me, but how thankful I am for the new song, 'O Lord, I will praise thee; though thou wast angry with me thine anger is turned away, and thou comfortedst me.'

'Worthy is the Lamb!'

'Worthy is the Lamb that was slain.' I thank God for enabling me this morning to adopt these words. Yesterday was my eighty-sixth birthday, and I had great humbling and searchings of heart for the sins, the neglects and the defects of a long life, but this morning my gracious Redeemer has put this new song into my lips. In the ordinary course it is not likely that I shall see another birthday, and I am far from desiring it.

How I love the eighth verse of the 143rd Psalm: 'Cause me to hear thy lovingkindness in the morning; for in thee do I trust: cause me to know the way wherein I should walk; for I lift up my soul unto thee.'

Our Lord's Second Advent

At the present time there is much said about the nearness of our Lord's second advent, which ought to be very quickening, but when too much dwelt upon is apt to weaken our views of heaven and of the great eternity. For myself it is not now a practical question, for I am far past the ordinary limits of life on earth; and the Apostles Peter and Paul, who so loved the appearing of the Lord Jesus, both speak of the certain nearness of death in their own case. Of two followers of the Lamb living at present, if one shall survive till the Lord come and the other be removed by death, the one who dies will rise from the grave and be the *first* of the two to greet the Lord at his coming. It always remains true that in such an hour as we think not the Son of Man cometh, so that we cannot fix either an immediate or a distant time for his personal coming, but are warned to be always ready. There is much in Bunyan's answer to the question, 'What do Christians think of Christ?'—'They long to see him betwixt this and the clouds of heaven.' But when death comes to the believer Jesus Christ comes to receive him, as he did to the martyr Stephen. The extreme advocates of the nearness of the second advent seem to have overlooked the inspired longing, 'having a desire ['the desire,' R.V.] to *depart*.'

'Thou shalt love the Lord thy God!'

Yesterday and today the command, 'Thou shalt *love* the Lord thy God with *all* thine heart, and with *all* thy soul, and with *all* thy might' (Deut. 6:5) has been much in my mind, humbling me because since I have tasted that the Lord is gracious, I have fallen so sinfully and so sadly short of any adequate obedience to this command, and likewise under the sense of present inability to comply with it. But in the course of today the Lord has graciously reminded me that what is a *command* in the Old Testament is a *promise* in the New, and I have been enabled to plead the promise for this special duty, 'I will write my law in their hearts and put it in their minds,' and this has lifted me up and helped me beyond expectation. It comes, however, through seeing that 'We love him because he first loved us.'

Self in Little Things

Have been humbled today by the Spirit bringing to my recollection an act of inconsiderateness sixty years ago, which I thought nothing of at the time through not seeing its unkindness in putting others to needless trouble and inconvenience. How deep self is in little things and great! But what humbles me most is the reflection how many instances of self-pleasing to the discomfort or pain of others, and unthought of by myself, must have stained my life. I thank God for granting me repentance in this instance, repentance unto life; and at the same time enabling me to confess the deep root of self in me, so prolific of manifold evil. 'Search me, O God, and try me.'

Jesus Christ within the Room

On awaking this morning Jesus Christ drew very, very near to me, in a way so as never quite the same before. He 'manifested himself' to me with inconceivable lovingkindness and tenderness and holy intimacy. He moved and constrained me to answer, 'My Lord Jesus,' with the softening and the love of my whole heart, and with more than the whole of my previous heart. 'A new heart will I give you,' and 'I am come that they might have life, and that they might have it more abundantly.' It came to me as a token that 'the night is far spent and the day is at hand,' and that suddenly he may now be saying, 'I will come again and receive you to myself.' 'Behold, I come *quickly.* Amen, even *so,* come Lord Jesus.'

It was not the lifting up of my heart to Christ in heaven, but it was Jesus Christ himself coming down into the room with me for a good long time, speaking to myself and moving me with tearful tone to answer him.

Recalling Many Mercies

Lay awake last night from eleven o'clock till four in the morning without the least shade of sleep, but was very grateful for the Lord's exceeding goodness, for his lovingkindness was better than sleep. Over against my sins which he brought to my remembrance on a previous night, he was now pleased to recall to me a long succession of mercies in providence and in grace, of deliverances, of pardons, of quickenings, of the manifold help of his own right hand and of his watchfulness over me to keep my feet from stumbling and mine eyes from tears, after he had saved my soul from death. What a debt I owe for the daily cleansing of sins that grieved the Holy Spirit through so many years, and now it seems to me as if he were about to grant me to love much because I have been forgiven so much. I have been wondering at his condescension in *allowing* me to love him after all my provocations.

The Daily Victory through Christ

The love I owe for sin forgiven,
    For power to believe,
For present peace and promised heaven,
    No angel can conceive.[3]

What heights and depths are in my daily life! I have been remembering the first day and hour when the word of God came to me with saving power and I found the forgiveness of sin. I trust that he has never since taken it utterly out of my mouth, and I cannot say that a day passes without 'beholding the beauty of the Lord' and being revived by his grace. For the most part the Lord is with me the greater part of the day, and is daily giving me some new insight into the depth and freeness of his love, together with the conviction of sin and contrition of spirit, in which there is

[3] From the hymn 'Ten thousand talents once I owed' by John Newton (1725–1807).—*P.*

much peace and rest. But almost daily I am thrown back again by the inborn hardness of my heart, and have conflict before I recover, sometimes (though not daily) such a conflict as makes me experience that 'through much tribulation we must enter the kingdom,' and that whilst increase of grace is granted, the tribulation may also increase, the nearer we come to entering for ever into the kingdom.

Gracious Victory over Satan

Last night before going to bed I was enabled to pray with intense and repeated earnestness for the presence of the Spirit through the night and for the Lord's lovingkindness in the morning, and lay down full of thankfulness for the help in prayer, and with the joyful hope of an abundant answer. But as soon as I lay down Satan suddenly beset me with unholy thoughts, and for an hour or two it cost me a conflict of great severity before God gave me the victory through the blood of the Lamb, by prayer and by psalms and many passages of Scripture brought seasonably to my recollection. At length the struggle ceased and the victory was more than complete. It was not merely warding off the adversary and restoring my soul, but the Lord made me 'more than conqueror through him that loved me'; loving me during the contest and now enlarging me over mine enemy, and giving me a new song by bringing Satan under my feet more completely than before.

The Lord's Teaching through Life

This morning, in reviewing my past life after reading Isaiah 26:12, 'Thou hast wrought all our works in us,' my thoughts reverted to what works the Lord might have wrought in me by his grace, for which I ought not to be unthankful. My life-work has been to preach Jesus Christ, with sad defects and very unequally, but it is in this mainly that I have laboured, and I trust that the Lord has wrought in me both by his teaching in preparation and by the presence of his Spirit with me in preaching. More than forty years ago I was for a time brought under an overwhelming conviction of sin, so that many supposed my sermons then to be legal; but my thought of sin in myself and in others was of an undervalued Christ, and resting in the gospel without the present exercise of grace and contrition of spirit. I thank my God for whatever witness I have been privileged to bear to Christ, and him crucified, who is all my praise and my glory.

Next to Jesus Christ and inseparable from him is the word of God through which alone we know him by the teaching of the Holy Spirit. In my old age the Lord wrought in me to bear testimony to the truthfulness and trustworthiness of the Old Testament, for which I thank him much. The misconceptions of the divine record in our land overwhelmed me with the severest sorrow, and after much labour I trust I was enabled to relieve the minds of some of our people who were greatly distressed by the setting aside of its plain truth.

The Flavour of Fruit Increased by Length of Time in Ripening

Today I was arrested by reading that the flavour of fruit depends on the length of time it takes to ripen, and I am therefore thankful for more time on earth for ripening, but humbled by the thought that when no longer fit for any work I have been left here after all my early associates, because I needed more mellowing than they did, with more in me that was harsh and raw to be chastened and softened. But how good is the great Husbandman, so to make his own fruit in me more meet to be plucked by his loving hand.

The Happy End Not Far Off

Waiting soul, thy days are ended,
    All thy mourning days below;
Go, by angel-guards attended,
    To thy waiting Saviour go.

Longing to receive thy spirit,
    Lo, Emmanuel waits above;
Pleads the value of his merit,
    Offers thee the crown of love!

Away, thou waiting soul, away,
    Fly to the mansions of the blest;
Thy God no more requires thy stay,
    He calls thee to eternal rest.[4]

These verses (two or three words slightly altered) have been much in my mind through the day, and nearly express my own thoughts about my way and work being ended. But I find that to retain an abiding and lively sense of the presence and the peace of God, I must often return to the counsel of the prophet Micah: 'Humble thyself to walk with thy God.' How clear and full is the grace of our Lord Jesus Christ to our souls, when we are enabled and lovingly inclined to take our own place as sinners, with no light or help except in the Saviour alone, who is then seen to be 'full of grace and truth' to ourselves.

Satan Buffeting the Soul

Last night was kept long awake and greatly fatigued by foolish thoughts harassing the soul, yet not entering into it or occupying it but beating incessantly from without and striving for entrance. It was clearly an assault of Satan, and the conflict was sore and incessant to keep him out, till after

[4] Hymn by Charles Wesley (1707–88).—*P.*

a long wrestling the Lord gave me a full and refreshing rest, and comfort in the thought, 'He giveth his beloved sleep.' Two thoughts came to me about it: that Satan came in great wrath because he knows that he has but a short time, and that we must through much tribulation enter the kingdom of God; for it truly amounted to tribulation. When the love of God has been shed abroad in the heart it has been heaven on earth, and I have been well content to tarry all the days of my appointed time; but if Satan were suffered to repeat such assaults I could not but pray, 'O that I had wings like a dove, that I might fly away and be at rest.' But I am resting in the peace of God today, while taking this 'temptation' as a possible token that the blessed end may be quite near. Lord Jesus, condescendingly speak to me in fullness of power and love, and say to my soul, 'Come unto me and I will give you rest,' whether on thy footstool here or beneath thy throne above. But, Lord, what am I that thou shouldest bear with me, and think lovingly upon me?

Heaven on Earth

One day last week there came upon me for some hours a soul-satisfying sight and sense of the presence, the peace and the love of God so full and tranquil as to turn earth into heaven, and to make my approaching departure most simple and unutterably joyful. I could thus conceive (but who can describe?) the everlasting abolition of 'the heart of stone,' and the whole man bathed for ever in the ocean of the love of God, so infinitely removed from all that is hard or dead and so full of tenderness and grace.

What a weak as well as low idea it is to conceive of our God and Creator as if he were impersonal, when he is the essence of personality, the one living God, the only living One in the fullest sense of the word, the root and essence of all life, from whom all creatures receive their life, 'living and moving and having their being in him,' and apart from whom all creation would die.

The Melting of the Heart of Stone For Ever

After awaking this morning I had a long musing on the blessed promise, 'I am pacified toward thee for all that thou hast done,' and the Lord seemed to give it to me for the immediate ending of a long life. I grasped the privilege of a joyful repentance on earth before leaving it for heaven, where our heavenly Father with his own hand wipes all tears from our eyes. Then the thought came that though there will be no repentance in heaven, we may be endued for ever with a singularly blessed contrition of spirit, loving much because forgiven much; and the heart that was once a stone may be melted into a contrite joy for ever, akin to what a stalwart Highland convert called 'an eternity of sweet weeping.' But in heaven there are no tears.

Rebellion and Restoration

Nearly a fortnight ago after retiring to rest a most painful rebellion against my heavenly Father sprang up in my heart, partly from the deep enmity of the carnal mind against God, and partly by Satan infusing his own malignant hatred to the Holy One. Never since my birth have I known so virulent a contest against my Almighty Maker, but after two miserable hours it was graciously subdued before falling asleep, and in the morning I awoke in peace with God, but for a day or two was not restored to my wonted light and liberty. Yet that day week[5] from my grievous trouble the Lord more than forgave all my rebellion, and for hour after hour flooded my inmost soul with such a stream of light and love and peace and joy as I had never known, quite as marked and singular as the contrary had been, more than covering and compensating my

---

[5] That is, a week after.—*P.*

evil with his own surpassing goodness, and constraining me to say, 'Who is a God like unto thee, that pardoneth iniquity, transgression and sin?'

Communion with God

The hope of eternal life is surpassingly wonderful and glorious: to be with God and in God for ever—the Father and the Son and the Holy Ghost. When a brief time of communion here is so satisfying to the whole heart and the whole mind, and so fills the soul in its inmost recesses to overflowing, what must it be to be 'filled with all the fullness of God' throughout all eternity! It passes knowledge, and it almost seems as if no room could be left within us to think of the redeemed and of the holy angels; yet our rejoicing with them will only increase our exceeding joy in the Lord, and our everlasting rest in his grace and truth and love.

'Our fellowship is with the Father and with his Son Jesus Christ.' Of late I have been jealous over myself lest my fellowship has been too exclusively with Jesus Christ. But while thankful for growth in reverent intimacy with my Ransom and my Redeemer, I must never forget that 'through him we have access by one Spirit unto the Father.'

* * *

The latest entry in this diary which I have found is presented to the reader in facsimile.

"Shame called you friends?"

5 January, 189.

12 Tuesday (12-058)

Having been taught that my sins need be crucified the Lord of glory & that He consciously bore them for me, it pleased Him on my awaking this morning to reveal Himself in his human... closely and lovingly as a personal friend. The gracious interview was brief but unspeakably joyful elevating & comforting. In itself the friendship to me, as to all his own, must have been the same ever since He called me by his grace, and is the same at this moment though not so sensibly manifested. What a glory & joy to us is "Jesus Christ the same yesterday, to-day, and for ever". If our mind is stayed on Him, there is no darkness or discomfort when we know & rejoice in the certainty that His heart is the same toward us now, as when He spent it fully to ours.

Later in the day I have been humbled by reflecting that if my Lord Jesus has been walking with me as a Friend these sixty-seven years, He must have been often grieved not only by my many sins and deplorable defects, but by my sad failure in the personal exhibition of his grace and loveliness in my whole walk and conversation which He looks for in all to whom He says "Henceforth I call you not servants, but I have called you friends."

Facsimile of the last entry in the devotional diary.
(See overleaf for transcript.—P.)

'I have called you friends.' [John 15:15]

Having been taught that my sins had crucified the Lord
of glory + that He consciously bore them for me, it pleased
Him on my awaking this morning to reveal Himself in his
human sympathy closely and lovingly as a personal friend.

The gracious interview was brief but unexpectedly joyful,
elevating, and comforting. In itself the friendship to me, as
to all his own, must have been the same ever since He called
me by his grace, and is the same at this moment though not
so sensibly manifested. What a stay and joy to us is 'Jesus
Christ the same yesterday, today, and for ever.' If our mind
is staid on Him, there is no darkness or discomfort when
we know + rejoice in the certainty that his heart is the same
toward us now, as when He opened it fully to ours.

Later in the day I have been humbled by reflecting that
if my Lord Jesus has been walking with me as a friend these
last sixty-seven years, He must have been often grieved not
only by my many sins and deplorable defects, but by my sad
failure in the personal exhibition of his grace and loveliness
in my whole walk and conversation which He looks for in all
to whom He says 'Henceforth I call you not servants, but I
have called you friends.'

Transcription of last entry in the devotional diary.—P.

— 20 —

Declining Years and Departure

Pure fell the beam, and meekly bright,
    Upon our father's hair,
And touched the sacred page with light,
    As if its shrine was there.

But oh, that patriarch's aspect shone
    With something lovelier far,
A radiance all the Spirit's own,
    Caught not from sun or star.

—Mrs [Felicia] Hemans

FIFTY-FIVE years had elapsed since Dr Moody Stuart began his Master's work as missionary in Holy Island, when he reached the jubilee of his pastorate in Edinburgh in 1887. His strength had now become seriously impaired, and though his health continued good every public effort in the pulpit was a great tax and strain upon him. Without formally retiring from his loved ministry, which his kirk session would not hear of his doing, he had gradually and most reluctantly to give up preaching. In these circumstances it was thought right by his family and himself that he should give up the manse, which adjoined the church. Accordingly Dr and Mrs Moody Stuart, with their daughter, Eliza, in the spring of 1888 removed to Annat, spending the winter months of each year in Glasgow with their son Alexander, who had shortly before been appointed Professor of Scots Law in that University.

The quiet of the college quadrangle was very congenial to one who, amid all the harassing cares and distractions of a long and active ministerial career in a great city, had never intermitted his scholarly habits and studies.

Although unable for the strain of public speaking, my father continued to take a keen interest in the course of public affairs, both ecclesiastical and political. His mental faculties remained unimpaired, his hearing was almost preternaturally acute, and his eyesight so perfect that he could read the smallest print, and even his own very minute manuscript notes, without the aid of spectacles up to the time of his last illness. Although he walked more or less every day, he spent a great deal of his time in reading, and enjoyed the perusal of the leading Reviews. He thus fully maintained his intelligent acquaintance with the more solid literature of the day, which he had always cultivated so far as time allowed, and especially studied with care all new theological views and theories, and watched the course of the Higher Criticism and cognate movements in religious thought. On these subjects he never saw any reason to modify the positions which he had taken up. One of the last times I was with him in Glasgow he said that he had never seen any refutation of the leading arguments in defence of the authenticity of the Pentateuch, which he had published in *The Bible True to Itself*, and seemed gratified when I said that neither had I come across even any attempted refutation of those already specified in this memoir. He warmly welcomed the fresh contributions to the subject by Professor Robertson of Glasgow and others, and took in at a glance the whole force of each new link or chain of reasoning.

In 1895 he wrote to the Rev. Charles Jerdan of Greenock: 'With my whole heart I thank you for your admirable defence of the Books of Moses, and your noble testimony to the truth of the word of God. For myself, I am just waiting till the Lord shall be pleased to call me to his own presence, where I am so unworthy to appear, and I owe a debt of gratitude to every brother who upholds and openly maintains the infallible authority of our blessed and adored and beloved Lord.'

The Bible was the centre of all his reading, and I do not think I could give a better portrait of our father in his study at this period than in the lines by Mrs Hemans, some of which have been quoted at the beginning of this chapter. She portrays the saintly patriarch seated with the open Bible before him, while the sunbeams shed a halo round his head, and illuminated the volume:—

> For there, serene in happy age,
>   Whose hope is from above,
> Our father communed with the page
>   Of everlasting love.
>
> Some word of life e'en then had met
>   His penetrating eye,
> Some ancient promise breathing yet
>   Of immortality:
>
> Some prophet's utterance, where the glow
>   Of quenchless faith survives,
> While every feature says, 'I know
>   That my Redeemer lives.'

In the spring of 1891 a union was happily effected between St Luke's and Tolbooth congregations,[1] and a letter from Dr Moody Stuart was read from the pulpit on 22 March, conveying his congratulations on the first day of the united assembling of the two flocks, 'the one company dear to me as the flock to which I was privileged to minister for so many years, and the other as the flock of a beloved friend whom I have long held in high esteem.[2] "Grace

---

[1] The united congregation was thenceforth known as Queen Street Free Church.—*P.*

[2] Alexander MacKenzie (1819–94) had been translated from Nairn to the Free Tolbooth congregation in 1863.—*P.*

be to you, and peace from God the Father, and from the Lord Jesus Christ."' He reminds them that the occasion was notably one of the Lord's beginnings in the course of their religious life, and prayed that what Delitzsch termed 'the creative intensity of all divinely effected beginnings' might hold good in this union, and that they might experience the fulfilment of the divine promise (a favourite one with him), 'I will do better unto you than at your beginnings.' He continued to take the deepest interest in any accounts which he received of a work of grace in any part of the country. Generally when I came from Moffat to Glasgow he would ask me if I had news of any spiritual awakening, and his whole face lighted up when he heard of persons who were anywhere seeking the Lord.

In April 1891, our father and all the family suffered an irreparable loss in the death of our mother. Early in March she was attacked by influenza, which was prevalent that winter in Glasgow in a severe form. In his diary our father wrote: 'In praying much for my beloved wife in her last illness there was granted to me twice such a nearness to the throne of grace, and such a conscious power in pleading, as I had very rarely known in the course of my life.' But it was not the will of the great Hearer of Prayer to grant restoration of her cherished life, though no doubt in answer to the earnest supplications of her husband and of others, desiring that if it were possible 'this cup might pass from them' at this time, he granted that grace of preparation to her and of support to them in submitting to the divine will, which is the condition and hinge of all acceptable prayer for temporal deliverance. She so far recovered as to be able to drive out, but a relapse supervened, and her state soon became very critical, and on the morning of Monday 27 April, a few hours before daybreak, she was gently summoned to enjoy that peace the promise and foretaste of which had 'kept her heart and mind in Christ Jesus,' not only during her life, but through her last illness, when the word 'peace' was often on her lips. The verse she repeated to me towards the end fitly describes alike the course and close of her life:—

> But yet or here, or going hence,
> To this our labours tend,
> That in his service spent our life,
> May in his favour end.[3]

On the following Thursday, 30 April, her remains were interred beside those of her father and mother, sisters and children, in the family tomb in Kilspindie, amid a large concourse of sorrowing friends and neighbours, including many labourers who had given up their work to attend the funeral. The children (who for many years were welcomed by her at a summer treat) sent a very large everlasting wreath for her grave.

What our mother was to our father during their long married life of fifty-one years it would be impossible to over-estimate. Differing from him in natural temperament, and to a certain extent in spiritual character and experience, she was all the more fitted to be to him the true helpmate which she was. She was not so impulsive as our father, and formed a calmer judgment than he of persons, and movements, and courses of action to be pursued, though she used to say that, as is common with the female mind, her opinion was rather intuitive or instinctive, than based upon a process of reasoning.

There were periods in our father's life when he suffered from spiritual depression, and I do not know that he could have got through these trying seasons without lasting injury to his health and usefulness, had he not enjoyed the support of our mother's tender sympathy, wise advice and courageous spirit. Much fell upon her at times of peculiar strain which few women could have come through. The whole management of the house and finance, as well as the training of the children, and the forming of all plans and arrangements fell wholly upon her, as our father was constitutionally unfitted for these things. She had an intense love for God's word, and did not stint the time she devoted to its prayerful perusal.

---

[3] Paraphrase of 2 Cor. 5:1–11, from the *Scottish Paraphrases* (1781).—*P.*

She also greatly delighted in the services of the sanctuary, often attending the House of God when very unable to do so. Never was text more appropriately inscribed over a grave than that which is put below her name on the marble slab in the family tomb, 'Lord, I have loved the habitation of thy house, and the place where thine honour dwelleth.'

Her natural affection was of a peculiarly strong character, and what she was to her own children cannot be told. But beside performing most efficiently the part of a minister's wife generally, she won the peculiarly deep attachment of members of St Luke's belonging both to the higher and humbler classes. The cottars and tenantry at Annat had the warmest regard for her, and she used to delight in visiting them in their homes, and in ministering alike to their spiritual and temporal needs.

In referring to Mrs Moody Stuart's death on the Sabbath after the funeral the Rev. Alex. Mackenzie said in Queen Street Church: 'We all know the excellences of her Christian character—what a help she was to her much-beloved husband, and with what singular devotedness she watched over him in seasons of weakness, as well as on all occasions; and in doing this she was a great succourer of you in making his ministry among you the lighter to him. Now that she is taken away we greatly rejoice in the clear testimony she bore to the grace and faithfulness of him who loved her, and in whom she believed.'

In the afternoon Dr Cunningham in closing his discourse, said: 'Let us along with other mourners today bless our God for the grace which moved his handmaid early to choose the better part, and to give herself unreservedly to the Lord in the dew of her youth, and for the devoted piety which sustained her in the faithful and ungrudging discharge of grave responsibilities incidental to her position as the helpmate of one who had to take a conspicuous place, and always exerted a wide influence for good, in a most remarkable period of our Church's history. But the public events in which her husband fearlessly took a prominent part seemed never to distract

Mrs Moody Stuart from the interests of her home. With an intense affection she did always dwell among her own, and lived for them. It is in that inner circle which knew her Christian example and her self-sacrificing constancy to duty that the loss which we mourn today must be felt to be irreparable.'

After her decease Dr Moody Stuart began to take an interest in revising for the press some of his former sermons from notes taken by hearers, which were published early in 1893, under the title *The Path of the Redeemed.* He also now began for the first time to keep a devotional diary, material from which has been incorporated in various parts of this memoir, and specially in chapter nineteen. He contemplated that portions of this, as well as his early autobiographical reminiscences, should be published, and they were carefully transcribed in a clear hand by an attached member of his flock, Miss Catherine M. Stewart. Sprung from a Highland family, she and her mother were drawn to St Luke's when they settled in Edinburgh by the experimental and thoughtful character of the preaching, and the compiler of this memoir would have found his task far more difficult had it not been thus facilitated by the unwearied labour of this devoted Christian lady, who, alas, was not spared to survive her loved minister, and to see the fruition of what had been to her a true labour of love.

Laid completely aside from public ministry, he thus sought to prepare by his pen for conveying religious instruction to others after his decease. He also prepared carefully for family worship, at which he used to give a short exposition of the passage read in course.

Although the bodily frame was gradually becoming more enfeebled he enjoyed taking short daily walks, and in these he would sometimes engage in conversation with those whom he met. Coming often across a little boy, he spoke to him about God, and as it was all new the boy was much interested. Having told him of God's power, the boy asked, 'Is he awful strong?' 'Yes, he's awful strong.' 'Is he stronger than a steam engine?' 'Yes, he's stronger than a steam engine. Does your teacher not tell you about God at school?' 'No:

it's awful stupid.' 'Yes: it's awful stupid.' The views of the child and the aged minister were at one as to purely secular education.

In his earlier life once when in Aberdeenshire he had asked the gardener's child who made her, she replied almost in Topsy's words: 'Naebody mak's naebody; a'body grows.'

Another very pleasing anecdote of a child is taken from his diary: 'February, 1895. On returning home from my short walk a little girl, four or five years old and most comfortably dressed, came down alone from one of the cross streets and to my surprise came smiling up to me, put her little hand into mine, and walked along with me. It was too responsible a charge, and I looked in vain for some one to claim her, but she was herself quite happy under my protection. When I asked her where she was going, she pointed in the direction that was my own, and I began to talk to her, and asked her if she knew about Jesus Christ. Her smiling reply was singularly sweet, "Jesus loves me." When we came to the top of the brae she bade me good-bye, and ran down to her home expecting to find the house door open; but it was shut, and she came running back to ask me to ring the bell for her. My Lord Jesus says, "Suffer the little children to come unto me," and he loves that I should be a little child, and put my hand confidingly in his to guide and shield me through my journey home, and through the valley of the shadow of death, for "even there shall thy hand lead me, and thy right hand shall hold me." He hath all the keys of his Father's house, and he openeth and no man shutteth, and I trust in him like a little child to open for me the door of the mansion he has prepared.'

He set very great store by the sacrament of the Lord's supper. When unable to have the privilege of himself sitting at the table, if he remembered that the coming Lord's day was the communion Sabbath in some congregation in which he was interested, he would be almost completely absorbed for days before in meditation and prayer regarding it. So much was this the case that in latter years, if those of his family who were with him thought him looking ill, and were seeking to discover the cause, it was always a relief if they recollected that the coming Sabbath was the sacrament in such a place, as they had reason to hope that when the Sabbath was past his strength would rally. In his diary he writes: 'Three days ago was the communion in my old church in Edinburgh, and both then and on the previous days my mind and heart were occupied with the holy Supper and with the ministers, elders and people, and I was much enlarged in meditation and prayer, yet not without the Satanic assaults so frequent at such seasons. On the Monday the Lord gave me abundant rest and refreshing in the love of the Father, and in the increasingly wondrous gift and sacrifice.'

Mrs Robert Moody Stuart died in June 1894, and of her the diary records: 'The dear wife of my son in Dundee, who has been long ill, seems now to be sinking. Like her honoured father, Captain Shepherd, she is one of the Lord's redeemed, and if the end is near it will be everlasting joy to her, but a sad bereavement to her husband and children. We have prayed much for her, but it does now seem as if longer life were not to be granted. My daughter in Edinburgh is not in so very critical a state, but has been long ill and is very weak. I pray earnestly for her also that she may be restored.' This prayer was not granted, and his second daughter, Jessie, wife of Mr George Watt, advocate, after a lingering decline, died a happy death in Jesus in January 1895, leaving four children. The following touching letter from her father, who, much to his distress, was unable to travel to Edinburgh to see her, only arrived at her sorrow-stricken home after her spirit had fled:—

Glasgow, 15 January 1895.

My greatly beloved Daughter,

Let me send you the words which the Lord Jesus, her Saviour and ours, spoke to your beloved mother before calling her home to himself:[4] 'Peace I leave with you; my peace I give unto you; let not your heart be troubled'—'the peace of God that

---

[4] Our mother had repeated these words over very slowly before her departure.—*KMS.*

passeth all understanding.' And let me add his words: 'I will come again and receive you unto myself.'

Farewell till for us both 'the day dawn and the shadows flee away,' and we meet together to praise 'him who hath loved us and washed us in his own blood.'

Your very loving Father.

In June 1896, Robert, his fourth son, died. He was established as an accountant in Dundee, where his high Christian character and conscientiousness, as well as his business ability, won him the esteem of many. Letters came from young businessmen both at home and abroad telling of the good they had derived from their intercourse with him.

In connection with these successive bereavements we may present to the reader some reflections of Dr Moody Stuart upon Affliction, which are extracted from a sermon (printed for private circulation) preached in 1866, just after death had made the first breach in his family circle, on John 18:11—'The cup which my Father hath given me, shall I not drink it?'

I. *The cup given by our Father in heaven to all his children.*— Before the bitter cup of trial our Father puts into our hand the precious cup of life and manifold blessing. Our cup was put by the Father into the hands of his Son to drink on our behalf; and he drank for us 'the dregs of the cup of trembling, and wrung them out.' Having taken our cup of condemnation, he hands to us the cup of salvation in his own blood, saying, 'This cup is the new testament in my blood, shed for many, for the remission of sins; drink ye all of it.' This is the sweetest of all cups to drink, but it is the last which rebel man will put to his lips; and he never drinks it till overcome by the grace of God, and made willing in the day of his power.

This was not the cup the Father gave to Christ, but it is pre-eminently the cup which he gives to us in his name: the first, the largest cup which he puts into our hands; no other is worthy to be remembered after it. This cup is running over; it can hold no more, there is no room for anything else, for anything contrary; all else that is mingled in the cup must henceforth be in God, who has filled your cup with himself and made you blessed for evermore.

Yet in Christ the Father does give his children, not another cup than the cup of blessing, but a cup of trial as part of the cup of blessing, as it is written, 'Blessed is the man whom thou chastenest.' If the chastening were absent, the blessing would be stinted. It is not a curse counteracting the blessing, not a curse mingling with and lessening the blessing; but a chastening entering into and filling up the measure of the cup of blessing.

This cup of ours is varied, composed of mingled elements, some of which enter into my cup, others into yours. It is a cup common to all believers, and the same to all, for 'no temptation hath befallen you but such as is common to man'; and a cup peculiar to every separate man, having an element of its own to each, or having its elements so differently mingled that each has a grief with which a stranger cannot intermeddle. It is bereavement to one, poverty to another, blighted hopes to a third, shame to a fourth, sickness to a fifth, the combination of several great trials to a sixth, and the mingling of innumerable little trials to a seventh.

But it is in every case the cup which your Father giveth you to drink. No matter who seems to mingle or to hand it, still it is your Father himself that gives you the cup. You think you could receive it at the hand of the great and good God; but you cannot drink it from the hand of man that is a worm like yourself. But Christ's cup seemed to come only from the hand of man, from the treachery of Judas, the denial of Peter, the deadly hatred of the Jews, the murderous coldness of the Romans, the pride of rulers, the insolence of servants, the cruelty of soldiers. Men combined together to mingle the cup, friend and foe met to put it to his lips; it was at the hand of men, of many men, yet it was the cup which the Father gave him, and so is yours. Behind the outward scene it was Satan that prepared the cup for our Lord; it was his hour, when his hands were unfettered that the Lord's might be bound by him; it was he that mixed and filled and presented the cup through human hands and hearts, yet Jesus said that it was not he but the Father who really gave him the cup to drink. Even if you say, 'But it is my own hands that have mingled my cup—my folly, my imprudence, my sin,' even then the sin is all your own, but the bitter dregs that you are wringing out flow from the 'cup which your Father giveth you to drink.'

II. *Our earnest and lawful prayer for the removal of the cup presented by our Father.*—Christ prayed for the removal of his cup, and in being conformed to his image we may and ought to pray for the removal of ours.

'Father, if it be possible, let this cup pass from me!' This was the most intense and earnest prayer that ever has been offered on earth, the greatest prayer in some respects ever offered by the greatest suppliant that ever was. Its singular intenseness is indicated by its threefold repetition, by his prostration on the earth, by his agony in supplication and by the great drops of blood wrung out by that agony. The prayer for the removal of the cup was the utmost outgoing of the soul in supplication of which the soul of man was capable, or which the human body could endure. It was likewise by the greatest moving of the Spirit as the spirit of entreaty. Through the human soul of Christ, that Spirit strove to the utmost in this prayer in the garden, with a striving unequalled on any other occasion. Further, it was altogether and eminently according to the will of the Father that this prayer should be offered; for its not being his will to grant the petition does not in the least interfere with its being his will that it should be presented, and no prayer offered by Jesus was in its offering more agreeable to the Father's will. *This prayer was not granted according to the letter.* One indirect but undoubted answer to the entreaty for the removal of the cup was in the strength given him to drink it: but it was not therefore better that Christ should have asked that strength, else he would have asked it. Prayer for strength to drink it would have interposed another thought between himself and the cup, but 'let this cup pass' is tasting the cup while he asks its removal; it may be even tasting some elements of its bitterness more painfully than in its actual drinking. In the end he rose with boldness, alacrity and holy joy to drink the unremoved cup; weakened in body, but stronger in spirit than if the path to Calvary had not lain through Gethsemane; strengthened through that dark hour for the far darker hour to come, for it was the shadow of Calvary that made Gethsemane dark; and strengthened far more abundantly than if strength itself had been asked, just because the prayer for strength would have been a feebler prayer followed by a less copious answer, while the stronger cry for the cup's removal drew down an ampler supply of strength to drink it unremoved.

In speaking of this prayer of Christ's not being answered in the letter, we must always bear in mind that the prayer itself was twice expressly made conditional, and was in the end withdrawn by the suppliant himself, so that in that light there was no refusal. It was conditional on the Father's will: 'Not my will but thine be done!' He expressly asks that, in this matter, not his own holy human will should be fulfilled, but the will of the Father, if in this the two wills should be different. There is also the further limitation, 'if it be possible, let the cup pass.' Even if the Father should consent, Jesus himself does not desire, and does not ask, that the cup should pass 'except it be possible'; which cannot mean the mere external possibility of removing the cup itself, for Jesus often said that he 'laid down his life of himself, and that no man took it from him.' It must therefore mean, if it were possible with the attainment of the glorious end of his coming into the world for the salvation of men.

It still remains true, however, that the prayer in its letter was not granted but refused. But the spirit of the prayer was answered, not merely in the strength imparted to drink the cup, but much more abundantly by the cup itself, which could not pass without being drunk, passing from him by being drunk, as

Jesus said, 'if it may not pass *except* I drink it.' The chief answer to the prayer appears to have been the greatest of all answers, in the resurrection of Jesus from the dead, and in the secured resurrection of all his redeemed; according to the scriptural testimony that 'in the days of his flesh, when he had offered up prayers and supplications with strong crying and tears unto him that was able to save him from [or out of] death, he was heard in that he feared' (Heb. 5:7). He was delivered out of death by the Father, by the quickening of the Holy Ghost and by his own omnipotence; but he was delivered in answer to his own strong crying and tears, not *from* death, but *out of* it; and in this he obtained a far greater and better answer than by a literal preservation from death, an answer in which he rejoices eternally. 'Thou hast given him his heart's desire, and hast not withholden the request of his lips; he asked life of thee, and thou gavest it him, even length of days for ever and ever.'

'It is enough for the disciple that he be as his master.' Like him we may lawfully pray for the passing of a threatened cup. We pray, and then resign not only the object prayed for, but the prayers themselves into the hand of God; which it is harder to do but more blessed than merely to resign the object of desire without asking. Acquiescence in the Father's will is at the root of all right affection toward God, and of all true prayer; but mere submissive acquiescence in the cup is far less than the same acquiescence after earnest prayer for its removal. And if Christ's own prayer for life was denied in the letter, we need not wonder that ours may be also denied, even when it hath seemed to us that our hearts were encouraged to pray by providential help and guidance, as our Lord was cheered by angelic help in the midst of his supplication; and when also our prayer has been helped and moved in our own measure by the Holy Spirit, as his was helped and moved by the Spirit without measure.

But Christ's prayers were not lost, and by seeming loss only gained their end; and our prayers are not lost but may be answered in a manifold fullness, in life spiritual and eternal to ourselves, and to those for whose recovery we have prayed without receiving the answer we craved.

III. *The filial drinking of the cup; acquiescent, willing, it may be cheerful drinking of a bitter cup.*—The willing drinking of our Father's cup in the highest sense belongs only to such a cup as it is in our power to refuse, as was the case with our blessed Lord. Man could not make him drink it except of his own free will. his Father did not force him, but loved him greatly because he willingly drank it.

In our lower place we may in our measure partake of his baptism, and freely drink for his sake a cup which it is in our power to refuse. We do so as often as we suffer for conscience' sake, choosing affliction rather than sin. But in most cases of suffering we cannot set the cup aside by refusing to drink it when the hour is come. In bereavements, if we refuse to drink our cup, it does not thereby pass from us, but only remains as a bitter potion before us. The death of friends may often be averted by the prayer for the removal of the cup; it may also be averted by acquiescence and submissive acceptance; and through sentence of death received by a father or a mother the life of a child may often be spared. But if not, there remains for us nothing but the filial drinking of the unremoved cup, and with that drinking infinite mercy and sweetness mingled. Every cup drunk in the childlike submission of a deep yet chastened grief is in the Father's sight as freely accepted by us as if our refusal would have removed it; and none but those who have tasted it can tell what sweetness he mingles in it. Christ himself hath drunk it for us, when 'in all our afflictions he was afflicted,' and when, by the will of God, 'He tasted death for every man.' He hath drunk the wormwood and the gall, and left us only the bitter flavour of a cup out of which the poison has all been taken. In Christ 'the bitterness of death is past' to all his followers, though death itself remains, and although they taste it in the death of those they love.

But he drinks it with us even now, when with childlike submission we drink our Father's cup, for whosoever shall do the will of his Father he owns for his mother, his sister, and brother; and we never more truly do his will than when we drink his cup. He can drink it with us as no other can. 'The heart knoweth its own bitterness.' A stranger cannot enter into it; the nearest left to you on earth may seem too remote for sympathy, or too ignorant of affliction to enter into yours. But, compared with Christ Jesus, the most sorrowful of the sons and daughters of men is only a stranger to grief. There is no sorrow in any of your hearts but Christ Jesus knows it better than you do yourself; not by his omniscience merely, but by having himself tasted it, and in far larger measure. The Man of Sorrows was acquainted with grief as none other can ever be; and your grief, whatever it may be, he hath tasted for you, and knows its bitterness as you can never know it. 'As many as I love I rebuke and chasten: behold I stand at the door and knock; if any man hear my voice, and open the door, I will come in to him, and will sup with him, and he with me.' He will share with you your supper of bitter herbs; he will drink with you your cup of tears, even when waters of a full cup are wrung out to you. And you will sup with him. Without drying up your sorrow, which he asks not, and you desire not, he will extract its bitterness and will give you the cup of salvation; he will impart the joys of his manifold redemption, and in the abounding tribulation will make the consolation much more to abound. Child of God, if you drink willingly the cup which is mingled for you by your Father's hand, be it the cup of bereavement, or some other cup that seems worse to you than death, you are blessed in so doing, however unblessed the cup in itself may seem in your eyes.

In the summer of 1896 Dr Moody Stuart's health became more enfeebled, and sometimes caused anxiety. It was now thought desirable that he should move to Crieff, where he took Ellerslie as a residence, and the more stimulating air and change of scene seemed to restore his strength considerably. Both in Glasgow and at Ellerslie he enjoyed being visited by old Edinburgh friends, one of whom says she was 'struck with his appearance of frailty, as the venerable figure with its noble and gentle bearing entered the drawing-room. But there was no frailty about his mind, which was as clear, vigorous, and as full of interest as ever. We had a long talk, most of it relating to the church where he had laboured so long and which he loved so well.' Dr J. H. Wilson says: 'My last visit was paid to him at Crieff in the summer of 1897, when I found his old interests strong as ever and his prayer carried me back to his best days, the burden of it being for Israel.'[5]

In February 1898, he caught cold which proved very weakening, and it was feared he might not be able to be again moved from Glasgow. In spring, however, he was sufficiently recovered to move to Ellerslie, and again the change had a restorative effect, and he was able to resume his short walks out of doors. About this time he wrote: '"As for God, his way is perfect: the word of the Lord is tried: he is a buckler to all those that trust in him" (Psa. 18:30). At the end of a long life I most cordially write my signature to each of these ascriptions of praise to God, our Maker and our Redeemer, for the perfection of all his way, the proved trustworthiness of all his word, and the faithfulness of his protecting shield to all who trust in him. I wish I could also affix my name to the testimony that follows in verse 32: "He maketh my way perfect"; but I can venture to say in humble hope, "The Lord *will* perfect that which concerneth me."'

In the beginning of July he took very seriously ill, and little hope was entertained of his recovery. His illness lasted some weeks, and though he rallied once or twice, so that we were hopeful that his life might be spared for a little, this was not his heavenly Father's will, and he was taken Home on 31 July 1898.

During the period of his illness, along with great weakness, there was a good deal of unconsciousness, but his mind was evidently

---

[5] The diamond jubilee of Dr Moody Stuart's ministry occurred this year (1897), and gratifying addresses were received by him from the Edinburgh Presbytery, of which he had now been for sixty years a member, and from the Jewish Committee, over whose deliberations he had so long presided, showing that his old friends and fellow labourers retained their affectionate and appreciative regard for one who had served so well two generations among them.—*KMS.*

mainly dwelling on spiritual things, and he was much engaged in prayer. He often quoted verses of favourite psalms, repeating, 'Bless the Lord, O my soul: and all that is within me, bless his holy name! Who forgiveth all thine iniquities'; 'Thou shalt guide me with thy counsel while I live, and afterward receive me to glory'; 'Yea, though I walk through the valley of the shadow of death I will fear no evil, for thou art with me'; 'Goodness and mercy have followed me all the days of my life,' and, 'Thou hast said, "Thou shalt dwell in my house for ever—and ever—and ever."'

He would repeat his favourite doxology, 'Unto him that loved us, and washed us in his own blood, to him be glory for ever!' Again, 'Lord Jesus, into thy hands I commit my spirit. Amen! Even so, come Lord Jesus!' 'We shall see his face, and his name shall be in our foreheads, and we shall reign over sin, and over death, and over the world. God hath made us more than conquerors through his Son Jesus Christ; and Oh, how we love him who first loved us!' At another time, 'Glory be to the Father, and to the Son, and to the Holy Ghost! Not unto us, but to thy name be the glory! Thou didst love us when we were cast out, and had destroyed ourselves: and Oh, we have so often destroyed ourselves, but thou didst always proclaim thy mercy.' 'The Son of Man came to seek and to save that which was lost.' 'He sends his angels and draws me up without effort of my own. My life is hid with Christ.' 'Father, let thy servant depart in peace! I have sometimes thought that I would not depart till mine eyes had seen the Lord's Christ, and if my eyes have *now* seen the Lord's Christ, let me depart! Not my will but thine be done! To me to live be it Christ, and to die it is gain, *gain*. To depart to be with Christ is very far better. There is none in heaven to be compared with thee, and O we thank thee that when we shall see thy face in glory we shall be like to thee because we shall see thee as thou art.'

Again he said: 'The Son of God who loved me and gave himself for me. Oh wondrous exchange! I set my seal to it: I accept it.' 'Lord, thou hast brought me so far; be with me unto the end! Thou saidst, Father, I will that they whom thou hast given me be with me where I am. O take me altogether to thyself! and deliver the great multitude from all nations, and redeem tonight that sheep which was lost.'

One day his thoughts had evidently gone back to much-loved sacramental seasons, and portions of meditations and addresses of much beauty, delivered in a clear voice, and with natural and almost youthful vigour, as if he were again presiding at the table, were heard by those watching in the room, while he quoted: '"This is the blood of the new covenant. He that eateth of this bread shall live for ever. He that believeth on me, though he were dead, yet shall he live again. This is a faithful saying, and worthy of all acceptation, that Christ Jesus came into the world to save sinners; of whom I am chief." I set my seal to that.' Once after saying, with great energy, 'He delighteth in mercy, he delighteth in mercy,' he clapped his hands with joy.

He seemed to be much engaged in adoration, repeating solemnly the name of the Trinity, and often saying, 'Worthy is the Lamb that was slain'; once adding 'The highest angel in heaven can say no more; the vilest sinner on earth need say no more, and dare say no less.'

Once when his lips were moistened with a drop of water he said, 'With joy shall ye draw water out of the wells of salvation.' Again, 'Dust unto dust! All things are thine, and death is thine.' 'I give my body to the grave, that grave in which the holy body of my Saviour lay. Thou wast laid in the grave, and we would lie with thee. Amen, so let it be!'

These dying sayings, when read over to an aged lady, who was called to pass through the dark valley of the shadow of death a month or two after him who had been the pastor and counsellor of her youth, brightened its gloom for her, and they are given here (when private feelings might have craved their omission) in the hope that they may be used to bring like comfort to others.

On Sabbath morning, 31 July, he gently folded his hands, as if in prayer, and fell asleep. Assuredly it was granted him to 'depart in peace' as he had requested, and on his entrance into the blessed company of the redeemed it seemed as if he could hardly be more engaged in the highest exercises of worship than he had been before he left this world.

A telegram intimating the death was despatched to Mr Durran, junior minister of Queen Street Church (in Dr Cunningham's absence), who made the mournful announcement at the morning service. An old member of the congregation, Mrs Gow, told me that not catching what was announced, she asked a person sitting in the pew what it was. On learning that it was an intimation of Dr Moody Stuart's death, she said that she could not control her emotion, and burst into tears, and at the same moment there rose up as if before her eyes a succession of scenes pictured on her memory, in which she saw again the deathbeds of her husband and sons, with their loved minister coming to visit each. She had attended my father's ministry from the time he preached in the first church in Young Street. She also recalled my mother visiting her two boys who were dying, and said that one day when she was leaving the house the younger boy called her back, and on her returning with a smile and asking what it was, he stretched out his arm and said, 'I just wanted to say good-bye to you.' The knowledge that such household ministrations remain so long in the memory should cheer ministers in a work which they are sometimes tempted to think not so fruitful as that of the pulpit.

The funeral took place on Thursday, 4 August. A service having been conducted at Ellerslie by Dr Henderson, Crieff, the remains were conveyed to Kilspindie, where a funeral service was held in the church, Mr Cowan, Elgin, and Dr Bannerman, Perth, leading the devotions. The coffin was lowered into the grave in the family tomb, in presence of a large assemblage of mourners, by the five surviving sons,[6] son-in-law and other near relatives, to rest beside the dust of his beloved wife, two of his children, and other loved ones, 'whose bodies being still united to Christ do rest in their graves till the resurrection.'

[6] Kenneth, Alexander, George, John and Charles.—KMS.

On the following Sabbath my friend Dr Douglas Bannerman, in kindly preaching for me in Moffat Free Church from Genesis 25:8, 9, said:

> On Thursday your minister and I stood together at the grave of his father, who, like Abraham, 'died in a good old age,' an old man, and 'satisfied', and was gathered unto his people, and his sons buried him in the possession of a burying-place which had long been made sure to him and his, where the wife of his youth had been laid, looking out over the broad Carse, with its fields ripening to harvest, and the great river flowing to the sea. The full glory of the summer sunshine was over the hills, and woods, and waters that he loved so well, and over the trees at Annat, whose growth and beauty he used to watch with such keen interest and delight. In the church beside the burying-place, under the great trees on the border of the field, we read those Scriptures which tell that 'as in Adam all die, even so in Christ shall all be made alive,' and how as 'one star differeth from another star in glory, so shall it be in the resurrection of the dead,' and which tell of 'the Lamb in the midst of the throne and of the elders,' and of the new Song of Redemption. There was praise and thanksgiving, led by those who had known and loved and honoured him who was gone, and we sang the familiar words of the sixty-fifth paraphrase:—
>
> > Lo! elders worship at his feet;
> > The church adores around
> > With vials full of odours rich,
> > And harps of sweetest sound.
> >
> > Worthy the Lamb that died, they cry,
> > To be exalted thus;
> > Worthy the Lamb, let us reply,
> > For he was slain for us!

In the accompanying picture of the church and churchyard of Kilspindie the reader will see the tomb where the mortal remains of

Photograph of the tomb in Kilspindie from the 1899 edition, showing the 'stooks of grain' in the foreground.

this loved and honoured servant of Christ repose, beneath the shelter and shadow of the ancient elm trees, till the resurrection of the just. Surely of him it might truly be said, 'Thou shalt rest, and stand in thy lot at the end of the days,' even in that day when 'they that turn many to righteousness shall shine as the stars for ever and ever.' The harvest stooks of grain in the foreground of the photograph form a not inappropriate symbol of one who 'came to his grave in a full age, like as a shock of corn cometh in in his season' (Job 5:26). The texts under the names of Dr and Mrs Moody Stuart on their memorial tablet in the tomb are, 'Whose faith follow' (Heb. 13:7), and, 'Lord, I have loved the habitation of thy house, and the place where thine honour dwelleth' (Psa. 26:8).

A funeral sermon was preached in St Luke's Church by Dr Moody Stuart's colleague Dr Cunningham, in which a short sketch of his ministerial career was given, from the days when he was 'leader of a band of messengers of God, whose names a grateful church and country will hold in everlasting remembrance, till the day when the call, which had summoned from his side almost every friend belonging to his generation, reached his own ear and found him ready.'

One who had sat in St Luke's fifty-five years ago but who left Edinburgh in 1855, on hearing that I was engaged in compiling my father's memoir, said to me, 'Dr Moody Stuart's life was a *living one* to those who sat under his ministry'; and I pray that this imperfect record of it may cause it to be lived again in some who never heard the gospel from his lips, and that it may recall helpful and sanctifying memories in those to whom he long proved a faithful and loving pastor.

— Appendix —

Appendix to the
First Edition (1899)

In Loving Memory of Dr Moody Stuart

Written, on hearing of his death, by Miss J. M. Gillies, *who grew up under his later ministry:—*

M ost honoured saint, thy life was lost to view
    In later years, but yet no time can blot
      The memory of that noble life which wrought
An influence sublime on those it knew.
The Church gave thee its highest honour. Jew
    And Gentile blessed thy life-long work. Thy lot
      Was loving and beloved. There will be sought
In vain thy pure and courteous grace so true.

So beautiful in life—with Christ to share
    Thy walk—it was a life of faith well trod;
      The souls it won thy God alone can tell.
So beautiful in death—thy lips did bear
    Ever the words of prayer and praise to God;
      So wondrous happy—and now all is well.

Acknowledgment of Deceased Contributors

O F those friends who have kindly furnished some material for this memoir, no fewer than six have deceased while these sheets were passing through the press, *viz.,* Dr Thomson, of Constantinople; Rev. Wm. Bennet, of Moffat; Professor Blaikie, D.D.; Dr Williamson, of Belfast; Mr J. R. Maclaren; and Mrs Brown Douglas, of whom the three last were intimately connected with my father both in personal friendship and Christian work. Mrs Brown Douglas joined St Luke's along with Mr Brown Douglas forty-five years ago, and she, as well as her husband, exercised a deep influence not only on the congregation but in the Christian community of Edinburgh. I remember her regularly conducting women's meetings in the mission district, in association with my mother, and her active and intelligent interest in Jewish Mission efforts is well known.—*KMS (Editor).*

Additional Material
for this Edition

Recent Awakenings[1]

R EVEREND Fathers and Brethren,—You have elected me to a responsible office in the church, which I neither expected nor aspired to, and for which I have no fitness. But all the more deeply on these accounts I feel your kindness, and thank you very respectfully and most cordially for the honour, while I entreat your prayers that the Lord may supply my lack out of his fullness.

Our Honoured Dead

Fathers and brethren, while each return of our annual Assembly on earth lifts our hearts to the general assembly and church of the first-born in heaven, this thought is pressed on us with a peculiar force on the present occasion. The sudden removal of the beloved and honoured father who proposed my name for this chair at your preliminary meeting, and for whose kind assistance I looked in the discharge of its duties; whose decease was so little contemplated, that he was proposed by almost all our presbyteries for a high and permanent office in this church; and who, from first to last, has occupied so great a place in all its history and in all its interests, in our ecclesiastical proceedings, in their narrative as an historian, in the support of our ministers, in the spread of the gospel among the neglected people of our land—his sudden removal has filled all our hearts with the profoundest sadness. This calamity, so startling in its telegraphic announcement, and still so recent, is revived afresh

[1] The Opening Address of the General Assembly of the Free Church of Scotland, 1875—the Assembly at which Dr Moody Stuart was Moderator.—P.

this week, first in committing his honoured dust to the earth, till the resurrection, and next in our assembling without him today. With the deepest sorrow I survey the awful blank. Dr Buchanan's great talents, his financial skill, his untiring industry, his large and earnest heart for every good work, his wisdom, his patience, his courtesy, his capacity for leading, his caution against extremes, his command of the respect of the community, make his loss not easily estimated. God grant that in the end we may not find it greater than we at present know. Other ministers, not a few, have been taken from their flocks since last Assembly; some of them well known and highly honoured in the Church; and one, an elected member of this Assembly, Mr Rose, of Poolewe, in a manner peculiarly solemn. In one of our brethren in the strength of life struck down in the pulpit with only power to say, 'The hand of the Lord is upon me,' God is speaking with a loud voice to all of us in the ministry, both to arise and trim our own lamps, and to work while it is day, because the night cometh when no man can work.

Of the ministers deceased during the year there were distinguished by age and eminence four whose names are fitly placed side by side with Dr Buchanan's. Yet how different are the images they present to our minds; as we name them, how each stands out before us separately in his own character—Dr Buchanan, Dr Henderson, Dr Fairbairn, Dr Forbes, Dr Grierson.

Dr Henderson was admired among us for a beautiful character singularly free from faults, was loved for his gentleness, was honoured for his learning. He has passed away, and his style of preaching has passed with him, or rather before him. Too refined and beautiful and symmetrical for the unresting spirit of the present day, we do not ask that it should be imitated and recalled. But when we remember how rivetedly we have listened to him in his earlier ministry, and to others deceased before him, we are reminded of elements in the older preaching which it might be good for us to retain. The press has sometimes been disposed to conclude that preaching had given place to printing, but it has been amply proved that what John Knox calls the 'speech and lively voice' in contrast to colder writing still holds its own high place in moving the hearts and minds of men. But while preaching can never lose its power, we must be jealous of losing any of the great elements of that power. Our fathers spoke of the doctrines of the gospel being 'solidly stated and ably vindicated.' Ably vindicated they are and tastefully illustrated, but we must not forget what they so highly valued in the full and solid statement of the grand doctrines of the cross.

Principal Fairbairn was removed suddenly and sadly for us all, yet most gently for himself, his death bearing a remarkable resemblance to that of his attached friend, Dr Buchanan; and although ripe in years, he was taken away in scarcely abated vigour for using his extensive learning. His writings have long held, and will retain a high place in our theological literature. A generation of our younger ministers look on him with filial affection and reverence; and the man whom this Assembly may elect to succeed him may expect the blessing which the good man leaves to his son, without the fear of being wronged by comparison with one who stood so calmly and so nobly on an elevation peculiarly his own.

Dr Forbes, gifted with the highest talents, excelling in his own profession, and distinguished in mathematical science, was imbued with deep and earnest godliness, and presented a fine embodiment of the scriptural image 'clothed with humility'—a clothing which seemed to cover him from head to foot. In my own mind he was always associated with his intimate friend, Dr Gordon, to whom many of us owe so much. Resting from their labours they are remembering, and are doubtless recalling together all the way by which their Lord led them on earth, to humble them, and to prove them, and to do them good in their latter end, which for ever endeth not.

Dr Grierson ranks among the characteristic men of our Disruption, as one of the best fitted to bring out the moral character of that great event, for he would have been the last man to cast in his lot with it, if it had been the fruit of fanaticism, or party spirit, or love of ecclesiastical power. Constitutionally averse to extremes, having a special regard to whatever was orderly in all the actions and relations of men, and ardently attached to his parish, his church, his manse, nothing but the sovereign command of conscience would have moved him to the sacrifice he made in that crisis of the Church of Scotland. But holding it to be the duty of the state to own and to support the church of Christ, he held it to be the privilege and bounden duty of the church to stand fast in the liberty wherewith Christ had made her free, and not to be entangled in any yoke of bondage. The Lord gave him his reward in a useful, honoured, and cheerful life, and in a triumphant death. He retained his faculties to the last hour; he repeated many texts to himself; named various passages of Scripture to be read to him, and rejoiced in hope of the glory of God, saying:—'Death has no power over me; Jesus is near me, is by me; safe in the arms of Jesus; make no tarrying, O my God'; and when it began to dawn he prayed once and again, 'Let me go, for the day breaketh.'

To the large list of former Moderators fallen asleep in a single year, is to be added the name of the distinguished son of a highly distinguished father, Dr M'Crie. Although for many years associated with the Presbyterian Church in England, he was once a minister of this Church, and presided over our Assembly, and he has left among us an honoured remembrance.

Among the honoured and lamented elders who have finished their course, are Mr Auld, who held an office of trust in the Church; Mr Paterson of Mulben, highly esteemed in a wide district of the north; and that most loveable man, so like his Master, Captain Shepherd, of Kirville, one of the last of the noble band of gentle men who were witnesses for the doctrines of grace in different parts of the country before the Disruption, and then stood faithfully for the liberty of the Church, and gave freely for its maintenance. All of us who survive that wondrous era are now floating few and far between on the great stream of time,

Rari nantes in gurgite vasto;[1]

---

[1] 'Rare survivors in the immense sea'—Virgil, *Aeneid*, I, 118.—*P.*

but our Redeemer has gone through the waters of death before us, and is waiting for us on the shore.

There are two elders that stood out more prominently in our Assembly—the Earl of Dalhousie and our legal adviser, Sheriff Cleghorn.

With his position as a member of the House of Commons in the time of our Church's struggle, with his sagacity, his energy, and his habits of business, Lord Dalhousie was enabled to take an active, a most honourable, and what would have been a most efficient part in our cause, if any effort could have been effectual in that trying but elevating and ennobling time. The separation was of the Lord, and the help of no human arm could avert it. But the noble stand he made for our Church's deliverance, followed by the interest he took in all its work, and in the meetings of our Assembly year by year, leaves a wide blank in the midst of us today, and distinguishes Lord Dalhousie as a man to whom in no ordinary measure honour is due by this Church.

To Sheriff Cleghorn we were deeply indebted for his efficient labours as Convener of our Continental Committee. A man of a tender conscience, of a pure heart, of a loving and Christ-like spirit, and of a most consistent walk, he was widely known among us, and died beloved and lamented by all who knew him.

The Church of the First-Born

These few names recall to our memory the names of Dr Guthrie and Dr Candlish, and the large company of the honoured dead amongst us from the beginning. How many well-known to us are mingling in the bright and holy throng above; how many who have met beneath this roof are now in that General Assembly of the first-born; but our whole Church is only one of many branches in the church universal; and, as our affections are not imprisoned within the walls of our own history, so neither are our possessions. All who have been called from this earth to the city of the living God are still ours—Paul, Apollos, Cephas, Abraham, David, Elijah, Augustine, Luther, Knox—and they still live each in his own individuality, all that was weakly or sinfully distinctive in them gone, all that was personally attractive in nature and in grace abiding. So will it be with you and with me, and so with the least of the hidden ones scarcely known here except to their own Redeemer, but made known in that day when he will be admired not only by all but in all them that believe. What a general assembly that will be, gathered out of all the churches on earth, with no separating shibboleth for ever. What a joyful conclave of all the just, the holy, the true, the pure, the brave, the loving, and the good who have lived on this earth, and each, not the image of another, but bearing the personal stamp impressed on him in earth by his first birth in nature, and his second birth in grace, by his country, his family, his education, his history, his mercies, his trials, his falls, his recoveries, his tears, his songs, his life in Christ, his death in the Lord.

In that assembly of the first-born, as there will be neither Jew nor Greek, so neither male nor female, but all one in Christ, and all like the surrounding angels. The difference will be for ever great between the fiery prophet of Carmel, rough on earth like his own hairy garment, and the pensive listener at the feet of Jesus; while both have received their distinctive graces out of the fullness of the meek and lowly One with the zeal of his Father's house consuming him, and both will for ever wear his likeness. Our conformity to Jesus Christ in the resurrection includes both inward and outward resemblance. But as in the distant and brighter regions of our own world you are struck both with the great difference of the gorgeous scene and with the likeness that underlies the whole; so probably in that other world we may find at once a greater change than we now anticipate, and a nearer resemblance to what we have already known. Yet of that future state which 'eye hath not seen'—

> The little that is known,
>   Which, children-like, we boast,
> Will fade like glow-worms in the sun,
>   Or drops in ocean lost.

Augustine and other fathers pressed the saying of our Lord too far, when they looked for the exact restoration of every hair of the head from the words, 'Not an hair of your head shall perish.' But they were surely right in their idea that our bearing the image of Jesus Christ includes the likeness of apparent age, and that childhood will be brought up, and old age brought back, to the likeness of the mature and perfect, yet youthful manhood, in which Jesus died and rose again. For, however beautiful the hoary head is on earth, it is the ripe fruit of decay; and infancy with all its loveliness would cease to be attractive, if it did not grow both in wisdom and in stature. It has been said acutely that 'the oldest angel in heaven looks the youngest,' or in other words, is the brightest, and looks the freshest, as if most newly fashioned by the hands of his Creator. Sin was never young, was never new, and never can be new. Sin was tarnishing, defilement, corruption, oldness from the first; and in all its changing forms is corrupt, and old for ever. But as in the new covenant and the new heart, that never become old, so in the new heavens and the new earth the Lord Jesus makes all things new and incapable of growing old; garments that wax not old, treasures that never rust. And as he has himself the dew of youth for ever, so, doubtless, his redeemed will grow in beauty, in freshness, and in dew-like youthfulness, while in their spirits, and in their bodies illuminated by their spirits, they become ever more nearly conformed to his transcendently glorious image, yet each retaining his own individuality with his own 'new name which no man knoweth save he that receiveth it.'

Ruling Ourselves

But, fathers and brethren, alike from the remembrance of those who have gone before us, and from our own bright hopes above, we must ever come down to the present things of earth, and of the church in the earth. In every such Assembly as this, in the different departments of work in the Lord's vineyard, in the various questions and matters arising occasionally yet continually, it often happens that the amount of time bestowed on each bears too little proportion to its intrinsic and general importance. The least important is sometimes the most urgent, and often the most difficult; all of us are apt to allow lesser questions or interests to become too absorbing; and when that which is little has been suffered to become great, that which is great may for the time become little. It ought, therefore, to be the earnest prayer of us all that the Lord himself would give us daily the unction from the Holy One, that in his light we may see light. Without his help our path soon becomes a hedge of thorns; we get entangled, pricked, and worried, or we labour fruitlessly beating the air. But when he bids the mountain become a plain, the height which we were toiling to climb over or to dig through, is a level pathway for our feet. This help from on high is granted to the faith that worketh by love. Suffer me, therefore, to remind you of our constant need of that mastery over our own spirits, which is so well defined in these old words, 'Thou oughtest, therefore, diligently to aim at this, that in every place or action, or outward business, thou be inwardly free, and master of thyself; and that all things be under thee, and thou not under them.' In our deliberations, discussions, and decisions, we carry with us the encouraging assurance that the things wherein we have differed, or may differ, do not affect our salvation through grace and the eternal truths in which we are agreed. In the innermost depths of our hearts we are all agreed, we are all one, and by this, said our Master, 'shall all men know that ye are my disciples, if ye have love one to another.'

The Recent Awakening

Fathers and brethren,—Of all the subjects to be brought before you, the greatest is the state of religion in our own land; always the most important, but having special interest at present in connection with the recent awakening throughout the country. Such awakenings, however great, if not diligently followed up, are apt to leave little permanent result; and even with abiding fruit, the season of spiritual movement is frequently succeeded by one of listlessness and death, and a tide of earthliness returning with renewed force. Mainly on ministers and elders depend the cherishing, deepening, and extending of the work of the Lord. Without much care on your part—and even with it—a weakened and sickly appetite toward the ordinary, permanent, and essential means of grace, may be the unhappy result in many of those who have most relished and profited by the occasional means; and then the much-prized good will be followed by a greater loss.

There is one great result of these awakenings which ought to weigh much with those who are doubtful of them—their effect in bringing out into distinct recognition in the Christian community the necessity and the power of conversion. This was one of the most marked effects of the awakening in 1839. The doctrine that a man must be born again to see the kingdom of heaven is accepted by all; its present necessity is brought home by the Spirit to those who are effectually called. But it is a great step in the spiritual extension of the Redeemer's kingdom, if by the mass of church-going people it is not only believed as a doctrine, but recognised as the great practical event in the history of every man who has a true hope of eternal life. The successive awakenings in the land have done much to extend the recognition of this great truth by the people, and even in churches where it might have been least expected. In such seasons we must neither make a man an offender for a word, nor look for everything in every man. If sleeping men are to be aroused they must be startled; and men, who have themselves escaped safe to land out of the great shipwreck of human lives, will not speak in tame and measured terms to others either of their danger or of the great rescue. Luther expressed himself with perhaps an excess of strength when he spoke of the Lord Jesus Christ becoming a murderer for David and a liar for Peter; but such a statement awakes men to ask what is under it, even as in our Lord's own words, 'If a man smite thee on the right cheek turn to him the other also.' As regards defect or partiality in doctrinal statement, we must remember what a might there is in the man who is firmly grasped by any of the great truths

333

of salvation so as to utter them with power. The gospel of the grace of God as the good tidings of great joy has been the theme of the late evangelistic preaching, and many of us in the ministry would be filled with boundless gratitude if we were enabled to preach to perishing men the glad tidings of reconciliation out of a full heart, as in the words of the penitent Psalmist, 'Restore unto me the joy of thy salvation, then will I teach transgressors thy ways, and sinners shall be converted unto thee'; or, as in the simple lines—

> Let not conscience make you linger,
>> Nor of fitness fondly dream;
> All the fitness he requireth
>> Is to feel your need of him;
> This he gives you,
> 'Tis the Spirit's rising beam.
>
> Come, ye weary, heavy-laden,
>> Bruised and mangled by the fall;
> If you tarry till you're better,
>> You will never come at all.
> Not the righteous;
> Sinners Jesus came to call.[1]

There is nothing more quickly communicative than heavenly joy; the experience of indwelling sin has saddened many of us, and has severely taught us to distrust ourselves; but we lose much when we lose our trust in the power of God's word over men's hearts, or when we are straitened by an excessive distrust of our fellow men. Seasons of visitation are always marked by the preacher's faith in the power of the word over his hearers; this is a very special gift of God, and is at the command of no man; but we should seek it with diligent and intense prayer, for we cannot too often remember the dying counsel of the old missionary Elliot, 'Pray, pray, pray.' Every increase of faith

---

[1] Verses from the hymn, 'Come, ye sinners, poor and needy' by Joseph Hart (1712–68).—*P.*

is a great gain. 'I preach to you the glad tidings, and by grace you will receive them,' tells far more on men than 'I preach the gospel to you, but through sin you will reject it.' Frankness of trust in others has even naturally a great effect. In intercourse with savage tribes, Captain Basil Hall found nothing so helpful as a frank trust in their goodwill. When the officers of the ship, approaching them with courtesy, and ceremony, and scrupulous fear of giving offence, met with only distance and reserve, the blue-jacket, in his rough sailor confidence, going up frankly to them, clapped them on the shoulder as brothers mutually glad to meet each other, and took their hearts by trusting them. And nothing is better fitted to take any heart, whether savage or civilised. Many of us in the ministry would be thankful to retain or to recover our first love to men, and our first faith in the word of God as omnipotent over their consciences; and we are grateful to brethren of any church, or any country, who go forth to preach in faith, trusting in the Lord and in the riches of his grace, and believing that 'God will have all men to be saved, and come unto the knowledge of the truth; and is not willing that any should perish, but that all should come to repentance.'

Our evangelistic brethren are sometimes thought to scatter the seed of the word with too wide a hand. But with most of us our sowing is too stinted; we forget the command of the Lord of the harvest, 'Freely ye have received, freely give,' and the warning, 'He that soweth sparingly, shall reap also sparingly.' A farmer in the United States of America purchased for seed some highly recommended Indian corn, and gave it in charge to a young man in whom he could confide. Feeling sure of a rich harvest, he was bitterly disappointed when the stalks of maize grew late and sparse over the fertile field. Next year, after the rest of the farm was sown, he bade one of his servants sow what was over of the fruitless seed on a piece of waste land, and to his surprise it yielded an abundant and beautiful harvest. Calling the young man to whom he had given the seed at first, he learned that under a sense of his responsibility he had taken unusual pains, planting every grain very deep; and the master saw at once that the good seed had never sprung to the surface because it had been sunk too far from the sun and the air. So some of us planting too sparingly and too deep obtain a scanty return, while other brethren, scattering freely, rejoice in fields whitening quickly to the harvest.

Dangers to be Avoided

There are, however, certain dangers to be avoided in conducting the work of the Lord. The first is the encouragement of an excessive confidence not in the word of God, but in personal salvation, when there may be merely a hopeful impression. In dealing personally with inquiring souls, we often communicate a sympathetic sense of our own spiritual impression, which will help them much if rightly used, but if mistaken for a saving change may only add them to the stony-ground hearers of the word who 'anon with joy receive it.' Not that joy in the Lord is to be held out as postponed to a late period in the Christian course. In the words of our Shorter Catechism, 'assurance of God's love, peace of conscience, and joy in the Holy Ghost' often accompany justification by faith, and may fill the heart before there has been any 'increase of grace or perseverance therein.' At first it may be only a momentary gleam through the surrounding darkness—

> Brief as the lightning in the collied night,
> That in a spleen unfolds both heaven and earth;
> And ere a man hath power to say, Behold,
> The jaws of darkness do devour it up.[1]

But the light may soon shine steadily, and the soul may know that the Lord hath translated it out of darkness into his marvellous light. But even then the modesty of faith shrinks from a rude inter-meddling by the hands of man, while in fit time and place the child of God will take up the words, 'Come and hear, ye that fear God, and I will declare what he hath done for my soul.'

[1] Lines from Shakespeare, *A Midsummer Night's Dream*, Act 1, Scene 1.—*P.*

Another danger is in the excessive notice of cases of conversion, real or supposed. Most of you, however differing otherwise in your judgment, rejoice in believing that during the visit of our American brethren there was an unusual presence of the Spirit of God. In former awakenings, as in the present, one marked effect of the Spirit's power was in the quickening and restoring of the Lord's people, and the raising of many to a higher spiritual level; and on this subject of a higher holiness I desire to speak, if the Lord will, at the close of our Assembly.[1] In those awakenings there were many souls effectually turned from the power of Satan unto God whose change, although it could not be hid, was better known afterwards than at the time, and it has proved abiding and fruitful. But, on the other hand, the cases that were more remarkable, and most brought forward, and the narration of which seemed most helpful to others, did not, in many instances, turn out the most satisfactory in the end, either because they were not so thorough in themselves, or were injured by excessive notice. The last were often first, and the first were last.

There is a third danger of that most fruitful duty of speaking and working by members of the church running to excess. 'With the heart man believeth unto righteousness, and with the mouth confession is made unto salvation.' In Christian countries our presence at public ordinances involves no trial of faith; the real trial of confession is in private, in the family, or with friends, or to strangers, and this confession of Christ is often singularly blessed both for the salvation of others and for the quickening and joy of the speaker himself. But there is need of much watchfulness against the snare of that 'talk of the lips which tendeth only to penury'; of 'a man thinking himself to be something when he is nothing, and deceiving himself'; of becoming busy teachers and ceasing to be earnest hearers of the word; or of being 'many masters' and being seduced into that insidious separatism which is such a bane to the progress of salvation through the earth.

[1] See p. 342.—*P.*

Doctrinal Truths

Besides these notes on the conduct of the Lord's work, suffer me to call your attention to certain great truths which it is seasonable for us to inculcate. And, first, it is essential to impress on the people that the letter of the gospel is powerless without the Holy Spirit. In a time of visitation the Spirit through the word so testifies of Jesus Christ and of the things that are freely given to us of God, and so demonstrates the truth to the mind, that it often seems to the learner as if the power could never be absent where the truth is present. But while it is the simple truth that sets us free, that truth for its reception by us depends every moment on the work of the Holy Spirit in our hearts.

Next, the holy sovereignty of the great God is apt to be overlooked in the midst of an awakening, and should never be so pressed as to fetter the absolute freeness of the gospel. But we must not omit it, else the conscience of the convert will be troubled and his mind bewildered when he meets this great doctrine, not in books, but in his own experience and in the church and the world around him. 'It is not of him that willeth, nor of him that runneth, but of God that showeth mercy,' is a truth which every child of God has to learn, and it is good for him to be taught it clearly from his own book. It will not hinder but help the free running of the word of God.

Further, let us fully preach repentance both as regards sins against law and conscience, and as regards unbelief toward the Lord Jesus Christ. To press every man to say 'Jesus loves me' is to put words into his lips, than which the apostle Paul could adopt none higher, and is fitted to lull him asleep in the persuasion that all is well with him, and that he needs nothing more. Repentance in all its bearings occupies a large place in all the Scriptures; its preaching reaches the conscience and inner being of every man as the voice of God to himself; and without it we shall nurse a feeble and crippled religion.

Lastly, let us fervently preach and impress that fear of the Lord which is clean and endureth for ever, and with which his secret and his covenant are ever found. In many of our younger people at the present hour, even with evident grace, there is a very real observable want of deep reverence and godly fear; and this moral defect is cherished by too exclusive a reference to the humanity of the Eternal Word made flesh, and too little regard to the great God laying his hand on us and encompassing us on every side. The elder Dr M'Crie said of the fear of the Lord that it is the only recorded element in the worship of the angels; and John Bunyan, after seeing in a great crisis of the soul's history the key of its gate put into the hands of Godly Fear, adds that he sometimes wished that it should be always in that keeping.

Popery and Infidelity

Reverend Fathers and Brethren, it is good for us to meet here together with One in heaven for our only Father, and one Lord Jesus Christ for our only Master, with the written and unchangeable word for our only rule, and with the Holy Spirit of promise to enlighten us in that word, yet in no way imparting to us or to our decisions the infallibility which belongs to the Bible alone. How different our light and liberty, and the light and liberty of our flocks, from dark bondage to a priesthood exalted into an authority over the conscience that pertains only to God, a usurpation consummated in these last years by the declared infallibility of the Chief Priest of Rome as if he were the Christ of God on earth. This act was the concentration and solemn annunciation of previous claims of blasphemy; it was the deed of an ecclesiastical assembly of world-wide magnitude formally adding the topstone to the impious edifice. And since the dark bright day when our Lord was crucified—bright with the outbeaming of the Father's love and with the light of the great atonement, dark with the sin of man reaching its height in the murder of the Holy One by the chief priests of Judah,

> Where the towers of Salem stood,
> Once glorious towers, now sunk in guiltless blood,

since that day in Jerusalem, stained with the blood of the Son of God, there seems to us for these eighteen hundred years to have been no other day in this world's history so dark as that in which the assembled priesthood of Rome crucified our Lord afresh by elevating Antichrist into his throne, in declaring their own chief priest to be the infallible head of the church on earth. Too faithfully interpreted in Rome was that decree at the time in a sermon reported as having been preached to a distinguished audience by one of their prelates, who said that there had been three incarnations of Deity— the first in the manger at Bethlehem, the second in the sacrament of the mass, and the third in the person of an old man at Rome. That church has entered on a great, an eventful—it may be for a time a successful path—yet surely on the last stage of her blasphemous course. Henceforward, on the part of Rome, it is war to the knife against every knee that will not bow to Baal, and every mouth that will not kiss him. Even more alarming for the hour is the growth of atheism through 'science falsely so called,' although in the end this materialism may possibly join in adoring a God of flesh and blood in the shape of the Roman Antichrist. Against the true church of Christ there is the credulity of superstition on the one hand, and the credulity of unbelief on the other—the one believing every invention that is forged in the name of the church, the other believing every fancy that is dreamed in the name of science—and asking us to accept not the facts of science, but the credulous imaginations of scientific men in contradiction to their own facts. But all the more does this credulity, in both its forms, prove the power of the seducing influence at work, and the strength of the enmity with which the faith in Christ has now to contend, and with probably a much harder conflict in the not distant future.

But God is with us when we are with him, and then greater is he that is with us than all that are against us. Alike against an enslaving priesthood and a withering atheism, our sure defence is that 'We know in whom we have believed,' and, in the face of both, 'We are not ashamed of the gospel of Christ, for it is the power of God unto salvation to every one that believeth.' In believing on Jesus Christ we have not been left without a sure witness. He hath said, 'I am the way to the Father,' and coming through him we have found the living God and our souls have entered into rest; believing on him we have obtained the answer of a good conscience toward God, we have been sealed with the Holy Spirit by God himself, and there has risen within us a well of living water springing up into everlasting life. We have thus a manifold evidence, as sure as any evidence of sense to outward things, as clear as the light of the sun to the eye, that 'That this is the true God and eternal life.'

In the name of the Lord Jesus Christ, therefore, we go forward to all our work of every kind, specially to every work in his more immediate service, and now to this present work of our Assembly, trusting to him to guide us by his counsel that we may guide the great flock entrusted to our care, 'the beautiful flock,' which is not ours, but his through the ransom of his own blood; not ruling as lords over God's heritage, but seeking to be ensamples to the flock, that 'when the Chief Shepherd shall appear we may receive a crown of glory that fadeth not away.'

Higher Holiness[1]

REVEREND Fathers and Brethren,—By the good hand of
our God upon us the labours of this Assembly have now
been brought to a close, and I have respectfully and heartily to congratulate you on the thorough concord which has marked
so very large a portion of your proceedings, as more specially shown
in your unanimity regarding our highly esteemed brethren of the
Reformed Presbyterian Church;[2] on the brotherly love that has pervaded the Assembly in discussing the matters wherein you have differed; and I trust I may add on the dew of heaven that has descended
on the mountain of Zion, refreshing our souls. I shall make no
attempt to review what you have done, but I cordially congratulate
the Assembly on the remarkable blessing which this year has rested
on the silver and the gold in the Lord's treasury, largely augmenting
the fund for the maintenance of the ministry, and at the same time
increasing the resources of all our missions at home and abroad.

Prayer for Israel

In reference to the ingathering of Israel, you will allow me to ask
your prayers for them on their weekly Sabbath, on Friday evening
or Saturday morning, when they are reading those Scriptures which

[1] The Closing Address of the General Assembly of the Free Church of Scotland,
1875.—*P.*

[2] Discussions were taking place at this time with regard to a proposed union
of the Reformed Presbyterian Church with the Free Church. The majority of the
RPC did unite with the FC the following year.—*P.*

are 'able to make them wise unto salvation' but only 'through faith in Jesus Christ'; and also on their great Day of Atonement, which falls this year on the 9th of October, when they assemble in crowds in their synagogues, change their usual attitude of standing in prayer into kneeling and prostration, confess their sins with fasting for more than twenty-four hours, read those passages of Scripture full of light to us which set forth the One ransom in so vivid types, and darkly seek the great truth that lies hid under the saying of their Rabbis, that Satan accuses Israel every day of the year except the Day of Atonement.

Nyassa Mission

Permit me, further, to recall your attention to Dr Duff's[1] fervent appeal for the noble mission to Lake Nyassa,[2] and for a moment to refer to our dear departed brother, John Braidwood,[3] whose beautifully calm and heavenly temperament, so full of grace, makes it seem as if to him the change from earth to heaven would not be startling; and reminds me of the dream of Dr Payson,[4] in which, thinking himself in heaven, he wondered that, in its fullness of joy, he remained so quiet, when on earth he had often been excited with its slightest foretaste; but an angel showed him a bottle with a little water which was greatly agitated when shaken, while the same bottle quite full was absolutely still. From this brother, so like on earth to the calm of heaven, Dr Duff led us into the heart of Africa, and his burning words on the horrors of the slave gang there

[1] Alexander Duff (1806–78), missionary in India and later convener of the Free Church's Foreign Missions Committee.—*P.*

[2] The Free Church expedition to Lake Nyassa (Lake Malawi) departed later in 1875. Further information surrounding the establishment of this mission may be found in *Livingstonia: The Mission of the Free Church of Scotland to Lake Nyassa; with an Appendix containing Speeches, Letters, and Lists of Subscriptions* (Edinburgh: John Grieg & Son, 1876).—*P.*

[3] John Braidwood (1810–75) served as Free Church missionary in Madras, India.—*P.*

[4] The reference is to Edward Payson (1783–1827), minister of the Congregational Church in Portland, Maine, USA.—*P.*

recalled to me the still darker woes that once awaited her sons in crossing the Atlantic. Thirty years ago, near one of the harbours of Brazil, where slavery has since been happily abolished, I saw a strangely painted ship, with her colour nearly resembling the hue of the ocean beneath her. She was an African slaver, and her hold was said to have been the coffin of four hundred human beings, who had been mercilessly suffered to perish by the cruellest of all deaths for want of water, nine hundred survived, and their sale brought a large profit on the voyage. The slaves once sold to Brazilian masters, were usually well treated by them, but if you put the simple and earnest question, 'Will you teach them to read?' the prompt and decided answer was, 'No, if they could read, there would be an end of slavery,' and so they must die in ignorance.

In that country I saw the fairest scene that I shall look upon till I see the paradise of God above. A valley filled with every tree that is fairest to the eye; lofty palms, tree-ferns with their utmost softness of grace, araucarias with their perennial spikes of green iron for leaves; bamboos tapering into tall trees, then curving to the earth in grass-like slenderness; climbing plants using the trees like masts for the rigging of ships, and interlacing them with an intricate green ropework; pitcher plants, whose cups of water you were apt to pour over you by carelessly touching them; flowering shrubs of exquisite beauty, with humming-birds fluttering from flower to flower; on the right hand and the left, and as far onward as the eye could reach, the lofty trees clothed with plants that needed no soil, and hanging the valley for miles with garlands of flowers, with a variety and amplitude of brightness and of beauty, that irresistibly constrained the praise, 'O God, how manifold are thy works, in wisdom hast thou made them all, the earth is full of thy riches.' In wonder and ecstasy, I was ready to exclaim, 'The eye is satisfied with seeing.' Still far from human dwellings, I turned my horse's head out of the valley at a point where two paths met, and seeing what seemed a guide-post, rode up, and read in Portuguese to this effect—'Hue and cry, reward for capture, runaway slave-woman, twenty-three years of age, of such height, such features, so many scars on the shoulders, each so long and so broad, so many teeth out, such and such mutilations of different parts of the body'—the published fruits of the lash and of the rage of a brutal master, and it might be of a fiery will, writhing against its wrongs. The eye was sickened with seeing, and I turned aside with horror from the blood-red fangs of the serpent at the very gates of paradise. Oh accursed African slavery, darkest and sorest of human ills. Father of the spirits of all flesh, look down in pity on the untold woes of Africa; 'hear the groaning of the prisoner, and loose those that are appointed to die.'

It was not my lot to witness the noble exodus of our Church in order to keep inviolate the liberty wherewith Christ had made her free, when the spectators felt prouder of their country than ever before. But at the same time in another form I had never been so proud of my country as when I saw how, under the sector of our honoured and beloved Queen, the chains fell in a moment from the neck of the bondsman. In a foreign harbour where Britain had no foothold on the land, and no sway over the sea, three thousand miles from our shores, one of the sable daughters of Africa, stolen in her youth from her own sunny home and sold for a slave in a distant land, followed footsteps of her mistress into our ship, and I remarked to the captain that on reaching England she would be free. 'No,' he replied, 'she is free already; the Queen of England has no slaves; the moment she set her foot on the planks of this ship she was a free woman, and her mistress cannot now bid her return to the shore without her own free consent.' It was a grand thought—no, it was a glorious fact—that this dark daughter of Ethiopia, a helpless bondswoman one minute before, was now as free and as safe as our Queen upon her throne, and that until all the guns of England were silent and her fleets sunk beneath the waves, not an hair of her head could perish. But, fathers and brethren, I shall be far more proud of my country if my brethren reach the heart of Africa with the Bible in their hands, and round the shores of the Lake Nyassa enter the homes of her people as heralds of the Great Peace; and if God, through us, shall be pleased to loose the fetters of iron from their souls, and bring them into the glorious liberty of the sons of God.

Presbyterian Council

The General Assembly has entered cordially into the proposal for a General Presbyterian Council, and, in these days of the rapid evolution of the works of the Lord, we cannot but hope, by his blessing, for good and even great results, from such an Assembly.[1]

Higher Holiness

Fathers and brethren, in addressing you at the opening of this Assembly, I referred to the recent awakening in some of its aspects, and I propose now to take up first the kindred subject of a higher holiness, and then to speak briefly on evangelistic preaching on the part of ministers. Wherever there has been conversion with power, the souls that have been reconciled to their Creator will not fail to inquire how they may become 'perfect as their Father in heaven is perfect'; and every one who seeks to turn a sinner from the error of his way must strive with his whole strength and his utmost skill for the evenest moral path and the highest spiritual walk that he can reach for his own footsteps. For us who are in the ministry this aim is of primary importance, because, under God, the moral and spiritual health of the nation depends chiefly on the inward health of its Christian ministers. What we say within ourselves is always more to others than what we say for them; and the command, 'Meditate on these things, give thyself wholly to them, that thy profiting may appear unto all,' shows the will of God concerning us that our growth in grace should be evident to all around, that it shall be plain to them that our own eye sees the loveliness of the Lord Jesus Christ, and our own heart is taken captive with the beauty of holiness. But when the heart of men is moved, and their intellect awakened in the greatest of human

---

[1] The first General Presbyterian Council took place in Edinburgh in 1877, which brought together representatives of Presbyterian churches throughout the world.—*P.*

interests, defective, or excessive, or erroneous views regarding holiness, commonly old opinions revived, are apt to be suggested and adopted; and with this most hurtful and deplorable result that the perception of the errors scares some, and by others is made an excuse, so as to turn them aside from the earnest, and hopeful, and thorough pursuit of holiness for themselves. At the present time it is very desirable to aim at making our path clear in this great matter, because, though not in our own Church, nor by our evangelistic brethren from the other side of the Atlantic, yet, by various earnest writers and speakers, opinions have been advanced which are extreme as to what is attainable, or mistaken in what is desirable, or erroneous regarding the nature of true holiness, or one-sided in the means of acquiring it.

Let us lay it down as a first principle, that the holiest man in this Church, or on the earth, is the man who, most of all, trusts, admires, and loves the Lord Jesus Christ. He is the best man in the world—the fullest of God and of human brotherhood—in whose heart is deepest written, 'Worthy is the Lamb that was slain'; who hates father and mother, and brother and sister, and his own life also, for the sake of Jesus Christ; and in whom the words, 'He must increase, but I must decrease,' have a daily and cordial amen. Every man becomes like the object of his strongest love and highest admiration; and if a man admires, and trusts, and loves his own vile self, he becomes in every way vile. The one absolutely beautiful object ever disclosed on this earth of ours is Jesus Christ, wholly admirable from his cradle to his cross. Even those who are not his friends admire his peerless beauty. A recent writer, who disowns his claim to divine authority, yet maintains, 'The teaching of Jesus carried morality to the sublimest point attained or even attainable by humanity. The influence of his spiritual religion has been rendered doubly great by the unparalleled purity and elevation of his own character.' (*Supernatural Religion.*[1]) But apart from his cross, this

[1] *Supernatural Religion: An Inquiry into the Reality of Divine Revelation*, vol. 3 (London: Longman, Green & Co., 1875), p. 487. This work was published anonymously but later revealed to be by Walter Richard Cassels (1826–1907). At the time

sublimest teaching and unparalleled purity only drive us the further off; for we may admire, but cannot touch the spotless One; our conscience acknowledges, but our heart cannot learn his lessons; so unlike us, so contrary, we cannot imitate, and never can possess, his holiness. Through his death alone we reach his life, and even in his cradle we embrace him as

> The babe lies yet in smiling infancy,
> That on the bitter cross
> Must redeem our loss,
> So both himself and us to glorify.[1]

Calvary is ours; outside the camp we find the Holy One 'numbered with transgressors,' and made ours in all his fullness. In that same hour his blood purges our conscience from dead works to serve the living God; we are renewed in the whole man after the image of God, in mind, in will, in heart; and sin hath not dominion over us, because we are under grace. We rejoice in a real likeness to Christ; and we joy in the assured hope that when he shall appear we shall be wholly like him, for we shall see him as he is. If in heaven all were not white as snow; if one spot were left, either one stain of the past not washed away, or one old sin retaining its poison, on that single spot we should gaze for ever, and all heaven would present no beauty and afford no joy. That one stain would occupy eternity with itself.

It cannot, however, be set forth as within the plan of redemption that perfect holiness should be ours on earth. If we wash our hands in snow water, and make ourselves never so clean, we are quickly plunged into the ditch again, and compelled to cry out, 'O, wretched man that I am, who shall deliver me from the body of this death.' We are not, therefore, defeated, for we have learned that sin is not omnipotent over us, but that grace is omnipotent over sin. There is

of its publication, the book caused controversy by its casting doubt on the validity of the New Testament.—P.

[1] Lines from John Milton (1608–74), 'On the morning of Christ's nativity'.—P.

no sin, no temptation, no obstinacy, no vitality of sin over which grace is not almighty to overcome, and at last to uproot it. Where sin and Christ met together on the cross, Christ finished transgression for us, and made an end of sin; and so in us, when sin and the grace of Jesus Christ meet together, grace triumphs, in the end always triumphs, and over every kind of sin. Yet every man who is acquainted with himself must adopt the language of the patriarch of Uz: 'If I say I am perfect, mine own mouth shall prove me perverse'; and both the word of God and the history of the church attest the humbling truth that 'No man is able in this life perfectly to keep the commandments of God, but doth daily break them in thought, word, and deed'; and the higher any man rises in nearness and in likeness to God, he is always the more deeply conscious of sin, as seen in Job, in Daniel, in Paul. There is a wide gulf between the character of the holiest of the redeemed and of him who was separate from sinners, and the liker they become to the Redeemer the gulf becomes consciously the wider. 'I am ashamed and blush to lift up my face to thee, I repent in dust and ashes, I am carnal, sold under sin,' are the confessions of the highest among the saints, while in Jesus of Nazareth we pass in an instant to another form of man altogether, who demands, 'Which of you convinceth me of sin?' who asserts, 'I do always those things that please the Father'; who announces to the whole world, 'I am meek and lowly,' which it would be pride in any other man to say, or in the angel Gabriel to speak of himself. Yet this sinless One is more truly human, more open, more accessible, more sympathetic, more attractive to the worst of sinners than any man of like passions with ourselves.

But while sin still stains all the redeemed on earth, there is a wide difference between one and another in holiness. While some are saved only as by fire consuming their wood, hay, and stubble, an abundant entrance is ministered to others into his kingdom, where without holiness no man shall see the Lord; and between these lowest and highest there is every degree of various holiness. It would be misery for one child of God to live for a single day in the heart and life of another child of God, for the man who strives to be in the fear of the Lord all the day long to live for a day in the measure of hardness, deadness, earthliness, selfishness, pride, acridness of temper, that are allowed by another. It is grace that enables one man to grow in grace above his fellow, but it is our sin that we frustrate the grace of God so sadly in ourselves. Which of us did not once expect to be far better men than we have been? which of us might not have become far better than we now are? and, thanks be to God, which of us may not still be far better in the future than we have been in the past? The past we cannot recall, but it can be confessed and forgiven; and if we yield ourselves as clay into the hands of the great Potter, his hands can mould each one of us as a vessel meet for the Master's use.

Mistaken Views on Holiness

But what is the holiness that we are to hope for and aim at in this present world? As regards what constitutes holiness in redeemed men on the earth, the dangerous opinion has been advanced which makes a very excessive distinction, or rather division, between the new man and the old, between the flesh and the spirit in the believer, as if the sinfulness of the flesh were to be disregarded on account of the holiness of the spirit; forgetting that it is still one person in whom the evil and the good are found, and that if the sinfulness of the old nature is accounted little, it will soon swallow up every trace of holiness in the entire man.

Another perilous opinion rests on an extreme distinction between the will and the emotions, holding that all holiness is in the will, and that if the will is right we need not be distressed for wrong emotions. We cannot be grateful enough for a renewed will, for when the will is not supreme in the man, as in dreams, he is ready to become the helpless prey of any emotion; and it belongs to the highest good in the redeemed, when the evil in the affections is met by the resistance of the will, as when the will quenches the sudden emotion of anger. Yet sin in the emotions constantly makes the child of God cry out, 'Oh, wretched man that I am'; and he is the far holier man of the two whom the sinful emotion makes wretched, than he who regards it as of no account. If there be no sin in evil emotions there is no holiness in good emotions, in love to God or man; and it will then be hard to discover any holiness at all.

A third opinion, very closely allied to the last, is that which reduces the standard of holiness; and instead of our Saviour's full demand, 'Be ye perfect, even as your Father in heaven is perfect,' adopts a measure of man's own, sometimes called evangelical perfection, which some men fondly think they have attained. But to lower the standard is not to heighten the man; and a fuller discovery of the holiness of God would draw from every living man the confession, 'I abhor myself in dust and ashes.' The difference is vast between a partial and an absolute resistance to sin, not only in the contest on our part, but in the strength of sin that contends against us. If we count that to be innocent, which is sin by the law of God, we shall encounter less resistance, and gain an easier victory; but the conquest is partial and deceptive. It is often most of all when we would do good that sin is present with us in greater power than at other times. In the weighty words of Dr Owen: 'Whosoever contends against indwelling sin shall know and find that it is present with them, that it is powerful in them. He shall find the stream to be strong who swims against it, though he who rolls along with it be insensible of it.'[1] This element throws some light on our blessed Lord's resistance to temptation, which is apt to be looked upon as easy because he had no sin within him. But, on the other hand, Jesus of Nazareth, oppressed by suffering, and surrounded by sin, stands alone in an absolute resistance to the least inlet of evil. Therefore against him the pent-up stream of sin without beat with a force which neither Adam nor any fallen man has ever encountered, because they have all yielded to the stream; and so his words of grace come home to us, 'To him that overcometh, even as I also overcame.'

---

[1] John Owen, *The Nature, Power, Deceit, and Prevalency of the Remainders of Indwelling Sin in Believers*, in *The Works of John Owen*, vol. 6 (1850–53; repr. Edinburgh: The Banner of Truth Trust, 2009), p. 159.—*P.*

Another view of holiness, which we prefer to call mistaken rather than erroneous, connects it with a perpetual joy, as expressed in the lines—

> If our love were but more simple,
> We should take him at his word;
> And our lives would be all sunshine,
> In the sweetness of our Lord.[1]

The relation between joy and holiness is very close; there is joy the fruit of holiness, and holiness the fruit of joy. 'The peace of God that passeth understanding keeps the heart and mind in Christ Jesus'; and there is no more common or hurtful error than in seeking peace with God as the fruit of holiness, instead of looking for holiness as the fruit of peace with God through Jesus Christ. 'Joy in the Holy Ghost' belongs to the highest of all holiness, and in this relation joy itself is holiness. But this is only one part of the truth, for sorrow also is holiness in the godly sorrow for sin that worketh repentance not to be repented of. It is far from scriptural to assert that true religion always begins with peace. True religion began in the famished outcast in the far country, when he resolved, 'I will rise and go to my father'; and it was already begun in the proud soul of Saul of Tarsus, when in darkness and distance it was said of him by the Lord, 'Behold, he prayeth.' And through the Christian course 'all sunshine' is neither attainable nor desirable. Paul, after being justified by faith and having peace with God, after reckoning himself dead unto sin and alive unto God through Jesus Christ, after finding that sin has not dominion over him when he is under grace, after delighting in the law of God in the inner man, has still a sharp, long, and frequent conflict with sin struggling not to be slain and to get the victory. Likewise in his providential life and ministry his spirit is far from resting in a perpetual sunshine, but is often perplexed and cast down by fightings without and fears

---

[1] Verse from hymn, 'There's a wideness in God's mercy', by Frederick William Faber (1814–63).—*P.*

within. On one occasion his mental anxiety is so severe that he is unable to avail himself of a most favourable opening for preaching the gospel. 'When I came to Troas to preach Christ's gospel, and a door was opened to me of the Lord, I had no rest in my spirit, because I found not Titus my brother, but leaving them, went from thence into Macedonia.' This perplexity on account of the Corinthian church so oppresses him, that he cannot preach to people thirsting for the word of life; but leaves them, not to go to Corinth, but to find Titus, and learn how the Corinthians had received his letter; and afterwards the Lord grants him a singular blessing at Troas, which he leaves in such perplexity. This is not all sweetness and sunshine; and if we cultivate a mere placid joy, however the Lord may cover our mistake and grant us that smile which we covet, we are nevertheless turning aside in the harvest from the burden and heat of the day, we are declining the battle-field, and in fighting no great battles we can look for no great victories.

Means of Attaining Holiness

Further, in the way of acquiring holiness, its attainment by faith has been spoken of as if it were a new discovery, and also as if a man were sanctified by faith alone in the same sense in which he is justified by faith alone. It is true that many who look to Christ alone for their justification, have been looking partly to themselves for their sanctification; but this obliquity of view springs from a defective sight of justifying righteousness. Sin has no condemnation because we are not under the law, but under grace; and sin has no dominion because we are not under the law, but under grace; and according to our apprehension of free grace are our apprehension and experience of sin's no condemnation and sin's no dominion. In our Shorter Catechism, with its wondrous fullness and precision throughout, while our effectual calling is defined as the work of God's Spirit, our sanctification is described as a 'work of God's free grace,' exactly as justification is an 'act' of the same free grace; not thereby setting aside the Spirit's work, but bringing out the great truth that sanctification comes from grace, and if from grace in God then through faith in us, for 'therefore it is of faith that it might be by grace.' Practically it has brought a bright surprise to most believers, when they have found that with the pardon of sin through the blood of Christ there has been the victory over it through the same grace that forgave it. But we are not sanctified at once as we are justified; we are never exhorted to perfect our justification, as we were called to be 'perfecting holiness'; and while sanctification is unto faith and never apart from it, it is likewise through trials, through mercies, through temptations, through deliverances; and in it we work out our own salvation, because God worketh in us to will and to do of his good pleasure. But knowing these things, how far short we fall in doing them; with how little confidence can we say to our flocks, 'Be ye followers of me, even as I also am of Christ?' What a treasure of unused holiness is mine, is yours, in Christ; there for us, there possessed by us; but how guiltily content we are to have it in Christ, instead of drawing it out of his fullness as grace for grace to ourselves.

We receive holiness by faith, but we obtain it also by intensity of prayer, of which Coleridge says most truly, that 'to pray with all the heart and strength, with the reason and the will—prayer with the whole soul—is the highest energy of which the human heart is capable'; and it is at the same time the most fruitful. If we prayed for holiness as for our very life we should find it above all our asking and thinking.

We obtain it, further, by solemn and unreserved dedication of ourselves to God in Christ, which with our fathers frequently took the form of a written personal covenant with God. Oh, that we did one and all, by the mercies of God, present our bodies, our entire persons, a living sacrifice, that so we may prove in ourselves, in our own hearts and lives, 'what is that good and acceptable and perfect will of God.'

But along with faith and prayer and self-surrender, there are daily lessons to be learned in detail by us all. Our Lord Jesus Christ would himself live over again in the world in the person of each one of you, and in the place where he has planted each as his own representative in the earth. In the marriage of the Lamb the Bride will come to him washed in his own blood and clothed with his own righteousness; and also 'in raiment of needlework' wrought out through her own hands by God working in her to will and to do; in a clothing minutely beautiful as by the million-fold puncture of the needle—stitch, stitch, stitch—till her patient continuance in well-doing is crowned with glory, honour, and immortality. In this trying, humbling, yet most glorious process, the soul is helped by all kinds of detail, such as are found in Thomas à Kempis: 'How little soever the thing may be, if it be inordinately loved and regarded, it defiles the soul and keeps it back from the supreme good.—No man is safe to speak but he that willingly holds his peace.—What thou art thou art; nor is it any use to thee to be accounted greater than what thou art in the sight of God.' Or again, in the words of John Wesley, 'It is hardly credible how straight the way is, and of how great consequence before God the smallest things are. As a very little dust will disorder a clock, and the least grain of sand will obscure our sight, so the least grain of sin which is upon the heart will hinder its right motion toward God.—And as the most dangerous winds may enter at little openings, so the devil never enters more dangerously than by little unobserved incidents, which seem to be nothing, yet insensibly open the heart to great temptations.'

Absolutely sinless holiness, as we have said, is our only scriptural standard, and the least sin is not to be tolerated in us, or excused, or in any way made light of. But it will be asked of whom the Bible speaks when it bids us 'mark the perfect man,' seeing 'there is not a just man on the earth that sinneth not.' What is his perfection? It is, we take it, a true and steadfast loyalty of heart to God, which in its root pertains to all God's children, but is more marked in those who 'wholly follow the Lord.' Above all others on the earth in his day, Job is described as 'a perfect man,' but Satan never proposes to try if he is sinless, for neither Job himself nor anyone else entertained such a thought. Satan's boast is that this favourite of heaven will, if tried, turn out not merely faulty but disloyal, will renounce God altogether, will curse him to his face; and Job's wife, whom Satan spares to aid him when he slays his dutiful children, asks her stricken husband, 'Dost thou still retain thy perfectness,' which is well translated 'thine integrity,' or thy loyalty to God. In like manner David, under severe chastening, in the 41st Psalm, after special confession of sin,—'Heal me, for I have sinned against thee,'—blesses God for preserving him in his fidelity through the trial, 'As for me, thou upholdest me in mine integrity,' that is literally, 'in my perfectness.' Now while sinlessness is the standard which we strive to reach in heaven and always to approach more nearly on earth, this steadfast loyalty of heart is a noble aim for our actual possession day by day. Its daily confession is, 'Whom have I in heaven but thee, and there is none on earth whom I desire besides thee'; and its daily estimate of all things is, 'Thy favour is life, thy loving kindness is better than life.' The holiest state of man on earth is described in the words of the 139th Psalm—'Search me, O God, and know my heart, try me and know my thoughts, and see if there be any wicked way in me, and lead me in the way everlasting.'

> By sins we feel how low we're lost,
>   And learn in some degree
> How dear that great salvation cost
>   Which comes to us so free.
>
> If such a weight to every soul
>   Of sin and sorrow fall,
> What love was that which took the whole,
>   And freely bore it all.
>
> O, when will God our joy complete,
>   And make an end of sin?

When shall we walk the land, and meet
    No Canaanite therein?

Will this precede the day of death,
    Or must we wait till then?
Ye struggling souls, be strong in faith,
    And quit yourselves like men.

Our great Deliverer's love is such,
    He cannot long delay;
Meantime, that foe can't boast of much,
    Who makes us watch and pray.[1]

Hope and Fear Motives to Holiness

Another and very different view of holiness from any that we have
noticed is taken by writers, who deny Christ's divine mission, yet
strangely imagine that they admire his moral teaching, as the author
of the work on *Supernatural Religion*, who says—'No practice of
Christian ethics for any ulterior object whatever can be more than
mere formality. Mosaism might be content with observance of law
secured by a promise of length of days in the land, or a threat of death
to the offender, but the great Teacher demanded holiness for itself
alone. The morality of Jesus lays absolute claim to the whole heart
and mind, and they cannot be bribed by hopes of heaven, or coerced
by fears of hell.'[2] The teachings of the Stoics was that goodness being
the true nature of men, they should no more have regard to reward
on its account than the eye should demand a reward for seeing, or
the feet for walking. But this author's conviction, in which he asserts
that the teaching of Jesus Christ is a morality apart from the motives
of hope and fear, betrays a strength of preconception that disqualifies
him for interpreting the plainest precepts of the Christian religion,
much more for weighing its evidence. The motives which he vilifies

---

[1] Verses from a hymn entitled 'Corruptions' by Joseph Hart (1712–68).—*P.*
[2] *Supernatural Religion: An Inquiry into the Reality of Divine Revelation*, vol. 2
(London: Longman, Green & Co., 1874), p. 488-9.—*P.*

as 'bribes,' as fit only for Moses, and not for Christ, are held out far more largely by Christ than by Moses. The Ten Commandments offer them very sparingly, but the beatitudes are full of them—'Blessed are the poor in spirit, for theirs is the kingdom of heaven; blessed are the meek, for they shall inherit the earth; blessed are ye when men shall say all manner of evil against you falsely for my sake, for great is your reward in heaven.' In the 'earliest teaching' of Jesus Christ, to which this writer attaches an exceptional weight, in the Sermon on the Mount, the promise of life on the one side, with the threatening of death on the other, is the woof through the warp of the whole discourse, even where singleness of eye is most strongly enjoined, and cannot be removed without destroying its entire texture. 'Make the tree good' is indeed the root principle of that great sermon; but it is driven home by the stern threatening, 'Every tree that bringeth not forth good fruit is hewn down and cast into the fire.' On the other hand, 'Take heed that ye do not your alms before men; but let not thy left hand know what thy right hand doeth, and thy Father, which seeth in secret, himself shall reward thee openly.' And so through the whole discourse, and through the gospels from their alpha to their omega.

Genuine morality is bound up with the great principle that 'It shall be well with the righteous, for he shall eat the fruit of his doings; it shall be ill with the wicked, for the reward of his hands shall be given him; he that cometh to God must believe that he is, and that he is a rewarder of them that diligently seek him.' The distinction between the two doctrines does not consist in a mere difference about a supplementary motive, but involves the whole character of sin, both as needing the divine forgiveness, and as requiring an atonement that it may be righteously forgiven, because it deserves punishment. Every man who loves holiness hates sin, and the strength of a man's hatred of sin is the measure of his love of holiness; but when you hate sin in another, that very hatred is punishing sin; if you love holiness, that love is rewarding holiness, feebly in us, but not feebly in the High and Holy One. His smile is life, his love better than life; his frown is death; his displeasure the second death. We never reach a right view of sin till we see it to deserve punishment; and if we see not this desert, we are still ignorant of its true character. The retribution of shame is one of the oftenest noted in the Book of God; sin rightly seen awakens instant shame in the sinner, and sin unforsaken covers him with shame in the eyes of every holy being. Shame is the least award of suffering that can be assigned to sin, while it is hard to conceive any other more severe; and if I do not look on sin as meriting this retribution, I have not discovered it to be sin. Holiness, on the other hand, necessarily attracts the favour and the smile of God; 'with a pleasant countenance he beholdeth the upright.' This smile is the highest of all rewards, without which heaven itself would be clothed with no beauty, and would afford no rest.

But disinterestedness, that chief element in holiness, loving self-sacrifice for others, has never been so taught as by Jesus of Nazareth; and whence is it, where is it, what is it, in its root, and birthplace, and home? It is from God, it is in God, it is God; for God is love, generous, disinterested, self-sacrificing love. 'The Son of Man shall be spit upon and crucified,' said Jesus to Peter. 'That be far from thee, Lord,' was his irrepressible reply. 'Get thee behind me, Satan,' the divine answer, 'for thou savourest not the things that be of God, but those that be of men.' Self-pleasing is of the nature of Satan and of men since their apostacy; but Christ 'pleased not himself'; and being the Son in the bosom of the Father, he assures us that self-sacrifice is of the very nature of God, that to give himself for his enemies savours of the very mind and heart of the Most High.

Oh that we ourselves, and every minister in this Church, were through grace resolved to take no rest till we reach a higher walk of faith, a nobler life of love, a deeper secret of holiness; that the Lord Jesus may say of us—'Behold my brethren, for whosoever shall do the will of my Father, the same is my brother.'

O for an heart to praise my God,
  An heart from sin set free;
An heart that always feels thy blood,
  So freely spilt for me!

An humble, lowly, contrite heart,
  Believing, true, and clean,
Which neither life nor death can part
  From him that dwells within.

An heart in every thought renewed,
  And full of love divine;
Perfect, and right, and pure, and good,
  A copy, Lord, of thine.[1]

Ministers Preaching Salvation to the Lost

Fathers and brethren, I have occupied so much of your time with the subject of personal holiness, that I have little left for my proposed remarks on the preaching of the everlasting gospel to perishing men. For that, as for every other Christian work, ministers alone are quite unequal, and we rejoice in the multitude of workers now in the field, in obedience to the command—'Let him that heareth say, Come!' But it will be a dark day for the church and the world if it shall ever come to be held that the evangelistic work should be left mainly to others, and that ministers ought to be only pastors and not evangelists. The double result would be a ministry clothed with no living power, and a surface evangelism with a shallow religion for its fruit. The divine charge to every minister is, 'Do the work of an evangelist, make full proof of thy ministry,' and none of us ever make full proof of our ministry without doing the work of an evangelist. That honoured minister and evangelist, William Burns, used to say, 'It is an easy thing to preach to saints, what tries a man is preaching to sinners.' For

[1] Verses from a hymn by Charles Wesley (1707–88)—P.

grappling with consciences still asleep in sin, the whole man with every power within him,—mind, conscience, will, affection,— must be awake. The apostolic Brainerd complains, 'I could not handle the people's consciences today, my hands were like stumps'; and fingerless stumps we all often feel our hands to be, when we set ourselves to grapple with the sleeping conscience of a man who is to die or to live for ever. Judgment to come is awakening, because it appeals to the conscience, but to preach the coming judgment without dealing with the conscience is alike easy for the minister and fruitless for his people. Our power lies in so speaking as to 'commend ourselves to every man's conscience in the sight of God'; and for this the minister's own conscience must be awake, and at the same time his love to his fellow men so kindled as to make him willing for their sake to become a fool, that by the foolishness of preaching he may save them that believe.

This requires an entrance into the presence of the great King. 'It does a man good,' said Samuel Johnson, after his interview with George III, 'it does a man good to speak to a king'; and if with an earthly king, how much more with the King of kings. 'If,' saith our King, 'they had stood in my council (in my secret), and had caused my people to hear my words, then they should have turned them from their evil way, and from the evil of their doings.' What a glorious promise of a successful ministry, what a bright assurance of unfailing fruit; yet linked to it the sharp warning, 'I am against the prophets that steal my words every one from his neighbour; I have not sent these prophets, yet they ran.' God's own words, apart from his own teaching: God's words borrowed from other men's lips, and not written with the finger of the living God in our own hearts, will neither save ourselves nor them that hear us. What an issue depending on every minister in our Church; what an issue on every Sabbath and on every sermon! The fire on our own altar is too often like a glimmering spark ready to die, needing help from without to keep itself alive, and feebly unfit to kindle the wood on another altar. Oh, if for even one Sabbath in all our churches we pleaded and found the promise—'I will make the governors of Judah like an hearth of fire among the wood, and like a torch of fire in a sheaf,' what a bright flame would our preaching enkindle through the land. Such a result is worth any effort of self-denial in us, any intensity and continuousness of pleading, any secret wrestling of the worm Jacob with the Angel of the Covenant, any deepest stirring of our inmost selves, till our will, strengthened and upheld by grace, shall meet the divine will; and in this case not to ask 'Thy will be done,' but in the depth of self-emptiness, rising to say, 'I will not let thee go except thou bless me.'

If we are to move our people they must see that we have for ourselves entered into the great mysteries of life and death. When a student in this city under that noblest of recent men, Dr Chalmers, an elder of this church, no longer with us on earth, drew my attention to two beautiful family portraits in his drawing-room and said:—'These are by the most eminent painters of their day, and both perfect in their kind, but that is by an artist, and this by a genius; in the one you have the whole before you but nothing beyond, in the other all the lines run off into infinity; and you ministers should have more of the infinite in your sermons. You will never reach the people by teaching us as if you knew it all, and giving us our lessons as if we were children. If you wish to move us, you must make us feel that you see more than you are able to express, and that you think and know that there is an infinite height and depth beyond what you see. But you go to the brim of the great ocean, you dip your tumbler into it, you set it down on your desk before us, and you tell us, "That's the ocean."' This elder said truly that this is the weakest of all preaching. And in these days of a ready-made and glib evangelism, when the speaker keeps repeating that it is all so plain, and no darkness or difficulty in it; as if there were no unfathomed depth in the heart of man, and no infinite depth in the mind of God; the thought will sometimes arise, That is the sparkling water in your glass, but what of the great ocean? We must both go ourselves to the ocean, and lead our people there; we must for ourselves and with them learn to say—'Thou hast beset me behind and before, and laid thine hand upon me: such knowledge is too wonderful for me.'

What Lord Bacon said of all truth, holds more specially of its highest kind, that 'Truth is a certain daylight, which doth not show the masks and mummeries of life half so stately and daintily as candle light'; and we must let the daylight of divine truth in upon our minds even when it most mars the glitter of our dainty candle-lights. There is an ample compensation for the loss, when our eyes see light in the light of the Lord.

Fathers and Brethren, it is the highest ambition of every minister of Christ to be enabled so to speak as to save both himself and those who hear him; to be divinely enlarged to testify the gospel of the grace of God; to share in that all-utterance, that holy boldness and freedom in preaching, with which Paul was so largely gifted, and for which he so prayed and asked the prayers of others, because it is at the command of no man, but is always the immediate gift of God by the Spirit. Of this preaching, one of the glorious peculiarities is that, however near the minister himself may be within the veil, and the further he is within it, he is the more enabled to identify himself with those who are without, as himself needing and rejoicing in the same gospel and the same grace which he is holding out to them. He sees and feels that nothing stands between himself and a portion among the dogs without, except Christ and him crucified; and that the grace of Jesus Christ is infinitely ample for the souls of all who hear him. From the depths of his inmost consciousness, he can pray, 'Purge me with hyssop and I shall be clean; wash me and I shall be whiter than snow'; and he can press every hearer to utter that prayer and to accept that cleansing; not that prayer must be before cleansing, for either may precede the other, but that the cleansing accepted always makes the soul white as snow.

Wondrous truth, that Jesus Christ came into the world to save sinners! The first time it is seen it fills the soul with surprise and unutterable joy. Many years ago, in a time of spiritual inquiry, a stranger, having an air of superior intelligence, called on me in distress of mind. In speaking to her, I was brought to a stand by her thorough knowledge of the letter and the doctrine of the Scriptures, and finding I could add no instruction I asked no further question, but briefly opened and pressed the words, 'Jesus Christ came into the world to save sinners,' and ended with prayer. While I was speaking, a stream of tears began to flow, and she looked relieved, but was silent. A week after she returned with her face bright with joy, to tell me that she had found that peace with God which she had before been vainly seeking. I asked her, 'Why did you weep when you left last day?' 'I wept for joy.' 'And what gave you the joy?' 'I saw, as you were speaking, that Jesus Christ came into the world to save sinners.' 'But you knew that before?' 'No.' 'Then what did you think?' 'I always thought that Jesus Christ came into the world to save saints, and I wept for joy when I saw that he came to save sinners.' To myself, Fathers and Brethren, it is always new every time that I see that Jesus Christ came to the world to save sinners. It does not appear to me as if I had never seen it before, but each successive sight of it is as new and bright—sometimes newer and brighter—as fresh as if it were now for the first time; and it always seems as if I had forgotten it daily, and daily recovered it again. How new it will be the first hour that we join the general assembly above! How new and marvellous it will be after millions of years in heaven! After preaching the gospel for more than forty years to others, I find for my own soul no sin so easily besets and so sorely hinders me as the thought that Jesus Christ came into the world to save saints; and I should finish my course with joy if I were enabled fully to testify the gospel of the grace of God, to bear witness that the Son of Man has come to seek and to save that which was lost. If through grace we abide there, we shall not fail to see under our ministry many turned from darkness to light, and from the power of Satan unto God.

And now, Fathers and Brethren, we separate never again to meet all of us on earth, and we have met in this Assembly after very special warnings how soon and how suddenly we may be called to another and an eternal scene. 'The Lord grant unto us all that we may find mercy of the Lord in that day,' and be found of him in peace. The tombstone of an English gentleman had inscribed on it by his will the one Bible word: 'Kept'. May it be written as by the Lord's own hand on my tombstone and on yours; and may we all be 'kept by the power of God unto salvation, ready to be revealed in the last time.'

Jesus Christ the Bond of the Holy Universe[1]

'That they all may be one; as thou, Father, art in me,
and I in thee, that they also may be one in us: and
that the world may believe that thou hast sent me.
I in them, and thou in me, that they may be made
perfect in one.'—*John 17:21, 23*

THE annual meeting of our General Assembly never fails
to recall, with all their hallowed associations, the well-
remembered words, 'Jerusalem is builded as a city that is
compact together, whither the tribes go up, the tribes of the Lord,
unto the testimony of Israel, to give thanks to the name of the Lord;
for there are set thrones of judgement, the thrones of the house of
David.' This compactness of Jerusalem below, this oneness of heart
and mind on earth, links us at the same time to heaven above; for
while the uniting Spirit comes from heaven, it is when the brethren
dwell together in unity that the anointing oil flows down from the
head of the high priest to the skirts of the garments. In the temple
of old, 'when the trumpeters and the singers were as one to make
one sound to be heard in praising the Lord, for he is good: then the
house was filled with a cloud, even the house of the Lord'; and in
the lowly second temple of the upper room in Jerusalem, when the
disciples prayed with one accord, the rushing breath of the Spirit

[1] Preached at the opening of the Free Church General Assembly, 18 May 1876.—*P.*

366

filled the house with the glory of the Lord. In the Sermon on the Mount, peace with our brother on earth is ordained to precede our drawing nigh to the altar of God in heaven; and the only supplication in the Lord's Prayer that defines our own state is that which embodies love to each other, in the petition, 'Forgive us our debts, as we forgive our debtors.'

But this oneness on earth, and this oneness of earth and heaven, is only in Jesus Christ: 'I in them, and thou in me, that all may be perfect in one'; and by the divine help I propose to examine with you for a little the great truth of my text, that JESUS CHRIST IS THE GOLDEN KNOT WHICH BINDS INTO ONE THE UNIVERSE OF HOLY BEINGS. In this I shall ask you to consider first that all evil is one, yet all in whom it dwells are divided; and then, more largely, the converse, that all good is one and all in whom it dwells are gathered into one in Jesus Christ; and thereafter the apparent difficulty arising out of the distance between man and God; and then some of the great properties of this oneness,—its efficacy in uniting men together, its power of dissolving every contrary union, its fullness, its permanence, and its effect in the salvation of the world. Let us then consider—

I. Evil in Its Oneness and in Its Severance

1. *The oneness of evil is among the most marked of its characteristics.* Whence or how evil came first of all, possibly no creature knoweth. But we know in whom it began, and from whom its poison has spread through creation; for 'the devil is a murderer from the beginning; he is a liar, and the father of it.' As regards the beginning of evil in him, the saying of our Lord falls to be noted, that 'he abode not in the truth, because there is no truth in him.' The union of the true believer to Christ is set forth in our text as affected and secured by the double bond of a mutual indwelling; and it is formed after the likeness of the union of the Father and the Son, 'As thou, Father, art in me, and I in thee, that they also maybe one in us,' or, as elsewhere expressed in our Lord's words, 'Abiding in me, and I in you.' But as

regards the temporary believer, who, in some lower sense, is said to be in Christ, being called 'a branch in him that beareth not fruit,' there is not in his case the converse assertion of Christ being also in him, and of this double bond of union with the true Vine. In a manner analogous, although the coincidence may not be designed, our Lord says of Satan, that 'he abode not in the truth, because there is no truth in him'; that he was therefore once in the truth, but continued not in it through the want of truth in him. As if, over and above the great fact that the holy angels kept their first state, because they were among the elect of God, there were also a connection of Satan's fall with this, that there never had been the reciprocal indwelling by him in the truth, and of the truth likewise in him.

But, however this may be, it was in him that evil had its dark origin; none tempted him to sin, and from him all sin in angels and men had its source, for 'he is a liar, and the father of it.' The principalities and powers of darkness were seduced by him from their allegiance, and it was his deadly sting that by one deep thrust infused the poison of sin through the whole human family. And all sin centres in him still, for the tongue that speaks bitter words on earth is 'set on fire of hell'; and hence much of the terrible power that lurks in what seems to be a very little evil. All sin hangs together; the least sin coheres to the greatest, is pervaded by its character, and partakes of its force. This is indicated in the prayer, 'Deliver us from evil,' or literally 'from the evil:' obviously so, if we interpret the petition as for deliverance from the evil one; but also if we take it as deliverance from the evil thing, because it designates all sin as 'the evil'; intimating that every evil thought or word or work belongs to the one great evil, the one body of sin and death. It is an appalling thought that there exists no isolated transgression; that there is no such thing as a stray sin; but that the least accepted sin binds the soul by a tremendous change to all iniquity to the whole universe of evil with all its horrors and all its vileness.

As all sin, so likewise all sinners are bound together in a miserable union. The world loves its own; Satan does not cast out Satan, and is not divided against himself; and the word of God acknowledges no distinction among men except that 'between the righteous and the wicked, between him that serveth God, and him that serveth him not.' All who are not among 'the children of light' are classed in one as 'the children of disobedience.' This massing together of all the ungodly, of 'the tender and delicate woman, which would not adventure the sole of her foot to the ground for delicateness and tenderness,' with the man of violence and blood, ought to move in each of us the earnest prayer: 'Gather not my soul with sinners, nor my life with bloody men.' But there is likewise to be taken into account the other element of evil, for—

2. *All evil is division.* Sin is in its nature severance, and the union of sinners is neither true nor lasting. It is founded on falsehood, and cannot endure. When the time is come the kingdom of Satan will be destroyed; when he can deceive no more he will reign no longer, and among all the children of disobedience no hand will be lovingly joined with another. Of all of whom it can be truly affirmed that they are 'hateful,' it will also be seen to be true that 'they hate one another.' Sin has in it no real principle of union, and no compatibility with lasting union. It is the essential and everlasting seed of division, discord, and strife. There is no discord in the intelligent universe except through sin, and there is no sin in the universe without enmity and strife.

For a time there may be concord amongst sinners, and their enmity may seem to be directed only against the holy one who is looked upon as their common foe. But sin that builds a wall of partition between man and God, erects in the same hour a dividing wall between man and man. Sin is separation and enmity all round. Its voice is, 'My will be done, over every other will in heaven or on earth'; and it is love and concord only on this condition. Sin can never truly say, either to God or to man, 'Not my will.' God creates ten thousand distinct wills, wills distinct at first, and everlastingly distinct; yet the owner of each can say, can will to say, and can love to say, 'Not my will, but thine be done.' But sin originates ten thousand separate and hostile wills, and from these arise ten thousand defiances to God and to man, 'Not thy will, but mine.' Sin and unity are everlasting opposites.

But to this there is a glorious contrast presented by the grand truth of our text, that all the redeemed and God their Redeemer are knit together for ever in Jesus Christ: 'that all may be one, as thou, Father, art in me, and I in thee, that they also may be one in us.' And let us now consider—

II. Jesus Christ the Golden Knot that Binds Us All into One

In the history of the intelligent universe three great steps have been taken by its all-wise Creator, and the last of these has attained an everlasting oneness: the creation of the angels, the formation of Adam, the birth and death of the Son of God. And—

1. *The creation of the angels* presents a marked absence of oneness in the highest sense of the term. The glorious angelic company as coming from the hands of the Creator is not a unity; it is not a tree with its branches, but a field of wheat with its separate stalks. There are diversities of rank, angel and archangel, cherubim and seraphim. There is organisation and unbroken order. There are thrones, dominions, principalities, and powers; around these, and in subordination to them, are ranged the myriads of the angelic hosts, and fullness of harmony reigns through them all. Yet before God each stands by himself and for himself; each is not bound up in every other; and if they have a prince or a leader, yet there is no common root and centre of the whole. In concord and at one they all are, but they are not one; not bound together as the welded links of a chain that embraces all. One stands, and his comrade beside him falls; or a thousand fall, and one abides faithful. So also towards God: he is the fountain of all their good, the sum of all that happiness, and the centre of all their harmony; yet they are not united to him by a union that cannot be dissolved and many of them fall away for ever, like bright stars quenched in darkness.

The elect angels abide in their allegiance, being upheld by the good hand of their God; yet their everlasting union to the centre of all good appears to be increased, confirmed, and secured through Jesus Christ, for God is set to 'gather together in one all things in Christ, whether they be things in heaven or things on earth, even in him,' and 'by him to reconcile all things to himself, whether they be things on earth or things in heaven.' He has become their one great head; to them as well as to us he is 'the first-born of every creature,' visible or invisible; and there is not the mere issuing of a sovereign command, but the promulgation of a new privilege, in the divine decree, 'Let all the angels of God worship him.' The song of the angels of heaven over the babe born in Bethlehem is 'glory to God in the highest, peace on earth and goodwill to men'; and the reciprocating song of earth when the Lord Jesus has finished his work, and enters Jerusalem for his great sacrifice, is 'Blessed be the king that cometh in the name of the Lord, peace in heaven, and glory in the highest:' God in Christ reconciling all things to himself, whether they be things on earth or things in heaven. But while the angels were created each in his own independent individuality,

2. *The formation of Adam* brings a great advance toward oneness and a centre of union. First of all, in the very composition of his being, consisting of the two great elements in creation, *matter* and *mind*, and uniting both in one. Hitherto these had been kept apart. Angels are spirits; if not spirits absolutely pure, as the great Spirit, yet not clothed with visible, tangible, solid bodies like ours. Power over matter they have, but as themselves apart from it; not as united to it and bound up with it. The beasts that perish consist of body without spirit; so far as we know, they have nothing in common with the angels of light; and they are not a little lower, but altogether different from and vastly beneath the angels. But man, whose innermost being is like the angels—soul, spirit, intellect, will—had no existence apart from his earthly frame, and that frame was fashioned out of the same earth from which the lower animals sprang. It was nobler far than theirs, but in its earthliness it partook of the same nature. Then his soul was so embodied in that earthly tent that the two made one man; the highest and

lowest elements in creation being combined in him and becoming one.

At the same time a still greater step toward the centre of union was taken, in one man being ordained to be at once the *root* and the *head* of all the race. God hath made of one blood all nations of men in the whole earth, so that the same blood that flowed in Adam's veins still circulates in yours and in mine. The millions of men constitute one family, one tree with its innumerable branches springing from the single root, and none of them detached and independent.

But still more than as our one root are we all bound to Adam as our one great *head*; as our one representative, in whom we were to stand or fall; in whom for a season we stood and lived in innocence; in whom we quickly sinned and fell. 'By one man sin entered into the world; and by one man's disobedience many were made sinners.' Yet by our own will and act we have all set our seal to that first transgression. If the first covenant were yet unbroken, each of us would be ready to take the initiative in transgressing it. And being broken, none of us have remained at the spot where Adam fell; but we have all gone forward in the broad road, every one of us turning to his own way, and advancing in a path of disobedience on which there is no footmark except our own; my own way, your own way, tried by none before us and by none after us. Yet there is a dark oneness staining all the diversity, and bringing us back to the sad truth that in Adam we have all died; with its thousand separate footpaths there is but one broad road of departure from the fold and the shepherd, of a common apostasy from God only good.

But when the bond of oneness for good in Adam was broken forever, there came, in the inscrutable wisdom and grace of God, the last and great step in this history, which is,

3. *The Birth and Death of Jesus Christ, the Son of God and the Son of Adam.* His birth, his death, his being bruised and broken and forsaken, all combined to make him the bond of holy oneness. In his *birth*, the highest and lowest created elements, mind and matter, soul and body, are combined. Had he so willed, he might

have assumed a high angelic nature, leaving out the lower bodily element, and not honouring it by union with himself. 'But he took not on him the nature of angels, but the seed of Abraham.' While there is thus in Jesus Christ, as in Adam, the union of soul and body, there is at the same time the far more wondrous and glorious union of creator and creature, of God and man. In his wonderful person, spirit uncreated, pure, absolute, infinite, is united with created spirit—holy and perfect in its kind, yet limited in holiness, wisdom, power, presence—and likewise with the material body of flesh and bones. There is thus not only the union of all creation, but of all being; of creation in its two great forms, higher and lower, spirit and matter; and of absolute, infinite pure spirit, at once to created spirit and to matter, the lowest portion of creation, yet also very good. Highest and lowest, mental and bodily, creator and created, are all thus united in one, without any part being confounded with another, or swallowed up and lost in the whole, but each preserving entire and unchanged its own distinctive nature. There is no province of being, no separate element of universal existence, left out in God manifest in the flesh, but all singularly gathered up and combined in One, undivided and indissoluble Being, one glorious Person, one Christ forever.

All had now been perfected in Jesus Christ, if he had been the designed head of a new creation which would leave out men already fallen. But while there was in him the almighty power of a new creation, the sphere of its operation was to be in men already existing and defiled by sin, which separates while it defiles. It was from our corrupted stock that he drew his holy manhood, being not merely man like us, but of us, out of us; holy, harmless, and undefiled, yet flesh out of our flesh, bone out of our bone; casting himself into the heart of the existing family, and from it deriving his own everlasting manhood. By his birth of the Holy Ghost he was himself sinless in his humanity; but he had come to adopt into union with himself men who were sunk in sin, to be the head of a people given to him by the Father, all of whom were defiled with all iniquity.

How to take sinners into union with himself, while he was and could not but remain infinitely far from the least communion with sin, seems to have been the link in the history of the universe which called forth to its utmost the wisdom of God only wise, even as it drew forth from its innermost depths the love of God, who is love. Christ united himself to his people by taking them to himself in his *death* on Calvary. He took us as his own in that hour, as one with himself; and he took us with all that was ours, with the burden of all our sins. That he might receive us into oneness, he stood in our place; he accepted our penalty, our curse, our death. He so took our sins as to make them altogether his own, and to remove them entirely and forever from us. Our sins and ourselves seemed to be one; they were all that we could claim as ours; they were felt by us to be as if an essential and inseparable element of our being; as if they could be destroyed and come to an end only by our annihilation, by the everlasting extinction of soul and body and sin together. But Jesus Christ on the cross came between us and our sins by taking them upon himself. The Father 'laid on him the iniquities of us all; and by himself he purged our sins, bearing them in his own body on the tree, that by his stripes we might be healed.' And when God manifest in the flesh has thus placed himself between us and our sins, then 'as far as east is from the west,' so far hath he removed our transgressions from us.

In that hour, in order that he might become the bond of union between God and sinful men, this wondrously united one was *broken as if in pieces*. As his vesture was woven without seam throughout, his soul and his body, when themselves parted asunder, remained united to the Godhead, and through it to each other; but in his manhood Christ Jesus was broken in two, and in every part of it he was rent and torn. His inward frame was crushed in Gethsemane till great drops of blood were forced through the skin; his flesh was cut by the scourge when 'the ploughers ploughed upon his back, and made long their furrows'; his bones were racked so that he cried, 'All my bones are out of joint'; his soul was torn as if in twain when he was so amazed and in an agony in the garden; and in reference to the shame of the cross he complains, 'Reproach hath broken my heart.' So sorely for our sakes 'it pleased the Father to bruise him,' and with such manifold fullness were his own words made true, 'This is my body, which is broken for you,' in order that we with him and with each other might become 'one bread and one body.'

At the same time, he who was to be the one bond of all union for ever was also for this end cut off from communion with every being in the universe, and was left *alone* as no other ever was or can be; according to his own words, 'Ye shall be scattered every one to his own, and shall leave me alone.' None has ever entered the fathomless depths of loneliness as Jesus did; and he was cast into them that through his isolation, his awful absolute solitude, he might expiate and take away sin, the cause of separation, and might become the bond of everlasting union between God and all his ransomed flock. Apart from every creature; earth combined against him in Jew and Gentile, ruler, priest, and people; hell combined against him in the hour and power of darkness; all his disciples ashamed of him and afraid to follow him; all heaven withdrawing and no angel sent now to succour him in his time of need. One all-sustaining solace remains so long as he can say, 'Yet I am not alone, because the Father is with me.' Yet this also fails him in the end, and through the darkness that covers the land there wails the saddest cry that ever arose from earth to heaven, 'My God! My God! Why hast thou forsaken me?' Like the scapegoat carrying 'all the iniquities of the children of Israel, in all their transgressions, and all their sins into the wilderness,' and bearing them into 'a land not inhabited,' so the Lamb of God taking away the sins of the world bears them into a solitude where nothing meets him but our sins, in their countlessness, their vileness, their exceeding sinfulness. Who can think what this loneliness, this desertion was to him who said of the Father, 'I was with him as one brought up with him, I was daily his delight'; and of us, 'My delights were with the sons of men'; and of whom it was said, 'Let all the angels of God worship him'? Through the endurance of this severance and immeasurable removal from all light and peace and friendship for our sakes, Jesus, because he cannot be holden by those cords of darkness, returns to his Father's smile, but not till he has left all our sins behind him in the depths of that sea for ever; and thus he unites us to himself, to his Father, and to each other: 'I in them, and thou in me, that they may be made perfect in one.'

Through his death the Lord Jesus Christ sends his HOLY SPIRIT into the hearts of his redeemed, and by that Spirit in the day of our effectual calling we are brought into a wondrously high and holy union with Christ and with God. The Holy Ghost, who proceedeth from the Father and the Son, who dwelleth in the Father and the Son, and who forms the mysterious link of union and communion between the Father and the Son, is the same by whose indwelling we are united to Christ; for 'God hath sent forth the Spirit of his Son into our hearts, crying, Abba, Father'; and 'hereby we know that we dwell in him and he in us, because he hath given us of his Spirit.'

But let us now advert to—

III. The Barrier of Distance Between God and Man

The greatness of God over against the littleness of man presents no insurmountable or unsurmountable obstacle to the oneness of God with man in Jesus Christ, and our oneness with Christ; and the light of modern science makes the distance between man and God no greater than man has always felt it to be. This distance is sometimes spoken of as if it were more to us than to Abraham and to John, on account of the magnificent wonders of the starry universe as disclosed by modern research; but it has really been the same in all ages of the world, and is brought out as clearly in what is probably the oldest book in the Bible as in any book of our own day. Through faith, with an enlightened and most vivid imagination, the patriarch Job took a larger grasp of the vastness of creation than any mere astronomer can ever reach by figures and by measurements. On earth the great mountains and the wide sea far exceed man's little grasp, and it is not so much a higher mountain and a broader

sea that will enlarge our thoughts of their Maker as a roomier intellect to take in what is already before our eyes. Job sees the awful
power and wisdom of God as shown in these his two greatest works
on earth; and then looks on his bright work above us as grander
than these, and names Arcturus, Orion, and the Pleiades, and the
chambers of the south, which yet he speaks of as only the 'fringes'
of the vast unseen in the star-spangled curtain of the heavens; and
awe-struck with the majesty of the unsearchable Creator in contrast to his own littleness, he exclaims, 'If I had called and he had
answered me, yet would I not believe that he had hearkened to my
voice' (Job 9:16; 26:14, *Hebrew*). This is the voice of nature in man
overwhelmed by dark trial: but the true relation of the divine greatness to our littleness is to be found in the trustfulness and acceptance of the 8th Psalm,—'When I consider thy heavens, the work of
thy fingers, the moon and the stars, which thou hast ordained; what
is man, that thou art mindful of him? or the son of man, that thou
visitest him?'

The truth is, that as regards union and fellowship the distance
from God in heaven to man on earth is neither of the same kind
nor at all so great, as the distance between man and the lower creatures of the earth beside him. The wise difference between man and
beast, and the comparative nearness and likeness of man to God,
are both expressed in the early divine decree,—'Every moving thing
that liveth shall be meat for you, even as the green herb; but whoso
sheddeth man's blood, by man shall his blood be shed, for in the
image of God made he man.' In the ranks of the humble creatures
passing before man there is no help-meet found for him; but the
eternal Son of God, by whom all things were made, takes redeemed
man for his companion, his friend, his Bride; and because man is
partaker of flesh and blood, he also himself likewise takes part of
the same. He takes it in infinite grace and condescension, but with
no trace of degradation, and without effacing one ray of his divine
glory; and having taken human nature, he retains it forever as his
own. Man could never become a dog without utter debasement

and the abandonment of his manhood; he would cease to be honoured by himself, or loved and reverenced by his former fellows. But the Father does not honour or love his Son the less for having become man, but rather the more, if that were possible, for Jesus says, 'Therefore doth my Father love me, because I lay down my life, that I might take it again.'

Between man and the lower animals there is a great gulf fixed which can never be bridged over. There is rule and subjection, command and obedience, and there may be mutual understanding, and even strong affection. But there is no fellowship; and no humblest condescension on the part of man, or highest attainable elevation of these lower natures, can ever effect a mutual fellowship and friendship between them and us. Within their own limits and in their own species they know each other, and cherish their own narrow intercourse; but into either the mind or the heart of man they can never rise, neither can man descend into that which is within them. Man is capable both of apprehending the works, the character, and the thoughts of God, and of entering into his love, in a manner and to an extent in which no beast of the earth or fowl of the air can make the least approach, regarding the works, the character, the thoughts, and the affections of man.

Viewed in some of its aspects, the distance may seem little between a man and the dog that follows at his foot. We are both creatures formed by one maker out of the dust of the same earth, and although not of one blood, were both born out of flesh and blood, and at death the bodies of both returned to the dust. Fascinated by this resemblance, some acute men of science, ignoring man's creation in the divine image, and his peculiar and completely distinctive capacity for God, and seeking a oneness for man beneath him and not above him, have pored over this earthly likeness till what is heavenliest in their own faculties seems to have been benumbed; and they have pictured to themselves a man near of kin to the other beasts, only a little higher, and almost if not quite self-promoted from among them. As in its childhood the world by wisdom knew not God, but changed his glory into the image of corruptible things, so again in its old age the world seems ready to relapse into a second childhood by returning after another fashion to the glorifying of 'four-footed beasts, and birds, and creeping things.'

Man has been said, rightly enough, to stand in some way in the place of God to the dog whom he feeds and commands. But in all that relates to likeness and fellowship, the difference is vastly wider between the dog and man who treads the same earth than between man and the great God who guides the stars in their courses. As regards power, the distance indeed is limited from the worm to the archangel, but is infinite from the archangel to God almighty; and it is equally so from man to God, man formed out of the dust, and the great unseen spirit, infinite, internal, and unchangeable. Between the littleness of man and the greatness of him who holds the sea in the hollow of his hand, the distance is immeasurable; and between the creature and the Creator it is absolutely infinite, between us who are moulded like clay by the hand of our Potter, and God who created all things out of nothing by the word of his power. Such power, with the manner of its exercise, is to us what has been called in recent phraseology, 'unthinkable'; and its apprehension is in the Bible denied to mere intellect of man, for 'the world by wisdom knows not God,' and is ascribed to the childlikeness of faith; yet it is so ascribed to faith that the intellect shares in that which faith enables it to grasp, for 'by faith we understand (we mentally apprehend) that the worlds were framed by the word of God; so that things which are seen were not made of things which do appear.' As creatures the distance between us and this great Creator is infinite; yet man was created in the image of God, but the dog was not created in the image of man; and as concerns oneness, friendship, communion, the distance between man and the dog that serves him is immeasurably greater than the distance between God and man formed in the image of God. Between man and the wisest beast of the field there is interposed a chasm, deep and dark, across which millions of years can weave no thoroughfare. But man was created in likeness and fellowship with God, and in that likeness we are renewed, and to that fellowship we are more than restored by Jesus Christ: 'I in them, and thou in me, that all may be perfect in one.' Then 'truly our fellowship is with the Father, and with his Son Jesus Christ,' and our whole training on earth is for its furtherance and perfecting. Under severest trial it was asked of old, 'What is man, that thou shouldst magnify him and set thine heart upon him; and that thou shouldst visit him every morning, and try him every moment?' and it is answered in the new covenant that 'he chastens us for our profit, that we might be partakers of his holiness,' that we may be one with him in likeness and in communion.

Let us lastly consider—

IV. Some of the Great Properties of this Oneness

1. *Oneness with Jesus Christ unites us to each other:* gathering into one all the redeemed in earth and heaven, 'that they all may be one.' There is no bond of union among men equal to that which binds Christians together as the children of their heavenly Father; for the members of the mystical body of Christ are in him united to each other in a manner similar to the union between the Father and the Son. It is incredible and inconceivable to the world how Jesus Christ breaks down every parting wall between his redeemed, not only in heaven but on earth, and knits heart to heart in the whole flock of the Good Shepherd. A mingled but beautiful flock, for 'the wolf shall dwell with a lamb, and the leopard shall lie down with the kid; and the calf, and the young lion, and the fatling together; and a little child shall lead them.' In the day of our new birth we are 'taught of God to love one another,' and that not by mere commandment, but by love divinely planted in our hearts to all that are in Christ Jesus. We know them as we never thought it possible to know another; for the same Christ and the same Spirit are in us and in them. The very same truth that is in our heart is in theirs, the very same thoughts, the same fears, the same hopes, the same desires. Jesus Christ who has loved us has loved them as he has loved

us, and Jesus Christ whom we love is loved by them as by us. If we love him we cannot but love them. The separation of country, of language, of rank, of age, of disposition is broken down; and we are united to them all by a bond that enters deeper into our heart and theirs than any other, that binds us closer together than any other, and that endures when all other bonds shall have given way.

2. *By this union to Jesus Christ every contrary union is dissolved.*— Our union to Adam and the Adamic covenant, and to the broken law of the covenant of works, is dissolved, for 'as in Adam all die, even so in Christ shall all be made alive,' and 'we are dead to the law by the body of Christ.' Our union to the world, in its allurements and its frowns, which is so bound up with every man's heart, is dissolved; and 'we glory in the cross of Jesus Christ our Lord, by whom the world is crucified unto us, and we unto the world.' Our union to sin, which seemed to be as if an essential part of our inmost being, is dissolved; for 'we are dead unto sin, but alive unto God through Jesus Christ our Lord.' Our union to self, which nothing seemed able to break except annihilation, is now dissolved; for Christ loved us and gave himself for us, 'that we should no longer live unto ourselves, but unto him that died for us and rose again.' In following him, we take up our cross and deny ourselves; nay, we take up our cross 'daily' and deny ourselves, Christ henceforth taking the place of self. Even as Peter in denying Christ, when his enemies railed on him, spit on him, and buffeted him, said, 'I know not the man'; so the Christian sees the old man of self reviled, trampled on, and beaten, while he stands by and denies as it were all interest or acquaintance, saying, 'I know not that man.' If I am crucified with Christ, self in me is crucified with a lingering but certain death. 'Nevertheless I live, yet not I, but Christ liveth in me.'

3. *This union has a glorious fullness of blessing,* For a oneness with the Lord Jesus Christ is all our life, our strength, our joy, our fruit. It is all our *life*. Words cannot express more strongly our entire death, apart from Christ, than the Lord's saying: 'Except ye eat the flesh and drink the blood of the Son of Man, ye have no life in you';

nor, on the other hand, can anything exceed the fullness of our life in him: 'I am the vine, ye are the branches; because I live, ye shall live also.' It is all our *strength*: 'When we were yet without strength, in due time Christ died for the ungodly'; and as we derive all our strength at first from his crucifixion in weakness, so for our hourly supply of spiritual strength we depend on him alone, for, 'Without me ye can do nothing.' It is all our *joy*. Our Lord has given us the humbling and saddening assurance, 'In the world you shall have tribulation'; and often when we have fondly begun to think that we have finally escaped out of the toils of earthly sorrow, we quickly find ourselves again entangled in a new network of grief. But his words of consolation never fail us, and are fullest of joy in our deepest sorrow: 'In me you shall have peace; my peace I give unto you.' And it is all our *fruit*. When the church of old confessed and complained, 'I am like a green fir-tree,' verdant but fruitless, her Lord returned the gracious answer, 'From me is thy fruit found'; and to us the Lord Jesus Christ has given the exceeding great and precious promise, 'He that abideth in me, and I in him, the same bringeth forth much fruit.'

4. *Our union with Jesus Christ, unlike other unions, is one that can never be dissolved.* 'We are members of his body, of his flesh, and of his bones.' He is the vine, and we are the branches, believers being, through his grace, as truly the branches as he is himself the vine, so that without them he would become like a branchless tree. 'Abide,' saith he, 'in me, and I in you,' laying it upon us to abide in him, and, at the same time, in his love laying it upon himself to abide in us. A blessed necessity for us, so vile and empty, to abide in him, so full and glorious; a marvellous condescension for him, so high and holy, to abide in us, so poor and sinful. He never dissolves this union, for whom he loveth he loveth to the end; and none other can dissolve it either in life or in death. 'For who shall separate us from the love of Christ? I am persuaded that neither death, nor life, nor angels, nor principalities, nor powers, nor things present, nor things to come, nor height, nor depth, nor any other creature, shall

be able to separate us from the love of God which is in Christ Jesus our Lord.'

5. Lastly, *This oneness is divinely endued with a great power for the salvation of the world.*—The ancient admiration of the world, 'Behold how these Christians love one another!' has sometimes been turned into the taunt,—'Behold how they hate one another'; yet their mutual love is as genuine, and, in the same circumstances, would prove as intense, as it was eighteen hundred years ago. The tenderness of Christian love is an unknown affection among the children of this world. A mother's affection for her son or a widow's sorrow for her husband the world can both understand and appreciate; the tenderness of purely Christian love is incomprehensible to the child of earth. In the loftiness of his heart he would count it despicable in himself to be capable of such an affection; if he sees it in the heir of heaven, it is only to despise it in his day of unbroken pride; yet it speaks as a living witness to him in the hour when the Spirit moves on his heart and his conscience. The attractive spectacle of heavenly love amongst brethren on earth is one of the grand means ordained for the world's salvation; of love seen in a Christian family, in a congregation, in a church, in separate churches towards each other, and still more as happily to be seen amongst ourselves in this Assembly, in the drawing together of churches long divided, and our blending in brotherly love again into one. The very God of peace grant a time of refreshing to both the churches in an event so desired by both; may he bestow his blessing on the union, and make the united church a blessing in the land.[1]

But toward the conversion of the world there is still greater power, in our seen union on earth to Christ in heaven. It was this power of Christ in his servants that most of all struck the high priest and the council at Jerusalem. Apparently more than at the sight of the lame man walking and leaping, they 'marvelled' at the boldness, the holy

---

[1] Moody Stuart refers to the union, which had come into effect that year, between the Free Church and the majority of the Reformed Presbyterian Church. See above, p. 342.—*P.*

liberty, and the wisdom of the apostles, and 'they took knowledge of them that they had been with Jesus,' recognising a very peculiar influence upon them through that intercourse. There is nothing more effectual for the conversion of the world than Jesus Christ seen to be in us. In the words of Paul, 'As in the sight of God speak we in Christ'; we in Christ, and Christ and we in God. In your own private circle there are no sayings or deeds of yours that will so move the hearts and so touch the consciences of those around you, as whatever convinces them that Christ is in you, and that you have been with Jesus. Without this inward conviction no words of yours will avail to turn their hearts to the Lamb of God which taketh away the sin of the world, and with it a few words will reach far. So also in the ministry of the gospel: if while we preach it shall be evident to our hearers that we are in Christ, and Christ in us, many will believe through grace to the saving of their souls. This divine token pertains to the foolishness of preaching and the shame and offense of the cross, but it is the power of God unto salvation to perishing men. Oh that in us, whether ministers or elders or members of the church, these words of our Lord were this day fulfilled, 'I in them, and thou in me, that the world may know that thou hast sent me, and hast loved them as thou hast loved me!'

The Manifold Sufficiency of Grace[1]

'My grace is sufficient for thee.'—*2 Cor. 12:9*

TO everyone to whom the word of the Lord comes, and who is willing to receive his word, the Lord says, 'My grace is sufficient for you.' Who are you? You could not tell if you would, and you would not say if you could, who you are and what you are. A strange mystery every man is to himself, and a strange mystery every man is to his neighbour. None knows you except yourself, yet every other knows you better than yourself. In the depths of the heart you alone know yourself; 'For what man knoweth the things of a man, save the spirit of man which is in him?' Yet how little you know yourself, and how well everybody else knows you!

The strange mysterious being that every man is! The same as every other man in the world, yet different from every other. The same as others, 'there is no difference, for all have sinned'; and 'as in water face answereth face, so the heart of man to man'; and every man who knows his own heart, knows the heart of every other man in the world. It is very humbling to us when we learn that there is no difference, and that if my neighbour knows his own heart, he also knows mine, which we had thought was concealed from all. Yet while there is 'no difference' in the great transgression, while

[1] A sermon preached in St Luke's, reproduced from a church member's notes in *The Path of the Redeemed: Sermons by A. Moody Stuart, D.D.* (Edinburgh: Mac-Niven & Wallace, 1893), pp. 142-51.—*P.*

we have all like lost sheep gone astray, it is also true that 'we have turned every one to his own way'; that there never has lived a man the same as you. Your character and history are different from the character and history of every man that ever was or ever will be, so that you could not be changed into any other or any other changed into you. You are yourself and no one else forever. Yet whilst there is a unity in the man, there is also a strange dividedness. Every man is one; if you meet a man after twenty years, he is the same man, you see that he is the same, and he knows himself to be the same. There is identity, unity; yet a strangely divided man he is. Every one who has grace has two men in him, an old man and a new; but every one also, apart from grace, has a great dividedness; for he has a heart inclined to all evil, and a conscience that witnesses to all good.

If in so many ways every man is a mystery, what can be sufficient for him? When we begin to be acquainted with ourselves, we come to see that nothing on earth can satisfy us. The prodigal son when he is perishing with hunger is ready to wish that he were one of the herd of swine, when he sees that they are satisfied with husks and he is not; as many a man has wished that he was a dog, when he felt that he was worse than a dog. But oh, wondrous, blessed grace of God! Even as that prodigal, who was perishing with hunger, desiring to be fed with the husks, and no man giving him bread, said at last, 'In my father's house is bread enough and to spare,' so our God, the Lord Jesus Christ, says to every one who will receive it, 'My grace is sufficient for thee.' There is nothing else sufficient; life is not sufficient, nor health, nor youth, nor pleasure. Riches and learning and friends are not sufficient; nor your own self-esteem, nor the esteem of others. Nothing is sufficient except only this, 'My grace is sufficient for thee.' It is the Lord Jesus Christ who speaks; he has taken this flesh of ours, knows all the heart of man, and although 'he knows no sin,' he knows what poor lost man is, for he came to give his life a ransom for many, to seek and to save that which was lost. He says to all that are taken out from among the lost, 'I have called you friends,' and he says to every last one who will receive it,

'My grace is sufficient for thee.' We are not sufficient of ourselves to think anything as of ourselves, our sufficiency is of God; and if we accepted this word of the Lord Jesus Christ, what a satisfied people we should be, not self-satisfied, but satisfied with grace, and fully satisfied.

From this promise let me further consider with you—Grace given in free offer to every child of man; given in sure promise to every child of God; sufficient for every season; and sufficient in all circumstances.

I. Grace *given in free offer* to every child of man

Jesus Christ came into the world to save sinners, and the chief of them. He came not to condemn or to destroy, but to save; and he comes to us with that which is so wondrously good that no man ever comprehends it except by his own teaching. It is the great loss of most men who hear the gospel that they think of it according to their own notions, without the least conception of what the grace of God really is. Man being himself so evil, cannot believe in anything so good as God justifying the ungodly, as grace reigning through righteousness to the worst of sinners, as the free gift of God being eternal life to everyone who will accept it. Every man tries to make a bargain with his Maker, and thinks that his Maker desires to make a bargain with him; he conceives of the great Redeemer as seeking to get as much out of him as he can, and he tries to get as much as he can out of the divine Saviour; for all men are deeply mercenary in their hearts. So men refuse grace, refuse that which alone can save them, not because they are too low for it, but because they are too high. We are too sunk, too lost, for anything but grace. But oh, the grace is sufficient though nothing else is. I saw that I was poor, very poor, but not that I was utterly poor; and I tried to add my brass and iron to the riches of the Lord Jesus Christ; I tried to bring something to help together with Christ to make me rich toward God, and so did you. But when I discovered that I was utterly poor and knew the grace of the Lord Jesus Christ, that though he was rich, for our sakes he became poor that we through his poverty might be rich, then I dared not add to his infinite righteousness, nor any longer cast my worthless brass into his gold tried in the fire. His spotless, saving righteousness was enough for me by itself, and I would have utterly marred it by adding anything of my own. And whoever you are that have not yet tasted that the Lord is gracious, this grace is now free to you, near to you, and sufficient for you by itself alone. Christ knows all your case, and he says, 'My grace is sufficient for thee'; for these words, spoken to the apostle, are recorded for you if you will receive them for yourself, because 'the grace of God that bringeth salvation has appeared to all men.'

II. Grace given *in sure promise* to every child of God

Oh, how you have sinned against grace! Not merely against grace freely offered, but against grace richly given, against grace in you, against God's grace in your own heart. When a man knows that he has sinned not only against the law, but against grace, he is ready to think, 'What can be sufficient for me?' but the Lord Jesus says, 'My grace is sufficient for thee.' A saint in this respect needs more grace than a sinner, needs new grace, and in some way larger grace; but as for every sinner that will receive it, so for every erring child of God, his grace is sufficient. You did not know at first what a depth of wickedness was in you, you did not know how vile a sinner it was that the Lord Jesus stooped to lift up as a lamb in his arms; you knew it in part, but you know it sadly and far more thoroughly now. Yet over against your sins there is this much more abounding grace. How sin abounds! How the least sin is full of evil; as it is said of the tongue, 'How great a matter a little fire kindleth!' The little word on the tongue, the little thought in the heart, and tongue set on fire of hell, what a flame of sin from one little spark! What, then, is it with all our sins? And yet all sin is as nothing to the abundance of grace; 'I will cast all their sins into the depths of the sea'; the pebble cast into the sea, and the sea bright and blue as before, and the grace so swallowing up the sin that there is nothing left but grace for ever and ever.

III. Grace sufficient *for every season;* for every age of the world, and of the church

The world and the church ever come on unexpected evils, but the Lord has ever prepared unexpected grace which is sufficient. So for every time of man's life; for childhood, 'Suffer the little children to come unto me'; for youth, with all its snares and temptations, 'Wherewithal shall a young man cleanse his way? by taking heed thereto according to thy word'; for manhood, with all its difficulties and trials, 'Cast thy burden on the Lord, and he shall sustain thee'; for old age, 'Even to your old age I am he, and even to hoar hairs will I carry you'; for life and for death, 'I am he that liveth, and was dead; and behold I am alive for evermore.' This grace is not about sufficiency that might be enough and no more, as we are too ready to think. Often indeed we may be thankful even to stand in the evil day, and having done all to stand; but the sufficiency of the promise is large and full, abundantly ample, and not barely enough. Grace is never little; it is always 'the unsearchable riches of Christ,' if we will receive it.

'Let us therefore come boldly unto the throne of grace, that we may obtain mercy, and find grace to help in time of need.' In the time of our need, when the time seems unfavourable for grace, when we lack it in ourselves, or see the want of it around us, when we need both mercy to pardon and grace to help, and both seem to be far off, if we come boldly to the throne of grace, we often find both that the Lord 'abundantly pardons,' and that he has made a special provision of grace for our special time of need. There is none good but one, that is God, for there is no goodness in the universe for a moment to be compared with the inconceivable love of God, when he gave all that he had for lost men, and spared not his only Son from shame and suffering and darkest death.

IV. Grace sufficient *in all circumstances*

Someone now present may be ready to object, 'Grace is not enough for me; I need something else besides grace; I need a change in the circumstances in which I am, and I cannot do without it.' My dear friend, you can do without it; you cannot do without grace, but you can do without any change in your circumstances, except indeed they be sinful. Grace is not sufficient for any sin wilfully retained, for the least cherished sin. Many indeed seemed to suppose that grace is so sufficient as to allow you contentedly to live in sin more or less. But it is never sufficient for such a course; 'Let every one that nameth the name of Christ depart from iniquity.' It is always 'faith and a good conscience,' and grace is not sufficient to make a bad conscience good when you are living in sin. It will make the worst conscience clean, if there be 'holding faith and a good conscience,' striving to depart from iniquity in naming the name of Christ. For while there is the free forgiveness of sins through the grace of Jesus Christ, there is with it the promise that 'Sin shall not have dominion over you; we are not under the law, but under grace.' There always is the grace of holiness where there has been pardoning mercy from God; and if mercy merely saved the man from sentence of death and did not sanctify him, did not remove his sin, it could never satisfy his conscience, for grace would have done that which is least without doing that which is greatest. Grace so saves us as to enable us to glorify God, 'that we might be to the praise of the glory of his grace.'

You all need grace, but none of you need a change in your circumstances, if they are not sinful; for your watchful Redeemer is always saying to you, 'My grace is sufficient for thee.' Yet it may be allowable to ask that your circumstances be altered, and you may err in not so asking. In any of the various relations of life, or in your own person, circumstances may be hard and trying for you, and you may rightly ask God to change them. The Apostle Paul did so ask. We know not what his circumstances were, and there is no need to seek to discover them; but we know that they were sorely trying, for he speaks of 'a thorn in the flesh, and messenger of Satan to buffet him.' He besought the Lord that in his loving-kindness it might be removed. He asked once and did not get an answer; he asked again and received no answer; he asked a third time, and the Lord was not displeased with his asking, for he did not know but that the divine will might alter the circumstances, and he thought it would be a great advantage to himself if they were altered. He conceived likewise that it would be to the advantage of the cause of grace, to the furtherance of the gospel, for the promotion of Christ's glory, if the circumstances were changed: and so he cried to the Lord for relief. But the Lord answered 'No,' and Paul was quite content. He saw at last that this messenger of Satan was *given* him; he had probably thought of the trial as merely the work of Satan, but now he sees that it has been given to him by God. He learns that God can glorify himself and bring out more good to his servant and his church, not by removing the trial, by altering the circumstances, but by giving more abundant grace; not by recalling the messenger of Satan, but by giving grace to overcome. So it is with you: it is quite right if circumstances are against you that you should ask an alteration of them; but then when you have asked, and with the utmost earnestness, you must resign both the matter itself and the prayer into God's hand. If you say that you cannot serve God in your circumstances that are not sinful, and if you cannot glorify him as you are, you will never glorify him anywhere. You are making the circumstances your God. 'This and that about me hinders me from rejoicing in Christ Jesus'; but if everything were changed you would be no better; it is not the circumstances, it is yourself. Oh, God's children have often said that this trouble or difficulty must be removed before there can be any good; but grace is enough for it. It seems a cold consolation, but it is the very opposite, it is always 'abundant consolation and good hope through grace.' God says, 'My grace is sufficient for thee; for my strength is made perfect in weakness': and like Paul you will be enabled to say, 'Most gladly therefore will I rather glory in my infirmities, that the power of Christ may rest upon me.'

The True Battle of Life[1]

'For the battle is not yours but God's.'—*2 Chron.* 20:15

LIFE'S true battle embraces both the life that now is and that which is to come; it concerns the real life of man in his own very self, both in all that is worth living for, and in all that constitutes a worthy life. If our true life does not begin here, it will never begin elsewhere; if it were to end here, few would think it worth living, and to most it would present no motive to make it worth seeking. The foes of this true life we all know are the world, the flesh, and the devil; and if we are to live really in this first term of our existence, or everlastingly in the next, these must be fought against and overcome. But whilst we know who the deadly enemies are, the great secret is to discover whose the battle is, and how they are to be overcome. This secret is disclosed throughout the Scriptures, and briefly in these memorable words, spoken to Israel before one of their great battles: 'The battle is not yours but God's.' In a previous battle the stripling David was their champion, and the Israelites were set aside; Goliath was the champion of the Philistines, for whom they were in like manner set aside. On the issue of that battle the happiness and liberty of Israel hung, yet it was not they who were to fight; if they had put forth their hands to help, they would have marred the whole and have lost the battle. If they had

[1] A sermon preached in St Luke's, reproduced from a parishioner's notes in *The Path of the Redeemed: Sermons by A. Moody Stuart, D.D.* (Edinburgh: MacNiven & Wallace, 1893), pp. 53-71.—*P.*

not faith in Israel's God, thousands in the host must have quaked as they stood still and looked on, while they said in their hearts, 'We have put all our lives in the hands of this stripling.' David trembled not, but went freely forward, assured of victory because the battle was the Lord's, and he fought in the name of the living God whom the Philistines had defied.

The life-warfare of us all has hung on two members of the human family, the First Man and the Second Man; there was none between these two, and the Second, although not merely man, was as truly man as the first; the First the one father of all men, the Second the one Son of Man. The first battle we lost; our own father stood for us, and in an evil hour our parents were seduced from their allegiance, and fell beneath the tempter's flattering falsehoods and his vile calumnies against the God of truth and love. Which of us would have stood firm in the trial, when our adversary's 'words were softer than oil, yet were drawn swords,' wounding unto death both our father and ourselves in him? And which of us has chosen to remain on the spot where Adam left us when he fell? With one consent we have all gone further in sin and error; each of us choosing a path of our own, trodden by none before us and by none after us; acting every one of us as a god to himself, like our erring father, and concurring in his bitterly sad apostasy from the living God who was all our life.

But when we were lost and dead, dead under condemnation for our sins, and lost in utter helplessness to return to the God of our life, he thought upon us with yearnings of tenderest mercy to bring us again to himself. In the depths of his unknown love it pleased him to send his eternal Son into the world to become one of us, that as the Son of Man he might meet and overcome our adversary, make satisfaction for our innumerable sins, and restore us to the forfeited favour of our Father in heaven; that 'as by one man's disobedience many were made sinners, so by the obedience of one many might be made righteous.' We cannot undo the first battle which Adam lost for himself and us; neither can we interfere or take any part in the second, which our Lord Jesus fought for us when 'of the people there was none with him.' In the whole conflict and in all the obedience he stood alone; on the cross neither man nor angel shared in his atoning and unknown sufferings, and none shared in the infinite and unapproachable obedience of his life and death. But when he was 'crucified in weakness' our help was laid on One that is mighty; and when they asked him, 'What shall we do that we might work the works of God?' his answer was, 'This is the work of God, that you believe on him whom he hath sent'; that you work not, but trust in him, and rest in the 'finished work' which the 'Father gave him to do.'

The battle is not ours, but God's for us by Christ Jesus; not ours, but God's in us by his Spirit through Christ Jesus; and the praise of the victory is not ours, but the Lord's alone through us.

I. *The battle is not ours but God's for us by Christ Jesus*

For every one of us this grand truth is at once most blessed and most humbling. Nothing so great and so good could have been conceived by man as that Jesus Christ, God manifest in flesh, should have taken our place in service and in suffering; and have given us his own spotless and infinite righteousness for the pardon of our sins, our justification in the judgment, and our immediate and everlasting acceptance with God. Few of us thought that we were good enough to stand before the great judge, but many of us were aiming by Christ's help to become such that we might be accepted. It is a revolution in a man's whole being when he first discovers, or rather when it is discovered to him by grace, that 'God hath made him to be sin for us who knew no sin, that we might be made the righteousness of God in him.' Fifty years ago, a Swiss pastor said to me that when he first heard these glad tidings through Mr Robert Haldane[1] in Geneva, he exclaimed in admiring wonder, '*C'est trop grand*

---

[1] Robert Haldane (1764–1842) was a Scottish philanthropist and preacher, who spent time ministering in Geneva between 1816 and 1819, where he was influential in the revival of the evangelical movement on the Continent. His well-known *Exposition of Romans*, now published by the Banner of Truth Trust, consists of sermons preached whilst he was in Geneva.—P.

pour être vrai.' (It is too great to be true.) A whole mind and heart are revolutionized when, instead of striving for something done by us or wrought in us in which we may stand before God, we see that the Lord himself has become our righteousness, and are enabled and gladly constrained to say, 'In the Lord have I righteousness and strength. The Lord Jehovah is my strength and my song, he also is become my salvation.'

Of ourselves we never see this; we read it, but see it not; we hear it, but perceive it not. It passes all understanding when the eye is open to it at first; and 'the peace of God passes all understanding' still, every time we receive it anew in all its freeness and fullness. What then will be our eternity of grace after we have received 'the grace that is to be brought unto us at the revelation of Jesus Christ': himself with 'the dew of youth' for ever, and 'making all things new' eternally. It has been acutely said that 'the oldest angel in heaven looks the youngest,' as if the freshest and brightest from the Creator's hands. Sin was never new, but was oldness and corruption from the first, marring our new paradise, and turning it unto death in one fatal hour. On the contrary, the grace of our Lord Jesus Christ is never old, and will be everlastingly and increasingly new. If, having not yet seen our Ransom and our Portion, we now rejoice in him with joy unspeakable and full of glory, what must be our holy joy in that hour and in that eternity when we shall see him face to face, by whose stripes we are healed, who has suffered the chastisement of our peace, and by whose infinite obedience and lowly service in our stead we have become sons of God for ever.

At the same time this salvation, whilst so exalting and gladdening to the receiver, humbles him past all previous thought as soon as it is fully before his mind. The great Redeemer takes away our guilt by finishing transgression and making an end of sin; but when he takes away our burden he makes no account of our goodness, but strips us of it and casts it also quite away. He bids us stand far aside and see the salvation of God for us. This crucifies to death our inborn pride and restlessness; we have marred the divine work, and are eager to repair it, to take some part in working out our own recovery by making good again that which we have made evil. But the gift of Christ is to him that 'worketh not but believeth,' trusting and resting on him alone for salvation. If our hands were to touch his work it would be polluted, and be no more the spotless ransom for redemption. The man is new-born who in the day of power is made willing to be set aside by God for Jesus Christ, willing to take his place with the thief and the murderer, to be numbered with the lost whom Jesus Christ came to seek and to save. This test sifts the heart to its inmost recess. It is as contrary and humiliating to nature, as it is intensely joyful to grace to say of the Lord Jesus that he is 'the *end* of the law for righteousness.' Our own thought was that Christ was the beginning of obedience for us, and that by his gracious aid we might attain such a conformity to the holy law as must be accepted for his sake. But when we are taught of God, we learn that Jesus Christ is first, and midst, and last in the fulfilling of the law, that it has been met in all its length and breadth, and satisfied by him more amply and gloriously than it will be by all the angels through eternity; and that his infinitely acceptable obedience is for us both the beginning and the end of the law for all justifying righteousness before God. When this is seen by us our self-righteousness and self-esteem are utterly gone, for nothing of ours is of any account at the bar of God. We then know that there is an infinite distance between sin and holiness, between the wicked and the righteous; but 'no difference' at the bar of the great judge between sin and sin, between one sinner and another, between the worst and the best of fallen men, 'for all have sinned and come short of the glory of God.' Most welcome to us then, are the good tidings of great joy that 'Christ Jesus came into the world to save sinners.' We then love to glory only in the Lord, and each for himself to say, 'He has fought my battle, he has finished my work, he has borne my condemnation, he is my present and everlasting ransom.'

At a season of some awakening many years ago, a stranger having an air of superior intelligence, called on me in distress of mind. In conversing with her I was brought to a stand by her thorough knowledge of the letter and doctrine of the Scriptures; and being able to add no instruction, I asked no further question, but briefly opened and pressed the words, 'Christ Jesus came into the world to save sinners,' and ended with prayer. While I was speaking a stream of tears began to flow, and she looked relieved, but was silent. A week after she returned with her face bright with joy to tell me that she had found that peace with God which she had been vainly seeking before. I asked her, 'Why did you weep when you left last day?' 'I wept for joy.' 'And what gave you the joy?' 'I saw, as you were speaking, that Jesus Christ came into the world to save sinners.' 'But you knew that before?' 'No; I always thought that Jesus Christ came to the world to save saints, and I wept for joy when I saw that he came to save sinners.'

In the great salvation there are two leading elements, distinct from each other yet beautifully combined, and each setting the other in a brighter light; the pardoning mercy and the redeeming righteousness. If we were merely pardoned through grace and not justified by righteousness, our standing would be very different, both in our own consciousness and in the sight of God, angels, and men. A convicted criminal condemned by the judges of the land, but graciously pardoned by his sovereign, would bear for life the badge of his disgrace; but an innocent man accused, tried, and acquitted, walks as an equal with his fellows. We are not innocent but guilty; through Christ Jesus we are freely pardoned by the sovereign grace of our God; but in the same hour we are acquitted and justified, owned by God as righteous in him and for his sake, and sealed by his Spirit to be openly acquitted in the great day. We are now emboldened to say in our hearts, and it will then be proclaimed for us before the universe, 'It is God that justifieth, who is he that condemneth?'

Yet our salvation is not the less, but all the more, of tenderest mercy because it is through strictest righteousness, for the gift of God's beloved Son for us is the noblest fruit of his yearning mercy over us; 'for God so loved the world that he gave his only begotten Son, that whosoever believeth in him should not perish but have everlasting life.' But as we are thoroughly humbled when we are stripped naked of the stained and rent garment of our own goodness, that we may be clothed in the spotless and seamless robe of our Redeemer, so likewise we lie down in the dust when we accept of mercy. Our proud hearts refused mercy from our Maker, because we did not need it, just as we should refuse and resent a pardon from our earthly sovereign, although clothed in kindest words, because we are not convicted criminals to be pardoned. But in the hour when we are awakened to our guilt in the sight of God, we would eagerly accept of mercy, and our difficulty is now that our guilt is too great to be pardoned. In such despair of ourselves we are not left to perish, but are divinely enabled to apprehend the mercy of God in Christ, and we learn with adoring wonder that 'the Lord is gracious and full of compassion.' A man full of compassion would be little, but who can sound that ocean of love of which it is written that 'God is *full* of compassion,' the whole infinite Godhead filled with tenderest pity to the lost and guilty. We now delight to leave ourselves at the mercy of the Most High; we would far rather trust ourselves for pardon to his compassions than have the pardon in our own hands; and from the depths of a thankful heart we exclaim, 'Who is a God like unto thee, that pardoneth iniquity, because he delighteth in mercy.' The free mercy and the redeeming righteousness harmoniously agree together. In the divine oracles of the Old Testament they are described as lovingly meeting together: 'Mercy and truth are met together; righteousness and peace have kissed each other' (Psa. 85:10). In the New Testament they are beautifully intermingled: 'Not by works of righteousness which we have done, but according to his mercy he saved us—that being justified by his grace we should be made heirs according to the hope of eternal life' (Titus 3:5-7).

II. The battle is not ours, but God's in us through Jesus Christ by his Spirit

Our enemies have all been fought and overcome by our Lord Jesus Christ in our behalf, else we could never overcome them. They are too many and too strong for us, the world, the flesh, and the devil, with the numberless temptations of each. The least of them were stronger than the wisest of us, and out of Christ they are all as strong as ever. There is no weakness in sin, or the world, or the devil apart from Jesus Christ and out of him; but in him sin is finished, the world broken, and Satan bruised under our feet. We overcome only through the blood of the Lamb, and through the blood of the Lamb we never fail to overcome. By faith in Christ we receive the Holy Spirit, who 'worketh in us mightily,' and then the battle is not ours, but God's. The Spirit convinces, enlightens, renews us day by day; reveals to us our sins, takes of the things of Christ, and shows them to us, makes them ours, and gives us the victory.

In Christ sin has lost its dominion over us, because we are no longer under the law but under grace. Formerly sin was over us and we were under sin; but in the hour of our believing in Christ grace reigns over us, and we reign over sin, being made by him 'kings and priests unto God and his Father.' Sin never conquers grace, never reigns over it. Sin indeed is both vast and powerful beyond all man's conception; none can measure its amount or ascertain its bounds. In the earth there is nothing earthly so great, nothing so prolific and so abundant. A little sin, how it abounds—it fills a heart, it fills a family, it expands and grows as if it would fill the world. But thanks be to God that 'where sin hath abounded, grace hath much more abounded,' mightily subduing and overcoming it, 'till it swallows up death in victory.' Wherever grace and sin meet, sin is always the weaker of the two. Sin is in me, but grace toward me and in me meets my sin and prevails triumphantly over all its strength and subtlety, for 'the battle is not mine but God's.'

If the battle is mine, it is already as good as lost; but if my battle is the Lord's, it is already as good as won, because Christ has already overcome for me, and he will not lose his battle in me. There is no enemy so weak but will overcome me, if he is fighting only or mainly against me. What child of God and soldier of the cross has not failed in a little battle after he had been victorious in a great one;

falling before a weak and puny foe, when thousands had erewhile fallen before him, and he could adopt the words as his own,

> Oh, I have seen the day,
>> When with a single word,
> God helping me to say,
>> 'My trust is in the Lord';
> My soul has quelled a thousand foes,
>> Fearless of all that could oppose.[1]

But when this soldier of the cross is met by a puny foe, by a little temptation, he may, through self-reliance, be ensnared to think, 'I have strength enough for this little battle, this conflict with my own temper, with my brother, with this adverse providence.' In such a case, did we ever overcome in the contest? Was not the despised foe too strong for us, till we were thrown in the dust, and in our helplessness cried, 'Lord, help me!' But when we said, 'This little cross from the Lord is too heavy for me to bear in my own strength, this misconception with my brother too twisted for me to unloose, this conflict with myself too hard for me to master,' and so took it over to the Lord himself, it was soon all righted; even as the toiling disciples were at the land whither they went, as soon as they received Christ into the ship.

Yet the battle of life within us is often truly great and severe; with our inborn heart of stone, our evil heart of unbelief departing from the living God, our selfishness, our pride, our judging of others, our ill-will to our neighbour, our envy, our covetousness; with the flesh lusting against the Spirit and the Spirit against the flesh, so that we cannot do the things that we would. But when we are constrained in sorrow to cry, 'O wretched man that I am! Who shall deliver me from the body of this death?' we are enabled to add with joy, 'I thank God through Jesus Christ our Lord,' and even to say in triumph, 'Nay, in all these things we are more than conquerors through him that loved us.'

---

[1] A verse from the hymn 'The Lord my banner' by William Cowper (1731–1800).—P.

In the inward battle of life there is however another adversary with whom we have to contend, for 'we wrestle against principalities and powers, against the rulers of the darkness of this world.' For our deliverance from Satan we fall back on our Lord's wondrous prayer for his ransomed ones in the depth of his dying agony on the cross, asking life for us when all God's waves and billows were passing over him: 'Deliver my soul from the sword; my darling (my only one, *margin*) from the power of the dog, save me from the lion's mouth,' and then rejoicing, 'Thou hast heard me: I will declare thy name unto my brethren' (Psa. 22:20-22). This great enemy outside of us complicates our battle, and often makes it hard to distinguish with whom we are fighting, all the more because his chief weapons are subtlety, craft, and falsehood. He was at first our only foe, but we surrendered to him the citadel of our hearts; we betrayed ourselves and gave him an easy victory over us, which he has ever since been striving to maintain and augment, and because he commonly fights against us through the passions of our own unruly hearts, it is hard to distinguish what is ours and what is Satan's; and we are the losers if we excuse our sins by imputing them to him. Even when the temptation is his, the sin of yielding to it is ours, as it was with our first parents. Yet the contest with Satan is not the less real because on his part it is subtle, and it is our wisdom and safety not to be 'ignorant of his devices.' It is no light relief and help for the struggling soldier in the great warfare to discover the trail of the serpent or the footprint of the lion and the enemy with whom he is contending, and so to 'resist the devil,' who flees when met in his own person, although he had not fled but returned and persevered where sin was resisted simply in itself. But this quenching of the fiery darts of the wicked one is never by pride and self-confidence, but by faith in the word of promise and childlike humbling under the hand of God (James 4:6, 7). So likewise in an adverse providence it is our wisdom to distinguish between the will of the Lord to be patiently acquiesced in, and the working of Satan to be overcome. St Paul writes to the Thessalonians: 'We would have come unto you once

ALEXANDER MOODY STUART

and again, but Satan hindered us.' He was allowed so to hinder the
Lord's servant, as more than once to prevent his desired coming to
Thessalonica; and in this case the obstruction was insurmountable.
Yet it was from Satan and not from the Lord, resistance to it was
lawful and right, and in other cases would have been effectual.

'The lion in the way' of the slothful man stalks within his own
indolent fancy, and some of us have been turned from our way
and been frightened from our duty by imaginary lions. When the
'roaring lion' is really crossing our path, he will flee from us if
we go forward in the name and the strength of the Lord. The
wise man has put on record that 'the wisdom of the prudent is
to understand his way,' and for the outward obstacle in our path
one element in this wisdom is to know whether it is from above
or from beneath, to be humbly kissed as the hand of the Lord, or
to be boldly met by going forward in faith as the hindrance of the
Lord's adversary and ours.

III. The praise of the victory is not ours, but the Lord's alone through us

We are apt to think that it would exalt ourselves to be freely reconciled to God through Christ; and the world judges that any man
who believes that his sins have been forgiven for Christ's sake, and
that through grace he has been called to become a child of God
and an heir of heaven, must be intolerably proud. How little they
know! As the salvation is all of grace and not of self, so it is all to the
praise of grace and not of man. If it were of yourself, of your own
work, of your own merit and desert, it would exalt you; but being of
grace it humbles you in the dust, and leaves you nothing to glory in
except in the grace of God that freely saves you. And believing you
are 'accepted in the Beloved to the praise of the glory of his grace,'
and when the Lord comes to be 'admired in all them that believe,'
you can humbly delight, not that you should be admired, but that
Christ should be admired in you, although you should be the last
and least of all in whom he is admired.

402

To have your sins forgiven and to know it, does not exalt you, because you see now, as never before, the greatness of the sin that has been pardoned and the depth of your unworthiness of the pardon. The fairest robe now put upon you, the ring on your hand, and the shoes on your feet, the tokens of reception to the family of our Father in heaven, humble you still more under a sense of your unfitness to be received amongst the sons of the living God. The gift of everlasting life and the Spirit's seal of the gift only concur to humble you yet more deeply, by the contrast between the eternal inheritance and your own character and desert.

Grace is never proud of grace itself, or of its privileges and hopes; the carnal mind that still remains in the children of God is ever prone to be proud both of past grace and of the bright hopes in the future; but grace in present and living exercise dominates in the heart of the redeemed, and keeps them lowly. When at the first we are justified freely by his grace, God humbles us to receive his mercy, and humbles us by its reception; and when afterwards we work out our own salvation with fear and trembling, it is by 'God working in us both to will and to do of his own good pleasure.' It is all of grace from first to last, and all the praise is to the glory of grace.

By nature we all began with trusting in God for nothing, and now through grace we hope to end by trusting him for everything. Our self-strength and self-exalting are broken at their deep seat within us in our first knowledge of the great redemption; and, if we grow in grace, they come to be broken for that which is least as well as that which is greatest. Day by day we learn to trust God for all things, and to distrust ourselves in everything. Everyone that enters the kingdom of heaven is converted, or turned from a strong man into a little child, and the greatest in the kingdom is lessened from the little child into the least of all the children. We delight in our helplessness, in our own utter inability, that we may be 'strong in the Lord, and in the power of his might'; for, when we are weak, then are we strong, and when weakest therefore strongest, when least of all then greatest of all. As helpless infants we are carried at first and as helpless infants we are carried to the last in the strong and tender arms of the Good Shepherd, who laid down his life for the sheep. 'Hearken unto me, O house of Jacob, which are borne by me from the belly, which are carried from the womb: and even to your old age I am he, and even to hoar hairs will I carry you' (Isa. 46:3, 4).

A dark and lonely life it is to walk through the world trusting ourselves for everything, and trusting God for nothing; to be daily saying in our hearts, 'The battle is not the Lord's but mine, the work is not the Lord's but mine, the burden is not the Lord's but mine'; and it brightens all our life to know that all is of the Lord, by the Lord, and to the Lord. We do not therefore sink into cowardice and sloth, but we sing with David, 'Blessed be the Lord my strength, which teacheth my hands to war, and my fingers to fight'; or, as the words have been well enlarged, 'My hands to war, and every finger to fight.' 'Through God we shall do valiantly, for he it is that shall tread down our enemies.' Let us give all the glory to him alone, and say continually, 'Praise the Lord, for his mercy endureth for ever,' as Israel did, when the Lord assured them that the battle was not theirs but his. Let us hold fast the hidden secret that is revealed to the babes, which so relieved and gladdened us when we learned from above that we are called to praise the Lord 'because he is good,' and not vainly to wait till we are good. 'Let Israel hope in the Lord, for with the Lord there is mercy, and with him is plenteous redemption; and he shall redeem Israel from all his iniquities.'

Early Minutes of the Kirk Session of St Luke's

*The following extracts from the Session Book (records of elders'
meetings) of St Luke's and Free St Luke's, transcribed by
the Publisher, have been included in this edition for interest.
All the records of the St Luke's congregation are now held by the
National Records of Scotland (NRS).—P.*

September 1837—Elders Appointed for St Luke's [1]

At Young Street, Edinburgh,
the Fourteenth day of September,
One Thousand Eight Hundred and Thirty Seven Years

Which day, the Revd. Dr. Dickson, and the Revd. Messrs. Candlish
and Hay, the Committee appointed by the Reverend Presbytery of
Edinburgh to appoint the Revd. Alexander Moody, Minister of the
Church and Parish of St Luke, Edinburgh, in the formation of a
Kirk Session, for said Church and Parish having met, and the meeting having been constituted with prayer by Mr. Moody, as Moderator, Dr. Dickson was chosen Clerk.

The following Gentlemen, all members of the congregation, were
then proposed and unanimously agreed to, as, in every respect,

[1] NRS catalogue reference: CH3/782/1/1.

suitably qualified to fill the office of Elders in said Church and Parish: viz.

Messrs. Wm. Stothert, Randolph Crescent
Adam M'Cheyne, Hill Street
James Howden, Windsor Street
Thomas Gardner, Frederick Street
Robert Hogue, Hill Street
James Russell, M.D., Queen Street &
James Robertson, Thistle Street

Whereupon the Committee did, and hereby do, authorise the Edict of the above named individuals to be served in the Church by the Revd. Mr. Moody, on the forenoon diet of Sabbath next, the seventeenth currt. [current]—with intimation that, if no objections to their Life and Conversation are lodged with the Moderator or Clerk on or before Thursday Evening the twenty currt. [current] at ½ past six o'clock, when the Committee hereby agree to meet in the Session House for the purpose of receiving the Return of the said Edict, the admission of Messrs. Stothert, M'Cheyne, Howden, Gardner and Hogue who were formerly Elders & members of other Kirk Sessions, and the Ordination of Messrs. Russell and Robertson, will, in presence of the Congregation, after sermon, be forthwith proceeded in, according to the rules and practice of the Church. The meeting was closed with prayer.

Alex. Moody Stuart, Moderator
David Dickson, Clerk

November 1841—Moody Stuart's Departure for Madeira [1]

63 Queen Street,
Edinburgh
8th November 1841

The Kirk Session having met at the request of the Moderator on this the eve of his departure for Madeira, whither he has been

[1] NRS catalogue reference: CH3/782/1/95.

recommended to go for the recovery of his health—and having been Constituted.

Sederunt, the Moderator, Messrs. Stothert, Howden, Gardner, Hogue, Russell, Robertson, Henderson, Boyark, Smith, Macdonald, Pringle and M'Cheyne. The Kirk Session having sung the three first verses of the Eightieth Psalm, the Moderator read the Fifth Chapter of the First Epistle of Peter, and then engaged in a solemn and affecting prayer, after which were sung the Nineteenth and Twentieth verses of the Thirty-Fourth Psalm. The Moderator then took leave of the Members after closing the Session by pronouncing the Blessing.

A Day of Fasting on the Removal of their Pastor

At St Luke's Session House, 10th November 1841, The Members of Session having met for prayer—Sederunt, Messrs. Stothert, Howden, Gardner, Russell, Robertson, Henderson, Smith, Macdonald, Pringle and M'Cheyne. After the usual devotional exercises the meeting unanimously resolved (with the approbation of Mr Burns who is expected to commence his labours on Sabbath the 14th) to set apart Thursday the 18th Instant as a day of fasting and humiliation under the afflicting hand of God, who has seen meet for a time to deprive the Parish and Congregation of their beloved pastor: and it has resolved to have public worship on that day at one o'clock, afternoon, as well as in the Evening at seven o'clock. The meeting authorised the Treasurer to accept Messrs. Field and Allan's offer of 2d. [?] Instant for keeping the roof of the Church in repair.

A. M'Cheyne, Session Clerk

June 1843—St Luke's and the Disruption[1]

St Luke's Session House, 19 June 1843.

At the Ordinary Meeting of the Members of St Luke's Session—Sederunt, Messrs. Stothert, Gardner, Hogue, Russell, Henderson,

---

[1] NRS catalogue reference: CH3/782/1/127.

Boyark, Macdonald, Pringle and M'Cheyne. Mr. M'Cheyne laid upon the Table three copies of the Act of Demission or Deed of Separation from the Establishment, by Elders of the Free Church, signed by all the Twelve Members of this Session: Of which Copies he was directed to transmit one to the Clerks of the Free Assembly and to keep the other two *in retensis*. The meeting took this opportunity of recording an expression of gratitude and thanksgiving to Almighty God for the honour conferred on St Luke's Church on many different occasions during the recent contendings for the Headship of Our Lord and Saviour Jesus Christ, and more especially on the following memorable occasions, *viz. Primo,* That on the Eleventh day of August Eighteen hundred and forty, the Solemn Engagement by a large body of the Members of this Church to stand by the two fundamental principles of Non-Intrusion and Spiritual Independence, At all hazards, was entered into and signed in St Luke's Church. *Secundo,* That upon the Eighteenth day of November Eighteen hundred and forty, the Church of St Luke's was honoured to receive within its walls the Commission of Assembly when the other churches of the City were shut against it. *Tertio,* That in St Luke's Church was held the Extraordinary Meeting of Commission which sat on the Twenty-fifth day of August Eighteen hundred and forty-one where, with reference to 'Reasons of Dissent' given in by certain Office Bearers of the Church at the Ordinary Meeting of Commission on the Eleventh day of the same month, Resolutions were adopted by the Commission to maintain and defend the fundamental principles of the Church at all hazards against the attempts of the said dissentients and their adherents to subvert the same. *Quarto,* That the Overture to the General Assembly for a Declaration against the unconstitutional encroachments of the Civil Courts, embodying the substance of, and resulting in, the Claim of Right, Declaration and Protest adopted by the Assembly on the Thirtieth day of May Eighteen hundred and forty-two, was unanimously agreed to and signed in St Luke's Church by a large and influential meeting of Members of Assembly on the Twenty-fourth day of said month. And finally, That St Luke's Church was selected for the meetings of the Convocation of Ministers and Elders held on the Fifteenth, Sixteenth and Seventeenth days of May Eighteen hundred and forty-three, preparatory to the meeting of the General Assembly appointed to be held on the Eighteenth day of the same month, at which meetings of Convocation, after much and prayerful deliberation, there was agreed to and signed, by a large number of the Commissioners to the Assembly there present, for themselves and all who should adhere to them, that Solemn and ever memorable Protest, which was next day, read and laid on the Table of the Assembly by the Reverend Dr. Welsh, the Moderator of the former Assembly, after which the Moderator and whole protesting Commissioners withdrew and proceeded in a body to their Hall at Canon-Mills where they constituted themselves, with other adhering members of the Church, as the only true and Free Assembly of the National Church of Scotland. The Members of Session deem it wholly unnecessary to record in their minutes either the foresaid protest or the subsequent Act and Deed whereby nearly five hundred ministers of the Church divested themselves of their connexion with the state, and of their whole status, endowments and emoluments thence arising,—these being documents already published to the World, and which can never be lost or forgotten while the Church of Christ endures. Glory be to God in the highest! Amen.

A. M'Cheyne, Clerk
Wm. Stothert

The Spiritual and Natural Children of Abraham; and the Obligation under which the Gentile Believer has been Laid to Love and Honour the Jew[1]

By the Rev. Alexander Moody Stuart, A.M.,
Minister of St Luke's Parish, Edinburgh

'If then ye be Christ's, then are ye Abraham's seed, and heirs according to the promise.'—*Gal. 3:29*

IN reference to the glories and the terrors of the latter day, Jehovah has graciously promised that he will 'turn the heart of the fathers to the children, and the heart of the children to their

---

[1] This address was originally delivered as part of a series of lectures by Church of Scotland ministers in 1839, in which year a deputation was appointed to visit the Holy Land and Continent of Europe to make inquiries about the establishment of a mission among the Jews. (This was the deputation of which Robert Murray M'Cheyne and Andrew A. Bonar were a part.) The Introduction to the published volume of those lectures notes that they were delivered 'in order to awaken and keep alive the interest at home in behalf of this people [the Jews], and to show the obligations on Christians to earnest prayer and renewed efforts on their behalf. The Lectures, when delivered, excited an extensive and profound interest among all classes…' See *The Conversion of the Jews: A Series of Lectures delivered in Edinburgh by Ministers of the Church of Scotland* (Edinburgh: John Johnstone, 1842).—*P.*

fathers, lest he come and smite the earth with a curse'; he will, by his Spirit, so move the minds of men, that they shall no longer think of themselves merely and their own welfare, but seek the good of every one to whom they are by any bond related. Men will begin to study the various relations in which they stand, both natural and spiritual, whether as fathers and children, as rulers and subjects, pastors and people, or by whatever tie of nature or of grace God hath knit the human family together. Toward all to whom they are in any way related, he will turn their hearts, enkindling within them feelings corresponding to the special relation; lest that which was designed for good, should by their unfitness be converted into evil, and the earth be smitten with a curse, because it was incapable of receiving the blessing. And in the midst of much cause of gladness in this respect, and much likewise of sorrow in the midst of heart-less neglect and bold denial, on the one hand, and on the other, of successful study and earnest desire in reference to many of these relations, it is with unfeigned gratitude that we see the heart of the Gentile turning to the Jew. We hail it as a token for good, not to Israel merely, but to us, that we who have so long forgotten that Abraham is our father, are now, at last, remembering it, for other-wise we might ourselves be smitten with a curse; but if our hearts are drawn out to them, and theirs, in turn, are by grace moved toward us, we and they shall be accepted together, and enjoy one common blessing.

And yet, while our object is, this evening, to endeavour to turn the hearts of the children to their fathers, to induce a man to think of his brother, we cannot but remind you in passing, that this can be done to no purpose, and will be followed by no blessing, unless every man have thought first of himself. A man's heart must be turned inward first; he must have found grace for himself, before he can really desire it for others; and, therefore, instead of asking all of you to give your minds to the train of observation on which we are entering, there are some of whom we earnestly request, that you will not attempt to follow us, but wisely pause on the first expression of our text, and let it occupy, for an hour at least, your intense and exclusive attention. 'If ye be Christ's,'— what an interesting,—what an awful *if!* Weigh it well and thoroughly, and till you have arrived at some just conclusion on so important a subject, let it lodge deep and fast within your mind.—*If* I be Christ's—*if* I be Christ's!

Proceeding now to the proper subject of our present discourse, we shall examine, and request you to examine along with us, these three simple propositions:—Every believer is by grace a child of Abraham,—every Jew is by nature a child of Abraham,—the child of Abraham by grace is bound to love and honour the child of Abraham by nature.

I. Every believer is by grace a child of Abraham

'If ye be Christ's, then are ye Abraham's seed.' To whatever nation of the earth any man belongs, from the hour in which he believes in Christ he is a child of Abraham. This spiritual relation, so fully and frequently declared in other Scriptures, is so plainly stated in the words before you, that we shall not detain you by seeking fuller proof, but rather proceed to inquire, what the relation *is*, and what the relation *implies*.

1. First, then, what is the relation in which the believer, and specially the believing Gentile, stands to Abraham? In what sense is he our father, and are we his children?—a question sufficiently interesting, and withal somewhat difficult, and yet too lightly passed over by many whom it very nearly concerns. In the word of God, we find the terms 'father' and 'child' employed to denote very various spiritual relations, in some of which the connection is strong and close, in others, comparatively weak and distant. If we review those relations in reference to that one which falls specially under our consideration, we shall arrive at the conclusion, that in it the terms 'father' and 'child' express a connection far indeed from the strongest that they are used to denote, yet by no means the weakest.

To begin with the highest of all, we are not children of Abraham as we are children of God, 'who of his own will begat us with the word of truth'; to him Abraham himself cries, along with us, 'Abba, Father.' Neither are we Abraham's children, as we once all were, and as we fear some amongst us still are, children of the Wicked One. This relation is not nearly so close as the first; we never were children of Satan as we now are children of God, for Satan himself is but a creature. Still, it is a connection of prodigious power, and influence, and likeness, the father working in all his children, and taking them captive at his will; and to this tyrant our father Abraham, along with us, lived many years a slave. Nor, farther, is our connection with Abraham such as our connection with Christ, who says, 'Behold I, and the children which God hath given me.' Abraham is no saviour but himself a saved sinner. Nor yet, again, are we united by grace to Abraham, as we are by nature united to Adam. The father of the faithful was indeed the head of a covenant, yet not such a covenant head as our first father. The Jew himself has a connection with Adam which he has not with Abraham; in every son of Israel you may read the moral features of the one, but in thousands you will search in vain for any trace of the other.

These relations are all stronger, but there are others expressed by the same terms, that are weaker. There is mere discipleship and imitation, as the disciples of the prophets are styled the sons of the prophets. This is included in our being children of Abraham, according to the Scripture, 'If ye were Abraham's children, ye would do the works of Abraham,' but by no means expresses the entire connection. We are walking in the footsteps of the apostles, and we have Paul exhorting us, 'Be ye followers of me'; and the beloved disciple, in the overflowings of fatherly affection, calls us his 'little children'; yet we need not prove, that the Scriptures nowhere intimate that we have any such connection with them, as we have with him who is the father of all them that believe. Even Noah, with whom the covenant of grace was renewed, and whose children all of us literally are, is not termed our father by any such marked distinction. But, again, there is a closer tie than that of mere imitation, in the bond that subsists between the convert and the instrument of his conversion. 'Though ye have ten thousand instructors in Christ, yet have ye not many fathers, for in Christ Jesus I have begotten you through the gospel.' This connection is very strong and very sacred, and should ever be remembered and cherished; but it also is both different in its nature from the relation into which we are inquiring, and less frequently and strongly marked in the word of God.

But in the midst of various spiritual relations that are stronger, and others that are weaker, than our relation as children to Abraham our father, we think we can discover one, if not exactly, yet very nearly analogous in the connection formed between father and child, in the ordinance of baptism.[1] That connection itself it is indeed difficult to define. Yet the father, on the one hand, is not the saviour of the child, but is himself a helpless sinner, presenting to God his lost and helpless offspring; and neither is he, on the other hand, the mere teacher of the child. The child is baptized because the parent is a believer, and it is to the faith of the parent that regard is had in the ordinance. Not that his inward unbelief will intercept all blessing from the child, if he has professed his faith in Christ, and is a member of the visible church, any more than the ungodliness of the minister of God can make the word he has preached entirely void; but if we have no right to expect a blessing on the word from the lips of an unbelieving messenger, no more may we expect a blessing on the child presented in the arms of an unbelieving parent. Were there more faith in parents, there would be more grace bestowed on their children. If fathers confidingly embraced the covenant for their offspring, we should oftener see the fruits of a covenant blessing in earliest infancy, or, it may be, the blessing kept in store to be granted after many years of rebellion.

---

[1] 'Abraham received God's covenant promises, and restipulating with God, not only as a *type* of Christ, the true Father of the Faithful, not only as *an example* to his seed, who should walk in the inimitable steps of his faith and obedience, but as *an ordinance* for conveyance of the same covenant to all the confederacies with God therein; that so, all who should receive this covenant from God in Christ afterwards, must also draw and derive it by faith through Abraham, to whom the promise was made.'—*Mystery and Marrow of the Bible* [by Francis Roberts (1609–75)].—*AMS.*

Now, Abraham had faith to embrace the covenant, not for himself merely, but for his seed. He was a man, indeed, who would train his offspring in the fear of the Lord. 'I know him that he will command his household after him'; but this was not all the benefit they derived from him, for his heart was specially enlarged to embrace the promises on their behalf,—'To thee will I give it, and to thy seed.' His faith was stronger than the faith of other men, and singularly strong in this; he seems to have known above others the force of such words, 'The promise is to you and to your children.'

But we are not the children of Abraham: suppose Abraham did embrace the covenant for himself and for his seed, still from his loins we are not sprung. True; and take, therefore, a case analogous. Take an adopted child; take an instance, not of simple adoption into a family, but the case of a father adopting an orphan infant child, and presenting him in baptism, undertaking the duties of a parent toward him, and embracing the promises for him. How would a parent feel toward such a child, especially if he had not merely endeavoured, but been enabled to commit him by faith to God, and the child having been baptized with water, had also given early evidence of the baptism of the Holy Spirit? Would not a father look on such an infant as his own child indeed? And such is our connection with Abraham. He embraced the covenant not for the Jews only, but also for the Gentiles. It was held out to him in promise, 'In thee shall all families of the earth be blessed.' That promise his heart was opened to receive, for 'he believed that he might become the father of many nations'; it was confirmed to him when God said, after he had believed, 'A father of many nations have I made thee.' And if Israel should claim exclusive affinity to the father of the faithful, under his first name Abram, believing Gentiles have their own full claim to him under his second and more honourable name. We are 'Abraham's' seed, and if our name is altered into Israel, that we may be adopted by him, his name was likewise altered into Abraham, that he might adopt us.

2. This relation implies our inheritance of the promises, and our entire severance from the covenant of works. It implies our participation in the promises, 'If ye are Christ's, then are ye Abraham's seed, and heirs according to the promise.' The grand promise to Abraham was that he should be the father of the Messiah, and that in him all blessings should be given to his seed. To this channel all the blessing is confined (ver. 16); and through Christ believing Gentiles, as children of Abraham, are partakers of all the promises, for in Christ all the promises are yea and amen; and 'he is *not* a Jew which is one outwardly; neither is that circumcision which is outward in the flesh; but he *is* a Jew which is one inwardly; and circumcision is that of the heart, in the spirit, and not in the letter, whose praise is not of men, but of God.' Out of many promises exceeding great and precious, which we inherit through this relation, these two may be specified:—(1.) 'Eternal life, which God, that cannot lie, promised before the world began'; for this indeed was that of which Abraham laid hold for himself and his seed. He believed for an earthly Canaan, but while he did so, he 'declared plainly that he sought a better country, that is an heavenly'; and as he embraced the promise of that earthly country for his earthly seed, so for his heavenly seed he embraced the promise of the heavenly country of which the other was a type. His children by nature became heirs of the one; his children by faith heirs of the other—heirs according to the promise. (2.) The Holy Spirit—the promise of the Father—the seal and pledge of eternal life—'the earnest of the inheritance until the redemption of the purchased possession.' This is expressly stated, in verse fourteen, to be the blessing which we receive through our connection with Abraham, 'that the blessing of Abraham might come on the Gentiles through Jesus Christ, that we might receive the promise of the Spirit through faith.' The blessing of Abraham, then, and the promise of the Spirit, are one.

But our relation to Abraham implies farther, our entire severance from the covenant of works. Between Jew and Gentile in this respect, there is indeed no difference, both being equally condemned by the law, and shut out from all salvation but that of free grace.

But if it was used as an additional argument with the Jew, that 'the covenant that was confirmed before of God in Christ, the law which was 430 years after, cannot disannul, that it should make the promise of none effect,' the reasoning applies still more forcibly to us Gentiles who never came under that law at all, but whose connection with a covenant God comes directly from Abraham. If any seeming hope is left to the Jew from legal covenants, subsequent to Abraham, the very appearance of such ground of confidence is taken away from us, who can establish no claims whatever from the law, but must look straight up to the promise—the promise made to us through Abraham. A legal Jew is without excuse, but a legal Gentile has no shadow of excuse.

Abraham was an uncircumcised Gentile when he believed, and herein is made evident our right to all the promises. In being left without circumcision, and in being left without the ceremonial law that followed, we are not left without promise, or without inheritance. After the promise was given, the law came as a school-master to bring to Christ, to train the children for the enjoyment of their heritage. Without that school-master we were left; we neither enjoyed the benefit, nor endured the restraint, of being placed under those 'tutors and governors.' Yet children we were notwithstanding, and heirs too. The promise was ours, and the inheritance ours. Israel alone received the outward badge of a child; he alone was corrected as a child,—alone instructed as a child. We were lost, ourselves forgotten, our claims out of mind. But when the fullness of time came, when the inheritance was to be enjoyed, when the Holy Ghost, the promise of the Father, was actually given, and when, therefore, the title-deeds were produced to ascertain who were the heirs, our names were found written in them side by side with the names of the seed of Israel. Contrary to the judgment of others, and far from our own expectation, we were found lawfully entitled to the inheritance, if only we believed, and served ourselves heirs, setting to our seal that God was true. And by grace we were enabled so to do. But Israel mistook the shadow for the substance; they thought that the tutelage, the bondage, the state of servants, which went before to prepare them for the full enjoyment of the possession, was the actual possession itself. They claimed the bondage instead of claiming the heritage; and while they fought for the seal, and for the title-deeds, denying our claims, we entered freely into the promised land itself. God graciously enabled us to see Christ as the way, and we had boldness of access in him, and 'being Christ's, we are Abraham's seed, and heirs according to the promise.'

II. But while the believing Gentile is by grace a child of Abraham, every Jew is Abraham's child by nature

This connection is one of high honour and privilege, and yet such that it may be forfeited and lost; being in this respect unlike our natural connection with Adam, and our spiritual connection with Christ. Every child of Adam derives from him sin and curse; every believer in Christ has eternal life remaining sure; but every child of Abraham does not inherit the blessing of his father. In every son of Adam you see the features of his father, but in many a son of Abraham you can trace no moral resemblance. We say not that the unbelieving Jew is the very same as the unbelieving Gentile; but he has no more blessing—he has less—his blessing is converted into a curse. Just as there is a promise to believing parents, and yet many a child of godly parentage is a child of Satan; so with Abraham, while God honoured him so highly, while he made him so signal an instance of converting grace, and gave him such blessing for his children, he still shows his sovereignty, by choosing whom he will out of those children. Even Abraham 'hath not whereof to glory before God'; he was himself a sinner, and many of his children dying in their sins—children of the kingdom though they were—have been cast into outer darkness. The blessing of Abraham is confined to Christ, and to all that are in Christ. He alone hath this undivided honour; many who are in Abraham perish, but all who are in Christ have eternal life. They are not all Israel who are of Israel; and while the wild branch, grafted into the good olive tree, draws sap and life from the root, just as the living natural branch, the natural branch broken off has no more connection with the root for any life or produce, than if it had never belonged to the tree.

The connection, then, may be forfeited, and yet it is, notwithstanding, one of high honour and privilege. In the broken off branch we see the marks of the origin whence it sprung. It is dead, but the very dry twigs and withered leaves bear the impress of the parent stem. It is useless at present, but it has a peculiar suitableness for being grafted in—a special fitness to the stem and root. It requires only the living sap to make it peculiarly lovely, excellent, and glorious.

On the child of a godly parent there descends a double benefit. His parent dedicates him to God—his parent trains him for God. The first does not depend merely on the second: if the parent died, he would leave a blessing on the head of the child. Both these benefits, although they may be forfeited, changed, converted into curses, are still far from being nominal. The father's descending blessing gives greater hope of conversion, and the father's training prepares the way both for conversion, and for the future growth of the convert. The cutting of the fuel, and laying it in order, is vain, if no kindling spark is introduced; cold and dark itself, you might as well have heaped so many stones together, for any warmth or light it will afford. But the quickening fire once applied, that previous labour tells for much. Now, the Jews, as a nation, enjoy something of both these blessings. They have the blessing of a believing parentage, for that is not limited to immediate offspring, but descends through many generations, according to the expression, 'showing mercy to thousands (i.e., of generations) of them that love me.' And then they have the other advantage, however abused, of preparatory training. The one pearl of price is possessed by every believer, but in Christ are hid many treasures corresponding to the manifold wisdom of God. To many of those treasures the keys are doubtless to be found in the types and ceremonies of the Mosaic dispensation;

and those keys have been specially committed to Israel. By reason of their blindness, they have hitherto applied them to no real use: it never has occurred to them to open the chests in which the treasure lies; they are not aware of any riches within, and they desire them not, but have busied themselves with the mere figure of the key, as if it were the treasure. Nevertheless, when they have once begun to hunger and thirst after righteousness, their previous knowledge will turn to prodigious account, and they will no doubt be enabled to unlock much that has been comparatively hid from us.

Judah is described as 'a lion's whelp,' the noblest among the beasts of the forest, easily the monarch of all. But this lion is dead, and the weakest creature that has life is stronger than he, and the vilest is nobler than he, and the most worthless is better—'a living dog is better than a dead lion.' We that were but dregs of the Gentiles, being alive in Christ, are immeasurably better than this lion, bound in the cords of death. But, again, he is not dead, but sleepeth; for there is life for the dead; and in reference to this sleep of death, the question put of old may be asked again, though in a somewhat different sense, 'Judah is a lion's whelp; who shall rouse him up?' We may do much more in awakening him, than in fighting our own battles. We are beset round about with foes strong and many, yet say not they are idle who seem to have left the battle-field before us, to inquire after Israel. They have gone to rouse this sleeping lion, that he may fight our battles, and we may conquer with him. Nor is this expectation vain, for the promise remains to be fulfilled (Micah 5:8), that 'the remnant of Jacob shall be among the Gentiles, in the midst of many people, as a lion among the beasts of the forest.' The image is one of strength and conquest, showing that Israel shall prevail over his foes, yet not of cruelty; for in the verse immediately preceding it is written, that 'the remnant of Israel shall be in the midst of many people as a dew from the Lord, as the showers upon the grass, that tarrieth not for man, nor waiteth for the sons of men.'

What, then, are they better than we? No, in no wise; both Jew and Gentile are under sin, equally guilty, and alike condemned.

But the apostle of the Gentiles asks two questions in the name of the Jews; the first, 'Is the Jew better than the Gentile?' To which he answers, 'No, in no wise:' the second, 'What advantage hath the Jew over the Gentile?' to which he answers, 'Much every way.' While, then, they are better than we are in no way, they have advantage above us in every way. Shall we murmur at this? nay, rather we rejoice that Jehovah should do what he wills with his own; and that he who, at his own pleasure, makes one vessel of gold, and another of earth, one to honour, and another to dishonour, should again make one of gold, and another of silver—one to greater honour, and another to less.

Are, then, all the Jews advanced for ever above all the Gentiles? This does not follow; Israel may as a nation be higher, and more honoured, and yet individuals among the Gentiles be raised above the multitude of believing Jews. In this, as in everything else, Jehovah shows his electing mercy, often giving most abundant grace to them on whom he has conferred fewest privileges. 'I have not found so great faith, no, not in Israel.' And then the distinction is not eternal: in the day of judgment there is no mention of either Jew or Greek, but every man is rewarded according to his works. If the believing Gentile has more of Abraham's faith than the believing Jew, then he is more fully Abraham's son; and when many come from the east, and from the west, to sit down with Abraham, and Isaac, and Jacob, in the king-dom, he will be seated nearer Abraham's bosom—for ever nearer the throne of the Eternal.

And what, after all, is the honour of the seed of Abraham? It is, that of all the kindreds, and tongues, and people, and nations, they shall be the least, and the lowliest, according to the Scriptures—'He that is greatest among you shall be your servant'; and, 'whosoever shall humble himself as a little child, the same is greatest in the kingdom of heaven.' If, therefore, they are the greatest, it will be only by their becoming the most humble and childlike of all. They will be first in giving all honour to God and the Lamb; first in looking on him whom they have pierced, and mourning; first in renouncing every thing of their own, and ascribing all to free grace; first to exclaim, 'Are we better than they? No, in no wise.' They shall be so eminently lowly and meek, they shall so put all honour from themselves, that we shall cheerfully give them the first rank, seeing no nation in all the earth which we would so delight to exalt. And wherein shall we be their inferiors? In the remains of haughtiness, and self-righteousness, and unholiness—less faithful, less prayerful, less humble and contrite. Go, then, believing Gentile, and humble thyself, if thou will be great; go, take the lowest room; think not more highly of thyself than thou oughtest to think, but think soberly, lest a more honourable than thou be bidden to the feast, and he that bade thee say, 'Give this man place,' and 'thou be put lower in' the presence of the Prince whom thine eyes have seen.

III. *The child of Abraham by grace is bound to love and honour the child of Abraham by nature*

On this we shall not enlarge, as it follows clearly from the considerations we have already adduced. We cannot but love those whom, for their father's sake, our heavenly Father loves, and those whom he honours we cannot refuse to honour. But the children of Abraham by nature, and the children of Abraham by adoption, have undoubtedly some special bond of brotherhood. Let us love them, let us pray for them, let us work for them, and above all, let us *believe* for them. Let us prove by this that we are really Abraham's seed; and, as he embraced the promises for us, let us embrace the promises for them. They have promises which they will not plead through unbelief, let us plead them on their behalf. We are Abraham's living representatives; if he were on earth he would embrace and plead the promises for lost Israel; let us, as his heirs, do what he would have done. And look what a blessed connection thence arises between Jew and Gentile. To their fathers we owe a debt of gratitude, and for their sakes we love their children; and to themselves we shall owe a tribute of honour when God has restored them to favour. But they again will look to us with love and gratitude. Hitherto, indeed, we have but triumphed over them, and trodden them down as the mire of the streets; but if we love them now, and pray for them, and are honoured in being instrumental to their conversion, then they in turn will love and honour us, and they and we together, in mutual affection and mutual gratitude, will go and walk in the light of the Lord.

We prodigal children have returned from the country whither in our folly we had wandered, poor and portionless, wearied and wasted, and without a rag to cover us. We have been welcomed back to our father's house with every mark of kindness. The fairest robe has been put on us, we have a ring on our hand, we have shoes on our feet, and for us the fatted calf has been killed, and there is joy in heaven over us. But our elder brother has been offended; he next has left his father's mansion. Because we have been received with honour that mansion has now no attraction, no comfort for him, and he has stood proudly and sullenly without. Meanwhile, in the gladness and mirth that have arisen on our account, in the midst of the music and dancing that have welcomed our return, he appears to have been forgotten. It seems as if the father himself, in the fullness of his joy over us, had left him in his own sullenness; or he has sent servants to fetch him in, and these servants have never gone forth, but have sat in the banquet with us, or else have carried out a cold and contemptuous message. But is not God himself arising now to have mercy on Zion? Is not the father going out to entreat? And shall we grudge the repentance and return of our elder brother; shall we say, 'Let him remain without since he will remain'; shall we envy him the seat at our father's right hand? Was this the thought of our heart when we first repented and were restored to favour? Did we not profess then, and did we not feel, that the place even of a younger son was too good for us, and that we should count ourselves happy in being numbered with our father's hired servants? Was a servant's place good enough for us then, and will we not now be satisfied unless our father displace for us his own first-born, our elder brother? My dear brethren, this was not our first judgment

of ourselves when we returned in our rags and were so honourably received; we did not then murmur at another's birthright, but
we marvelled at our own exaltation. And whatever other feelings
of jealousy may for a time have arisen in our bosoms, we disown
them, and are humbled and repent. Shall we not rejoice, then, at the
thought of our brother's return, although he should sit first at our
father's table? Shall we not gladly give place and yield precedence
to him, even when our Father shall say to him, 'Son, thou art ever
with me, and all that I have is thine.' Yea, let us, of our own free will,
remind our Father and our God, that his first-born is still standing
without; let us beseech him to have compassion, and to go out and
entreat him; let us count, that the first seat is not filled by us, nor
by any other, but is still vacant in his absence; let us mourn over the
blank, and when our Father arises let us go with him, and let us also
entreat. It was meet that there should be joy over our return, and
no joy was spared; the house was filled with music and dancing, till
the sound was heard in the fields; and now it is most meet that our
elder brother should join in the feast, and that our heavenly Father
should have joy in both his children redeemed by one Saviour, sanctified by one Spirit, joint-heirs of one inheritance.

Report of the Jewish Committee to the Free Church General Assembly, 1869[1]

Mr A. Moody Stuart submitted the report of the Committee on the Conversion of the Jews, from which we extract the following:—In laying the report on the table, Mr Moody Stuart called attention to various interesting details contained therein. He proceeded—In Scotland there are various reasons that make our exertions on behalf of the Jews peculiarly suitable. The Old Testament has always been more to Scotland than to most other nations; and so Israel has occupied a higher place with us than with others; and in our Directory for Worship we are instructed to pray for the propagation of the gospel to all nations, the conversion of the Jews, the fullness of the Gentiles, the fall of Antichrist, and the hastening of the second coming of our Lord. Merely New Testament Christians rarely take any special interest in the conversion of Israel. Our simplicity of worship, our Presbyterian government, our love of the Sabbath, are all natural elements that give us a nearer approach to them, and make it peculiarly fit for us to cast ourselves with interest into the cause of their conversion. But as regards missions to Israel, my apprehension is that the time for these missions may be half over already. It is thirty years since we commenced them, and it is quite possible that thirty

---

[1] This speech is extracted from *The Proceedings and Debates of the General Assembly of the Free Church of Scotland*, 1869, pp. 19-20.—*P.*

years hence all such missions will be practically finished. Speaking generally, what is likely to be the case of the Jews thirty years hence? There is a vast change now from the condition of the Jews thirty years ago—a greater change than took place in the last eighteen centuries. The grand difficulty about the Jews formerly was, that they were crushed, and they could not love the religion of their oppressors. Very strange it seems, but now our missionaries write that the grand difficulty with the Jews is, that they are so elated, they have got such freedom, they are getting such wealth, and they have such privileges, that their ear is closed now to the gospel. This is a new thing in their history, and our difficulty is just the opposite of what it was. Again, they are becoming better educated, and they are making great progress. They are uniting together as they did not use to unite. There was a Congress called in Hungary, not long ago, by the Ecclesiastical Minister of Hungary, that they might form themselves more completely into one body. At present it is proposed to hold a Synod in Germany, but very probably nothing will come of it, and the English Jews do not care about a central ecclesiastical authority. But it shows that the nation is striving after unity, and it is seeking to become one, and that it is becoming more jealous about Judaism. In one way or another there is at present a certain progress towards the uniting of the nation. Before the end of the century they may have returned to their own land, and the time for missions to them may be past. It is therefore of great moment for us to be diligent now in sowing amongst them the seed of the gospel which the Lord, in his own time, will quicken in their hearts unto an abundant harvest.

Report of the Jewish Committee to the Free Church General Assembly, 1882[1]

Dr Moody Stuart then proceeded with the report of the Committee on the Conversion of the Jews.

In submitting the report, Dr Moody Stuart said—The report on the conversion of the Jews, which I now lay on the table of the Assembly, presents a large amount of work with a fair measure of success. The faithful preaching of the gospel, the constant dealing with inquiries, and the occasional baptism of carefully-tried converts by our ordained missionaries, the daily instruction in the knowledge of Christ of many hundreds of Hebrew boys and girls by our excellent teachers, with the addition of flourishing Sabbath schools; the distribution of Bibles and tracts, and the constant conversation with Jews by devoted men working under our missionaries; the access by our medical missionaries to many hundreds, and in a period of two or three years to thousands of patients; the effect of our Hungarian and Bohemian bursaries in young ministers from those countries, returning home with a new spiritual life, and with zeal for the salvation of Israel. All this presents a large amount of work accomplished, with various tokens of the divine blessing, and a fair measure of fruit, for which we have great cause of thankfulness to

[1] This speech is extracted from *The Proceedings and Debates of the General Assembly of the Free Church of Scotland*, 1882, pp. 20-24.—*P.*

our God and Saviour in being thus permitted to carry back to Israel the words of eternal life which have come to us through them.

But, passing from the report, which is in the hands of members, I desire to direct the attention of the Assembly to the present condition of the Jews. The past year has been a memorable one in the national history of Israel, for their sufferings in Russia,[1] for the sympathy shown to them in England and America on account of their sufferings, for the proposals to return to their own land, and prospectively, for the effect of such a return when accomplished on their own religious condition and on the great future of the world.

The recent sad sufferings of Israel show that the inextinguishable and reviving nation has again taken its place in the world, so as to awaken the jealousy of the surrounding populations. The sufferings of the Jews in Russia recalls their early sufferings in the land of Egypt, and the very special Providence that has watched over his people is strikingly brought out by the fact, that in this one country alone there are many more Jews in the present day than the nation which came out of Egypt three thousand years ago, and that they are as distinct now from all of the nations as they were then. This is a fact quite singular in the history of the world, and can only be accounted for by the remarkable union in the case of Israel of the severest providential chastening by our God of their fathers on account of their aggravated sin in rejecting their own Messiah, with the tenderest and most watchful care as of a father over his children, that their suffering should never issue in their destruction. 'Behold, he that keepeth Israel shall neither slumber nor sleep,' said the inspired psalmist; and, it was added by one of the kings of Portugal, 'He will not suffer that those that keep Israel to slumber or sleep.' Like the Persian monarch in the days of Esther, the king lay restless on his bed, and having tried in vain to sleep, he rose and stood at a window of the palace in the clear moonlight, and, as he looked, he saw two men throw a dead

---

[1] Moody Stuart's reference is to the anti-Semitic pogroms that took place in parts of the southern Russian Empire (present-day Poland and Ukraine) between 1881 and 1884.—*P.*

body over a wall into the garden of a Jew. Next day, the body was found, the Jew was charged with the murder, and would have been condemned, but the king, entering the court, both interceded on his behalf, and testified to the sleepless watching of the Lord over Israel. Their preservation to this day is, in the eyes of the whole world, the evident and striking fulfilment of their own ancient oracles, in which the sternest threatenings are so remarkably combined with the most definite and assuring promises. 'For lo, I will command, and I will sift the house of Israel among all nations, like as corn is sifted in a sieve, yet shall not the least grain fall upon the earth.' Their present terrible calamities recall the memory of their mediæval sufferings. The great progress of the Jews for the last generation has led to the great atrocities in Russia, where it is said that there are one hundred thousand Jews left absolutely penniless.

In the present instance, over and against the renewed suffering—which in past ages has so been the badge of all their tribe, that there is nothing strange in it except its occurrence in the nineteenth century—there has been, on the other hand, an amount of Christian sympathy in England and America, which the Jews welcome with joy and gratitude as a new feature in the history of their race. Our disinterested desires for their conversion they often resent as they would resent persecution; and kindness towards them on the part of earnest Christians they are apt to distrust, as if it were only with a view to proselytism. But in their present trials they have seen that, apart from all other motives, the heart of the Christian beats in sympathy for them, not only as men, but as the children of Abraham, and as themselves beloved their fathers' sakes. They have felt and acknowledged this genuine sympathy, not only in Christians in general, but in those who have shown most zeal for Christianising them; as in the venerable Lord Shaftesbury, for many years president of the London Society for Promoting Christianity among the Jews. The Mansion-House meeting in London was hailed by them with unbounded delight, and the *Jewish Chronicle* wrote of it in these terms: 'The peculiar position of our race is illustrated in the most powerful and conciliatory way by the requisition addressed to the Lord Mayor by an extraordinary list of illustrious Englishmen for the Mansion-House meeting on behalf of our Russian brethren. We see in it an event of exceptional importance in the annals of our people. In fact the signatures to this requisition must be something like a new departure in the interaction of Jewish and non-Jewish destinies. No nobler act is recorded in the whole troubled annals of religions and churches. It can never be forgotten.' After naming the leading speakers at the meeting, the *Chronicle* adds—'At last, but not least, the ringing sincerity of the veteran philanthropist, Lord Shaftesbury, who came from his seat in the west of England to plead the cause of the poor Jews of Russia. England has now declared, as the United States had already declared, that the calamities of Jews are no longer to be disregarded, and that commiseration with them is felt by the most powerful as well as the most enlightened of the earth.' The *Chronicle* recorded with interest and gratitude the sympathy shown for the Jews in Edinburgh, Glasgow, and other towns, as well as in London.

One effect of this sympathy, which they have so highly prized, may be, by the blessing of God, to make them more open to consider the claims of Jesus Christ to their gratitude and allegiance. They have often drunk to the dregs the bitter cup of human hatred left itself, or strengthened by a false or merely nominal Christianity; and now for the first time in so large a measure, and so open a manner, they have tasted themselves sweet fruit of the Christian religion with genuine love and disinterested sympathy. This is known to the whole nation of the Jews, and well known in Russia, where they have suffered most; and by the divine blessing it may have a very great effect in removing the prejudice against our religion, for which ages of hardship had given too much occasion.

This Christian sympathy may also aid in opening the eyes of Israel to the great fact, well enough known but much overlooked, the controversy between Judaism and Christianity is by no means a contest between Jew and Gentile, but solely a contrast between Jew and Jew. We are not asking them to come over to our religion; but, through grace, we have gone over to theirs. We are not asking them to adopt the heathenism of our fathers; but we have ourselves been adopted into Judaism in its highest and perfected form. The object of our worship is Jesus of Nazareth, the king of the Jews; our highest honour for ourselves is that we have been grafted into their olive tree; and our earnest desire for them is, not that they should be engrafted into us, that we may glory over them, but only that they should be engrafted into their own olive tree; and that they and we together should rejoice in one Lord Jesus Christ, in whom there is neither Jew nor Greek, but all are one in him. The past and still existing hatred of the Jews to Christ is because he is a Jew; if he had been a Gentile, they would have rejected and neglected him, but they would not have hated him. But when once their eyes are opened and their hearts turned they will cleave to him with an intenser love, and glory in him with a more burning zeal, because, like themselves he also is a son of Abraham. Let us pray for them to our Messiah and theirs—

> Messiah, full of grace,
>   Redeemed by thee we plead
> Thy promise made to Abraham's race,
>   To souls for ages dead;
> Their bones, as quite dried up,
>   Throughout our vale appear,
> Cut off, and lost their last faint hope
>   To see thy kingdom here.
>
> Open their graves, and bring
>   The outcasts forth to own
> Thee for their Lord, their God, and king—
>   That true anointed one.
> To save the race forlorn
>   Thy glorious arm display,
> And show the world a nation born—
>   A nation in a day![1]

[1] Hymn by Charles Wesley (1707–88).—*P.*

The world is now at a loss what to do with the Jews, and the Jews are now at a loss what to do with themselves. Not very long ago they were little taken into account amongst the nations of the earth; but now they can no longer be merely despised. They may be hated on the one hand, or they may be loved on the other, but they cannot be overlooked. Those who fear them are afraid of their gaining an excessive influence and power; and they are themselves afraid of jealousy of the nations being always awakened by their success. Many of them therefore desire to return to their homeland, partly from their love to the land of their fathers, and partly from the desire to possess a country themselves, where they might prosper without being exposed to the envy and malice of others. Hitherto, not wholly but in great part, the Jews have gone to Jerusalem to die. The main object with most of them has been to lay their bones on the sacred soil of Palestine, and they have been largely supported by their brethren in other lands. Such pilgrims, however numerous, could never form either a morally healthy or an outwardly prosperous community. But in their present distress they are forming various plans for planting colonies of industrious Jews in Palestine. The leading Jews in Paris are decidedly opposed to any immigration of their brethren to Palestine, and the rich Jews in London are said to be of the same mind. But the *Jewish Chronicle*, which used to maintain that neither was the land yet ready for them nor they ready for it, has now, in the altered circumstances of the nation, come to regard the proposal with favour. In the *Jewish Chronicle* of last Friday it is stated that the first body of settlers in Palestine, numbering about 500, left Russia on the 20th April. The land in which they are about to settle had been previously purchased for them by delegates who had recently visited Palestine and a correspondent writes: 'It is difficult to hold the emigration back. Some hundreds have already gone, I fear prematurely, and they will have a hard time, but it is certain that nothing can prevent the exodus.'

But the most important consideration is the probable effect on the religion of the Jews that might follow their return to Palestine.

To return to their own land without repenting toward their own crucified Messiah will bring them no peace with God in heaven, and probably but little peace with men on earth. In past ages it would not have seemed impossible or highly improbable that the crushed remnant of the Jews would be absorbed in the Christian nations, and that the religion of Judaism might have ceased to exist, whilst their restoration to the land of their fathers would have seemed quite out of consideration. But their absorption amongst the Gentiles has not taken place, and the commencement of a return to their country is now seriously proposed. But if that return should be accomplished, it will hasten a great crisis in their religion. At present they pray continually for the rebuilding of their temple, and the restoration of its sacrifices; but many of them have no desire for the fulfilment of these prayers; and if there is an opening for return to their country, it will be first embraced by the most zealous in the nation, and by the most oppressed. Will they, then, rebuild the temple and celebrate its dedication with burnt offerings of hundreds of oxen and thousands of sheep, and then offer daily sacrifices morning and evening on its altar? In the present age it is scarce conceivable that such an attempt will be made, and the Jews themselves look for the rebuilding of their Temple and the renewing of their sacrifices only after the coming of the Messiah after their own mind, whom they will look for in vain. But in that case the Jewish religion will have conspicuously failed. In the sacrificial atonement of the Lord Jesus Christ the ancient religion of Israel is gloriously complete. Its sacrificial types have a lofty fulfilment in the Lord of the whole earth giving himself as the Lamb of God taking away the sins of the world; and it was not too much that the offering of the cattle from a thousand hills should have preceded and prefigured the shedding of the infinitely precious blood of God's own Son on Calvary. But when the prospect of Jewish sacrifices shall have ceased, the very substance of Judaism will have vanished without a meaning and without a result. And this evident failure of their own religion, together with their finally disappointed hopes of a Messiah after their own mind, will doubtless be used by the God of Israel to convince the nation of their own and their fathers' one great sin in rejecting and crucifying the Christ of God; and their eyes being open to see the substance of their ancient sacrifices in him who was led as a lamb to the slaughter, they will look on him whom they pierced with a bitter sorrow to be followed by more than pentecostal joy.

But known unto God are all his works from the beginning of the world, and the Lord of the harvest prepares for the abundant reaping by the previous sowing of much precious seed. The great body of the Jews have never yet heard the free gospel of Jesus Christ, although they know and hate the name of the crucified Nazarene. But far more than would have been the case in the last generation, even now, if they shall return to their own land, many amongst them will carry with them some acquaintance with the gospel and the weakening of old prejudice, along with the knowledge that many of their own brethren are already confessing Jesus Christ. Probably at this hour there is in many of them the same resistance to the gospel as in Saul of Tarsus, and the voice may soon reach their ears—'It is hard for thee to kick against the pricks.' When that old belief shall receive a shock in their fathers' land without the long cherished hope of their fathers' sacrificial worship in the Temple, the buried seeds of the gospel may by grace spring up in many hearts, and the light may rapidly diffuse its rays through the nation. If there shall also be special interposition for their conversion, the divine effectual call will still make use of all the scriptural knowledge they shall have received through the preaching and teaching of the gospel of Jesus Christ.

And when Israel is once enlightened with saving knowledge of Christ, there will be a nation of missionaries for the salvation of the whole human family. To the world the receiving of them will be 'life from the dead.' The Lord has said of old—'I will be as the dew unto Israel'; and then will be fulfilled the promise, 'Awake and sing, ye that dwell in dust, for thy dew is as the dew of herbs, and the earth shall cast out the dead.' Israel, dead in trespasses and sins, shall spring up in freshness of life, like the grass springing up from the earth under an abundant dew or a refreshing rain; and then will come the worldwide blessing in the promise that 'The remnant of Jacob shall be in the midst of many people as a dew from the Lord.' So the calling of Israel by the Lord to himself will be 'life from the dead' to all this withered and dying world. The Jews are often reproached by the Gentiles with an inordinate love of money; but it was an assembly of Jews that set the brightest example the world has ever seen of freedom from the spirit of covetousness, when 'the multitude of them that believed were of one heart and one soul, neither said any of them that aught of the things which he possessed was his own.' So it was in Jerusalem at the pentecostal feast of first-fruits, and so it will be again at the feast of ingathering, when 'all Israel shall be saved.' It is often promised that as they have been a reproach among the nations, so there will be an honour and a blessing; a trustful, rejoicing, and generous multitude at Pentecost is the earnest of the nation when saved. All reproach will be rolled away, and Israel will be famed and honoured through the whole earth for disinterestedness and generosity; willingly giving themselves, their substance, and their labours for the salvation of the world, till their reception into the fold of Christ shall have become 'life from the dead' to the whole human family, as a dew 'from the Lord of hosts, as showers upon the grass, that waiteth not for man nor tarrieth for the sons of men.'

> Daughter of Zion, from the dust
>   Exalt thy fallen head;
> Again in thy Redeemer trust,
>   He calls thee from the dead.
>
> Awake, awake, put on strength,
>   Thy beautiful array;
> The day of freedom dawns at length,
>   The Lord's appointed day.

Rebuild thy walls, thy bounds enlarge,
   And send thy heralds forth;
Say to the South, Give up thy charge,
   And keep not back, O North.

They come, they come, thine exiled bands,
   Where'er they rest or roam,
Have heard thy voice in distant lands,
   And hasten to their home.[1]

(Loud applause.)

[1] Hymn by James Montgomery (1771–1854).—*P.*

437

*Photograph that accompanied the tribute
in the* Free Church of Scotland Monthly

Dr Moody Stuart[1]

Rev. Robert Cowan, Elgin

D R Moody Stuart was born at Paisley on 15 June 1809. His father was Mr Andrew Moody, banker and for some time chief magistrate of Paisley. He was a man much respected and beloved by all classes. It is mentioned that on one occasion of popular tumult, when windows were being broken, the leader enjoined: 'Let Bailie Moody's house alone; he's a good sowl, Moody!' Alexander was the youngest son in a family of six sons and two daughters.

After attending school at Paisley, he joined the rector's class in Glasgow Grammar School, and thereafter, in his fourteenth year, entered the university. The holidays at Muirsheil—an estate in the uplands of Renfrewshire owned for a time by his father—were a not unimportant educative influence at this date, cultivating that love of nature and intelligence with it which throughout life char-acterized him. An interesting little tract published only a few weeks before his death, makes happy use of an incident connected with his father's sheep on the hills which he had noticed in a holiday ramble seventy-five years before.

He graduated in 1826, and although not quite seventeen was a very competent scholar, particularly in classics, and he became afterwards almost as proficient in Hebrew as in Latin and Greek. The same winter

[1] Tribute appearing in the October 1898 issue of the *Free Church of Scotland Monthly.*—P.

he entered the divinity classes at the university, and after two sessions at Glasgow took the remaining two at Edinburgh. It was when at Edinburgh that the spiritual crisis of his life occurred. Finishing his arts course, he had not yet decided on his profession. The death of his father, however, and of two brothers, about this time, with other circumstances that spoke of the vanity of earth, impressed him solemnly, and in quite a conscientious spirit—according to his light— he chose the ministry. 'Yet,' he says, 'I was a stranger to the covenant of promise and the new birth by the Holy Spirit.' A sermon by Dr Gordon, on what the new birth really is, deepened this conviction. Marshall *On Sanctification*, which he happened to read, taught him the entire sinfulness of fallen man, and over against this the infinitely perfect righteousness of Jesus Christ.

On the spring Fast-day in 1829, a cousin had, unasked, procured for him token to the communion. He had no intention of using it, but his anxiety and distress were acute, and next day he formed a resolution to 'care for nothing until he had found salvation.' Opening his Bible in a dark and desponding mood, he lighted upon the words: 'Awake, thou that sleepest, and arise from the dead, and Christ shall give thee light' (Eph. 5:14). 'They came to me,' he says, 'like a flash of lightning in the sudden awakening, but with infinite sweetness of light in Christ; his word had quickened me… the token received with sorrow was now used with joy, and for the first time I sat down at the Lord's table with true faith.' Besides the preaching of Dr Gordon, he was much helped by that of Mr John Bruce of St Andrew's Church, and at the university he got a great and abiding impulse from Dr Chalmers, then at the zenith of his intellectual strength and evangelical fervour.

He was licensed by the Presbytery of Glasgow in 1831, and in 1832, at the request of Mr Buchan of Kelloe, known for his Christian zeal and good works, went to labour as missionary at Holy Island, off the Northumberland coast. The population was mostly a fishing one. From the first there was blessing on his labours, but many of the people were in a backward state spiritually. Lovingly faithful, he warned them that God might chastise for inattention to the gospel; and when the cholera broke out in 1834, they said, 'It's the preaching that has done this.' The young missionary remained at his post during the terrible visitation, and, when for seven weeks in the autumn of that year the island was cut off from communication with the mainland, ministered to and nursed the sick and the dying. He was preserved in health, and his mind kept in perfect peace; a tender attitude of spirit was wrought in the people towards him and his message, and there was much spiritual fruit. His first publication, *Death-Bed Scenes*, owed its origin to what he had witnessed in this visitation. In 1835 he was invited to become assistant to Dr Candlish in St George's, Edinburgh, and territorial missionary in the parish. The mission proved so successful that a *quoad sacra* parish, under the name of St Luke's, was formed. The congregation at first met in an old Unitarian church in Young Street; but this speedily proving too small, a commodious new church was built on the same site. It was opened in May 1837, and in June Mr Moody was ordained as minister. St Luke's soon became a place of note, from the deeply spiritual ministrations of the pastor, and also as a rallying ground for the Evangelical party during the latter half of the 'Ten Years Conflict,' when other Edinburgh churches were not accessible to them.

In 1839 he was happily married to Jessie, eldest daughter and heiress of Kenneth Bruce Stuart, Esquire of Annat, in the Carse of Gowrie. The family to which he thus became allied, and whose name he now added to his own, is worthy of remembrance. Mr Stuart was an Indian officer, an eminent linguist, and a man of devout spirit. He died in 1832, and Mrs Stuart thereafter resided chiefly at Annat Lodge, Perth. She was a lady beautiful in character as in countenance, often doubting her own good estate spiritually, but whose lowliness and love, unthoughtfulness of self and thoughtfulness of others, acts of neighbourly and charitable kindness, and generosity to every good cause, seemed to those who observed her the very expression of the spirit of Christ. One of her daughters became the wife of the Rev.

John Milne, Perth, by his first marriage, and another of the Rev. N. Roussel of France. She herself died in 1873, in the full assurance of her interest in Christ and her going to be forever with him. Mrs Moody Stuart was a true helpmeet of her husband, diverse in temperament, but appreciative the more of what was distinctive in him, of acute intelligence and much practical wisdom, with a fine vein of sentiment underneath, and of a piety steadfast and deep, which fed itself at the word of God, and loved that word increasingly to the end. How much she was to her husband and children in the home, and how helpful to him in many ways in connexion with his work, he himself gratefully felt, and others could in part perceive.

In 1841 his health had broken down—so seriously that it was feared he would never preach again. The winters of that and the following year were spent in Madeira, and in the spring of 1843 he also visited Brazil. The enforced pause, though painful, was very fruitful both spiritually and in other ways. He had not a little of the poetic temperament and genius, had a true poet's eye for nature, and could turn to good account what he observed in travel. In his closing address as Moderator of Assembly, thirty-three years after this date, there is a description of a scene in Brazil which, for vividness of presentation and richness of colouring, is quite fit to rank with some of Ruskin's glowing word-pictures of Italian scenery. In his absence from home his prayers were being answered: God was visiting Scotland with times of refreshing, and under the preaching of William Burns, Robert M'Cheyne, and other helpers, St Luke's shared largely in the blessing. He returned in invigorated health, and resumed his labours in July 1843. Many long remembered the thrill that went through the crowded congregation when he rose up and gave out to be sung Psalm 118:17:

> I shall not die, but live and shall
> The works of God discover.
> The Lord hath me chastised sore,
> But not to death giv'n over.

The Disruption had taken place before his arrival home, but he was fervently with his brethren in what he afterwards refers to as 'the noble exodus of our church, in order to keep inviolate the liberty wherewith Christ had made her free'—'that trying but elevating and ennobling time.' All his elders and almost all his people had come out, and the congregation continued to meet in the old place until March 1849, when the Established kirk session of St George's gave them notice to quit, although, as in many similar cases, only a fraction of the cost had been contributed by those who remained in the Establishment. For three years thereafter they worshipped in Queen Street Hall, and in June 1852 the handsome new church in Queen Street was opened. It is worth noting that, in order to clear off a considerable debt that remained on the new church, they adopted the expedient of having a special collection every Sabbath—one elder putting £10 into the plate as his weekly mite, another £4, and others proportionally—until, in about a year, the whole was cleared.

St Luke's was remarkable for the combination of people it brought together—able professional men and intelligent working men, scholars and illiterate, highborn ladies and servant girls, 'remote Highlanders and high-class English people,' the rich and the very poor—all equally attracted by the preaching and the personality of the minister, and cordially owning one another as brothers and sisters in the one Lord. Among the names honourably associated with it, those of Mr Stothert of Cargen, Mr Brown Douglas, Dr John Duncan, Mr John Macdonald, treasurer of the Free Church, Dr Russell, Mr James Cunningham, W.S., the Hon. Miss Mackenzie of Seaforth, and the Duchess of Gordon when in Edinburgh, call up interesting memories; while others, of what Hugh Miller calls 'the upper working class,' like Peter Jackson the cabman, and many in very humble life, had a not less honourable Christian record.

What Dr Moody Stuart was as a preacher and spiritual teacher it is difficult to make plain to those not familiar with his ministrations. As he entered the pulpit, one felt the man before he opened his lips; there was an atmosphere of prayer and of heaven about him. The voice, though not strong, and somewhat high-set and plaintive in its tones, was clear and penetrating, and effective to express every shade of thought and feeling. The theology was that of the Reformers and Puritans, but taken in at first hand from the word, absorbed in his own life, and touched with his own individuality. The great characteristic of his style, both in writing and speaking, was expressiveness—the right word and phrase found to body forth the thought; and the great characteristic of his message was the life that was in it, and the way it fitted into the spiritual life in others. Students hearing him for the first time sometimes thought of him only as a good man saying simple things, but they quickly discovered the subtle thinker, the profound theologian, and the master in spiritual pathology. Sometimes the preaching was expository, sometimes textual, but it always dealt closely with experience and the heart, finding out the hearer, and often surprising him with the diagnosis of his particular case, and the tender and healing touch on his hidden sore. John Milne said, 'My brother Moody has an intricate mind,' and this was illustrated in the way his word wound itself into all the sinuosities of the inner experience. Carnal hearers might find little in the message, but to seekers, and Christians in doubt or darkness, it was medicine and balm, and living souls found in it the very nutriment their life needed. As a student who sat some time in his church says, 'It was a spectacle to see the eager wistfulness of the hearers, watching for every word, and drinking it in as if they were drinking champagne.' The word as preached by him, though searching, was always singularly cheering and encouraging; the secret being that he had got down for himself to the bedrock of the sinner's foundation in the grace of God in Christ, was always dwelling there, and felt quite sure of the entire sufficiency of this for others, whatever their cases might be. Especially on communion Sabbaths did his excellences appear. To apply a remark he quotes about Dr Duncan, 'The man was at his best then, and a wonderful best it was.' The word was good, the gracious influence was still better. One felt the beauty of holiness, and realized what it is to sit in the heavenlies. He himself seemed often to be filled with a holy joy. Those who had seen it could understand the remark he made when presiding at the first Conference communion at Perth, that he could wish for himself nothing better for the remainder of his days than just to be permitted to go about breaking the bread and offering the cup.

One thing which on acquaintance dawned almost as a surprise upon those who had before known him only as the saintly preacher was his versatility. He had read widely as well as travelled, was alive to all human interests, and seemed to know something about everything. One of the present writer's first meetings with him was at the hospitable house of Mr Turnbull of Huntingtower. Part of the talk turned upon cattle, in which Mr Turnbull was then taking a special interest. The listener was astonished at the eminent divine's familiarity with the subject, and charmed with his description of the white herd of the Earl of Tankerville, and some famous herds he had inspected of an Austrian Archduke; it seemed to give the question of cattle quite an aristocratic elevation! More memorable was a day spent at his beautiful country house of Annat, perched on the sides of the Sidlaws, with a fertile Carse and broad estuary of the Tay below. The black Austrian pines, of his own planting, and his other trees and shrubs, led to a disquisition on German forests and the caterpillar that threatened them, with an excursus to Indian trees, gardening, and allied topics. The hearer could read some parables in his discourse, and half suspected he meant them, but the plain drift was also very informing and interesting. This characteristic no doubt gave him openings, and helped his usefulness in many quarters. Whilst on the one hand singularly like his Lord in 'meekness and lowliness of heart,' so that the humblest could tell him their story, and understood him and were understood by him; on the other, his wide knowledge and culture, together with his sweet courtesy and dignified grace of manners, made him a welcome guest and associate with the highest. To few Scottish ministers has it been given to have such influence for good with people of rank and position.

His zeal and labour for the ingathering of Israel to their true Shepherd were an outstanding feature in his life-work. He rejoiced in all efforts for this end; but, in particular, his own church has cause gratefully to remember that he was for twenty-five years convener of her Jewish Mission. It was an interest that was always before him; he worked much for it privately, while his annual Assembly speeches, and even his notices for collections, had a rare freshness and vitality pertaining to them. Others had much to do with the prosperous inauguration of that remarkable mission, but to his influence and name are largely due the sustained interest and the wonderful liberality accorded it. In his study at Ellerslie at the time of his death the text still hung prominently, 'To the Jew first.'

In 1875 his old University of Glasgow confirmed on him the degree of D.D., and the following year he was called to occupy the Moderator's chair of the General Assembly. In every way he dignified the office: as his former assistant and friend, Mr Boyd of Carlisle, says, 'When called to special service he always reached a high ideal.' In particular, his opening and closing addresses, given with fine energy and unction, and in which, adverting to the recent awakening, he spoke of ministerial aims and work, evangelistic preaching, and the duties and dangers of revival times, were peculiarly striking and impressive. It happened to be known that Principal Rainy, as he quietly pressed his hand at the close, said, 'I have been giving thanks to God for you'; and such was the feeling of all.

In July of that year he had the gratification of having associated with him an accomplished and like-minded colleague, in the Rev. J. G. Cunningham (now Dr Cunningham), previously of Lochwinnoch. Subsequently, on the union of Tolbooth with St Luke's, he retired from the active duties of the pastorate, and the Rev. James Doran of Willesden was called to be co-pastor with Dr Cunningham. After his retirement, the family home came to be at his son's university residence in Glasgow, varied by a change to Annat in the summer months and for the last two years to Ellerslie, Crieff.

Dr Moody Stuart's published writings include *Life of the Duchess of Gordon*; *Recollections of John Duncan, LL.D*; *The Land of Huss*; *The Three Marys*; *Capernaum*; *The Path of the Redeemed, and other sermons*; *Song of Solomon*, and *The Bible True to Itself*. The last named is to some extent controversial; its scholarship and critical force have been cordially recognised by some who differed from him, and, like Samuel Rutherford's controversial writings, it has spiritual gems. His great work on the Song of Solomon is replete with spiritual suggestion, and is an abiding treasure to the church.

He had not a few family sorrows. His second son, Andrew, a most gifted and devoted Christian youth, died in 1866, after nearly completing his studies for the ministry, and giving high promise as a preacher. His two elder daughters died in the faith of Jesus, one of them the wife of Mr George Watt, advocate. His own loved wife died in 1891; and in 1896 his son Robert, accountant, Dundee, an excellent man of business, and a devoted and useful Christian. Of the five sons and one daughter who remained, his eldest son is the well-known minister of Moffat Free Church, and the second is Professor of Scots Law in Glasgow University. In his retirement his mind was still active and his pen not idle. He had a serious illness in the spring of the present year, from which he rallied wonderfully, but he again took ill in the beginning of July. Though much prostrated in body, the spirit was often very alert, and was chiefly occupied in adoration and prayer. 'Thou didst love us when we were cast out and had destroyed ourselves; and oh, we have so often destroyed ourselves, but thou didst always proclaim thy mercy.' 'Into thy hands I commit my spirit, thou hast redeemed me. I have only destroyed myself; but the Son of Man has come to seek and to save that which was lost.' 'Father, let thy servant depart in peace. I have sometimes thought that I should not depart till I had seen the Lord's Christ; and if mine eyes have seen the Lord's Christ, let me depart. Not my will, but thine, be done. To me to live be it Christ, and to die is gain, gain.' Such were some expressions overheard. One day he shouted aloud, 'For he delighteth in mercy, he *delighteth* in mercy,' and he clapped his hands for joy at the thought. Sometimes when the mind wandered he was dispensing the communion—'This is the blood of the new covenant; he that eateth of this bread shall live forever.' On his lips being moistened with a little water, he repeated, 'With joy shall ye draw water at the wells of salvation.' And again the words were heard—'Dust unto dust. All things are dying, and death is thine. I give my body to the grave, to that grave in which the holy body of my saviour lay. Thou wast laid in the grave, and we would lie with thee.'

On Sabbath morning, 31 July, he gently folded his hands and fell asleep. His body rests, with others of his loved ones, in the family burial place at Kilspindie, near his old summer home, till the Lord shall come, and they that sleep in Jesus shall come with him.

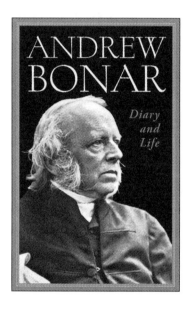

The Diary and Life of Andrew A. Bonar

Edited by Marjory Bonar

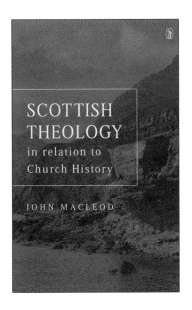

Scottish Theology in Relation to Church History

John Macleod

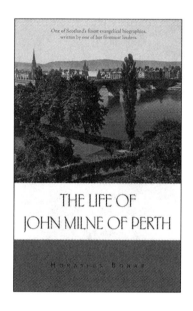

The Life of John Milne of Perth

Horatius Bonar

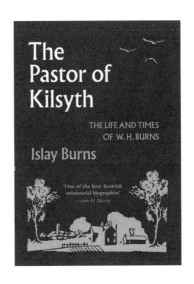

The Pastor of Kilsyth:
The Life and Times of W. H. Burns

Islay Burns

BUDAPEST

*View from Buda across the Danube to Pest
in the late nineteenth century*

9613. P. 2 - BUDAPEST. BLIC   EN FRANZ JOSEFS - BR